T0320834

Social Entrepreneurship and Enterprises in Economic and Social Development

Social Entrepreneurship and Enterprises in Economic and Social Development

Edited by Katharine Briar-Lawson

School of Social Welfare, University at Albany,
State University of New York, NY, USA

Paul Miesing

School of Business, University at Albany,
State University of New York, NY, USA

and

Blanca M. Ramos

School of Social Welfare, University at Albany,
State University of New York, NY, USA

OXFORD
UNIVERSITY PRESS

Oxford University Press is a department of the University of Oxford. It furthers
the University's objective of excellence in research, scholarship, and education
by publishing worldwide. Oxford is a registered trade mark of Oxford University
Press in the UK and certain other countries.

Published in the United States of America by Oxford University Press
198 Madison Avenue, New York, NY 10016, United States of America.

Library of Congress Cataloging-in-Publication Data
Names: Briar-Lawson, Katharine, editor. | Miesing, Paul, editor. |
Ramos, Blanca M., editor.
Title: Social entrepreneurship and enterprises in economic and social
development / [edited by] Katharine Briar-Lawson,
Paul Miesing, Blanca M. Ramos.
Description: New York : Oxford University Press, 2021. |
Includes bibliographical references and index.
Identifiers: LCCN 2020009360 (print) | LCCN 2020009361 (ebook) |
ISBN 9780197518298 (hardback) | ISBN 9780197518311 (epub) |
ISBN 9780197518328
Subjects: LCSH: Social entrepreneurship—Developing countries. |
Entrepreneurship—Social aspects—Developing countries. | Developing
countries—Social policy. | Economic development—Developing countries.
Classification: LCC HD60.5.D44 S63 2020 (print) | LCC HD60.5.D44 (ebook) |
DDC 338.9009172/4—dc23
LC record available at https://lccn.loc.gov/2020009360
LC ebook record available at https://lccn.loc.gov/2020009361

1 3 5 7 9 8 6 4 2

Printed by Sheridan Books, Inc., United States of America

CONTENTS

FOREWORD

Universities can play a key role in training and support of social entrepreneurs and social enterprises. In fact, universities reflect some key attributes of social enterprises and entrepreneurship. Here, we lay out some of the roles of universities by drawing on our own experience here at the University at Albany. In fact, this is also where the vision for this book was generated. Like the enterprise movements and developments described in this book, we, too, are learning our way through the challenges and opportunities, acting both as ecosystem and facilitator to foster entrepreneurs and social enterprises.

THE UNIVERSITY BUSINESS MODEL WITH ATTRIBUTES OF A SOCIAL ENTERPRISE

Research universities have always been a place where knowledge creation and public access to knowledge is our mission. In recent years this includes entrepreneurship and small business assistance. Many institutions provide such coursework and training programs as a community service, including community colleges and affiliated programs of the Small Business Association in the United States. These programs provide a vital service in the entrepreneurship ecosystem by offering assistance to a wide range of startup businesses across a variety of sectors. Additionally, larger research institutions provide more comprehensive technology transfer and commercialization services to assist innovation-oriented startups to get their products to market. These programs require a different mindset for both the entrepreneur as quick-paced risk taker and for university staff who are unaccustomed to administering such services to non-faculty or staff and are adverse to risk. In many instances, these startups are either born out of or look to leverage the intellectual assets of university research faculty and specialized laboratories. While these business ventures require a longer lead time to revenue generation and profitability, they do possess the potential to generate more jobs than traditional nontechnology or innovation-oriented startups if the technology or product is commercially viable. It is this full range of service delivery that exemplifies the significant economic engine that colleges and universities have been and continue to be in the development of the entrepreneurial ecosystem.

At the University at Albany, we are fortunate to have grant-funded resources through the Blackstone Charitable Foundation and New York State Empire State Development (NYS-ESD), the state's economic development agency, to provide entrepreneurial assistance to students, faculty, and community-based startup businesses. We have seen a significant increase in the creation of both technology-oriented and socially responsible startup businesses since the implementation of these resources. Through our Blackstone Foundation-funded LaunchPad program, we provide programming, coaching, competitions, workshops, and lectures to more than 1,000 students annually.

Another effort is our Innovate 518 program, also funded by the NYS-ESD. It serves as the Capital Region of New York State's Innovation Hot Spot, a program that coordinates the promotion of a network of more than 25 affiliated partner incubators, accelerators, and entrepreneurial service providers serving close to 300 startup companies. While we have seen significant progress, we continue to evolve and learn as a university in understanding the complexities of starting and growing a business in the region and how to capture (and indeed measure) the overall societal and economic impact we are having. One impetus for this book was born from our Small Enterprise Economic Development (SEED) program, an adaptation of the Grameen Bank model for microlending. This is made possible by the State Employees Federal Credit Union (SEFCU) and is administered by our Small Business Development Center in partnership with the School of Social Welfare and School of Business.

UNIVERSITY INTEREST IN ENTREPRENEURSHIP

Interestingly, colleges and universities face similar business development challenges as many of the startup businesses to which they aim to provide assistance and guidance. They have revenue and expenses, customer discovery and marketing challenges, price point influencers, and policy and compliance issues to deal with. However, in our role as a workforce and economic development driver within higher education, new business models and thought processes must be imagined, recognized, and then adapted.

The two most fundamental questions any business owner must address in order to be successful are "What is my product?" and "Who is my customer?" If these questions were posed to most higher education faculty and staff, you would most likely get the answer that the "product" is the education provided and that the "customer" is the student who purchases that product in the form of tuition. This seems like a very logical and sensible response, but it fails to address the questions in the larger context of the workforce/economic development supply chain. We have an opportunity to look at that supply chain from an economic development and community engagement perspective, where the "product" is our student and the "customer" is the business who chooses to purchase that student for the cost of a compensation package. In the process, our locally grown products get local compensation and strengthen the communities from which they emerged.

We in higher education never look at students as widgets or numbers, but if we took a lesson from businesses in terms of investing more in quality assurance to ensure that all of our students emerge from the safe space of our institutions with the required 21st-century soft skills, leadership attributes, and core disciplines, then the skills gap that we hear so much about today may not be as prevalent. This would lead to a higher level of economic output from those business customers and enable them to secure more contracts and in-source more jobs to our graduates. Moreover, higher education's greatest asset is the ability for different opinions and beliefs to coexist in a diverse and inclusive environment. Through healthy debate and discussion, these differing belief structures provide a case study for how some of the world's most complex societal problems can be solved by an international workforce. The economic/workforce development supply chain language is a metaphor for a classic lecture in supply and demand economic concepts. Universities have an impact on both sides of the equation.

One relevant factor that influences higher education as it tries to interface with business is the sometimes unseen expectation that students, faculty, and outside enterprises bring to the educational system, given that it developed over a thousand years from monasteries and has been called "an ivory tower." In this traditional environment, knowledge transfer is directional, from professor to student, in an articulated blueprint of accredited programs and classes. Businesses do not suffer the notion that this arrangement is in any way the real world from which they must hire college and university graduates. Fortunately, the modern reaction to the resulting gap between industry needs and academic training has been an encouraging collaboration from both sides around experiential learning in the form of internships, job shadowing, simulation, and other such activities that have much more of a real-world feel because they are unscripted, depend on real customers, are often supported by industry with mentors, and even may culminate in job placements.

When an important enterprise like Blackstone puts its name on an entrepreneurship program, and when it supplies real-world mentors and case study problems from its businesses, the undergraduate student can capitalize on the principles taught in class to develop teamwork and other real-world skills as well as the entrepreneurial and business knowledge that are needed after graduation to complement the facts and theories learned in the classroom. The fact that such experiential education opportunities are happening on campus does not dilute the non–ivory-tower component that stimulates students. The direct experience offers faculty and staff a chance to mentor students in a different way and often to do it in the presence of enterprise mentors. This is good for the students, who make enterprise connections, learn the implicit styles for that industry, get the feel for where their academic majors may take them, and typically become more successful in the job market when they graduate. For their part, companies get a look at the powerful latent talent that is the next generation of their employees, and they may save on funds that can be directed toward hiring and on-boarding in their industries in a highly efficient way. That both industry and academics gain defines the win-win between higher education and enterprise that makes the effort sustainable. Importantly, faculty and staff also are exposed to these attainments, leading to a culture change as the continuing evolution of the ivory tower becomes better aligned with industry needs. When this happens, the higher education institution becomes more attractive to future students, and, if students do not figure that out on their own, it is easy to advertise in recruitment such these experiences make that particular university a better investment of families' time, treasure, and talent. Of course, the big winners here are the students. More of them graduate with a better sense of their career path. More of them are better prepared to avoid the pitfall of malemployment that makes it harder to get a job and pay back tuition costs. This is the experience of cooperative education schools with a big commitment to work and study programming. And this is becoming an issue for all higher education institutions, regardless of how they are structured, as Big Data becomes better at figuring out which schools do a better job of helping their students not only to succeed while in school but also after graduation in the next phase of their lives.

Industry has what most students want: a career, even if that means further schooling. Higher education has what industry and the world wants: the next generation of critical thinkers, creators, and citizens of a civil society that has been very good at creating a better world for itself as well as generating the next set of problems to be solved. The three-way partnerships among students, universities, and the enterprise community represent one of the great hopes for the future.

University-led and -facilitated efforts to build social enterprises and meet the needs of students and their communities may become a global movement. To this end we hope that the inspiration that led to this book and to our enterprise work at the University at Albany will be generative. In effect, if more university supports and institutional resources are fostered, it is possible that more entrepreneurial pioneers, networks, and partners can be nurtured. Universities can play a defining role in social enterprise and entrepreneurship not only in facilitating them but also in modeling some of the core practices of a social enterprise, combining entrepreneurial activities with social impact outcomes.

—Matthew J. Grattan, Director of Community and Economic Development; James Stellar, Professor of Behavioral Neuroscience and former Provost and Senior Vice President for Academic Affairs; and James A. Dias, Vice President for Research, University at Albany, State University of New York

PREFACE

We believe this is a one-of-a-kind book, combining business, social welfare, sociology, public administration, urban planning, and other fields to advance new knowledge and perspectives on social enterprises and entrepreneurship. It does so by featuring models and cases from an array of countries and highlighting the lessons learned from them. We hope that the global snapshots that are featured and analyzed add to the growing knowledge base about new models and approaches to advance human well-being. Specifically, this work advances the delineation of key attributes of social enterprises and entrepreneurship, examines the human costs of development projects, and offers lessons learned for community-based social enterprises. In addition, by featuring policy and practice developments in different nations and regions as social enterprises and entrepreneurship accelerate, this book generates a compelling need for more public policy and investor supports. In fact, we offer suggestions for key services, resources, and policy supports to advance social enterprise and entrepreneurial movements that will begin to mitigate the human costs of failure. These recommendations are derived in part from snapshots of innovative approaches from different nations and regions around the world.

Moreover, this book also shows how social enterprises and entrepreneurship can address economic and social inequality while advancing social impacts. Using business strategies to promote improved outcomes for others, local innovators can combine core elements of economic and social development. As an antidote to "trickle-down jobs," social entrepreneurship can grow new jobs from the ground up. Globally, microenterprises are on the rise, as are supports for entrepreneurs. The growing movement in support of social enterprises and entrepreneurship is contextualized by different policy and supports across the world. Snapshots of these developments and challenges, delineated in this important book, help to inform the "state of the art." They further advance the growing interest in how to aid local entrepreneurs in promoting social good and impacts, especially those working in low income communities.

But entrepreneurial activity is not for the faint of heart. Resilience and success cannot rest on the shoulders of pioneering individuals and their families alone. Such initiatives require more supports to survive and thrive.

It may seem surprising to some that social work and business faculty would join forces to develop a book on social enterprises and entrepreneurship. However, there seemed to be myriad reasons for extending the tools of business to advance social welfare. And we knew that social welfare needs could drive a social impact focus for businesses. Adding to that, we saw the need for a parallel process in which, at a more macro level, economic and social development also could be better integrated.

Our journey toward this book project may help readers appreciate its aims and chapter composition. Our work began when several of us became intrigued with the Grameen Bank in Bangladesh advancing UN goals to build microenterprises for the poor worldwide. In partnership with the Dean of our School of Business, our Small Business Development Center and our State Employees Federal Credit Union (SEFCU) with a revolving loan fund, we were able to launch our own microlending program for low income individuals called Small Enterprise Economic Development (SEED). We simultaneously were able make a case for parallel faculty hires in social entrepreneurship in both our School of Social Welfare and School of Business to help lead this emerging agenda around social enterprises and entrepreneurship.

Requests came to us to help with the privatization of the workforce in Cuba, which led to a series of forums including faculty from Cuba and Russia to address transitions to a market economy. Our efforts were further aided by the development in our School of Business interdisciplinary Center for Advancement & Understanding of Social Enterprises (CAUSE). Grants to the University fueled the momentum as student interest was growing in initiating social enterprises and startups as student entrepreneurs.

As these faculty forums continued, there was interest in developing a text which captured the transitions in nations around the world. In addition, we sought to move beyond the "neoliberal agenda," advance more integrative approaches to addressing low-income populations, and build more inclusive economic and social development.

Our contributors share much of our passion, as we continue to learn from one another across the globe. So that is our backstory, and we have all learned and grown through the process of building this book!

—Katharine Briar-Lawson, Paul Miesing,
and Blanca M. Ramos, University at Albany

CONTRIBUTORS

Kelly Askew, PhD, is Professor of Anthropology and Afroamerican/African Studies and founding director of the African Studies Center at the University of Michigan in Ann Arbor, MI, USA.

Katherine Baker is Interim Director of the Small Business Development Center at the State University at Albany in Albany, NY, USA.

Swapnil Barai is a development professional in India, for more than a decade working with nonprofits, social enterprises, incubators, fund raising, and consulting firms in Maharashtra, India.

Meera Bhat is a doctoral student at the School of Social Welfare at the State University at Albany in Albany, NY, USA.

Stephanie L. Black, PhD, is Assistant Professor in the Department of Management at Texas A&M University-San Antonio in San Antonio, TX, USA.

Katharine Briar-Lawson, PhD, is Professor and Dean Emeritus in the School of Social Welfare at the State University at Albany in Albany, NY, USA.

William Brigham is Director Emeritus of the Small Business Development Center in the School of Business at the State University at Albany in Albany, NY, USA.

Kelly J. Gross is a PhD candidate in social work at the State University at Albany in Albany, NY, USA.

Vishal K. Gupta, PhD, is Associate Professor in the Department of Management at the University of Alabama in Tuscaloosa, AL, USA.

Michelle T. Hackett, PhD, works for the Community and Public Sector Union in Melbourne, Australia.

Michelle Harris, PhD, is Professor in the Department of Africana Studies and the School of Social Welfare, and she directs the Institute for Global Indigeneity at the State University at Albany in Albany, NY, USA.

Linda Marie Hogan is an associate with Groundswell Research Associates in London, England, UK.

Wonhyung Lee, PhD, is Assistant Professor at the School of Social Welfare of the State University at Albany in Albany, NY, USA.

Steve Lobel is Vice President of Anchor Agency, Inc., in Albany, NY, USA.

Michael B. Marks, PhD, is an associate with Groundswell Research Associates in London, England, UK.

Mizanur R. Miah, **PhD,** is Professor and Director Emeritus of Social Work at Valdosta State University in Valdosta, GA, USA.

Paul Miesing, PhD, is Founding Director of the Center for Advancement & Understanding of Social Enterprises (CAUSE) and Professor in the School of Business at the State University at Albany in Albany, NY, USA.

Leila Mucarsel is Lecturer in innovation and development governance and PhD candidate at the School of Political Science at Universidad Nacional de Cuyo in Mendoza, Argentina.

Eric E. Otenyo, PhD, is Professor of Political Science at Northern Arizona University in Flagstaff, AZ, USA.

Blanca M. Ramos, PhD, is Associate Professor in the School of Social Welfare with a joint appointment in the Department of Latin American and Caribbean Studies at the State University at Albany in Albany, NY, USA.

Michael J. Roy, PhD, is Professor of Economic Sociology and Social Policy at the Yunus Centre for Social Business and Health, Glasgow Caledonian University in Glasgow, Scotland, UK.

Ruslan Sadyrtdinov, PhD, is Associate Professor in the Institute of Management, Economics, and Finance at the Kazan Federal University in Kazan, Republic of Tatarstan, Russia.

Carina Skropke is an associate with Groundswell Research Associates in London, England, UK.

Gabriella Spinelli, PhD, is in the Department of Design at Brunel University London in London, England, UK.

Bruce R. Stanley, MSW, is former Director of the Social Welfare Field Unit with Small Enterprise Economic Development at the State University at Albany in Albany, NY, USA.

Henry-Louis Taylor, Jr., PhD, is Professor in the Department of Urban and Regional Planning and Founding Director of the Center for Urban Studies at the State University at Buffalo (University at Buffalo) in Buffalo, NY, USA.

Jildyz Urbaeva, PhD, is Assistant Professor at the School of Social Welfare at the State University at Albany in Albany, NY, USA.

Stephanie H. Wacholder is currently a development consultant in Albany, NY, USA.

William J. Wales, PhD, is Standish Chair and Associate Professor of Entrepreneurship at the State University at Albany in Albany, NY, USA.

Paul M. Weaver, PhD, is the founder and CEO of Groundswell Research Associates and Professorial Research Fellow at Maastricht University in the Netherlands.

Yi-jung Wu, PhD, is Associate Professor in the Department of Public Policy and Management at Shih Hsin University in Taipei, Taiwan.

SECTION I

Theoretical, Applied, and Biographical Contexts for Social Enterprises and Social Entrepreneurship

Introduction

PAUL MIESING, BLANCA M. RAMOS, AND
KATHARINE BRIAR-LAWSON

OVERVIEW OF SECTION I

The fundamental premise of this volume is that social enterprises are viable mechanisms for addressing a variety of ills faced by emerging and transitioning economies. The seven chapters in this section lay out the framework of these increasingly popular structural forms; the next section examines this phenomenon in specific countries throughout the Americas, Europe, Asia, and Africa; the final section further explores and synthesizes the issues and insights, concluding by offering lessons for this century. This section begins with Chapter 1, on "Social Enterprises as Integrative Resources, Strategies, and Models" that explains the social enterprise phenomenon and offers specific examples of different business models and strategies that have helped mitigate income, education, health, and technology disparities around the world. These disparities are not only immoral but are also a drag on economic growth and development because they hinder social and economic mobility. This volume attempts to illustrate the coincidence of social and economic development, with social enterprises helping improve both simultaneously.

Chapter 2 continues to highlight disparities that ironically are often caused by the very large economic development projects made by investment-based organizations that are intended to help them. In this chapter on "Displacement: A Typology for Social Entrepreneurs," a

Paul Miesing, Blanca M. Ramos, and Katharine Briar-Lawson, *Introduction* In: *Social Entrepreneurship and Enterprises in Economic and Social Development*. Edited by: Katharine Briar-Lawson, Paul Miesing, and Blanca M. Ramos, Oxford University Press (2021). © Oxford University Press. DOI: 10.1093/oso/9780197518298.003.0001.

typology is proposed that suggests innovative social entrepreneurs can create beneficial and sustainable social change by considering the informal economic sector, non-financial resources, and social and cultural capital. It also suggests that future research should examine additional displacement types that would inform more inclusive development approaches.

Given the important role of social enterprises in mitigating disparities, we next examine the entrepreneurial orientation (EO) of these organizations in Chapter 3 on "Organizational Entrepreneurial Orientation: Implications for Social Impact and Social Enterprise." Given their multiple missions of solving social problems in ways that are both financially and environmentally sustainable, social enterprises must not only identify disparities but also recognize the opportunities to solve them and be able to provide actual solutions. By focusing on the organization's strategic orientation rather than the role of individual entrepreneurs, EO not only recognizes the importance of social interactions but also the collective mindset and behaviors that create social impact and social value. This chapter proposes future areas of research.

We follow with Chapter 4 on "Immigrant Entrepreneurship: Economic and Social Development" that discusses the importance of immigrants in economic and social development, using the United States as an example. Many immigrants seek to better their lives economically or socially, and some arrive as political refugees. Regardless of motivation, they create commercial and social enterprises ranging from starting a new business venture *de novo* that has national impact to remaining in a protected subeconomy or culturally creative "symbolic economy" that exists in ethnic enclaves. Regardless of form or location, immigration and ethnic entrepreneurship are primary drivers for local economies, representing a disproportionately high level of private-sector employment. Moreover, much of this development occurs as immigrants and refugees move to economically depressed areas, thereby revitalizing those neighborhoods. To achieve such dramatic successes, immigrants must possess the correct skills and "know how," and indeed many have brought new technologies and innovation to various industries and often patent new research, products, and ideas. This chapter concludes by offering examples of immigrant social enterprises in North America taking the form of nonprofit organizations, for-profit corporations, and for-profit cooperatives.

Having presented our overarching framework for social enterprises in ameliorating various social ills and disparities and the role of entrepreneurs in creating social innovations, Chapter 5 on "Sustaining and Growing Social Innovations Using Integrated Development Models: Experiences from the United States, United Kingdom, and

Japan" shows how integrated socioeconomic development models can sustain and grow social innovations that achieve economic objectives along with equitable and environmental objectives. Because such integration requires novel ways of thinking about resources, organization forms and operations, and ultimate social impact, they often emerge through the efforts of grassroots social innovators. This chapter provides case studies and a typology of time bank business models that mobilize the time and talents of under-deployed people and discusses the conflicts and tensions inherent in opting for different business and development models. It concludes with a brief discussion of challenges for policy development and future research.

With microlending becoming an increasingly popular method to fund entrepreneurs, it is often considered to be a social enterprise because it enables new ventures to be created and succeed. While these programs serve a variety of underserved populations (including immigrants) unable to get a conventional loan, a few practice "character-based" lending. Chapter 6, on "UAlbany's Small Enterprise Economic Development (SEED) Program as an Exemplar," presents one model of microlending that provides financing services, technical assistance, and social and peer supports to unserved and underserved low-income borrowers to advance their business start-up opportunities. It is a collaborative project among a local university's two disciplines of business and social welfare, a Small Business Development Center (SBDC), a credit union, and a state agency that have together created an innovative and unique program. This chapter offers some lessons for those hoping to replicate its model.

We appropriately wrap up this section by offering inspiration on entrepreneurial benefits and challenges and the importance of resilience. Based on an intimate memoir of personal weaknesses and strengths, in Chapter 7 Steve Lobel addresses "Failing My Way to Success" and chronicles his personal experiences as an entrepreneur through decades of defeats and triumphs. Approaching mid-life with challenges and failures, the slow climb back to solvency and eventually to personal and business success now contributes to philanthropic causes. The personal odyssey and life lessons learned as an entrepreneur resonate with people from all walks of life. It took losing almost everything to develop an attitude toward life and work that was sustainable and satisfying. The route to self-knowledge tends to run through failure, according to the author, resulting in becoming kinder, wiser, more generous, and humbler. Most importantly, it was admitting inner truths that allowed him to turn failure into success and discover how much of entrepreneurship is to "know thyself." The care and compassion that drive social entrepreneurs are core personal values that all entrepreneurs must appreciate alongside business objectives of profitability, customer satisfaction, and growth.

Pursuing and achieving self-interest leaves an empty feeling; satisfaction comes when an entrepreneur becomes a social entrepreneur. This chapter—and section—concludes with 10 principles gleaned from a lifetime of trial and error, suggesting that failures light the way to success and success should be the means by which to help repair the world.

OVERVIEW OF SECTION II: EXAMPLES FROM TRANSITIONING AND MARKET-BASED ECONOMIES

A main thrust of this volume is to examine the integration of economic and social development through the lens of social enterprise and entrepreneurship. The first section assessed the benefits and challenges of this approach. This second section explores snapshots from transitioning and market-driven economies covering Latin America, Europe, Asia, and Africa. We address these based on the framework first introduced in Chapter 1 on how these country and regional examples help to illustrate possible structures for different national circumstances (Figure I.1).

We begin with Chapter 8, focused on Albania, a country in the Balkans that has embarked on a long process of social and economic transformation since communism's collapse in 1991. "Focus on the Balkans: Social

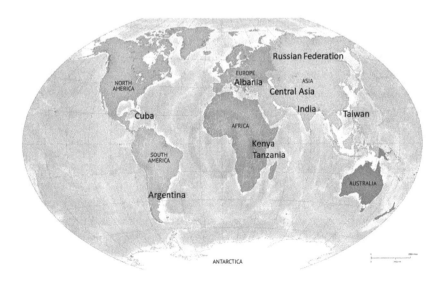

Figure I.1 Global snapshots.

Enterprise in Albania," presents a study of a youth professional services program that employs groups marginalized from mainstream labor markets. It demonstrates how ideologies concerning the role of social enterprise may influence its actors in post-communist countries and what this means for the future of the sector. Social enterprises, representing a "middle way" that blends social and economic values and impacts, straddle the excesses of communism and capitalism and therefore represent a paradigm in transition.

Chapter 9 discusses the rather new concept of social entrepreneurship in Central Asia, a region where competitive business markets are still emerging. It asserts that traditional craft production is a viable mechanism to achieve sustainable social and economic development and outlines the challenges and opportunities it entails. This chapter on "Redefining Silk Roads: Social Businesses and Crafts as Approaches for Improving Women's Situations in Central Asia" describes two projects that support women's craft production and entrepreneurial skills in Kyrgyzstan and Tajikistan. The author refers to these projects as "social businesses," recognizing their positive financial and social impacts on women, particularly those at a disadvantage in the labor market. The author delineates specific strategies designed to promote social enterprise and entrepreneurship among women who comprise a rapidly growing small-business sector dedicated to the production of Central Asian traditional crafts.

Next, we feature a snapshot of some of the social and economic developments taking place in the Russian Federation. Chapter 10 focuses on "Social Entrepreneurship and Corporate Social Responsibility in the Russian Federation" and discusses these widespread concepts circulating in Russia today. It also identifies appropriate tools to assess its sustainable development. The author proposes strategies that could further the development of social entrepreneurship and corporate social responsibility. These include creating an appropriate and favorable regulatory framework for socially active businesses, involving the state in the initial stage of the process when funding projects, and increasing awareness among the general public, regional authorities, and potential social entrepreneurs of the opportunities social businesses can offer. A radical change in how the business community perceives social responsibility and stronger support for social entrepreneurship from the general population and public sector would be optimal and produce an ideal scenario for social and economic development in Russia.

This is followed by Chapter 11, Socioeconomic Development in India: Lessons from the Third Sector, which depicts India's growth and development trajectory. The authors examine the social entrepreneurship sector framing it with an historical view of the diverse civil society sector, of which it is a part. The authors warn that there are tensions among social businesses, business enterprises, and social enterprises in an large yet disparate ecosystem. They argue that social enterprises need to be supported with facilitating and enabling ecosystems and investments that foster innovation social change. These analyses are contextualized by an overview of the rapid economic growth in India and the need for more inclusive economies.

Chapter 12 on "Where There Is No Formal Social Welfare System for an Indigenous People: Entrepreneurship, Watchmen, and the Reinvention of the Maasai Warrior" takes us to Africa, with a compelling depiction of the Maasai *moranism* (warrior society). The Maasai are a historically marginalized, underserved indigenous group in Kenya and Tanzania. Globalization trends and oppressive governmental exclusionary programs have greatly contributed to poverty, a host of social inequalities, and unmet needs among the Maasai. To help address their social and economic disadvantages, young Maasai men are forced to leave behind their traditional sources of economic support as pastoralists to participate in emerging forms of wage employment as watchmen. The authors propose that Maasai watchmen are social entrepreneurs in their own right.

Chapter 13 on "Social Enterprise in Taiwan: Economic and Social Welfare Transition" offers a glimpse of the social and economic development trajectory in Taiwan from inception to the present day. It provides a historical account of the political and socioeconomic forces that frame current social enterprise and entrepreneurship models and shape the social welfare system in this country. Social enterprise has become an attractive option for the younger generation interested in making a difference in society, and concerns regarding risks and challenges are noted. The author concludes her analysis with some recommendations, including the practice of some core social work methods and techniques for successful, sustainable social enterprises. As the presence of social enterprise and entrepreneurship enters its "mature era" in Taiwan, its past experiences, errors, and successes offer an excellent learning opportunity for other nations worldwide.

The last two chapters of this section focus on the Latin American extremes of Cuba and Argentina. Chapter 14 on "Social Entrepreneurship in Argentina: The Role of Mission-Driven Organizations on the Pathway to Inclusive Growth" examines social enterprises within the context of this country's economic and social recovery after the 2001 crisis. Discussions are centered on the contributions of social entrepreneurship organizations to development, with a focus on State-civil society partnerships to unleash social innovations, engage citizen participation and reach marginalized communities, as well as the challenges the social entrepreneurship ecosystem endures in Argentina today. Chapter 15 on "The Odd Couple: 'Incomplete Socialism' and Social Enterprises in Cuba" shows that social development in this country is pronounced. At the same time, the economic sector (including policies and supports for the rise of social enterprises) is rather mixed if not problematic. Although Cuba is a socialist republic, some of the same market forces that are present in a capitalist economy, including racism and classism, are apparent. This chapter contextualizes and hypothesizes the potential rationales for this quandary. Moreover, it is argued that, even with incomplete socialism, aspects of social and economic development are integrated for better and for worse.

The snapshots of eight emerging and transitioning world economies included in this section clearly illustrate the key roles that social enterprise and entrepreneurship play in social and economic development and elucidate best practices for a more integrative approach to social and economic development. The snapshots, indeed, attest to the global nature of this phenomenon.

OVERVIEW OF SECTION III: TOWARD MORE INTEGRATIVE SOCIAL AND ECONOMIC DEVELOPMENT— SELECTIVE BARRIERS AND FACILITATORS

In this section we discuss some of the benefits and challenges of fostering more integrative practices at policy and practice levels. We explore the need for more explicit attention to the ways in which social welfare benefits and social protections are integral and necessary for economic development and especially if social enterprises and entrepreneurship are to succeed.

Essential to the arguments for integrative thinking and practices is the mutual regard that is necessary to advance more harmonized, people-centered development. This means averting some of historic tensions, if not clashes, often seen among policy-makers between development projects and investments versus social welfare protections and benefits. In fact, we argue that entrepreneurs may be one of the groups to target for more systematic aid and support for their success, with more tailored social welfare protections. Moreover, we argue that we cannot afford not to.

Most nations are undergoing transitioning economies. Global trade and markets, while beneficial to many, have also created massive restructuring in local economies. As a result, ancestral livelihoods of resource-based industries such a farming, fishing, lumber, and mining have been lost due to resource depletion, global competition, and global franchises such as agribusiness. Instead of the demise of workers, their families, their livelihoods, and communities, such dislocation could be offset with targeted new social welfare and entrepreneurial supports with community-level development projects. To that end, this section offers a few principles and propositions to guide 21st-century thinking, policy, and practices. Chapter 16 on "Integrating Social and Economic Development" explores some of the challenges and benefits of more integrative practices involving social and economic development. The arguments in this chapter are buttressed by the UN Sustainable Development Goals. Chapter 17 on "Selected Observations and Lessons Learned for 21st-Century Supports for Social Entrepreneurship and Social Enterprises" offers a series of propositions for 21st-century practice and policy selectively drawn from the chapters of this volume. Together they comprise a template of suggestions for next steps in the advancement of policy, practice, and research on social enterprises and some of their requisite economic development and social welfare supports. They also represent testable hypotheses about theories of change for future social enterprise development in the context of rapid and often destabilizing economic and social change.

Given the uncertainties of the global marketplace, complete with tariff wars, escalation of competition, and growing disruptions of local economies and livelihoods, more attention seems warranted to bolster the inventiveness and resilience of workers, their families, and communities. Thus, we end this section and volume with some premises about key practices, policies, and rights that can be fostered. We caution that presuppositions that entrepreneurial activity can be seen as a replacement for core social welfare benefits in housing, health, food, and income supports. Inclusive economies require synchronized and inclusive welfare states that work for the betterment of all. This can best be achieved, we argue, by more integrative and tailored thinking, practices, and policies that advance the human drive for entrepreneurial contributions. In doing so, such key investments may help to ensure that workers, their families, and communities are able to tap their own talents, meet local needs, and foster human development and capacities while growing economies from the ground up. "Trickle-down" economics has been declared an insufficient if not an incomplete or even flawed paradigm for economic growth. Human and community well-being depend on the stewardship and investment role of the state to move beyond tax incentives, investments, and even bail-outs for large companies. Instead, nation states are now compelled, we believe, to invest in the entrepreneurial contributions of individuals, families, their dreams, and capacities. No economy can expand rapidly enough to absorb all who seek work. Thus, entrepreneurship will remain a core asset as social enterprises offer one way to improve and integrate social and economic development worldwide.

For too long, the risks and often devastating consequences of failure have been borne by the entrepreneur and their family. Moreover, the individual entrepreneur and family are often marginalized and unsupported, unlike the large corporation where such risks are often shielded by an array of investments, bail-outs, and supports. These, too, need to be directed toward entrepreneurs who are meeting needs, especially those advancing social enterprises along with job creation and simultaneously fostering economic and social development. Such supports for entrepreneurs, especially those advancing social enterprises, should emerge as social guarantees and constitute a collective global human rights agenda for the 21st century.

CHAPTER 1

⌒

Social Enterprises as Integrative Resources, Strategies, and Models

PAUL MIESING

INTRODUCTION TO THE SOCIAL AND ECONOMIC PROBLEM

There are numerous disadvantaged groups throughout the world (e.g., individuals with disabilities, ex-convicts, homeless, substance abuse, etc.). Complicating their plight is increasing disparities in income, education, health, technology, and other determinants of socioeconomic status. At the same time, there are many emerging global problems that require immediate attention such as environmental sustainability, systemic poverty, HIV/AIDS, terrorism, human rights abuses, and natural disasters. Before discussing disparities in emerging and transitioning economies, it is instructive to examine the United States as a baseline to see what lessons might be relevant to other countries.

There is a consensus that income inequality is greater in the United States than in any other democracy in the developed world, and, since this has been growing for decades, it now threatens democracy. Economics Nobel Prize winner Stiglitz (2012) claimed that growing income inequality is responsible for the slowing of economic growth worldwide as well as all manner of political instability. Piketty (2014) used tax data to calculate the percentage of income going to the top 1% and 10% of national populations. His results created a furor when he published these disparities. Figure 1.1

Paul Miesing, *Social Enterprises as Integrative Resources, Strategies, and Models* In: *Social Entrepreneurship and Enterprises in Economic and Social Development.* Edited by: Katharine Briar-Lawson, Paul Miesing, and Blanca M. Ramos, Oxford University Press (2021). © Oxford University Press. DOI: 10.1093/oso/9780197518298.003.0002.

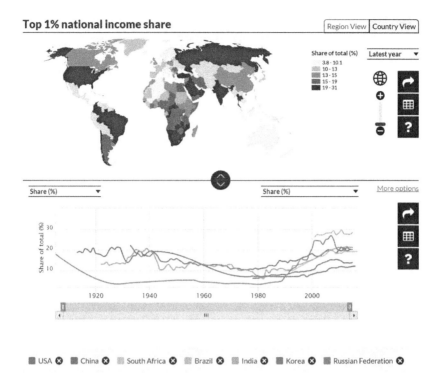

Figure 1.1 Global income disparity.
Source: http://wid.world/data/

shows the 2015 results from around the globe as well as a century of data for some of the large emerging and transition economies. The data clearly show that income disparity fell during the 1960s and 1970s but has increased since 1980. In the United States and much of the developing world, 10–30% of the population accounts for 1% of total income. Besides raising moral issues about the personal well-being of a country's citizens, these continuing disparities hurt social and economic mobility, so they are also a drag on economic growth and development. While controversial, his study forced a dialogue and debate over the coincidence of social and economic development. This chapter examines how social enterprises can help improve both.

What is new about the chasm between rich and poor in the United States is that all American politicians, regardless of ideology, are talking about it. Journalist, writer, and economist Kuttner (1984) explains the title of his book, *The Economic Illusion*, as "the belief that social justice is bad for economic growth" (p. 1). He concludes in the Epilogue: "I have tried to suggest that injustice is not necessary economics; that the economics can work, and has often worked, when the constituency for it is animated.

The politics of equality—that is a little harder" (p. 278). Still, the causes and costs of income inequality remain disputed.

Atkinson (2015) challenges the widespread assumption that technological progress and globalization are responsible since neither are new; he also cautions that this belief is dangerous because it suggests that growing inequality is inevitable. Rather, he argues that institutions and infrastructure determine globalizing economies: laws and public policies, taxes, unions and wage rates, the media, corporations, and finance organizations, all of which are determined by public officials, citizens, and elected legislators. "It is not enough to say that rising inequality is due to technological forces outside our control. The government can influence the path taken" (p. 119).

Linz and Stepan (1978) tried to figure out why the United States has for so long had much greater income inequality than any other developed democracy. They identified 23 long-standing democracies with advanced economies, including eight federal governments with both upper and lower legislative bodies. Using the number of seats and the size of the population to calculate malapportionment, they assigned an "Index of Inequality of Representation" to those eight upper houses and found that the United States had the highest score, with the most malapportioned and least representative upper house. These scores also correlated with the countries' income inequality: the less representative the upper body of a national legislature, the greater the gap between the rich and poor. As will be seen, these lessons also hold for emerging and transition economies.

An emerging market has a subsistence economy with low per capita income and underdeveloped factor markets and infrastructure, but a rapid pace of economic development with government policies favoring a free market economy (Hoskisson, Eden, Lau, & Wright, 2000). More specifically, the Morgan Stanley Capital International Emerging Markets index (https://www.msci.com/emerging-markets) tracks these countries. In the Americas, these are Brazil, Chile, Colombia, Mexico, and Peru; in -Europe, Central and Eastern (Czech Republic, Hungary, Poland), Greece, Russia, and Turkey; in Africa/Middle East, Egypt, Qatar, South Africa, and the United Arab Emirates; and in Asia, South (India and Pakistan), East (China, Korea, and Taiwan), and Southeast (Indonesia, Malaysia, Philippines, and Thailand). Other sources have also included Argentina, Hong Kong, Jordan, Kuwait, Saudi Arabia, Singapore, and Vietnam. The former communist and socialist countries of Central and Eastern Europe countries, China, Russia (along with the newly independent states of the former Soviet Union), and (to a somewhat lesser degree) Vietnam are considered transition economies since their political and economic ideology is changing from centralized planning toward freer markets based on private property, an open society, and encouraging entrepreneurial activities.

SOCIAL ENTREPRENEURS AND THEIR ENTERPRISES AS SOLUTIONS

The word "entrepreneurship" comes from the French *entreprendre* from the Latin *inter + prendere* "to take" (a variant of *prehendere*), which literally means "undertaker" or a contractor who undertakes some project. Interestingly, Smith's *The Wealth of Nations* (1776) refers to the word on several occasions as someone who faces risk and uncertainty, formulates plans and projects to earn profit, seeks out necessary capital, combines and organizes factors of production, and inspects and directs production. The word was popularized by Schumpeter's paradoxical notion of "creative destruction" in his *Capitalism, Socialism and Democracy* (1942) that explained how innovations create new businesses that lead to progress as they displace the status quo.

As these various usages of the word demonstrate, entrepreneurs are particularly good at recognizing opportunities, discovering innovative approaches, mobilizing resources, managing risks, and building viable enterprises. These skills are just as valuable in the social sector as they are in business. The fundamental purpose of social entrepreneurship is creating social value for the public good. This activity can occur within or across the nonprofit, business, or government sectors. Today we see increasing demands for social services while their costs climb and the availability of governmental and charitable funds decrease. Social enterprises fill this vacuum by addressing social problems or needs not met by private markets, governments, or charities.

The distinction between social and commercial entrepreneurship is not dichotomous but rather more accurately conceptualized as a continuum ranging from purely social to purely economic. Austin, Stevenson, and Wei-Skillern (2006, pp. 2–3) posit four distinctions that present opportunities: (1) market failure, when commercial market forces do not meet a social need or consumers are unable to pay for what they need; (2) mission differences between creating social value rather than rewarding private gain for successfully creating profitable operations; (3) restricted resource mobilization, especially for labor and capital; and (4) varying performance measurement by stakeholders, which complicates managing these relationships and demonstrates social impact.

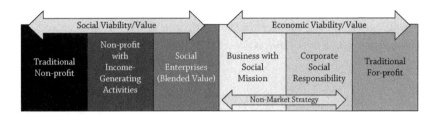

Figure 1.2 Blended value creation.

Social entrepreneurs are change agents who apply business practices and techniques to generate a profit while at the same time achieving a social mission. This is often referred to as "blended value creation" (see Figure 1.2). Note that private-sector enterprises with a social mission or pursuing social responsibilities are considered to have a non-market strategy that considers such stakeholders as governments, communities, the press, and communities. Social enterprises provide multiple possible benefits, such as reducing poverty; creating markets for locally produced products; retaining local wealth, as the newly employed both buy and spend more; developing community trust and strengthening local networks; making communities self-sufficient, which enhances their self-esteem, self-worth, and confidence; and increasing the local tax base to support public services. Hence, the necessity of these enterprises having to attain social impact while achieving long-term economic viability integrates and furthers social and economic development. Such a Herculean effort requires being opportunistic, resourceful, and innovative in creating a novel approach to allocating resources that have a social impact. There can be no doubt that social enterprises are significant contributors to economic growth and prosperity by providing a source of income and employment, producing new products and/or services, and improving up- and downstream value chain activities.

AN OVERVIEW OF BUSINESS MODELS

There are many views of business models but a consensus is emerging around certain characteristics. Models in general are abstractions of reality so, in the case of business, they are concepts of how the business works. As such they should be coherent, complementary, and consistent yet concise. According to Magretta (2002, p. 87), "A good business model answers Peter Drucker's age-old questions: Who is the customer? And what does the customer value? It also answers the fundamental questions every manager must ask: How do we make money in this business? What is the underlying economic logic that explains how we can deliver value to customers at an appropriate cost?" Models are also systemic in that they describe the various elements and the relationships between them that ideally are mutually reinforcing, with positive feedback loops that strengthen their virtuous cycle over time. (Appendix A provides an outline of what a social enterprise plan should consider.)

Because social enterprises are challenged to create value to both society and the economy, they must also maximize returns on social investments. Porter and Kramer (2011) consider the challenge of business models to (1) create value and (2) share that value. They claim that "one of the most powerful forces driving growth in the global economy" will be firms creating economic value in a way that also creates value for society by addressing its needs and challenges. They can do so by reconceiving products and markets, redefining productivity in the value chain, and building supportive industry clusters at the company's locations. To them, shared value is not corporate social responsibility or philanthropy but instead lies at the core of the business strategy. Indeed, they consider social enterprises as merely temporary organizations as businesses increasingly close disparity gaps by creating novel shared values that will challenge conventional thinking.

In addition, social enterprises must consider constellations of multiple and diverse stakeholders willing and able to share in defraying the costs of these transactions. Given these complexities, the social enterprise business model must correctly identify its sectors, segments, and support. *Sectors* refer to specific social issues to focus on, such as providing such basic needs as clean water and sanitation, health, and food security. These are precisely where innovative profitable business models are needed to offer improved products and services or more efficient delivery systems or to target underserved populations. The *segments* are the clients or beneficiaries of the entrepreneurial activities, many of whom are at the "bottom of the pyramid," where a billion of the world's population is unable to participate in market activities. Innovative solutions will need to be found to bring these vast numbers into the global economic mainstream. The final consumer is not always the customer who selects the product or service, nor is it the one who pays for it, so creativity is necessary to identify cash flows derived from the product or service. Most difficult is garnering *support*. This requires aligning with reliable partners as well as maintaining viable funding streams to support the social mission. Whereas charitable organizations rely on contributions, social enterprises attempt to create a continuous and reliable revenue source, attract impact investors, and use crowdsourcing. It is also important to maintain favorable relations with funders, governments, and complementors.

A synthesis of the diverse literature on business models focuses on four major components (see Figure 1.3), all of which have already been discussed in this chapter.

1. The *value network* is a cooperative economic ecosystem that delivers the firm's product or service by facilitating relationships within and between businesses that rely on each other to foster mutual growth. Social enterprises can better find partners and recruit impact investors by recognizing novel stakeholder constellations of suppliers, customers, competitors, and complementors.

2. Its *value proposition* specifies the customers and how a product or service solves their problems or improves their situation. Social enterprises create and capture value by differentiating their offerings. A novel business model focuses on clients who were not served or badly served by providing a new or improved product or service through a new process or model. The total value can be measured by the "triple bottom line" of profits, people, and planet.

3. Its *strategic resources* are the unique tangible and intangible assets that make up its core competencies, resulting in a sustainable competitive advantage. These are used to innovatively build the business architecture and organization infrastructure that produces and delivers value as well as reconfiguring the activities that make up the firm's value chain, including how it will sense and seize opportunities.

4. The *profit formula* (or *equation*) specifies the sources of revenues and costs to make and deliver its products and services, and, for a social enterprise, this also includes the overall social value. Novel revenue streams are not always from the end user but can come from third parties and other interested stakeholders. Moreover, controlling costs requires the firm to be efficient in all its operations.

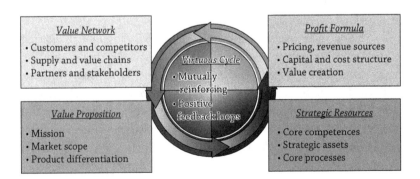

Figure 1.3 Business models.

Given the unique challenges of blended value creation, social enterprises must be creative in developing innovative business models that can provide sustainable solutions to many of today's largest challenges. The business model canvas is a popular template that organizes these elements, and there is one developed for social enterprises (see Figure 1.4). According to UAlbany's Center for Advancement & Understanding of Social Enterprises (https://www.albany.edu/cause/), there are 10 criteria to assess how these ventures are performing.

1. *System-wide*: Social enterprises should impact numerous stakeholders, often requiring alliances but resulting in large-scale institutional change.
2. *Scalable*: Good business models should have the potential to grow and be replicated, having a positive impact on many lives and communities.
3. *Self-sufficient*: Income should be generated via its mission-related activities despite inherent disadvantages, with consumers, clients, and third parties paying for the product or service.
4. *Sustainable*: The enterprise should have a long-term horizon, surviving beyond its founder(s) as it continues to provide viable solutions to achieve its mission.
5. *Significant change*: The impacts should have important benefits to peoples' health, their environment, economic security, and similar life-enhancing situations.
6. *Entrepreneurship*: The enterprise should have an innovative business model as well as be creative in its various activities.
7. *Environment*: The physical environment must be considered, especially in how natural resources are used and disposed.
8. *Equity*: The approach and results must consider issues of justice, human rights, and human development.
9. *Economy*: Social enterprises use a market approach to solve social ills, hence they have double mission mandates.
10. *Education*: These efforts should result in new learning and improvements in the organizations that are shared with others so that we can progress as a society.

THE STRATEGY TRIPOD AS AN INTEGRATIVE DEVICE

Peng, Sun, Pinkham, and Chen (2009) propose that three dominant strategy paradigms form the legs of their tripod, providing a better understanding of the strategy phenomenon. Combining these simultaneously

Key Resources	Key Activities	Type of Intervention	Segments	Value Proposition
What resources will you need to run your activities? People, finance, access?		*What is the format of your intervention? Is it a workshop? A service? A product*	*Who benefits from Beneficiary four intervention?*	Beneficiary Value Proposition Impact Measures
Partners + Key Stakeholders		**Channels**	Customer	*How will you show that you show are creating social impact?* Customer Value Propositi
Who are the essential groups you will need to involve to &deliver your programme? Do you need special access or permission?	*What programme and non-programme activities will your organisation be carrying out?*	*how are you reaching your users and customers?*	*Who are the people or organisations who will pay to address the issue?*	*What do your customers want to get out of this initiative?*
Cost Structure		**Surplus**	**Revenue**	
What are your biggest Expenditure areas? How do they change as you scale up?		*Where do you plan to invest your profits?*	*Break down your revenue sources by %*	

Figure 1.4 The social business model canvas.
Source: http://www.socialbusinessmodelcanvas.com/

address the micro, macro, and mezzo levels of strategy and can explain the various strategies employed by social enterprises.

Enterprise-Specific Resources and Capabilities

At the firm (micro) level is the "resource-based view" (RBV) of the firm (Barney, 1991) that is concerned with internal factors. This perspective considers the firm to be a collection of idiosyncratic technological, financial, and organizational resources that can be tangible (e.g., equipment, inventory, real estate, local facilities, roads, and communications infrastructures, among others) or intangible (e.g., reputation, human capital, and social relationships). *Reputation* is the "brand equity" customers attach to products or services as well as the image stakeholders have of the organization and the support they provide. *Human capital* is based on the entrepreneur's knowledge, skills, self-efficacy, need for achievement, and orientation. *Social relationships* are the connections with such important stakeholders as funders and other holders of critical resources. Enterprises often use alliances, joint ventures, and partnerships to learn from their partner, also considered a core competence. In emerging markets, political connections, corruption, or deceptive practices may come to be a very important source of competitive advantage.

Some of these resources may develop into valuable and inimitable capabilities that enable firms to attain a sustainable competitive advantage. These intangible resources tend to be more unique and hard to imitate, but some might become less valuable as an economy matures. The resource-based theory helps us understand how firms generate a sustainable and durable competitive advantage. When resources are valuable, they enable firms to achieve above-average profits or higher market share compared to competitors in their industries (Barney, 1991). Successful new ventures are those that can create value while at the same time insulate themselves from competition. Without the benefits that accrue from valuable assets that are rare, inimitable, non-tradable, and non-substitutable, anything that a new venture might do can be competed away by other firms. It is this heterogeneity of strategic assets that distinguishes enterprise strategies. The underpinnings of RBV hold that a firm can earn above-normal returns only if it has superior resources. Closely related to the RBV is the idea of core competencies—a strategic capability that is valuable, rare, costly to imitate, and not substitutable (Barney, 1991)—which the firm must continuously nurture and develop. Furthermore, those resources must be protected so they are not diffused throughout the industry.

West, Bamford, and Marsden (2008) point out that a community's economic development effort has a similar relationship to a firm's competitive advantage. Resource positions and configurations can be used to characterize a community's ability to generate entrepreneurial activity and economic benefits from such activity. Each community is bound physically to its local natural resources and may also be endowed with other institutional resources, such as schools, or with supportive infrastructures, such as roads. These endowments are systemic and can be long-lasting. Some subsistence economies may also have social resources such as informal networks or financial resources such as relationships with local banks or nongovernmental organizations (NGOs) that can better serve an entrepreneurial population. These existing resources may be valuable to a community that wishes to encourage entrepreneurial ventures only insofar as they can be mobilized so that prospective entrepreneurs find them more attractive than other resources found in competing communities.

Institutional Conditions and Transitions

At the country (macro) level are such "institutional conditions" as laws, regulations, and legal/political systems; educational resources, media systems, and the Internet, which provide information and knowledge; markets for capital, labor, and products that are transparent and accessible to everyone; technology and innovation; culture, including attitudes toward business ethics and social responsibility; the primary types of business structures and ownership/governance approaches; and the presence of an energetic, entrepreneurial, and creative population. North (1990) argued that institutions provide formal and informal rules of the game regulating economic activities, which are important in facilitating market interactions by reducing uncertainty and hence costs. These are underdeveloped but especially stronger in emerging economies than in developed economies. For instance, an emerging economy might have a culture hostile to entrepreneurship, a corrupt or unstable government, high taxation, restricted international trade or market entry, exploitation of public resources, and scarce or unavailable resources. Moreover, transition economies that have a history of depending on the state (at least in theory) to take care of its citizens might view entrepreneurial ventures as threats to their political ideology and authority.

Modern capitalism requires formal institutions. For instance, we expect stable political, regulatory, and legal environments to protect private property, enforce contracts, make commercial organizations accountable and transparent to all stakeholders, provide sufficient venture capital and financial instruments, have sound monetary and fiscal policies, and engage in beneficial relations with public interest groups and NGOs, including trade associations, professional associations, and labor unions. These governments are not expected to expropriate private property, to privatize public resources for private benefit, or to offer preferential trade agreements to cronies; they are expected to provide the physical and technical infrastructure necessary for trade today, including investing in human resources that will increase education levels and skills as well as further social stability.

Emerging and especially transition economies have an overhang of ruthless cadres benefiting from holding official positions and engaging in criminal activities. In many cases, privatization of state enterprises furthers the power of clan members of the political and administrative elites. Such weak formal institutions might give rise to informal networks, connections, and ties—sometimes through paying for entertainment, gifts, or outright bribery—or the creation of a large underground economy with numerous criminal and illegal enterprises ranging from money laundering to global cybercrime. These parasitic "antisocial" entrepreneurs can actually be destructive to economic development.

The concept of *institutional voids* refers to the "absence of specialized intermediaries, regulatory systems, and contract-enforcing mechanisms" (Khanna, Palepu, & Sinha, 2005, p. 63) all of which increase the costs of doing business and stifle economic growth and development. Thus, formal institutions lacking rule of law, governance systems, and property rights fail to promote economic and social development. These economies might restrict access that entrepreneurs have to critical resources and markets, offer limited protection against expropriating their startup-critical resources, and do not have predictable cultural norms and social conventions. Facing these challenges, entrepreneurs can respond by relying on informal institutions, including social networks; changing societal norms of behavior, customs, and traditions; or even having self-imposed codes of conduct. To the extent that social enterprises can fill these voids, they address social ills that formal institutions fail to solve.

Industry-Based Competition

Finally, between the "country" and "resource" perspectives is the industry (mezzo) context that includes rivalry and the basis for competing, buyers and sellers in the supply chain, and potential competitors and barriers to entry, as well as the broader political, economic, social, and technological environments. Industrial organization economics maintains that industry structure determines firm conduct, which, in turn, leads to company and country performance. Firms are viewed as perfectly rational profit maximizers, and resources are assumed to be mobile as well as identical and available to all industry members. Porter (1980) used this paradigm to develop his industry forces model of competition that advocated positioning a firm within its industry to gain market power and reduce competitive pressures. An industry analysis consists of identifying major sectors and that industry's competitors as well as other important industry players. Every industry has its specific key success factors that firms must match with their corporate core competencies. The nature of rivalry determines the bases for competing based on the firm's value proposition, competitive advantage, and best practices.

In contrast to these industry forces, the value network paradigm examines how companies create their own cluster of complementary partners including investors, suppliers, customers, partners and allies, and such important stakeholders as employees, government, and the press. Countries that have such clusters will support specific industries and be able to develop products and services that penetrate specific markets. Those with unique competitive advantages will contribute to national prosperity, as seen by international trade patterns, contributions to the global supply chain, and alliances and various forms of collective strategies. They might eventually become havens for contract manufacturing and outsourcing.

EXAMPLES OF SUCCESSFUL SOCIAL ENTERPRISE STRATEGIES

This section provides brief sketches of 10 exemplar social enterprises in a variety of countries, all addressing different disparities with their unique business models. While these 10 examples are few and not necessarily representative of the many social enterprises, they meet the 10 performance criteria suggested earlier and rest on each of the three legs of the strategy tripod.

Disability Disparity

BasicNeeds (http://www.basicneeds.org/) brings about lasting change in the lives of people with mental illness and epilepsy in 12 countries, including China, India, and several African countries. It seeks to enable the disabled and their families by providing them with access to regular community-based treatment along with livelihood support and initiatives to overcome stigma and abuse. It does so by building up the capacity of existing services and simultaneously nurturing self-help groups. Its business model is to work within existing healthcare systems to train doctors, nurses, and community workers to recognize and provide adequate treatment and support to people with mental illnesses. Public agencies (such as government health ministries) and other healthcare providers bear the cost of actual healthcare services and, along with philanthropic organizations, provide support for program development and training. They have over a half-million beneficiaries by serving 94% of mentally ill people in their communities; 79% of patients have secured employment or productive, nonremunerative work; and 70% report reduced symptoms.

Gender Disparity

Violence against women and girls is a largely unrecognized human rights abuse, affecting a third of the world's female population. Breakthrough (http://us.breakthrough.tv/) in India and the United States changes norms by engaging the entire community—especially men and boys—to become agents of change, shifting the public perception from a "woman's issue" to "everyone's issue." Media, arts, and technology target places where social norms are shaped: schools, churches, workplaces, and social media. Programs include classroom modules, leadership development, and educational entertainment such as interactive theater, video vans, call-in radio shows, online games, and mass media public service advertising. Breakthrough also trains police, government officials, teachers, and frontline healthcare workers as a means of preventing future systemic violence against women and girls. Moreover, it integrates gender equity into development agendas and national health and education outcomes. Public agencies attempt to change cultural norms, including early marriage and sex selection, by changing individual behaviors. Its business model is to garner philanthropic and corporate partner support for core programs that can be replicated and advanced as large public and private institutions adopt this approach; it also leverages media by reaching audiences in the tens of millions. Half a million people have participated in its educational programs, and its work in India has increased the marriage age for girls by nearly a year in villages where the program operates.

Education Disparity

Public schools remain the primary vehicle for educating all children in India. Educate Girls (http://www.educategirls.ngo/) is an NGO organization that holistically reforms more than 7,500 schools across more than 4,500 villages through community ownership that ensures greater than 90% enrollment and higher attendance as well as improved school infrastructure, quality of education, and learning outcomes. Its business model is to apply a strong community structure that believes in, demands, and contributes to a high-quality education from its government and schools. Better educated girls will improve their health, income levels, and overall livelihoods, bringing about social transformation. It has managed to improve the performance and educational outcomes for nearly 1 million children in six "gender gap" districts in Rajasthan where indicators of girls' education have been the lowest. It expects to empower 1.6 million girls to enter the classroom by 2024, or 40% of India's out-of-school girl problem, by building a volunteer network for community outreach and engagement. Philanthropy supports the organization, which enhances the reach and outcomes of public education resources by engaging with schools, parents, communities, and the education system. It is also launching India's first Development Impact Bond to support education, thus serving as an example for the education system and impact investors.

Ecological Disparity

Spread across diverse ecological and social geographies in India, the Foundation for Ecological Security (FES; http://www.fes.org.in/) works toward conserving forests, natural resources, and rural landscapes through the collective action of local communities. FES has worked with more than 4 million villagers in more than 7,000 villages to bring 1.5 million hectares of common land under village management, resulting in major benefits in soil quality, groundwater tables, and ecological diversity. It influences how shared natural resources are locally governed within the prevailing economic, social, and ecological dynamics by using a "socio-ecological systems" approach that views natural resources as economic assets for the poor and seeks to keep adjoining farmlands viable. Land productivity increases and the village determines the best way to take advantage of this, which translates into increased crop yields and income for villagers. Such village-level management of common lands results in more sustainable use, environmental conservation, greater resiliency, and durable income for villagers. Measurable improvements are expected to drive public invest-ment in replicating this approach. Moreover, collective action to effectively manage natural resources cascades to other spheres of village life such as education, health, and access to economic opportunities. Its business model is to garner philanthropic support for advocacy and technology to adopt new land management compacts.

Economic Disparity

Fundación Capital (https://www.fundacioncapital.org/) eliminates ex-treme poverty by providing knowledge and tools that enable the poor to save, build assets, and manage risk. It pioneered inclusive finance, continues as a testing ground for innovative asset building, and expands access to capital, information, training, and productive opportunities that improve and develop public policies that facilitate financial inclusion and social protection on a massive scale. It is active in 12 Latin American coun-tries and is expanding into 6 additional countries (3 in Africa, 3 in Asia) with the potential to reach 100 million families in 6–7 years. By aligning public policy, market mechanisms, and advances in digital technology, Fundación Capital enables millions of poor families to manage, grow, and invest their resources. By facilitating the exchange of ideas and experiences among both public and private sectors, it collaborates with critical players around the world in the fight against poverty. Most importantly, it strives to understand the problems and needs of low-income families to jointly create sustainable and scalable solutions. An integral part of its programs is to provide technical support and access to financial services. Its busi-ness model is to have governments provide *conditional cash transfers* to the very poor, and it enters into partnerships with them to improve services, motivated by the opportunity for more efficient and successful programs.

Human Rights Disparity

Each year, 15 million girls younger than 18 years are married. This endangers their personal development and well-being. Girls Not Brides (http://www.girlsnotbrides.org/) is a global partnership of more than 500 civil society organizations from more than 70 countries committed to ending child marriage and enabling girls to fulfill their potential. They share the conviction that every girl has the right to lead the life that she chooses and that ending child marriage will achieve a safer, healthier, and more prosperous future for all. Member organizations bring child marriage to global attention, build an understanding of what it will take to end it, and call for the laws, policies, and programs that will make a difference in the lives of millions of girls. They support each other and share learning about effective strategies. Their business model relies on philanthropic support. In November 2014, the UN General Assembly agreed that all member states should pass and enforce laws banning child marriage, with 116 countries co-sponsoring a resolution urging states to take steps to end child, early, and forced marriage. In addition, two UN commissions joined forces to issue a comprehensive document outlining countries' obligations to prevent child marriage.

Peace Disparity

Independent Diplomat (ID; https://independentdiplomat.org/) is a nonprofit venture focused on international relations, diplomacy, and conflict prevention in Africa, Asia, and Europe. This organization provides advice and assistance in diplomatic techniques and strategies to governments, political groups, international institutions, and NGOs facing complex international and political challenges. Making the rules of diplomacy more inclusive will lead to successful resolution of more conflicts. For instance, ID has worked behind the scenes of some of the biggest international policy issues of the past 2 years, including climate change with the president of the Marshall Islands, peace negotiations with the Syrian National Coalition and its president, and the New Deal for Engagement in Fragile States with Somaliland's Ministry of National Planning and Development. It is staffed by experienced former diplomats, international lawyers, and other experts in international relations, and it works with a broad network of individuals and organizations, including law firms, commercial consultancies, and universities that support and assist this work on a pro bono basis. Its business model relies on philanthropic and public support. ID holds itself and its clients to strict ethical standards by requiring its clients to be committed to democracy, human rights, and the rule of law.

Health Disparity

Medic Mobile (http://medicmobile.org/) uses mobile technology in numerous countries in the Americas, Africa, and Asia to create connected, coordinated health systems that save lives. It offers a free, scalable software toolkit designed specifically for health workers and health systems in hard-to-reach areas that combines messaging, data collection, and analytics that support any language. The tools run on basic phones, smartphones, tablets, and computers, with or without Internet connectivity, locally, or in the cloud. These mobile devices "connect the dots," linking healthcare workers to professional support and enabling the healthcare system to support better outcomes for more patients and to monitor crucial health data. It selects healthcare organizations, systems, and public agencies as partners based on their potential to deliver actual healthcare services and pay fees to use the platform. Its business model combines fees for service with philanthropic support for advancing system capabilities and core operations. It has developed support for use in new cases including malnutrition monitoring and treatment adherence in malaria and clubfoot, and it has trials in glucose monitoring, appointment management, prenatal care, and stocks of crucial drugs.

Legal Disparity

While nearly every nation in the world has declared its commitment to the basic human rights of its citizens, more than 4 billion people around the world are driven from their land, denied basic services, intimidated by violence, extorted by officials, and denied essential services. Namati (https://namati. org/) helps people in the United States and seven countries in Asia and Africa understand their fundamental legal rights, such as citizenship recognition, land tenure, and access to quality healthcare and how to challenge abuses. Its partnerships with more than 40,000 clients enable local NGOs to train and deploy a global network of more than 300 community paralegals and grassroots legal advocates beyond what Namati supports directly. By growing, it will be able to deploy more paralegals. Drawing on data from thousands of cases, it advocates for improvements to policies and systems that affect millions of people; it also convenes the Global Legal Empowerment Network of more than 550 groups from 150 countries learning from one another and working together to transform the relationship between people and law. Its business model relies on philanthropic support for its core programs and independent use of shared information to influence policy change.

Health Delivery Disparity

World Health Partners (http://worldhealthpartners.org/) is an international health organization whose mission is to provide to the rural poor and marginalized communities in low-income countries access to affordable, high-quality services, especially reproductive healthcare, within a reasonable distance. It harnesses local market forces and leverages existing social and economic infrastructure as well as human and physical resources, and it uses the latest advances in communication, diagnostic, and medical technology to establish large-scale, cost-effective health service networks. It makes significant changes by using appropriate low-cost technologies. This approach has helped create a network of more than 6,500 village-level entrepreneurs (rural health franchises) in India serving a total population of about 25 million; it recently launched a project in western Kenya to adapt its model to that context. Its business model is to offer franchises of for-profit clinics and centers that assure quality care through training and other franchise support and strategically use public subsidies to allow the very poor to access the system as paying customers. The number of franchise centers has been growing at a rate of more than 40% per year. In 2014, the network included 11,795 SkyCare rural providers and 1,154 SkyHealth telemedicine centers serving 43,942 villages. Surveys and patient responses indicate that these clinics provide improved quality of care, emphasizing preventative care and proper diagnosis and prescription. There is also a significantly lower incidence of both pneumonia and diarrhea in areas served by these centers. Sky patients paid 25–46% less for their treatment of these diseases than those served by other centers.

SUMMARY, CONCLUSIONS, AND TAKE-AWAYS

This chapter reviewed social enterprises as integrative mechanisms to further social and economic development. Social enterprises have helped where government, charities, and for-profit businesses have failed. As such, disparities in emerging and transition economies can be narrowed if not closed. The intent of this chapter has been to show how these enterprises can help mitigate the social and economic disparities commonly found. Indeed, social enterprises are the link that integrates and furthers both social and economic development. Social enterprises and commercial enterprises have many differences, but they share one common element: "roughly half of all new businesses are gone after five years. I don't know of any studies of the failure rate of social enterprises specifically, but it's likely to be similar" (Nee, 2015, p. 4). While precise numbers are controversial and businesses fail for many reasons, Cobb, Rosser, Vailakis, and Tomasko (2015, p. 24) offer a set of clear "Lessons on Tap" for aspiring social entrepreneurs by highlighting one instructive case, as follows:

1. *Begin with a sound financial plan.* Businesses fail because they run out of cash. Capital is necessary to grow a business and run day-to-day operations. To minimize financial risks, have sufficient capital to see the venture through the first few years of operation.
2. *Integrate your mission into your operations.* The purpose of social ventures is based on the community's needs, so weave it into daily business operations and use it to motivate employees.
3. *Know your business.* Learn about your industry or pick a partner who knows it well. Networking skills are an advantage; use your network or advisors. Picking the wrong business partner will, at the very least hurt, or, at worst, destroy a company.
4. *Clarify your target market.* No business can afford to ignore customers or be outcompeted, offer products or services with no market need, or have poor marketing. A clear definition of customers will address their needs with a unique value proposition (quality, reliability, cost of delivery, level of convenience and service, engineering innovation and design, image, overall satisfaction).

In competing directly with for-profit companies, not-for-profits, and even governments, successful social ventures are entrepreneurial in using innovative business approaches that challenge and redefine the traditional roles of not-for-profit organizations. Many social ventures succeed at achieving their mission despite being constrained, yet supports are still needed in these three areas:

1. *Legal and political constraints*: Governments must recognize social enterprises as partners and not threats to their legitimacy
2. *Financing and human resources*: Impact investors and crowd funding can help, and it is possible to rely on managers willing to work for below-market wages and volunteers.
3. *Conflicting stakeholder demands*: Solving massive social problems requires multiple partners achieving consensus on purpose and sharing resources.

REFERENCES

Atkinson, A. B. (2015). *Inequality: What can be done?* Cambridge, MA: Harvard University Press.

Austin, J., Stevenson, H., & Wei-Skillern, J. (2006). Social and commercial entrepreneurship: Same, different, or both? *Entrepreneurship Theory and Practice, 30*(1), 1–22.

Barney, J. (1991). Firm resources and sustained competitive advantage. *Journal of Management*, 17, 99–120. doi/abs/10.1177/014920639101700108

Cobb, M., Rosser, C., Vailakis, A., & Tomasko, R. (2015). Cause for reflection. *Stanford Social Innovation Review*, 13(2), 20–25.

Hoskisson, R. E., Eden, L., Lau, C. M., & Wright, M. (2000). Strategy in emerging economies. *Academy of Management Journal*, 43(3), 249–267. doi: 10.2307/1556394

Khanna, T., Palepu, K., & Sinha, J. (2005). Strategies that fit emerging markets. *Harvard Business Review*, 83(6), 63–76.

Kuttner, R. (1984). *The economic illusion: False choices between prosperity and social justice*. Boston: Houghton Mifflin.

Linz, J. J., & Stepan, A. (1978). *The breakdown of democratic regimes*. Baltimore: Johns Hopkins University Press.

Magretta, J. (2002). Why business models matter. *Harvard Business Review*, 80(5), 86–92.

Nee, E. (2015). Learning from failure. *Stanford Social Innovation Review, 13*(2), 4.

North, D. C. (1990). *Institutions, institutional change and economic performance*. Cambridge, UK: Cambridge University Press. doi.org/10.1017/CBO9780511808678

Peng, M. W., Sun, S. L., Pinkham, B., & Chen, H. (2009). The institution-based view as a third leg for a strategy tripod. *Academy of Management Perspectives, 23*, 63–81. doi.org/10.5465/amp.2009.43479264

Piketty, T. (2014). *Capital in the 21st century*. Cambridge, MA: Harvard University Press.

Porter, M. E. (1980). *Competitive strategy: Techniques for analyzing industries and competitors*. New York: Free Press.

Porter, M. E., & Kramer, M. R. (2011). Creating shared value. *Harvard Business Review, 89*(1–2), 62–77.

Schumpeter, J. (1942). *Capitalism, Socialism and Democracy*. New York: Harper Collins.

Smith, A. (1776). *An Inquiry into the Nature and Causes of the Wealth of Nations*. London: W. Strahan and T. Cadell.

Stiglitz, J. (2012). *The price of inequality: How today's divided society endangers our future*. New York: Norton.

West, G. P., Bamford, C. E., & Marsden, J. W. (2008). Contrasting entrepreneurial economic development in emerging Latin American economies: Applications and extensions of resource-based theory. *Entrepreneurship Theory and Practice, 32*, 15–36. doi.org/10.1111/j.1540-6520.2007.00214.x

APPENDIX A
WRITING A SOCIAL ENTERPRISE PLAN

Business plans are a common tool for entrepreneurs when starting or growing a business enterprise; developing one is essential for a social enterprise. It is especially important to consider how the mission, organizational structure, and financial and social impacts will align. The following outline for a social business plan is merely a suggestion of topics; use discretion in applying them to your specific situation. The following provides a roadmap for your plan, but the length and amount of detail in every section will vary depending on the nature of the enterprise, the complexity of the organization, and the purpose and audience for the plan. Good luck!

1. PRELIMINARY SECTIONS

- Cover page
- Table of contents
- Executive summary (briefly describe only the most important information that readers need to understand and support the concept but not necessarily know the detailed plans, ideally 2–4 pages with clear highlights including financial information):
  ‣ Who is the social entrepreneur and what unique skill, service, or background does he/she/they bring to the venture?
  ‣ What is the venture and where is it now? Is it truly new and important? Who will benefit from it? How?
  ‣ Where do you want to go? What will constitute success?
  ‣ How you will get there? How (in general terms) will the idea be executed?
  ‣ What kind of support for the enterprise do you need? What resources are required?

2. THE BUSINESS MODEL/CONCEPT

- Social purpose, mission, and vision statement/aims and perhaps its theory of change:
  ‣ Why is there a need for this social enterprise? Who will benefit? How will you meet the need?
- Quantifiable financial and social goals and objectives:
  ‣ Financial highlights and capital requirements
  ‣ Definition of success and "value"
- Products, services, activities, etc.:
  ‣ Value proposition or competitive advantage
  ‣ Key success factors
- Key innovations or adaptations
- Potential partners and stakeholders
- Starting the enterprise:
  ‣ Acquiring staff, space, and equipment
  ‣ When will you deliver services?

- Achieving financial sustainability:
  - ‣ Short-term (less than a year), intermediate (1–3 years), long-term (3–5 years)
  - ‣ Realistic assessment of chances for success
- Measuring, monitoring, and evaluating strategy and tracking progress toward "social impact"
- Exit strategy (how and when investors recoup their money):
  - ‣ Sell? Merge with another social venture? Dissolution—mission accomplished?

3. BACKGROUND AND STRUCTURE

- Brief description including organization's context, history, and programs
- How the venture will be organized; is there a chart?
- Legal ownership structure (equity positions, financial deal) and governance (boards, advisory committees, reporting, etc.)

4. THE MARKET

- Summary of current market situation
- Target market(s) segment and customer/client characteristics, needs, and how the enterprise will meet a gap and demand in the market:
  - ‣ Who will buy your goods/services? Why from you?
  - ‣ Market research (including trends)
  - ‣ Expected position and share
- Products/Services:
  - ‣ Positioning of proposed products/services
  - ‣ Advantage/value of product or service
  - ‣ Future products/services

5. COMPETITIVE ANALYSIS

- Industry description:
  - ‣ Primary competitors (e.g., similar social enterprises) and competitive advantage
  - ‣ Risks and opportunities

6. THE PEOPLE

- Key personnel:
  - ‣ Leader(s)/founder(s): Background, education, experience, accomplishments, reputation, skills, character/integrity, motivations/personal drive
  - ‣ Others: Advisors/counselors, consultants, supporters/partners
- Staffing and forward-looking human resource management strategy:
  - ‣ The team: From top management to front line
  - ‣ Key personnel (skills, experience, knowledge)

7. THE MARKETING PLAN

- Summary of sales forecasts:
  - ‣ Marketing strategy and activities
  - ‣ Distribution channels
- Revenue model:
  - ‣ Demand management (e.g., pricing and expected surplus)
  - ‣ Income from for-profit activities vs. noncommercial
  - ‣ Communications (e.g., advertising, public relation, promotions, direct mail, media, social networking)
  - ‣ Publicity and showcases
  - ‣ Marketing "the brand"
- E-commerce strategy

8. THE OPERATIONS

- Creation and delivery of the product or service:
  - ‣ Production plan or service delivery
  - ‣ Client service/support
  - ‣ Facilities required, including specialized equipment
- ? Location characteristics

9. THE FINANCE PLAN AND PROJECTIONS

- Historical, current, and projected views
- Summary narrative of key assumptions and comments

- Startup costs for capital equipment, inventory, initial marketing and staffing, technology, etc.
- Financial returns:
  ‣ Projected income, expenditure, cash-flow for next 3 years
  ‣ Pro forma balance sheet; profit and loss
- Subsidy needed to cover losses during the startup period ("burn rate")
- Source(s) for resources:
  ‣ Donors, philanthropist/angel, grants, initial public offering (IPO), debt financing
- Financial management systems
- When will the venture become financially self-sufficient?

10. RISK/REWARD ASSESSMENT

- Critical external and internal risks and contingencies (potential impact of failures, problems, unforeseen events and trends):
  ‣ Financial, legal, talent, technological, environmental, other
- Scenario planning: Best case to worst case
- Risk mitigation and possible responses

11. CONCLUDING SECTIONS

- Summary
- Key milestones/timelines and associated activities and schedules (calendar of expected dates and events)

12. APPENDIXES

- Supporting documents:
  ‣ Résumés for founders and key enterprise participants
  ‣ References/letters of recommendation (e.g., banker, lawyer, accountant)
  ‣ Sources of data used in the plan, including professional advisers' reports if used
  ‣ References for literature cited in the plan, if any
  ‣ Other (e.g., photographs/drawings, market surveys, Web page mock-up, product prototype(s), video, sample press release, etc.)

13. OVERALL APPEAL

- Feasibility of the plan (e.g., attractiveness of the market opportunity; realistic)
- Alignment of social and financial returns on investment
- Market, operational, and technological viability (e.g., value created by the new product or service; competitive advantage of the proposed venture)
- Keep it simple but clarify, clarify, clarify
  - ‣ Is the plan . . . comprehensive? sufficiently analytical? reasonable?
- Physical appearance (well-written and presented, easy to read, crisp, clean):
  - ‣ Check spelling and grammar
  - ‣ Have someone else read to check for omissions and weakness

CHAPTER 2

∾

Displacement

A Typology to Inform Social Entrepreneurs

KELLY J. GROSS

BACKGROUND

Many economists, governmental officials, and development experts have decried the harms of large economic development projects that have relied on a trickle-down approach to job creation but have also caused the displacement of people and ancestral livelihoods (Stiglitz, Sen, & Fitoussi, 2009). Given these critiques and concerns about development, it seems timely to explore displacement processes and effects and to classify various kinds of displacement in a typology. This chapter proposes a displacement typology drawn from economic development projects undertaken by nongovernmental organizations (NGOs), the World Bank, the International Monetary Fund, and similar investment-based organizations. Many of these organizations have in some way committed themselves to alleviating poverty in developing countries by supporting development efforts (Commission on Growth and Development, 2008). However, it is important to realize that while development projects intend to alleviate poverty and the marginalization of peoples around the world, their good intentions can also cause harms. This chapter categorizes these harms by offering a typology of displacements.

Kelly J. Gross, *Displacement* In: *Social Entrepreneurship and Enterprises in Economic and Social Development*. Edited by: Katharine Briar-Lawson, Paul Miesing, and Blanca M. Ramos, Oxford University Press (2021). © Oxford University Press. DOI: 10.1093/oso/9780197518298.003.0003.

While the displacement typology is drawn from themes in global development, it is meant to encourage reflection by social entrepreneurs during the planning, implementation, and maintenance of their social and economic innovations. The purpose of this chapter is to inform ways to reduce harms to communities—displacement—while providing social entrepreneurs action items to consider.

Social entrepreneurs are uniquely positioned to prevent displacement by virtue of their use of inclusionary, participatory, local innovation strategies. Several factors for consideration are offered to contribute to a discussion that may help to prevent displacement while informing more sustainable social and economic development. The factors for consideration that follow the proposed typology are offered in the form of a beginning checklist, enabling social entrepreneurs to appraise the variables they need to consider in their local development efforts.

Social entrepreneurs often live within the local communities that they hope to impact for development and innovation. Thus, they may be more attentive to the negative impacts of displacement processes while also being attuned to the potential assets within the community. Consequently, they are potentially more accountable to their local networks and more amenable to pursuing more locally driven, effective practices.

The typology is based on an examination of development efforts and their outcomes, including themes of loss and harms. Exploration of the causes, processes, and outcomes of displacement help to inform discrete categories for the displacement typology. Of special interest are examples of development efforts that may have been dismissed or discounted but could be taken up by social entrepreneurs because they are uniquely positioned within local networks and understand the systems' interplay at the local level. Variables under consideration in the development of the typology include (1) the role of the informal economic sector; (2) the role of all resources, not only financial resources; and (3) the use of social and cultural capital as more than an economic-only based resource (social and cultural capital is not only something to be used to sell—in the form of crafts, traditional herbs, etc.—but is also an asset that can be used to acquire skills and knowledge in the development efforts). This preliminary typology may also help inform future research. Such future research can address additional displacement types as well as offer more ways to proactively plan for and prevent these displacements. Furthermore, the considerations suggested may help inform more inclusive development approaches.

Displacement as Development's Unintended Consequence

Why is development-induced displacement an important topic to explore? Displacement is often presented as a by-product of violence, war, and disasters (IDMC, 2017; Terminski, 2013). Development-induced displacement is featured in some studies but mainly as it relates to mega development—constructing dams, extracting mining resources, developing irrigation systems, and other large-scale projects (Terminski, 2013). Development-induced displacement has generally been studied as it relates to the effects of physical displacement of peoples from their homes and livelihoods (Adeloa, 2016; Cernea, 1988; IDMC, 2016; Terminski, 2013). Physical displacement often causes people to be relocated, sometimes outside of their own country, where they become *refugees*. Those displaced inside their country are simply *displaced persons* and might be compensated for their losses. Of note, what are not studied as closely by researchers are social displacement phenomena such as loss of formal and informal networks, along with loss of social and cultural capital that occurs *within* a country.

Development-induced displacement is an important topic to explore especially if one considers its prevalence. As it relates to development, between 10 and 15 million people are displaced each year due to development projects worldwide (Adeloa, 2016; Stanley, 2017). Cernea (1988) advises that development causes more displacement than natural disasters. Furthermore, Terminski (2012) indicates that development projects, including dams, infrastructure, and resource extraction, led to 300 million people being displaced between 1988 and 2008. Overall, the prevalence of within-country displacement is thought to be underdocumented, especially for those persons who are within a short distance from their original physical home (UNESCO, 2017). Development-induced displacements help to highlight the weaknesses in development projects and show the need for data collection on the various types of displacement while orienting social entrepreneurs about what they should work to prevent as they engage in start-ups and potentially attempt to remedy marginalization and poverty.

Both cultural and social capital are important in this discussion since development is more than just an economic means to a monetary outcome. Therefore, the displacement effects are felt not just in economic terms. Instead, the cultural and social capital comprised in a community may be as important as community members' economic transactions and monetary outcomes. Formal and informal networks interact with one another to create social and cultural capital and therefore may help foster the environment for development and economically beneficial outcomes to occur. As Terminski asserts, "Despite its clearly humanitarian context, development-induced displacement is still a marginalized and underrated problem in the area of human rights and humanitarian protection and assistance for vulnerable groups" (2013, p. 20). Furthermore, he suggests that displacement be studied from more of an economics perspective than through a social or psychological lens (Terminski, 2013).

For purposes of this chapter, *social capital* is defined as "networks together with shared norms, values and understandings that facilitate co-operation within or among groups . . . we can think of networks as real-world links between groups or individuals. Think of networks of friends, family networks, networks of former colleagues" (Keeley, 2007, p. 6). "Social capital" has been largely used as an economic term to quantify that which can be used as a commodity. The broadening of the term "social capital" is important as it relates to the inclusion of the embedded assets used within social networks that allow for creativity, the ability to get things done, and the knowledge that is held by a group of people to allow for innovation, movement, and sustainability for development.

Bourdieu's *cultural capital* is loosely defined as capital that is symbolic and associated with one's culture (Bourdieu, 1986; Lareau & Weininger, 2003). It includes those skills, tastes, mannerisms, and ways of seeing the world that are inherited and valued within one's family, close associates, communities, or life experiences. Cultural capital is embedded in one's community and possibly in one's nation, and it usually differs from community to community. It also is less tangible and is thus harder to quantify. Again, cultural capital is important in this discussion when thinking about preventing displacements or remedying those displacements for more optimal social entrepreneur practice.

Types of Displacement

Displacement is defined as "the relocation related to deprivation of access to existing land and resources, unaccompanied by adequate support mechanisms for the affected people . . . not limited to physical departure . . . with no benefits gained in return" (Terminski, 2015, p. 59). This definition combines not only physical effects but also the less studied and understood social and economic dynamics and consequences.

The typology proposed in this chapter depicts displacement types based on the domains of loci, communities, resources, and financial systems. Each displacement type or domain will be defined followed by an analysis. In all displacement types, social and cultural capital are included because informal and formal networks are potentially affected. Some potential displacement types have been left out due to lack of complete data during the review of literature to date. For example, *infrastructure displacement* is one such type of displacement that needs further investigation. To provide a context, an ethnography summary is presented next to illustrate several of the displacement types.

Summary of an Ethnography to Illuminate Displacement Types

The summarized ethnographic study by Elyachar (2005) spotlights the negative outcomes of development. The case study is presented here because it illuminates some displacement types and issues for social entrepreneurs.

Historically, in Cairo, Egypt, there were craftsmen and workshop masters utilizing a *relational market*. Craftsman used their skills and knowledge in their craft-making. The skills and knowledge were passed down from craftsman to craftsman for centuries, and these were considered part of the informal economic sector. Workshop masters gain their position through lineage, where it is passed on through family and social relationships. Masters not only provide a place for craftsmen to practice their trade, financial help for tools, and the market in which to conduct business practices, but they also support many facets of social and economic life. In Cairo, the workshop masters' market includes the workshop, family, home, craftsmen, social supports, and the community. In this way, the market is not one where one individual competes with other individuals; instead, the market is comprised of social and economic aspects of daily life. Masters share workers, supplies, and machines with one another. They also share customers to gain favor and equal selling power within the market in Cairo. A master will often provide gifts to other masters or craftsmen in order to curry favor and also to foster an invisible social mechanism of trade. The gifts are often not associated with monetary items. For example, a master or craftsmen might encourage a customer to go to another workshop to purchase an item so that the "gift" of sharing a customer reflects well on them. It is a complicated, embedded, social, cultural, and economic system that cannot easily be described in this short summary. However, the key is that the value is not primarily economic but rather one of community and relational value (Elyachar, 2005). The market is more than economic and includes all of life within the community.

Learning and using a craft is a popular business model in Cairo, and business knowledge is gained from childhood through hands-on learning under workshop masters. These craftsmen have utilized the cultural practices endemic in their businesses since around early 900 AD (Elyachar, 2005). According to Elyachar (2005), workshop masters and craftsmen carry out business through a complicated exchange of relations with customers, workshop masters, and craftsmen through shared customers, shared production, and shared patterns of consumption. The marketplace is an economic exchange setting as well as a relational setting with a complicated network of actors. For example, if a craftsman is having a good week in selling his goods, he might refer a customer to another craftsman so that the customer could purchase the goods from a neighboring craftsman. This form of a transaction in the market is much more communal and cooperative in nature instead of being based on competition. This traditional community-based, relational market would be displaced through an attempt to modernize in the name of development using entrepreneurship.

Out of a desire to bring free trade and democracy to Egypt, el-Hirafiyeen was launched as a newly built city outside Cairo. It was designed by various international organizations as a place for the operation of a more Westernized market. El-Hirafiyeen was designed to be a common space for those businesses deemed too noisy to be housed in the city streets of Cairo and also to incorporate young entrepreneurs who were taught Westernized practices of free market enterprise and individual competition. Thus, the masters and their craftsmen were forced by Cairo officials from their neighborhoods to a newly designed workshop city outside of Cairo—el-Hirafiyeen—in order to focus their production and market-related activities. At the same time, young entrepreneurs were taught about a different type of market, one more in line with free market ways of conducting business using competition as a way to develop a market. The young entrepreneurs were funded by the World Bank's Social Fund for Development. They were not integrated into the masters and craftsmen network. Neither were they prepared to work with the existing masters and craftsmen, and they were therefore set up to fail (Elyachar, 2005).

The design of el-Hirafiyeen was completed by engineers and social scientists from international organizations and within the Egyptian government. El-Hirafiyeen was constructed disregarding local markets, which incorporated the social, economic, and cultural pieces within a neighborhood market. Traditionally, since masters and craftsmen in Cairo performed work within the relational context of their family and community, they preferred to live and work within a neighborhood that included a diversity of trade types all in one place. The designers of el-Hirafiyeen considerably missed the mark, thinking that creating individual neighborhoods around types of crafts would make business thrive (Elyachar, 2005). In this new design, craftsmen and workshop masters were not utilizing the relational market they were used to since the design was by craft type. The young entrepreneurs (about age 30) who were trained in free market development were added to the neighborhood to create micro enterprises. These entrepreneurs were placed in el-Hirafiyeen without traditional knowledge of the market in Cairo. Instead, they were taught about a kind of market that was an abstract concept that would be available to them if they practiced what they had learned in a classroom about markets and building a business. That type of market was foreign to the craftsman moved to El-Hirafiyeen and did not seem to mix with what was used for centuries as a tried and true relational market.

Outcomes included displacements for both the masters and craftsmen, as well as for the new young entrepreneurs. At the time of the ethnographic study by Elyachar (2005), el-Hirafiyeen was operating as a city in which young entrepreneurs had no market and were thus thought of as lazy failures. Some craftsmen decided to relocate back to their original community, renting out their spaces in el-Hirafiyeen to others or using them as places of storage for supplies. They moved back because for them el-Hirafiyeen had no informal market—as they were used to in Cairo—and no formal market.

Other craftsmen decided to stay but were living in el-Hirafiyeen without their families, links to their workshop masters, or links to their social and economic networks, all of which were important to not only their business but also to their lives. Like the craftsmen who moved from el-Hirafiyeen back to Cairo, the craftsmen who stayed were without their "market" as they defined it when they had lived in Cairo. Craftsmen who stayed in their new location of el-Hirafiyeen in some cases changed their crafts and attempted to build the kind of market based on relations that was so successful within Cairo. Supports and amenities based on a relational market were also lacking, such as a hospital, first aid station, a fresh food market, or cafés. Living in el-Hirafiyeen required a not only a different lifestyle in conducting business, but also in living daily life. Elyachar (2005) points to these ideas as reasons for the craftsmen to leave their workshops in el-Hirafiyeen.

The craftsmen who stayed in el-Hirafiyeen seemed to do so by being mindful of creating a relational market. They created an NGO to promote a way of recreating a relationally based marketplace that integrated social, cultural, and economic transactions. Under this NGO, they were able to partially create a relational market that was limited in its positive outcomes when compared to the market they had in Cairo. In their view, the market was not an abstraction but a way of daily life that had to do with networks and multiple interactions with the community.

Young entrepreneurs who had no understanding of a relationally based market used their experience from more Westernized forms of markets to build their microenterprises under their own NGO. Their NGO was funded under the World Bank's Social Fund for Development. Interestingly, the young entrepreneurs who were trained in "economic development" and more competitive, capitalistic style markets had difficulty establishing themselves in el-Hirafiyeen. Elyachar (2005) described the following vignette regarding these young entrepreneurs:

> The group called the "youth graduates" around which NGOs were organized, was supposed to embody . . . the market . . . but the kind of market they were meant to foster was an abstraction to which they could not sell. They searched for "the market" but could rarely find it . . . their enterprises failed. (2005, p. 11)

The relational market found in some parts of Cairo was not aligned with the Westernized nonrelational market sought by entrepreneurs. Furthermore, these young entrepreneurs were burdened with high rents or mortgages. Their activities were separate from the craftsmen although they shared the same neighborhoods, and they were unable to build a customer base for their goods. Subsequently, they had losses related to finances since they could not pay back loans given to them under the NGO. They had lack of a market, lack of positive economic outcomes, and lack of a social structure to help them be successful.

One questions whether an integrated approach using social entrepreneurs in this case might have been successful if they had worked with various officials and market businesses to understand context, needs, and embedded strengths. Here, social entrepreneurs could have been poised to innovate, building on what already worked, limiting displacement, and furthering economic and social good. An integrated approach with social entrepreneurship will be further discussed later in this chapter, but first the displacement typology will be outlined and explained.

DISPLACEMENT TYPOLOGY

The ethnographic summary illustrates different kinds of development-induced displacement. These include loci, community, resources, and financial systems as an initial way to look at development-based displacement (see Table 2.1). We note that these forms of displacement are linked to development projects in developing nations. In post-industrial nations, such as the United States, other kinds of displacement might be more germane

Table 2.1 DISPLACEMENT TYPOLOGY

	Loci	*Community*	*Resources*	*Financial systems*
Features of loss	Home	Reciprocal supports	Exported	High-interest loans
	Land	Networks	Replaced/ supplanted	Large loans that become unpayable
	Livelihood	Informal sector	Depleted	Unstable economies
	Infra-structure	Shared and common interests, attitudes, goals	Polluted	Unrealistic development expectations
	←Underutilized or Unrecognized Social and Cultural Capital→			

Note: *Loci loss* is the loss is of physical location; *Community loss* is the loss or undervaluation of networks and relations; *Resource loss* is the loss of indigenous natural assets and natural resources; and *Financial systems* loss involves financial capital, supports, and economy. *Underutilized or unrecognized social and cultural capital* feature of loss is one feature that fits under each displacement type: loci, community, resources, and financial systems.

and added to the typology, such as job displacement. Likewise, additional displacement types will be added to this typology as new data become available in the literature and research.

Displacement of Loci

Displacement of loci refers to development that causes changes to a community that result in some people losing their homes or their workplaces. Generally, individuals are removed by the government or through "force" due to modifications in the physical environment requiring a relocation somewhere else. Thus, displacement of loci is dislocation from location and physical space—home or workplace, usually a combination of both. With such displacement, the rupture caused is more than just the physical loss of space; it also includes loss of social supports, economic activity or livelihood, and land. Terms such as "involuntary resettlement" and "villagization" are used to describe the dislocation process (Cernea, 1988). Displacement is also conceptualized in terms of direct (home) and indirect (livelihood) losses (Cernea, 1988). Place-based dislocations involving direct loss of home and indirect loss of livelihood are combined in this typology under the definition of "displacement of loci" since in both loss of home and workplace the displacement is of location. The loss includes the following:

- *Home*: The physical building along with some (if not all) of its contents.
- *Land*: Including ancestral lands and one's homeland or livelihood (for those growing crops or raising animals for their own use and for their own entry into the economy).

- *Livelihood or economic activity*: A business, farm, trade, or barter/gift systems. In many developing countries individuals cannot be physically moved without hardship and displacement involving their livelihoods.
- *Infrastructure*: Including water systems, access to health and education, means of selling products (markets, agreements with other businesses or patrons), access to supplies, and transportation systems, among others.
- *Social and cultural capital*: Many developing localities depend on their physical locations to carry out daily life tasks. Social and cultural capital is part of the informal infrastructure and includes supports from family, community, ancestral ways of living and working, and other means of getting help on a daily basis. The informal system is not easily replaced in the new location since this system is often physically tied to place. Moreover, communities of people who are displaced are rarely sent to a new location together. When individuals are physically relocated, often both the formal and informal infrastructures are not moved with them to their new physical location.

Loss of loci often affects the poor most critically, whose identity and livelihood may be tightly interwoven with the land and the community, and this often makes monetized or land swap compensation insufficient (Terminski, 2015). Displacement involving loci may implicate the loss of social and cultural capital that has often been built over the course of generations, involving deep social ties and ancestral and cultural supports. Without these ties, social capital may be eroded, leaving some with insurmountable barriers. These may involve setbacks in recreating deep ties to support networks and opportunities to regain one's livelihood. Without ties and access to one's livelihood, people may have a more difficult time rebuilding elsewhere and are often worse off than they were in their home location or loci.

In the ethnographic study cited earlier, displacement of loci is illustrated by the way in which the workshop masters and craftsmen were moved to el-Hirafiyeen in the name of development and progress. Physical relocation and displacement occurred involving both home and market (workplace). Loss of their market included the loss of livelihood, social and cultural capital, and informal and formal infrastructures. Beyond having their market displaced, infrastructure also was displaced since el-Hirafiyeen had no grocers, cafés, or hospital, and the craftsmen did not have access to the infrastructure of their previous neighborhoods. The craftsmen who remained in el-Hirafiyeen eventually established a traditional, culturally based market like their old one, one that utilized their traditional social norms of doing business. However, many craftsmen relocated back to their old shops or to markets in other areas of Cairo.

Displacement of Community

Displacement of community (defined as networks) is another kind of loss involving ruptures in one's networks and support systems in the same physical location. However, displacement of community should not be confused with displacement of loci since displacement of community has nothing to do with a physical move. Instead, displacement of community occurs when local members stay where they work or live but their networks are either not valued, not utilized in development efforts, or are changed so drastically that their network access is ineffectual. Displacement of this type changes the way a community functions even though no person has changed his or her physical location.

Informal and formal networks within a community are complex mechanisms full of social and cultural capital through which individuals sustain and maintain their economic and social transactions—in effect, their way of living. Especially true in developing areas, community cannot be separated from development efforts since the way a community functions in many cases provides for a means of survival. In most instances in developing countries, individuals within communities have a history of depending on one another to survive, and many within the community work together to see that basic needs are met (Terminski, 2012, 2015). Thus, "community" includes intricate informal and formal systems that work together to provide social and economic support and is often deeply rooted in cultures that are generations old. This social and cultural capital is rich with capacity and may be underused, if not supplanted, by some developers. Developers are often remiss in not understanding or using the assets of community for buy-in and long-term sustainability of their development efforts. Instead, development efforts may consider social capital, but often with commodification goals—using the social capital as a product and thus a salable source. For example, traditional forms of arts and crafts and specific skill sets (such as in farming) become commodified. These forms of social capital are the basis of local knowledge that should be used alongside development efforts, not just for selling something, but for the knowledge to sustain projects in the long term. That which is local has helped individuals maintain and survive historically; therefore the use of social capital within a community context should be an important consideration in development work.

Displacement may occur when development projects do not encourage local stakeholders to participate in the planning process and implementation. As a result, key resources of social and cultural capital within informal and formal networks may be overlooked. These key resources include all of the embedded and useful social networks, relationships, skills, systems, and ways of conducting business and daily life that are important to the culture and the sustainability of development efforts. Social and cultural capital may be comprised of intricate networks that are not separate from economic or self-sustaining activities. Elyachar's case study (2005) can give a glimpse into the complex but useful systems that could propel development into an integrated and sustainable process. She uses the idea of relational markets to help explain some of the social and cultural capital embedded in networks that provide not only an economic means but a way of life. The social and cultural capital in a community may be overlooked as an asset and not well understood for development purposes, and therefore this sort of development causes loss or displacement. In fact, these forms of capital are sometimes thought of as limitations to engaging in free trade–based markets. But if development is one answer to poverty reduction, then sustainable development might include the understanding and use of these networks.

Paradoxically, displacement also happens when developers are uninformed about the reason that a community is chosen for development—that there was something promising about the community warranting an investment. Using Elyachar's study, a primary feature of this displacement is shown when generations-old, relationally based markets are disregarded. In el-Hirafiyeen, while displacement of loci (since the craftsmen and workshop masters were forced to move their homes and livelihood) overshadowed the displacement of community, the traditional knowledge of their relationally based market was not used to develop a new marketplace. In other words, the embedded cultural and social capital was not understood or utilized in new development efforts. Established norms around how to undertake a business, social traditions, and a lifestyle were disregarded. While this kind of relational market, as explained in the case study summary, is not completely aligned with a capitalistic-style competitive market, the boundless capacity of the market with all of its embedded, nuanced cultural and social capital was lost when development experts and governmental officials ignored it. This dynamic is best captured in Elyachar's description: "where strangers met to buy and sell . . . it marked out a place of Egyptian cultural practice. The market was not an abstract place" (2005, p. 12).

Displacement of Resources

Displacement of resources involves the depletion or dislocation of a locality's assets. In effect, resources are depleted through marketization as products or through environmental degradation, or they are not available for local residents' own consumption. Resource harms and/or depletion are illustrated in the following:

1. *Changes in production and exportation*, altering how the resources were once used by the local residents
2. *Free trade agreements* that change the way a country's resources are used, usually with a country's resources being replaced by exogenous (another country's) resources. In this way, the country's resources are undervalued (not used to full value) or replaced totally by the exogenous resources
3. *Environmental harms or resource exhaustion* so that resources are no longer available to the local residents

Experts suggest that "over 60 percent of the world's natural resources are located on indigenous lands" (Terminski, 2013, p. 18). Many traditional economic development projects use such resources for economic gain. For poor regions that are resource dependent (for food, traditional celebrations, for their own economic gain), the potential for depletion is great, exacerbating aggravated poverty. Sometimes such displacement creates environmental hazards that make the resources dangerous or unusable to those who depended on them for sustenance or livelihood. Likewise, when indigenous resources are exported in the name of development, displacement occurs. Resources such as food, building materials, and others are then grown and produced for export only, and local residents must either buy the same food on the market (at a higher price since now they must pay for it) or must grow another crop for their own use. In effect, development might hinder the use of resources that may be critical to local residents' traditional livelihoods, especially since many developing regions depend on local use of resources for food to eat, for use during local traditions and celebrations, and as a source of financial support (Terminski, 2013). Social and cultural capital is also displaced in that the traditional food stuffs and use of resources for ceremonies, healing, or daily life are replaced, polluted, or reduced.

The previously cited summary of el-Hirafiyeen's development is not illustrative of this displacement type since physical resources were not affected. Instead, one of the more common examples of resource displacement is the import of corn to Mexico. At one time Mexico grew its own corn for local use, for use in its production of corn products, and for use in export (Johnson, 2011; Relinger, 2010). Corn was not only a food product for export, it was (and is) a large part of the Mexican diet and is used in crafts and in cere-monial/traditional festivities. However, due to the North American Free Trade Agreement (NAFTA) (Relinger, 2010), the United States supplanted the growing of corn and exported US-grown corn to Mexico. Mexico's mass production of corn (and corn products) in many communities was mostly replaced by US corn (Johnson, 2011). Mexico still undertakes corn produc-tion, but it is using mostly US corn. Due to displacement involving Mexican corn, this crop is not as readily available to Mexicans for their own foods and ceremonies, or to use in Mexican mass production of corn products. This is not only a cultural loss, but is also an economic loss for the Mexican economy.

Displacement of Financial Systems

Financial systems' displacement often comes about due to problematic loan practices, unstable economies, or unrealistic development plans. This may involve the provision of loans at high interest rates that cannot be re-paid. Or this can be the result of loans that are based on unachievable goals. Often, where development is occurring to combat poverty, the economy may be unstable and thus financial transactions may not be sustained. In effect, borrowers cannot honor their loan repayments. Nonpayment of loans may also be due to fluctuations in interest rates, lack of regulation of inflation rates, and devaluation of currency.

The loss is exacerbated by the fact that some developing countries do not have the financial capacity to support or prevent financial displace-ment when compared to more developed countries. For example, in devel-oping nations, there may be little to no economic infrastructure (banks, loans at reasonable rates, access to capital, or collateral, etc.).

Financial system displacement can happen anywhere—take, for in-stance, the consequences of real estate loans that ended up in foreclosures across the United States in 2007. This was devastating to those who lost their homes and ended up in financial ruin. Their homes were foreclosed upon because of the recession and loans that were too high (Streitfeld, 2009).

Such high rates of repayment on loans, often seen in development projects, create economic insecurity and a precarious future for the loan recipients. When currency is also unstable, as is the case in many devel-oping economies, such financial chaos may create development failures and economically devastated regions. Social and cultural capital are changed in financial system displacement since the financial loss further complicates poverty.

In Elyachar's ethnographic account (2005), el-Hirafiyeen was developed as a neighborhood outside of Cairo where small and micro businesses could thrive. Financial system displacement took place when the craftsmen's businesses were relocated and these craftsmen were forced to move to this new neighborhood from their old neighborhood—they had no market in the new location. The craftsmen were left with no customers and therefore little to no income. This loss of income was compounded when they could not afford their rents or mortgages in el-Hirafiyeen, forcing them to move elsewhere or attempt to rent their buildings to others. Likewise, the young entrepreneurs had loans that they could not repay. The terms of the loans included unrealistic performance measures that were not matched to the reality of the relational economic structure locally. In the end, the relocated craftsmen and the new young entrepreneurs were displaced financially with loans that were hard to repay, thus causing unpaid rental costs and lack of income.

Summary of Displacement Types

This displacement typology illustrates some of the negative effects of economic development derived from inattention to loci, social, and cultural capital; formal and informal networks; resources; and financial systems. While development experts often have poverty reduction as a primary goal, they may inadvertently cause more harm than good. Although the consequences of displacement are germane to development projects, they are also relevant to local social entrepreneurs. Social entrepreneurs are better positioned than outside developers to think about these potential displacements since they combine social and economic development in their innovative planning. They are often locally based, and thus know their own communities.

The displacement typology just discussed is offered as a first step in development risk analysis to prevent or remediate displacement wherever possible. Such prevention and remediation are needed so that development efforts can be more effective in reducing harms and being better sustained over time. For poverty alleviation to be more successful, displacement needs to be addressed. Future research might explore the way that infrastructure is a key feature of loss and debilitation in development. (Currently there is insufficient research on infrastructure-related displacements to warrant this as another formal type of displacement.) Additionally, research might help to inform and elaborate on other types of displacement.

FACTORS FOR CONSIDERATION
BY SOCIAL ENTREPRENEURS

Social entrepreneurs undertake innovative solutions to complex community problems. Creating these social and economic change efforts may comprise an integrated, locally based answer to development (Guo & Bielefeld, 2014; Kickul & Lyons, 2012; Light, 2008; Praszkier & Nowak, 2012). In this, social entrepreneurs build on existing infrastructure and locally held knowledge by integrating elements of practical, grassroots solutions with the use of economic development by social means (Guo & Bielefeld, 2014; Light, 2008; Praszkier & Nowak, 2012). This chapter offered a first opportunity to look at a development-induced displacement typology. The case study by Elyachar (2005) incorporated displacement caused by development and suggests how social entrepreneurship that is not locally based can cause more harm than good. Since the social entrepreneurs in the study were taught using outside constructs, knowledge, and ideas, local knowledge was not incorporated and used as an asset (2005).

This development-induced displacement typology can help to further inform what social entrepreneurs do locally while allowing them to consider what may go into their work to combat further displacement. The factors suggested for consideration here are offered to help prevent displacement and contribute to a more unique, local perspective using market-based knowledge along with social and cultural capital.

- *Social entrepreneurs recognize the importance of using within-community assets and resources* (Ashoka, 2019; FES, 2019; Wheeler et al., 2005). They may analyze both strengths and barriers using informal (family, friends, other disabled) and formal (agencies, schools, etc.) networks throughout the entrepreneurial process (Ring, Peredo, & Chrisman, 2010; Saunders, Gray, & Goregaoka, 2014; Wheeler et al., 2005). Here some of a community's assets are used to develop outcomes for economic and social development (Ashoka, 2019; FES, 2019). Using strengths helps to reduce displacement of community and of loci since the individuals can collectively keep what is meaningful to them and what has been working and build on them while attempting to use the assets in the community (although they may still have to go outside of their community to gain access to needed items).

- *The use of local knowledge is paramount to the efforts for community and economic development* (Ashoka, 2019; Saunders et al., 2014). For instance, the local traditions and skills as capacity and assets are often used within the community by social entrepreneurs. The traditions and skills that are present are treated as the foundation to the development work as opposed to the one-size-fits-all answer that replaces local traditions and skills (as illustrated in Elyachar's [2005] case study). The use of traditions/ skills helps to create a cohesive and meaningful answer to moving forward in development that is based on what is *present, valued,* and *already deemed useable.* Local traditions can include the way in which economic systems operate (these may not be market driven), along with informal networks and both formal and informal infrastructure. In other words, considerations may weigh what has worked historically, how it has been functioning, and whether successful factors might foster community buy-in and further sustainable development (FES, 2019; Wheeler et al., 2005). The valuing and use of traditions and skills by social entrepreneurs helps to limit displacement of community and potentially displacement of resources.

- *Stakeholders are involved in all aspects of planning to track resources* (Ashoka, 2019; Ring et al., 2010). These stakeholders are those who are from the community and *who will ultimately benefit* from the project. The stakeholders are decision-makers and provide a historical context, giving information about local infrastructure that will lead to a collective sense of what is already available and what needs must be addressed. Additionally, stakeholders can help evaluate an immediate use of resources (natural and local infrastructure) and make room for unplanned use of needed resources as the project changes. Displacement of resources thus is kept in check, allowing local stakeholders to make decisions that inevitably affect the project's success since the natural resources must be protected for ultimate yield and future use. Displacement of community is prevented since stakeholders are local and are continuously making decisions.

- Tied closely with the preceding issue, stakeholders must also be intimately involved in decisions about what resources are being utilized and what additional resources are needed to create new infrastructure (FES, 2019; Saunders et al., 2014). Additionally, because collective action and local planning are used, the community and social entrepreneurs work together to take advantage of what already works for that community (infrastructure), building or shifting plans as needs change (FES, 2019). Displacement of community is the main focus here as community members help inform the decisions that allow assets to be used.

Moreover, displacement of financial systems is potentially prevented since the use of existing infrastructure is kept at the forefront.

- *Trust is created through community ownership that allows for social entrepreneurs to acquire more buy-in from community members* (Saunders et al., 2014; Wheeler et al., 2005). Here the community stakeholders may buy into the project since they may be more likely trust the social entrepreneur to use their local knowledge. Ownership of the project is implied during the lifecycle of the project from outset to end. Displacement of community and resources are potentially mitigated since local buy-in is fostered along with the social entrepreneur's accountability to local networks (Ashoka, 2019).

These considerations are offered to highlight how social entrepreneurs may already be preventing some of the displacements cited in the preceding typology. Tying the displacement type to factors for consideration by social entrepreneurs helps to illustrate how social entrepreneurs may be potentially well-positioned to innovate in their own communities, growing economic and social development while preventing the unintended harms outlined.

SUMMARY

This chapter explored and offered a typology of development-induced displacement to address unintended harms. This may also help inform social entrepreneurs who can both innovate and create more sustainable social and economic development. The typology helps to define and illustrate some of these harms, and the factors for consideration by social entrepreneurs may help to advance more successful, locally based social enterprises.

The intention is to use individual and collective local strengths while addressing or eliminating barriers. As outlined, in the factors to be considered by social entrepreneurs, the use of community assets and resources may be paramount in preventing displacement and also in creating more sustainable development for the long term. Social entrepreneurs may excel at long-term solutions for economic and social development. Furthermore, as suggested by factors offered for social entrepreneurs for consideration, social capital in the form of local traditions, skills, and informal networks are important to communities and have likely served them well for decades if not generations. Here again, using local assets and knowledge may benefit the project for sustainability. Social entrepreneurs often incorporate stakeholders not in a token way, but as valued members of the team, as innovators themselves. These stakeholders are often the same individuals or groups of people who will benefit from the project or development. Working *with* stakeholders encourages trust between social entrepreneurs and the people for whom the help is intended. Last, wherever possible, social entrepreneurs should seek to use the infrastructure that is in place, when appropriate. Too often, development projects may replace old infrastructure with newer, more "technologically sound" structures and processes, and then a project fails. New infrastructure may either not be the best way to move forward (for the short term) due to lack of training on use and maintenance challenges of the new infrastructure, or the infrastructure already in place may actually be quite effective. One caveat is that if stakeholders say they need new infrastructure or suggest problems around existing infrastructure, then social entrepreneurs may need to engage in a conversation about how to solve the problem.

The factors offered for consideration by social entrepreneurs are derived from local community projects using a ground-up approach, but they are not meant to discount the other valuable research and work done by social entrepreneurs who use more top-down approaches. The factors for consideration in this chapter should be used to complement other proven social entrepreneurial approaches for possibly more optimal outcomes.

REFERENCES

Adeloa, R. (2016). What does development-caused displacement look like in Africa? *Internal Displacement Monitoring Centre* (December 7). Retrieved from http://www.internal-displacement.org/expert-opinion/what-does-development-caused-displacement-look-like-in-africa

Ashoka. (2019). New paradigm for leadership—everyone leads. Ashoka United States. Retrieved from https://www.ashoka.org/en-us/story/new-paradigm-leadership-%E2%80%93-everyone-leads

Bourdieu, P. (1986). The forms of capital. Retrieved from https://www.marxists.org/reference/subject/philosophy/works/fr/bourdieu-forms-capital.htm

Cernea, M. (1988). Involuntary resettlement in development projects: Policy guidelines in World Bank-financed projects. *World Bank Technical Papers*. Retrieved from http://documents.worldbank.org/curated/en/699511468325205947/Involuntary-resettlement-in-development-projects-policy-guidelines-in-World-Bank-financed-projects

Commission on Growth and Development. (2008). *The growth report: Strategies for sustained growth and inclusive development.* Washington, DC: World Bank. Retrieved from https://openknowledge.worldbank.org/handle/10986/6507

Elyachar, J. (2005). *Markets of dispossession: NGOs, economic development, and the state in Cairo.* Durham, NC: Duke University Press.

FES (2019). FES: Foundation for Ecological Security. Retrieved from fes.org.in.

Guo, C., & Bielefeld, W. (2014). *Social entrepreneurship: An evidence-based approach to creating social value.* San Francisco, CA: Jossey-Bass.

Internal Displacement Monitoring Centre (IDMC). (2016, July). *Pushed Aside: Displaced for 'development' in India* (pp. 1–54, Rep.). Geneva, Switzerland: Internal Displacement Monitoring Centre (IDMC).

Internal Displacement Monitoring Centre (IDMC). (2017). *GRID 2017: Global report on internal displacement.* Geneva, Switzerland: Internal Displacement Monitoring Centre (IDMC).

Johnson, S. (2007). *The role of markets in the construction of wellbeing: The need for a Polynesian perspective* (Working Paper No. 42, 1–31). Bath, UK: ESRC Research Group on Wellbeing on Developing Countries.

Johnson, T. (2011, February). Free trade: As U.S. corn flows south, Mexicans stop farming. *McClatchy Washington Bureau.* Retrieved from https://www.mcclatchydc.com/news/nation-world/world/article24609829.html

Keeley, B. (2007). A bigger picture. In B. Keeley (Ed.), *OECD insights: Human capital—How what you know shapes your life* (pp. 94–105). Danvers, MA: OECD.

Kickul, J., & Lyons, T. (2012). *Understanding social entrepreneurship: The relentless pursuit of mission in an ever-changing world.* Oxon, UK: Routledge.

Lareau, A., & Weininger, E. B. (2003). Cultural capital in educational research: A critical assessment. *Theory and Society, 32*(5/6), 567–606. doi.org/10.1023/B:RYSO.0000004951.04408.b0

Light, P. (2008). *The search for social entrepreneurship.* Washington, DC: The Brookings Institution.

Praszkier, R., & Nowak, A. (2012). *Social entrepreneurship: Theory and practice.* New York: Cambridge University Press.

Relinger, R. (2010, April 19). NAFTA and U.S. corn subsidies: Explaining the displacement of Mexico's corn farmers. *Prospect Journal.* Retrieved from https://prospectjournal.org/2010/04/19/nafta-and-u-s-corn-subsidies-explaining-the-displacement-of-mexicos-corn-farmers-2/

Ring, J. K., Peredo, A. M., & Chrisman, J. J. (2010). Business networks and economic development in rural communities in the United States. *Entrepreneurship Theory and Practice, 34*(1), 171–195.

Saunders, M. N., Gray, D. E., & Goregaokar, H. (2014). SME innovation and learning: The role of networks and crisis events. *European Journal of Training and Development, 38*(1/2), 136–149.

Stanley, J. (2017, March 2). Development induced displacement and resettlement. *Forced Migration Online.* Retrieved from https://www.alnap.org/system/files/content/resource/files/main/fmo022.pdf

Stiglitz, J., Sen, A., & Fitoussi, J. P. (2009). *Report by the commission on the measurement of economic performance and social progress.* Institut national de la statistique et des études économiques. Retrieved from https://ec.europa.eu/eurostat/documents/118025/118123/Fitoussi+Commission+report

Streitfeld, D. (2009, November 19). U.S. mortgage delinquencies reach a record high. *New York Times.* Retrieved from https://www.nytimes.com/2009/11/20/business/20mortgage.html?searchResultPosition=1

Terminski, B. (2012). Development-induced displacement and human security: A very short introduction. *SSRN Electronic Journal.* Retrieved from http://dlc.dlib.indiana.edu/dlc/bitstream/handle/10535/8960/SSRNid2182302%20(15).pdf?sequence=1

Terminski, B. (2013). Development-induced displacement and resettlement: Theoretical frameworks and current challenges. Retrieved from https://dlc.dlib.indiana.edu/dlc/bitstream/handle/10535/8833/Bogumil%20Terminski,%20development-Induced%20Displacement%20and%20Resettlement.%20Theoretical%20frameworks%20and%20current%20challenges.pdf

Terminski, B. (2015). *Development-induced displacement and resettlement: Causes, consequences, and socio-legal context*. Stuttgart, Germany: Ibidem.

Wheeler, D., McKague, K., Thomson, J., Davies, R., Medalye, J., & Prada, M. (2005). Creating sustainable local enterprise networks. *MIT Sloan Management Review, 47*(1), 33.

UNESCO. (2017). Displaced person/displacement. Social and Human Sciences: International Migration, Glossary. UNESCO. Retrieved August 2019 from: https://wayback.archive-it.org/10611/20171126022420/http://www.unesco.org/new/en/social-and-human-sciences/themes/international-migration/glossary/displaced-person-displacement/

CHAPTER 3

⌁

Organizational Entrepreneurial Orientation

Implications for Social Impact and Social Enterprise

WILLIAM J. WALES AND VISHAL K. GUPTA

INTRODUCTION

The past few years have seen tremendous growth in social organizations so that there is now a proliferation of organizations with an embedded social purpose (Choi & Majumdar, 2014). As a result, research and media spotlight has been drawn toward social enterprises. From an academic perspective, a deep and meaningful understanding of the organizational landscape from which social enterprises emerge and operate may be significantly advanced through consideration of the strategic orientations of organizational actors. It has been suggested that social enterprise is defined in terms of organizational behaviors and activity. That is, social enterprises are organizations with missions emphasizing the creation of social value by providing solutions to social problems (Dacin, Dacin, & Matear, 2010; Dacin, Dacin, & Tracey, 2011). In brief, social value creation may be conceived as encompassing the following three components:

William J. Wales and Vishal K. Gupta, *Organizational Entrepreneurial Orientation* In: *Social Entrepreneurship and Enterprises in Economic and Social Development*. Edited by: Katharine Briar-Lawson, Paul Miesing, and Blanca M. Ramos, Oxford University Press (2021). © Oxford University Press. DOI: 10.1093/oso/9780197518298.003.0004.

"(1) identifying a stable but inherently unjust equilibrium that causes the exclusion, marginalization, or suffering of a segment of humanity that lacks the financial means or political clout to achieve any transformative benefit on its own;

(2) identifying an opportunity in this unjust equilibrium, developing a social value proposition, and bringing to bear inspiration, creativity, direct action, courage, and fortitude, thereby challenging the stable state's hegemony; and

(3) forging a new, stable equilibrium that releases trapped potential or alleviates the suffering of the targeted group, and through imitation and the creation of a stable ecosystem around the new equilibrium ensuring a better future for the targeted group and even society at large" (Martin & Osberg, 2007, p. 35).

Social enterprises drive value creation through their socially targeted efforts, which devote significant resources to the pursuit of new, forward-thinking solutions to societal issues. The organizational landscape of social enterprises is diverse and encompassing, ranging from nonprofits pursuing social change using limited revenue sources (e.g., the United Way) to for-profits pursuing opportunities that contribute to gains for both shareholders as well as community stakeholders (e.g., TOMS shoes). Argument has even been advanced that many forms of traditional or conventional entrepreneurship meaningfully lead to institutional change/reform and societal betterment and therefore may be considered as contributing to social value creation (Dacin et al., 2010). Given the broad, encompassing definitional nature of the social entrepreneurship concept, this chapter seeks to briefly review the literature on entrepreneurial orientation (EO) as it pertains to the landscape of socially conscious organizations and highlight the important questions and directions remaining for future research.

This chapter focuses on understanding EO as an organization's strategic orientation, given the observations of Light (2006) that, all too often, social entrepreneurship is focused on celebrating individual entrepreneurs while excluding organizations that exhibit similarly impactful change-making missions and behaviors. In the words of Light (2006), "By focusing so much on visionary change agents, prominent advocates of social entrepreneurship have excluded large numbers of organizations that deserve the financial support, networking, and training now reserved for individuals who fit both the current definition of social entrepreneurship and the prevailing model of the self-sacrificing entrepreneur."

As discussed by Light (2006), there are numerous issues with defining social entrepreneurship as an individual phenomenon, including tendencies to (1) focus on individuals' personalities as opposed to their impactful actions which define them as social entrepreneurs, (2) ignore the criticality of multiple actors operating within an organizational framework to achieve social change, and (3) neglect or associate the key pattern-breaking idea as part and parcel of the individual social entrepreneur. Rather than being developed fully by a single entrepreneurial "hero," impactful solutions for vexing societal problems are likely to be developed through social interactions aided by organizational frameworks.

This chapter examines the well-established concept of EO as a means of characterizing an organization's overall strategic orientation; that is, its collective entrepreneurial mindset and behavioral approach. In the modern era, it is often no longer the case that traditional commercial enterprises are created for the sole purpose of profit maximization. Yet there has been little investigation of the potential role of EO as a driver of gains in social value within traditional commercial settings. It seems that, in the context of social enterprises, EO may be an immensely relevant consideration given that research and understanding of social enterprises demands a means of gradation of organizational populations based on each organization's degree of entrepreneurial activity. Nonetheless, there has been limited consideration of how EO is manifest within social enterprises or may be assessed in a social context. Finally, we close with a discussion of potentially fruitful areas of research.

HISTORICAL ROOTS OF EO WITHIN TRADITIONAL ENTERPRISE

The concept of EO has a rich history of study and knowledge accumulation within the entrepreneurship and broader management literature. Indeed, it has been observed that EO is among the most investigated concepts in the entrepreneurship literature, outpacing even the more encompassing topic of corporate entrepreneurship (Covin & Lumpkin, 2011; Wales, 2016). EO refers to an organization's decision-making practices, managerial philosophies, and strategic behaviors that are entrepreneurial in nature and manifest as a stable organizational behavioral orientation (Anderson, Covin, & Slevin, 2009; Covin & Wales, 2012). EO has traditionally been defined in terms of three fundamental dimensions: innovativeness, proactiveness, and risk-taking, which together reflect the organization's proclivity for entrepreneurial action.

The first EO dimension, *innovativeness*, reflects an organization's support of new ideas, creativity, and experimentation in the development of new solutions and offerings. On this dimension, organizations may range from either pursuing incremental (or new improvements to existing offerings, i.e., low-end) to highly radical (or new to the world, i.e., high-end) innovations. The second EO dimension, *proactiveness*, represents a forward-looking and opportunity-seeking perspective that provides organizations with a basis for leadership within their respective organizational landscape. On this dimension, firms may range from being completely reactionary (or only following the lead of other organizations) to fully shaping the direction that their peers and stakeholders can take in their future endeavors. Finally, *risk-taking* captures an organization's bold and daring resource commitments toward organizational initiatives with high potential but ultimately uncertain results. In this regard, organizations can range from committing a small to large portion of their slack resources to projects that "swing for the fences" in search of big leaps in growth and impact.

It has been theorized that organizations are more entrepreneurial when they exhibit higher combined levels of these dimensions (Miller, 2011). That is, organizations that have higher aggregate levels across these dimensions may be considered more entrepreneurial than their peers that emphasize a less robust overall EO. To constitute an orientation, entrepreneurially inclined behaviors must be relatively stable, sustained over time, and thus come to reflect a reasonably consistent organizational state or quality (Ireland, Covin, & Kuratko, 2009). Research exploring the concept of EO has focused primarily on its potential financial impact for improved organizational performance (Wales, Gupta, & Mousa, 2013). Along these lines, it has been theorized that organizations with greater EO embrace more significant levels of experimentation (Wiklund & Shepherd, 2011) thereby contributing to the discovery of opportunities for above-average growth and financial performance (Rauch, Wiklund, Lumpkin, & Frese, 2009). However, there has been only limited consideration of what effects EO may have on organizational stakeholders beyond those interested in financial outcomes. Given the growing prevalence of social organizations within most modern societies, understanding the implications of EO for social impact and social enterprise is a particularly timely and relevant consideration.

SOCIAL IMPACTS OF EO WITHIN COMMERCIAL ENTERPRISES

The notion that organizations' exhibition of EO may have meaningful consequences for nonfinancial social outcomes surfaces in the work of

Lumpkin and Dess (1996), which delves into the concept of EO and its relationship with organizational performance. Specifically, Lumpkin and Dess (1996) suggest that stakeholder satisfaction and organizational goodwill are potentially significant outcomes of relevance within EO research. Yet, as recent research by Gupta and Wales (2017) reveals, EO–performance research has focused substantially more on hybrid financial and growth, rather than social, outcomes. This suggests a timely need to revisit earlier calls for broader implications of EO for performance.

In the spirit of investigating broader social implications of EO within more traditional commercial contexts, Sung, Choi, Kim, and Le (2014) observed that EO organizations tend to generate more responsible corporate citizens when a strong market orientation is present. That is, emphasis on making organizational decisions based on customer and competitor information may be critical to an organization's development of corporate citizens who support cultural values pertaining to legal, ethical, economic, and discretionary responsibility. Thus, the results of Sung et al. (2014) suggest that when organizations are better adept at paying attention to the market and disseminating this contextual information to employees, an organization's EO will produce a better sense of perceived social responsibility among its organizational citizens concerning the impetus to address key social issues within the organization's environment. Thus, engendering awareness (and avoiding isolation) appears to be an influential criterion to the encouragement of socially responsible organizational citizens.

It has also been suggested that firms with higher EO may engage in more significant environmental, economic, and social sustainability practices (Gawel, 2012). In this vein, Gawel (2012) suggests that EO will lead to greater sustainable development when those practices may be linked to economic advantages. In other words, sustainable development, when valued by the market, will be incorporated as a key competitive dimension among enterprises, and EO will then drive its advancement. Going beyond this proposition, Shahzad, Wales, Sharfman, and Stein (2016) theorize and observe that two dimensions of EO (i.e., innovativeness and proactiveness) yield higher levels of stakeholder value captured in terms of value accrued to primary stakeholder groups within the categories of community, diversity, employees, product, and the environment. Moreover, Tang and Tang (2018) observe EO to have a significant positive relationship with environmentally friendly policies, facilities, and programs focusing on strengths in areas such as pollution prevention, recycling, and clean energy.

Central to the concept of stakeholder value is the recognition that key stakeholder groups demand managerial attention if the organization is to prosper (Mitchell, Agle, & Wood, 1997). The work of Mitchell et al. (1997)

broadens our understanding regarding the potentially far-reaching social implications of EO. Moreover, concerning the ethical implications of firm entrepreneurial processes and behavior, it has been argued that being entrepreneurial does not necessarily imply being more ethical (Neubaum, Mitchell, & Schminke, 2004). In the work of Shahzad and colleagues (2016), more innovative and proactive organizations are at a minimum observed to pay more attention to their stakeholders, which at its core is considered to be an outcome of ethical decision-making by the firm (Berman, Wicks, Kotha, & Jones, 1999; Jones, 1995). It is therefore suggested that this research observes a more ethically conscious facet of entrepreneurial firms. Nonetheless, whether this observed relationship between being entrepreneurial and stakeholder value creation is motivated by financial gains, as Gawel (2012) would suggest, or by more altruistic firm ambitions is a topic that demands additional research attention.

In another study exploring the linkage between EO and organizational sustainability, Marshall, McCarthy, McGrath, and Claudy (2015) observed EO to positively enhance, or moderate, a firm's efforts to translate its social sustainability orientation into advanced supply chain practices emphasizing social sustainability. As one of the three core aspects of sustainability—environmental, economic, and social—social sustainability is arguably the least researched and understood dimension. Marshall et al. (2015) capture social sustainability culture using indicators that span organizational efforts to educate employees on the importance of social sustainability, as well as prioritize social sustainability initiatives, activities, and values. In terms of the outcome of interest in this study, advanced sustainability practices are evidenced through behaviors such as firms actively influencing their supply chain partners via close relationships, along with motivating the collective pursuit of recognized opportunities for social improvements. Organizations with advanced supply chain sustainability practices are thus more likely to collaborate with suppliers in the pursuit of products or processes that either benefit workers, encourage fair trade/ margins, engage the community, reduce health risks for consumers, or enhance transparency regarding sustainability practices in the supply chain.

Related research has investigated how various perceived ethical, economic, and legal responsibilities may drive EO within an organization. Intriguingly, in a study of 19 Chinese theater companies it was observed that ethical corporate social responsibility was a significant positive driver of firm EO, whereas economic and legal responsibilities were found to be negatively related with EO (Tuan, 2015). Thus, the most influential factor driving entrepreneurial activity among these theater companies is the ethical perceived responsibility to meet social expectations. As such, similar to the work of Shahzad et al. (2016), this study appears to illustrate a linkage between EO and ethical behavior. This finding is surprisingly in contrast to the expected perceived responsibilities to earn an economic profit or adhere to legal obligations. This suggests that, among certain organizations, the driver of entrepreneurial activity is indeed more closely tied to pursuing ambitions based on what is ethically appropriate and beneficial to a broader group of stakeholders than simply those with interests in economic gains.

In the next section, we move from the context of exploring EO within more traditional commercial contexts to exploring the manifestation of EO among more clearly defined social enterprises. Despite some suggesting that levels of EO are similar between for-profit and nonprofit organizations (Davis, Marino, Aaron, & Tolbert, 2011), little research has examined how EO is manifested, what causes it to flourish, and its impact on key organizational outcomes in social enterprises.

EO IN SOCIAL ENTERPRISES: WHAT HAS BEEN DISCUSSED?

Conceptualization of EO in Nonprofits

An important context in which some research has explored the implications of EO for social enterprise is that of nonprofit organizations (Coombes, Morris, Allen, & Webb, 2011; Morris, Coombes, Schindehutte, & Allen, 2007; Morris, Webb, & Franklin, 2011; Pearce, Fritz, & Davis, 2010). Morris et al. (2011) advanced the notion that nonprofits exhibit an EO for numerous reasons including, but certainly not limited to, enhancing their ability to compete for limited external funding opportunities, identify ways to do more for their target populations with less resources, and determine ways to make use of new technologies and environmental shifts. Because in the nonprofit context firm efforts are directed at primarily achieving a social (as opposed to economic) mission, there are fundamental differences in the manifestation of EO firm processes and activities within nonprofit organizations. As such, nonprofits afford a rich context in which to investigate how EO is manifest within social enterprise. Nonetheless, a deep understanding of how EO is actually manifest within nonprofit organizations has received relatively scant attention in the literature as compared to its more traditional commercial equivalent. As a result, Morris et al.'s (2011) theoretical examination of how EO may manifest in nonprofit organizations and their conception for each of the three core dimensions of EO (innovativeness, risk-taking, and proactiveness) in the not-for-profit context is commendable.

According to Morris et al. (2011), the emphasis on *innovativeness* in nonprofits is focused on core mission achievement, generating new sources of revenue, or some combination of each in concert. Given the primacy of a core social mission within social enterprises (Dacin et al., 2011), innovativeness within this context is focused on determining new ways to achieve the organization's critical social mission. Tied closely to developing new ways to impact the organization's core mission is the advancement of new sources of revenue that provide the slack resources necessary to (a) expand core service offerings and (b) enable experimentation and risk-taking with potentially new and better core mission achievement. Moreover, innovation may also be called for at times when an organization's mission requires revision or more significant refocusing or change. In this vein, as Morris et al. (2011) illustrate, the March of Dimes mission shifted to saving babies with birth defects following the discovery of a cure for polio based on the efforts of Dr. Jonas Salk in the mid-1950s.

Morris et al. (2011) suggest that *proactiveness* emphasizes how nonprofits are able to enact change in how and what social objectives are achieved, financial requirements are met, or stakeholder expectations are satisfied ahead of their peers with similar social missions. For instance, some organizations will be at the forefront of advances in achieving social mission objectives (e.g., Charity: Water, https://www.charitywater.org/), whereas others will be closer to fast-followers or late entrants that recognize the need for aid at a later point in time. In this example, Charity: Water recognized that personal donations toward clean water projects in the developing world would increase if there was a means for greater transparency in the actual impact of an individual's donations in a community. In a talk by Charity: Water's founder Scott Harrison, it was mentioned that they (a) covered their administration costs through separate donations from private benefactors so that individual donors could rest assured that 100% of their donations would go to a clean water project, (b) sent GPS and camera kits to project teams in the field so that they could take pictures of the projects during their undertaking/completion, and (c) integrated this data with Google Maps so that individuals could be updated in real time regarding the actual impact of their donation. This proactive approach to social mission achievement enabled Charity: Water to achieve growth in social impact during a period when the overall nonprofit sector was comparatively stagnant (Harrison, 2013).

Finally, *risk-taking* captures a nonprofit's willingness to engage in activities characterized by a significant probability and magnitude of loss in social mission impact, financial standing, or other nonfinancial stakeholder support (Morris et al., 2011). Risk-taking is inseparable from innovation.

More significant, radical, or frame-breaking attempts at developing innovative solutions to enhance social mission achievement will carry greater risk with their experimentation and implementation. On the other hand, they will also carry greater potential reward. For instance, social marketing efforts may be called for in certain situations in which individual behavior appears to be a principal culprit within a societal ill; however, the large amount of funding dumped into a social marketing campaign will have a much less certain impact on the overall social mission than spending an equivalent amount of funding on treating the issue. However, if the social marketing campaign succeeds, then the overall social mission achievement may be significantly higher overall. For instance, committing resources to treating a disease like malaria has more clearly defined social mission achievement than a social market campaign stressing that individuals should sleep with netting around their beds at night.

Nonprofits may also spread their resources too thin in the pursuit of social impact growth and thereby enhance their organization's risk profile. Moreover, as Morris et al. (2011) further note, at times nonprofits may have to take stands on controversial issues that have the potential to polarize stakeholder groups. This may pose a risk to the organization's financial and social support. Furthermore, a potentially adverse unintended consequence, one carrying the risk of creating pay barriers to accessing services, may enhance the organization's financial position but creates risk that individuals can no longer afford to access a particular public service presented in a more commercialized form. For instance, museums may enact mandatory entrance fees or medical clinics may require, albeit often subsidized, fees for their services.

In the next section, we turn our attention to the antecedents of EO within the context of social enterprises and explore potential drivers of this organizational phenomenon.

Antecedents of EO Within Social Enterprises

Presently, there is limited understanding of what drives the manifestation of EO within social enterprises (Schmidt, Baumgarth, Wiedmann, & Lückenbach, 2015). In an effort to theoretically delve into this important organizational context, Lumpkin, Moss, Gras, Kato, and Amezcua (2013) discuss four possible antecedents to the manifestation of EO within social enterprises: social motivation/mission, opportunity identification, access to capital/funding, and multiple stakeholders. Consider that a principal motivation behind pursuing higher levels of EO among social enterprises are the problems, issues, and demands associated with achieving the social mission at the heart of the enterprise. Generally, social missions address widely acknowledged detrimental social issues and injustices. As such, social missions drive higher levels of organizational EO in an effort to develop new, innovative solutions to these painful social problems.

A second and related driver of EO is an organization's forward-thinking opportunity scanning and identification efforts. In this vein, new aspects of social problems or solutions may rise to the forefront of an organization's social consciousness, shifting attention to new or more refined problem spaces. For instance, Elon Musk identified a new opportunity for addressing the problem of global pollution through the development of electric cars that departed from extant market offerings by being untraditionally "sexy" and fast sports cars that people wanted to drive because they were exciting as well as environmentally friendly.

Third, access to capital/funding also drives higher levels of EO and organizational entrepreneurial activity. EO, and its characteristic pioneering innovation, has been described as a resource-intensive strategic posture (Covin & Slevin, 1991). With greater access to capital/funding, firms have additional resources to devote to developing new or improved solutions to their targeted social issues. Thus, with greater resource availability organizations have the slack resources necessary to support social entrepreneurial experiments in the pursuit of new and more refined societal solutions. Finally, Lumpkin et al. (2013) suggest that a wide variety of constituents within a broad set of organizational stakeholders have the potential to drive the manifestation of EO within social enterprises. For instance, one such stakeholder is the actual population that the social enterprise aims to support. Through interactions with this often disadvantaged population, the social enterprise gains new insights into potential opportunities for innovation in how the population's social issue may be addressed, thereby spurring greater EO. As such, through interactions with individuals experiencing a given social hardship, social enterprises provide a voice to those whose difficulties may otherwise go unnoticed, misunderstood, or addressed using inadequate or ineffective solutions.

There has been surprisingly limited empirical literature exploring the antecedents of EO within a social enterprise context. One notable study is the work of Morris et al. (2007), which observes EO among nonprofits to be higher when they demonstrate transformational leadership, provide employees more discretion in their jobs, and have boards that actively support the organization. Intriguingly, these influential organizational antecedents have similarly been shown to beneficially impact EO within more traditional commercial contexts as well (e.g., Engelen, Schmidt, &

Buchsteiner, 2015; Gabrielsson, 2007; Lumpkin, Cogliser, & Schneider, 2009). In another study, Caruana, Ewing, and Ramaseshan (2002) observe that low degrees of organizational structural centralization are conducive to EO within Australian public-sector entities by affording employees within these organizations the discretion necessary to experiment with their ideas and potential innovations. In a similar vein, within more commercial family firms, Zahra, Hayton, and Salvato (2004) observed a beneficial relationship between decentralization of control and EO.

Moreover, in their study of Australian public sector entities, Caruana et al. (2002) observed that several dimensions of the external environment may foster higher levels of EO within nonprofits including environmental heterogeneity, technological turbulence, and resource munificence. More significant levels of environmental heterogeneity are likely to support and foster social entrepreneurial activity given that a more diverse population of organizations, customer needs, and product/service offerings may afford greater opportunity for innovation. Additionally, technological turbulence implies that change is happening rapidly and thereby driving social enterprises to adopt more EO strategic postures to meet or exceed the pace of the changing technological landscape. As previously discussed, Charity: Water's pioneering use of social media efforts provides a prime example of an organization's responsiveness to rapid advances within the external technological environment (Harrison, 2013).

Additionally, as discussed, slack resources are extremely important to enabling experimentation in the pursuit of new and improved means of social mission achievement. Greater environmental munificence implies that external resources are more freely flowing and therefore easier to access and leverage in the pursuit of the social mission of the organization. Environmental influences upon EO and EO–performance relationships have been extensively investigated within the more traditional research on EO within commercial enterprises, with similar findings and implications (Covin & Lumpkin, 2011; Rosenbusch, Rauch, & Bausch, 2013).

Outcomes of EO Within Social Enterprises

Past research has also theorized links between EO and outcomes. In a few instances this research has empirically linked EO within social enterprises to important outcomes of interest. Among the theorized outcomes associated with the manifestation of EO within a social enterprise context, Lumpkin et al. (2013) highlight three broad areas in which greater EO may enhance social enterprise effectiveness: social value creation, sustainability of solutions, and satisfying multiple stakeholders. First, and perhaps most importantly, through higher levels of EO organizations may generate greater social value. A key characteristic of social enterprises is their emphasis on social value creation for stakeholders beyond their organizational boundaries. Thus, in general, social enterprises focus on social value creation as opposed to the emphasis of commercial enterprises on organizational value appropriation (Santos, 2012). Nonetheless, hybrid models which blend social and economic value creation are possible. TOMS Shoes is a prime example: for each shoe purchased by a first-world customer (economic value creation), a shoe is given to a person in need within the developing world (social value creation). With greater EO, organizations identify opportunities to enhance their social value creation impact.

Second, EO may lead to the advancement of more sustainable solutions to societal issues. That is, as EO increases, developed solutions may have either greater permanency due to resource self-sufficiency (i.e., revenue streams provide a sustainable basis for the organization's social mission; e.g., TOMS Shoes) or by enacting institutional change (i.e., societal norms are positively impacted as a result of the social entrepreneur's actions). For instance, social entrepreneurs may undertake campaigns to promote condom use as a deterrent to the spread of HIV. Third, Lumpkin et al. (2013) suggest that consideration should be devoted to how EO may impact key stakeholder groups in different ways. Thus, the outcomes associated with EO for social enterprises are likely to be numerous and diverse. EO may help organizations engender greater legitimacy for their cause, directly impact disadvantaged populations, and improve the well-being of employees, as well as provide a positive emotional return to donors/investors.

Finally, it is also noted by Lumpkin and colleagues (2013) that relationships between EO and its outcomes within social enterprises may not always be positive. In many instances these relationships are subtly nuanced and complex, and, as such, the linkages are neither always straightforward nor theoretically tautological. For example, the preponderance of multiple stakeholders may actually constrain performance given its potential to orient the organization of short-term exploitative solutions at the expense of developing longer term and potentially more greatly beneficial exploratory solutions (March, 1991). As many stakeholders may be risk-intolerant, developing and leveraging EO is more challenging here than within commercial enterprises, where risk may be seen as a greater necessity in the pursuit of competitive advantage and achieving a firm's economic mission of higher financial gains.

Although the empirical literature linking EO to outcomes of interest within social enterprises is limited, a few studies have explored and evidenced significant relationships. In terms of linkages with performance, Caruana et al. (2002) observed a positive relationship between EO and overall organizational performance (efficiency and effectiveness) within Australian public-sector (governmental) entities. Moreover, a study of 548 registered social enterprises in Kampala, Uganda, by Abaho, Begumisa, Aikiriza, and Turyasingura (2017) observed EO to explain more than 37% of the variance in social enterprise growth. However, intriguingly, a direct relationship between EO and various aspects of organizational performance has often not met with significant support in prior research (i.e., Helm & Andersson, 2010; Miles, Verreynne, Luke, Eversole, & Barraket, 2013; Morris et al., 2007, etc.). In this vein Morris et al. (2007) observed a nonsignificant relationship between EO and nonprofit performance within a sample of 501-c nonprofit organizations in upstate New York. In addition to the work of Morris et al. (2007), Sung et al. (2014) observed a nonsignificant relationship between EO and social performance as measured by enhanced corporate social responsibility. However, Sung et al. (2014) observed that the influence of EO on corporate social responsibility was mediated by the organization's marketing orientation. This speaks to the criticality of developing a strong marketing orientation as a necessary complement to EO in the nonprofit context. In a similar vein, Chen and Hsu (2013) observed market orientation to play an influential moderating role in the ability of nonprofits to translate their EO into social performance across several areas of stakeholder satisfaction. Moreover, the work of Bhuian, Menguc, and Bell (2005) observed a nonlinear interaction of EO and marketing orientation on the performance of nonprofit hospitals, such that performance was the highest at moderate levels of EO. Although the question of whether marketing orientation is more appropriately positioned as a moderator or mediator within the EO–performance relationship among social enterprises remains open, the criticality of exhibiting both orientations for enhanced organizational performance appears well founded in prior research.

Other studies have observed mixed performance findings. For instance, the work of Coombes et al. (2011) found EO to be associated with greater perceived social mission achievement compared to peer organizations, but not financial performance as measured by a combination of IRS Form 990 reported revenues, net assets, and fund-raising ratios. In a similar vein, Miles et al. (2013) found EO itself to have no effect on social or economic performance unless combined with socially oriented Vincentian values within a more encompassing concept of organizational social value orientation. This novel construct was found to be related to social but not economic performance. Finally, it is worth noting that not all dimensions of

EO may drive performance similarly. For instance, in a study of the non-profit theater context Voss, Voss, and Moorman (2005) found that innovativeness drove revenue generation, but proactiveness and risk-taking had mixed relationships with ticket, royalty, and donation revenue streams.

Finally, in a novel line of research, Onishi (2014) observed that among social investment funders or organizations that apply venture capital practices to philanthropic investments, higher levels of EO are positively related to their level of engagement in unproved philanthropy investment practices drawn from the commercial realm of venture capital investing. Taken together, these studies suggest that research on the outcomes stemming from EO within a social enterprise context remains in its infancy, with great strides still left to be accomplished.

HOW DO WE MEASURE EO IN SOCIAL ENTERPRISES?

One of the most important considerations to advancing research on EO within social enterprises is how EO might be measured within this important nonfinancial or hybrid organizational context. The conceptualization of EO by Morris and colleagues (2011) is in line with earlier empirical work by Morris and Joyce (1998), which sought to operationalize EO within the nonprofit context based on the works of Covin and Slevin (1989), Miller and Friesen (1978, 1982), Miller (1983), and Morris and Paul (1987), all of which focused on EO within commercial enterprises. In terms of the relationships between these studies, the items developed by Miller and Friesen (1978, 1982) were incorporated into the development of proceeding instruments within the commercially focused entrepreneurship literature, including the scales advanced by Miller (1983), Covin and Slevin (1989), and Morris and Paul (1987). Several studies have investigated subsets of the Morris and Paul (1987) scale to capture EO within prior research (i.e., Bhuian et al., 2005; Caruana et al., 2002; Coombes et al., 2011; Morris et al., 2007).

Although these scales are similar in many respects, the nine-item semantic differential scale by Covin and Slevin (1989) is now well-established as the dominant method by which EO is measured within a commercial context (Wales et al., 2013; see Appendix A as a reference for the traditional Covin & Slevin [1989] instrument). Therefore, it is perhaps not surprising that many studies have more or less directly adapted the Covin and Slevin (1989) nine-item scale for assessing EO within the social enterprise context. For instance, the work of Pearce et al. (2010) examined EO within the context of nonprofit religious congregations and developed essentially a one-to-one adaptation of the Covin and Slevin (1989) nine-item instrument. To illustrate modification of this instrument, an item developed by Covin and Slevin (1989) for capturing innovativeness asks "In general, the top managers of my firm favor . . . A strong emphasis on marketing of tried and true products or services . . . A strong emphasis on R&D, technological leadership, and innovations." The same item adapted by Pearce et al. (2010) asks "In general, the leadership in our church favors . . . A strong emphasis on offering tried and true ministries and worship services . . . A strong emphasis on developing new ministries and worship services." Similarly, in a study of nonprofit philanthropy practices, Onishi (2014) employed the Covin and Slevin (1989) measure with minor wording modifications.

Alternatively, several studies assessed EO within a social enterprise context based on the work of Morris and Joyce (1998), which similarly builds on the earlier work of Miller and Friesen (1978, 1982) and examines EO across 17 items that capture the extent to which nonprofits characterize their organizational characteristics, decision-making practices, and degree of innovation as being either more (or less) entrepreneurial in nature (see Appendix B). Essentially, the efforts of Morris and Joyce (1998) sought to make the traditional EO scale items more generalizable and therefore less specific to commercial contexts that emphasize new product and/or service development in the pursuit of competitive superiority. Building on the work of Covin and Slevin (1989), the Morris and Joyce (1998) scale similarly builds on Miller and Friesen's (1978, 1982) pioneering work on firm strategic orientations in general and EO in particular. While not a direct one-to-one translation, the Morris and Joyce (1998) scale clearly draws inspiration from the Covin and Slevin (1989, p. 125) instrument. Similarly, Kusa (2016) offers proposed adaptations of items from Covin and Slevin (1989) for the nonprofit context such as "In general, the leaders and top managers of my organization have a strong proclivity for high-risk projects (with chances of solving the most difficult social problems)." Taken together, EO in social enterprises has generally been viewed as being based on the dimensions of innovativeness, proactiveness, and risk-taking (Covin & Slevin, 1989), an approach supported by qualitative investigation (Syrjä, Puumalainen, Sjögrén, Soininen, & Durst, 2019).

Morris et al. (2007) investigated EO using a 3-item subset of the original 17-item instrument advanced by Morris and Joyce (1998). The work of Morris et al. (2007) examined EO as a high rate of new program/service development compared to other organizations, seeking novel solutions via "idea people," and risk-taking in exploiting new opportunities. Recommendations within the commercial context, however, suggest that EO dimensions should not be measured with less than three items per dimension (Anderson, Kreiser, Kuratko, Hornsby, & Eshima, 2015). Other recommendations from the commercial literature include considering a separation of risk-taking attitudes from innovative and proactive behaviors. That is, Anderson and colleagues (2015) suggest that risk-taking may be considered in terms of a managerial attitude, whereas innovation and proactivity are more clearly defined in terms of behavioral processes and outcomes within the context of an external peer referent. For instance, it does not make sense to discuss proactivity absent a peer referent group. There has also been discussion as to whether EO should be measured formatively (Anderson et al., 2015) or reflectively (Covin & Wales, 2012). However, each measurement model has its own merits, and neither is inherently the "correct" way in which EO should be assessed (Covin & Wales, 2012).

Finally, in a few instances, studies have sought to develop novel measures of EO that are specific to a given social enterprise context. For instance, Voss et al. (2005) developed a measure of EO for the nonprofit theater industry that asked questions such as "we regularly commission playwrights to develop new works," "we seek new ways to market the theater," and "there is a major element of artistic risk in all of our productions." Again, it is clear that these measures draw significant inspiration from the commercial measures of EO advanced by Miller and Friesen (1978, 1982), Covin and Slevin (1989), and Morris and Paul (1987).

WHERE TO FROM HERE? WHAT QUESTIONS NEED TO BE ADDRESSED?

Based on the preceding review of the literature, it is safe to claim that research on EO within the social enterprise context is still in its infancy. However, several pioneering works discussed in this chapter help provide a productive way forward for research on EO within organizational contexts with a strong social mission. Most notably, the works of Morris et al. (2011), Lumpkin et al. (2013), and DiVito and Bohnsack (2017) provide thoughtful conceptual forays into understanding how EO may be manifest and expressed within social enterprises and with what antecedents/effects.

By synthesizing work exploring EO among organizations characterized by a strong social mission, the preceding discussion also highlights potential directions for future research that have received relatively little attention. To begin, there is a notable dearth of research on EO within hybrid organizations or organizations that simultaneously address issues within the private (or public) sector and the socially motivated voluntary sector. TOMS and its innovative one-for-one model represents a notable blending of private and voluntary sectors. The TOMS one-for-one model implies that each purchase of a given product such as shoes or eyeglasses in a first-world market triggers a similar product donation within the developing world. Yet little research has been done on such hybrid organizational forms, which arguably represent quintessential social enterprise organizations that apply market principles to help solve societal hardships. Undertaking such research promises to significantly advance our understanding of social entrepreneurship as an organizational phenomenon captured through strategic orientation.

In conclusion, although research has begun to explore how EO is manifest within social enterprises as well as the potential antecedents/effects of EO among organizations with prevailing social missions, there is still a great deal left to be accomplished in understanding social entrepreneurship as an organizational phenomenon expressed through strategic orientation. It is our hope that this review and discussion will serve to inspire future research within this important and emerging area of research on social enterprise.

REFERENCES

Abaho, E., Begumisa, D. B., Aikiriza, F., & Turyasingura, I. (2017). Entrepreneurial orientation among social enterprises in Uganda. *Business Management Review*, 20(2), 1–14. doi: 10.15678/EBER.2019.070305

Anderson, B. S., Covin, J. G., & Slevin, D. P. (2009). Understanding the relationship between entrepreneurial orientation and strategic learning capability: An empirical investigation. *Strategic Entrepreneurship Journal*, 3(3), 218–240. doi:http://dx.doi.org/10.1002/sej.72

Anderson, B. S., Kreiser, P. M., Kuratko, D. F., Hornsby, J. S., & Eshima, Y. (2015). Reconceptualizing entrepreneurial orientation. *Strategic Management Journal*, 36(10), 1579–1596. doi:https://doi.org/10.1002/smj.2298

Berman, S. L., Wicks, A. C., Kotha, S., & Jones, T. M. (1999). Does stakeholder orientation matter? The relationship between stakeholder management models and firm financial performance. *Academy of Management Journal*, 42(5), 488–506. doi:http://dx.doi.org/10.5465/256972

Bhuian, S. N., Menguc, B., & Bell, S. J. (2005). Just entrepreneurial enough: The moderating effect of entrepreneurship on the relationship between market orientation and performance. *Journal of Business Research*, 58(1), 9–17. doi:10.1016/S0148-2963(03)00074-2

Caruana, A., Ewing, M. T., & Ramaseshan, B. (2002). Effects of some environmental challenges and centralization on the entrepreneurial orientation and performance of public sector entities. *Service Industries Journal*, *22*(2), 43–58. doi:https://doi.org/10.1080/714005076

Chen, H. L., & Hsu, C.-H. (2013). Entrepreneurial orientation and firm performance in non-profit service organizations: Contingent effect of market orientation. *Service Industries Journal*, *33*(5), 445–466. doi:https://doi.org/10.1080/02642069.2011.622372

Choi, N., & Majumdar, S. (2014). Social entrepreneurship as an essentially contested concept: Opening a new avenue for systematic future research. *Journal of Business Venturing, 29*(3), 363–376. doi:10.1016/j.jbusvent.2013.05.001

Coombes, S. M. T., Morris, M. H., Allen, J. A., & Webb, J. W. (2011). Behavioural orientations of non-profit boards as a factor in entrepreneurial performance: Does governance matter? *Journal of Management Studies*, *48*(4), 829–856. doi:https://doi.org/10.1111/j.1467-6486.2010.00956.x

Covin, J. G., & Lumpkin, G. T. (2011). Entrepreneurial orientation theory and research: Reflections on a needed construct. *Entrepreneurship: Theory & Practice*, *35*(5), 855–872. doi:https://doi.org/10.1111/j.1540-6520.2011.00482.x

Covin, J. G., & Slevin, D. P. (1989). Strategic management of small firms in hostile and benign environments. *Strategic Management Journal*, *10*(1), 75–87. doi:https://doi.org/10.1002/smj.4250100107

Covin, J. G., & Slevin, D. P. (1991). A conceptual model of entrepreneurship as firm behavior. *Entrepreneurship: Theory & Practice*, *16*(1), 7–25. doi:https://doi.org/10.1177/104225879101600102

Covin, J. G., & Wales, W. J. (2012). The measurement of entrepreneurial orientation, *Entrepreneurship: Theory & Practice*, *36*(4), 677–702. doi:https://doi.org/10.1111/j.1540-6520.2010.00432.x

Dacin, P. A., Dacin, M. T., & Matear, M. (2010). Social Entrepreneurship: Why We Don't Need a New Theory and How We Move Forward From Here. *Academy of Management Perspectives*, *24*(3), 37–57. doi:10.5465/AMP.2010.52842950

Dacin, M. T., Dacin, P. A., & Tracey, P. (2011). Social Entrepreneurship: A Critique and Future Directions. *Organization Science, 22*(5), 1203–1213. doi:10.1287/orsc.1100.0620

Davis, J. A., Marino, L. D., Aaron, J. R., & Tolbert, C. L. (2011). An examination of entrepreneurial orientation, environmental scanning, and market strategies of nonprofit and for-profit nursing home administrators. *Nonprofit and Voluntary Sector Quarterly, 40*, 197–211. doi: https://doi.org/10.1177/0899764009351112

DiVito, L., & Bohnsack, R. (2017). Entrepreneurial orientation and its effect on sustainability decision tradeoffs: The case of sustainable fashion firms. *Journal of Business Venturing*, *32*(5), 569–587. doi:10.1016/j.jbusvent.2017.05.002

Engelen, A., Schmidt, S., & Buchsteiner, M. (2015). The simultaneous influence of national culture and market turbulence on entrepreneurial orientation: A nine-country study. *Journal of International Management*, *21*(1), 18–30. doi:https://doi.org/10.1016/j.intman.2014.12.002

Gabrielsson, J. (2007). Boards of directors and entrepreneurial posture in medium-size companies. *International Small Business Journal*, *25*(5), 511–537. doi:https://doi.org/10.1177/0266242607080657

Gaweł, A. (2012). Entrepreneurship and sustainability: Do they have anything in common? *Poznan University of Economics Review*, *12*(1): 5–16.

Gupta, V., & Wales, W. J. (2017). Assessing organizational performance within entrepreneurial orientation research: Where have we been and where can we go from here? *Journal of Entrepreneurship, 26*(1), 51–76. doi:https://doi.org/10.1177/0971355716677389

Harrison, S. (2013). *Thirsting for a life of service* [audio podcast]. Entrepreneurial Thought Leaders. Retrieved from http://ecorner.stanford.edu/authorMaterialInfo.html?mid=3177

Helm, S., & Andersson, F. O. (2010). Beyond taxonomy: An empirical validation of social entrepreneurship in the nonprofit sector. *Nonprofit Management & Leadership, 20*(3), 259–276. doi: https://doi.org/10.1002/nml.253

Ireland, R. D., Covin, J. G., & Kuratko, D. F. (2009). Conceptualizing corporate entrepreneurship strategy. *Entrepreneurship: Theory & Practice, 33*(1), 19–46. doi:https://doi.org/10.1111/j.1540-6520.2008.00279.x

Jones, T. M. (1995). Instrumental stakeholder theory: A synthesis of ethics and economics. *The Academy of Management Review, 20*(2), 404–437. doi:https://doi.org/10.5465/amr.1995.9507312924

Kusa, R. (2016). Measuring entrepreneurial orientation in the social context. *Entrepreneurial Business & Economics Review, 4*(3), 117–129. doi:10.15678/EBER.2016.040309

Light, P. C. (2006). Reshaping social entrepreneurship. *Stanford Social Innovation Review, 4*(3), 46–51.

Lumpkin, G., Moss, T., Gras, D., Kato, S., & Amezcua, A. (2013). Entrepreneurial processes in social contexts: How are they different, if at all? *Small Business Economics, 40*(3), 761–783. doi:https://doi.org/10.1007/s11187-011-9399-3

Lumpkin, G. T., Cogliser, C. C., & Schneider, D. R. (2009). Understanding and measuring autonomy: An entrepreneurial orientation perspective. *Entrepreneurship: Theory & Practice, 33*(1), 47–69. doi: https://doi.org/10.1111/j.1540-6520.2008.00280.x

Lumpkin, G. T., & Dess, G. G. (1996). Clarifying the entrepreneurial orientation construct and linking it to performance. *Academy of Management Review, 21*(1), 135–172. doi: https://psycnet.apa.org/doi/10.2307/258632

March, J. G. (1991). Exploration and exploitation in organizational learning. *Organization Science, 2*(1), 71–87. doi:https://psycnet.apa.org/doi/10.1287/orsc.2.1.71

Marshall, D., McCarthy, L., McGrath, P., & Claudy, M. (2015). Going above and beyond: How sustainability culture and entrepreneurial orientation drive social sustainability supply chain practice adoption. *Supply Chain Management, 20*(4), 434–454. doi: https://doi.org/10.1108/SCM-08-2014-0267

Martin, R. L., & Osberg, S. (2007). Social entrepreneurship: The case for definition. *Stanford Social Innovation Review, 5*(2), 28–39.

Miles, M. P., Verreynne, M.-L., Luke, B., Eversole, R., & Barraket, J. (2013). The relationship of entrepreneurial orientation, Vincentian values and economic and social performance in social enterprise. *Review of Business, 33*(2), 91–102.

Miller, D. (1983). The correlates of entrepreneurship in three types of firms. *Management Science, 29*(7), 770–791. doi:https://doi.org/10.1287/mnsc.29.7.770

Miller, D. (2011). Miller (1983) revisited: A reflection on EO research and some suggestions for the future. *Entrepreneurship: Theory & Practice, 35*(5), 873–894. doi: https://doi.org/10.1111/j.1540-6520.2011.00457.x

Miller, D., & Friesen, P. H. (1978). Archetypes of strategy formulation. *Management Science, 24*(9), 921–933. doi: https://doi.org/10.1287/mnsc.24.9.921

Miller, D., & Friesen, P. H. (1982). Innovation in conservative and entrepreneurial firms: Two models of strategic momentum. *Strategic Management Journal, 3*(1), 1–25. doi:https://doi.org/10.1002/smj.4250030102

Miller, D., & Friesen, P. H. (1983). Strategy-making and environment: The third link. *Strategic Management Journal*, 4(3): 221–235. doi: https://doi.org/10.1002/smj.4250040304

Mitchell, R. K., Agle, B. R., & Wood, D. J. (1997). Toward a theory of stakeholder identification and salience: Defining the principle of who and what really counts. *Academy of Management Review*, 22(4), 853–886. doi:10.2307/259247

Morris, M. H., Coombes, S., Schindehutte, M., & Allen, J. (2007). Antecedents and outcomes of entrepreneurial and market orientations in a non-profit context: Theoretical and empirical insights. *Journal of Leadership & Organizational Studies*, 13(4), 12–39. doi: https://doi.org/10.1177/10717919070130040401

Morris, M. H., & Joyce, M. (1998). On measuring entrepreneurial behavior in not-for-profit organizations: Implications for social marketing. *Social Marketing Quarterly*, 4(4), 1–23. doi:https://doi.org/10.1080/15245004.1998.9961027

Morris, M. H., & Paul, G. W. (1987). The relationship between entrepreneurship and marketing in established firms. *Journal of Business Venturing*, 2, 247–259. doi: http://dx.doi.org/10.1016/0883-9026(87)90012-7

Morris, M. H., Webb, J. W., & Franklin, R. J. (2011). Understanding the manifestation of entrepreneurial orientation in the nonprofit context. *Entrepreneurship: Theory & Practice*, 35(5), 947–971. doi:https://doi.org/10.1111/j.1540-6520.2011.00453.x

Neubaum, D. O., Mitchell, M. S., & Schminke, M. (2004). Firm newness, entrepreneurial orientation, and ethical climate. *Journal of Business Ethics*, 52(4), 334–347. doi:10.1007/s10551-004-1532-7

Onishi, T. (2014). Moderating effects of entrepreneurial orientation on institutional forces and venture philanthropy. *Academy of Management Annual Meeting Proceedings*, 2014(1), 1595–1600. doi:10.5465/AMBPP.2014.178

Pearce, J. A., Fritz, D. A., & Davis, P. S. (2010). Entrepreneurial orientation and the performance of religious congregations as predicted by rational choice theory. *Entrepreneurship: Theory & Practice*, 34(1), 219–248. doi:https://doi.org/10.1111/j.1540-6520.2009.00315.x.

Rauch, A., Wiklund, J., Lumpkin, G. T., & Frese, M. (2009). Entrepreneurial orientation and business performance: An assessment of past research and suggestions for the future. *Entrepreneurship: Theory & Practice*, 33(3), 761–787. doi: https://doi.org/10.1111/j.1540-6520.2009.00308.x

Rosenbusch, N., Rauch, A., & Bausch, A. (2013). The mediating role of entrepreneurial orientation in the task environment–performance relationship: A meta-analysis. *Journal of Management*, 39(3), 633–659. doi: https://doi.org/10.1177/0149206311425612

Santos, F. M. (2012). A positive theory of social entrepreneurship. *Journal of Business Ethics*, 111, 335. doi: https://doi.org/10.1007/s10551-012-1413-4

Schmidt, H. J., Baumgarth, C., Wiedmann, K.-P., & Lückenbach, F. (2015). Strategic orientations and the performance of Social Entrepreneurial Organisations (SEOs): A conceptual model. *Social Business*, 5(2), 131–155. doi: https://doi.org/10.1362/204440815X14373846978660

Shahzad, A., Wales, W. J., Sharfman, M., & Stein, C. (2016). Casting a wider performance net: The role of entrepreneurial orientation in boosting overall firm stakeholder value. *Journal of Management and Organization*, 22(2), 272–290. doi: https://doi.org/10.1017/jmo.2015.36

Sung, C. S., Choi, D. Y., Kim, D., & Lee, W. J. (2014). Do entrepreneurial companies make good corporate citizens? Exploring the relationships between entrepreneurial orientation, market orientation, and corporate citizenship. *Journal of Enterprising Culture*, 22(01), 1–25. doi:10.1142/S0218495814500010

Syrjä, P., Puumalainen, K., Sjögrén, H., Soininen, J., & Durst, S. (2019). Entrepreneurial orientation in firms with a social mission: A mixed-methods approach. *Cogent Business & Management*, *6*(1), 1–25. doi: https://doi.org/10.1080/23311975.2019.1602016

Tang, Z., & Tang, J. (2018). Stakeholder corporate social responsibility orientation congruence: Entrepreneurial orientation and environmental performance of Chinese small and medium-sized enterprises. *British Journal of Management*, *29*(4), 634–651. doi: https://dx.doi.org/10.1111/1467-8551.12255

Tuan, L. (2015). From corporate social responsibility, through entrepreneurial orientation, to knowledge sharing. *The Learning Organization*, *22*(3), 74–92. doi: https://doi.org/10.1108/TLO-09-2014-0052

Voss, Z. G., Voss, G. B., & Moorman, C. (2005). An empirical examination of the complex relationships between entrepreneurial orientation and stakeholder support. *European Journal of Marketing*, *39*(9/10), 1132–1150. doi: https://doi.org/10.1108/03090560510610761

Wales, W. J. (2016). Entrepreneurial orientation: A review and synthesis of promising research directions. *International Small Business Journal*, *34*(1), 3–15. doi:10.1177/0266242615613840

Wales, W. J., Gupta, V. K., & Mousa, F.-T. (2013). Empirical research on entrepreneurial orientation: An assessment and suggestions for future research. *International Small Business Journal*, *31*(4): 357–383. doi:10.1177/0266242611418261

Wiklund, J., & Shepherd, D. A. (2011). Where to from here? EO-as-experimentation, failure, and distribution of outcomes. *Entrepreneurship: Theory & Practice*, *35*(5), 925–946. doi: https://doi.org/10.1111/j.1540-6520.2011.00454.x

Zahra, S. A., Hayton, J. C., & Salvato, C. (2004). Entrepreneurship in family vs. non-family firms: A resource-based analysis of the effect of organizational culture. *Entrepreneurship: Theory & Practice*, *28*(4), 363–381. doi: https://doi.org/10.1111/j.1540-6520.2004.00051.x

APPENDIX A
COVIN AND SLEVIN (1989) EO IN COMMERCIAL ENTERPRISES SCALE

Innovativeness

In general, the top managers of my firm favor . . .

A strong emphasis on the marketing of tried-and-true products or services	1 2 3 4 5 6 7	A strong emphasis on R&D, technological leadership, and innovations

How many new lines of products or services has your firm marketed in the past five years (or since its establishment)?

No new lines of products or services	1 2 3 4 5 6 7	Very many new lines of products or services
Changes in product or service lines have been mostly of a minor nature	1 2 3 4 5 6 7	Changes in product or service lines have usually been quite dramatic

Innovativeness

Proactiveness

In dealing with its competitors, my firm . . .

Typically responds to actions which competitors initiate	1 2 3 4 5 6 7	Typically initiates actions to which competitors then respond
Is very seldom the first business to introduce new products/ services, administrative techniques, operating technologies, etc.	1 2 3 4 5 6 7	Is very often the first business to introduce new products/services, administrative techniques, operating technologies, etc.
Typically seeks to avoid competitive clashes, preferring a "live-and-let-live" posture	1 2 3 4 5 6 7	Typically adopts a very competitive, "undo-the-competitors" posture

Risk-taking

In general, the top managers of my firm have . . .

A strong proclivity for low-risk projects (with normal and certain rates of return)	1 2 3 4 5 6 7	A strong proclivity for high-risk projects (with chances of very high returns)

In general, the top managers of my firm believe that . . .

Owing to the nature of the environment, it is best to explore it gradually via cautious, incremental behavior	1 2 3 4 5 6 7	Owing to the nature of the environment, bold, wide-ranging acts are necessary to achieve the firm's objectives

When confronted with decision-making situations involving uncertainty, my firm . . .

Typically adopts a cautious, "wait-and-see" posture in order to minimize the probability of making costly decisions	1 2 3 4 5 6 7	Typically adopts a bold, aggressive posture in order to maximize the probability of exploiting potential opportunities

APPENDIX B
MORRIS AND JOYCE (1998) EO IN NONPROFITS SCALE

Our organization is characterized by (1, Strongly Disagree to 5, Strongly Agree):

1. A high rate of new program and service development compared to other organizations in our field or area.
2. An emphasis on continuous improvement in methods of operation or service delivery.
3. Risk-taking by key managers or administrators in seizing and exploiting new opportunities.

4. A "live and let live" philosophy in dealing with other organizations that compete for the same resources we do.
5. The seeking of unusual, novel solutions by senior managers to problems via the use of "idea people," brainstorming, etc.
6. A management philosophy that emphasizes proven services, programs, and approaches.
7. A management philosophy that emphasizes the avoidance of heavy expenditures on developing new programs.
8. A charismatic leader at the top.

At our organization, decision-making is characterized by (1, Strongly Disagree to 5, Strongly Agree):

9. Cautious, pragmatic, step-at-a-time adjustments to problems.
10. Active searches for major new opportunities.
11. Major social change as a dominant goal.
12. Large, bold decisions despite uncertainty.
13. Compromises among the conflicting demands of the different publics we serve, including sources of funding, clients, employees, government, board members, etc.
14. Adherence to the status quo and stability as primary concerns.
15. Over the past two years, how many new programs or services were introduced by your organization? _____
16. Over the past two years, how many major improvements were made to existing programs and services? _____
17. Over the past two years, how many major improvements did your organization make in its internal processes or methods of operation (e.g., new marketing approaches, new record-keeping methods, new approaches to funding, new human resource management systems, etc.)? _____

CHAPTER 4

⌁

Immigrant Entrepreneurship

Economic and Social Development

WONHYUNG LEE AND STEPHANIE L. BLACK

THE ROLE OF IMMIGRANT ENTREPRENEURSHIP AND ECONOMIC DEVELOPMENT

Business Venturing

In the United States, approximately 620 out of 100,000 immigrants start a new business every month (Fairlie, 2012), and an estimated 1 out of every 10 immigrants owns his or her own business (National Economic Council, 2012). The pace of immigrant business venturing is significantly high in comparison to the businesses established by non-immigrants. Studies show that immigrants are almost twice as likely to start a new business as native-born Americans (Fairlie, 2012; Herman & Smith, 2010). Immigrants have boosted their share of new entrepreneurs from 13.4% in 1996 to nearly 30% in 2010 (Reedy, Teitelbaum, & Litan, 2011). In fact, between 2007 and 2012, while Caucasian business ownership decreased, immigrant ownerships have increased. Mexicans make up the biggest number (12% of entire immigrant small business owners) followed by immigrants born in India, Korea, Cuba, China, and Vietnam (Fiscal Policy Institute, 2012).

Immigrant business owners represent 16.7% of all new business owners in the United States (Bellows, 2011). Research shows that the largest

Wonhyung Lee and Stephanie L. Black, *Immigrant Entrepreneurship* In: *Social Entrepreneurship and Enterprises in Economic and Social Development.* Edited by: Katharine Briar-Lawson, Paul Miesing, and Blanca M. Ramos, Oxford University Press (2021). © Oxford University Press. DOI: 10.1093/oso/9780197518298.003.0005.

number of immigrant business owners is concentrated in the professional and business services sector (141,000 business owners), followed by retail (121,000), construction (121,000), educational and social services (100,000), and leisure and hospitality (100,000) (Fiscal Policy Institute, 2012). Immigrant entrepreneurs play key roles in some of the nation's growing industries, such as food and transportation. For example, immigrant entrepreneurs have a strong presence throughout the entire spectrum of food production in restaurants, groceries, specialty retail markets, and food manufacturing. Immigrant entrepreneurs in food-related industries have often led to changes in consumer preferences and market demands (Hohn, 2012). Many immigrant entrepreneurs have also created businesses in the transportation sector, including taxi, limousine, and bus services. Immigrant transportation businesses meet a variety of needs, such as transporting disabled persons and sparking spin-off industries related to mobile advertising and transportation support businesses (Immigrant Learning Center, 2012). Moreover, immigrants tend to dominate in the leisure and hospitality sector where they represent approximately 28% of small business owners, comprising 43% of hotel and motel owners and 37% of restaurant owners (Fiscal Policy Institute, 2012).

Also of importance is the fact that 40% of the Fortune 500 companies were founded by immigrants (90 companies) or children of immigrants (114 companies) (Partnership for a New American Economy, 2011). Immigrant-founded Fortune 500 companies drive a wide range of industry sectors within the United States such as aerospace, defense, Internet, consumer products, specialty retail, railroads, insurance, electronics, hospitality, natural resources, finance, and many other. Some of the examples of these corporations can be seen in firms such as Apple, Google, eBay, Yahoo!, Tesla, and Intel. Moreover, many recognizable "American" brands were founded by immigrants, including AT&T, Kraft, Proctor & Gamble, Goldman Sachs, Kohl's, Honeywell, and Nordstrom.

In addition, immigrant entrepreneurs are widely recognized as an integral part of America's small business environment. Immigrant small business owners play an important role, one that has grown over the past 20 years in step with the increasing immigrant share of the labor force. With one in six small business owners being born in another country, it is evident that immigrants are an important part of America's small business environment (Fiscal Policy Institute, 2012). In fact, a US Survey of Business Owners (US Census Bureau, 2007) showed that immigrants account for 900,000 small businesses in the United States, generated $776 billion in sales receipts in 2007, and they contributed to 30% of the small business growth between 1990 and 2010.

Ethnic Enclaves

Immigrant entrepreneurs contribute to local economies through the form of ethnic enclaves as well. The term "enclave" implies the natural formation of a certain identity of a place, but the most common usage of "enclaves" refers to economically self-contained communities formed by racial or ethnic minorities (Abrahamson, 1996). Research on entrepreneurs has revealed that ethnic enclaves offer a subeconomy as a source of customers, employees, and suppliers while fostering reciprocity, support, knowledge, and motivation for new entrepreneurs (Dana & Morris, 2007; Light, 1972; Lin, 2011; Portes, 1987). Aldrich and Waldinger (1990) explained the background for the formation of ethnic economy as the following:

> Ethnic consumer tastes provide a protected market position, in part because the members of the community may have a cultural preference for dealing with co-ethnics, and in part because the costs of learning the specific wants and tastes of the immigrant groups discourage native firms from doing so, especially at an early stage when the community is small and not readily visible to outsiders. (p. 115)

The concentration of ethnic businesses in specific localities has become a common phenomenon not only in the context of global cities such as New York City and Los Angeles but also in growing suburbs around Silicon Valley, the Research Triangle Park, and Boston (Aldrich & Waldinger, 1990; Bonacich, 1994; Lin, 1998; Saxenian, 2002; Wadhwa, Saxenian, Rissing, & Gereffi, 2007; Zhou, 2004). In some cases, ethnic enclaves serve the local economy as tourist locations. For example, the enclaves such as Chinatown in San Francisco or Little Havana in Miami serve not only the ethnic locals but also tourists. In this regard, ethnic enclaves promote a "symbolic economy" which reaps profits from the industries requiring cultural creativity, such as architecture, fashion, media, and entertainment (Zukin, 1995). The growth of the tourism and symbolic economy encourage infrastructure development as well as serve to formalize cultural districts.

Job Growth and Neighborhood Revitalization

Ethnic entrepreneurship as a whole is one of the primary drivers for local economies because it helps to generate new employment opportunities for local residents as well as promoting greater regional economic development (US Chamber of Commerce and Immigration Policy Center, 2012). Immigration has had a positive influence on job growth in many metropolitan areas. Presently, immigrant-owned small businesses employ on average eight employees with a payroll of $253,000 (Fairlie, 2012). Overall, these businesses represent 30% of the total private-sector employment (Fiscal Policy Institute, 2012). Also, research has shown that immigrants stimulate employment growth and decrease the overall unemployment rate within the United States. For example, a study by the Fiscal Policy Institute (2012) evaluated the economic role of immigrants in the country's 25 largest metropolitan areas and found that immigration and economic growth for these metro areas go hand in hand.

In a more localized context, immigrant-owned businesses contribute to revitalizing commerce and positively impact investment in areas in decline. Many immigrants move to economically depressed areas because it is often more affordable (Immigrant Learning Center, 2012). The economic implications of immigrants and refugees for these areas are significant because the individuals fill vacant houses, manufacturing jobs, businesses, and cultural amenities. For example, Brooklyn and Schenectady in New York, and Midtown in Minneapolis demonstrate dramatic changes of neighborhood revitalization driven by the influx of immigrants (Echanove, 2003; Kershaw, 2005; Popuch, 2009). There is much evidence that recent Somali refugees and Latino workers fill in manufacturing labor (e.g., meatpacking, agriculture) in the Midwest regions which have experienced economic restructuring and population loss (Fennelly, 2005; Gouveia & Saenz, 2000; Paral, 2009; Schaid & Grossman, 2007). This phenomenon suggests that regions suffering from "white flight" and a downturned economy can start by attracting immigrants for manufacturing industries and microscale neighborhood revitalization projects. In fact, several cities and states within the United States have actively pursued strategies to attract and retain immigrant workers and business owners to help stimulate growth, alleviate skills gaps, and revitalize local economies. As of 2014, 18 initiatives across the country have created Welcoming America affiliates, and 25 city and county-based programs participated in the Welcoming America's Welcoming Cities and Counties initiative. These initiatives recognize entrepreneurship as a springboard for economic advancement as well as social integration for many immigrants as they have become an integral part of the economic success both locally and nationally.

Skills, Know-How, and Innovation

Highly skilled immigrants have played a vital role in the US growth by bringing new technologies and innovation to various industries. Highly skilled immigrants, especially in technology and science, have had a significant positive impact on the United States by spurring innovation through their patents on new research, products, and ideas, which has helped create jobs. For example, more than three out of every four patents (76%) at the top 10 patent-producing US universities had at least one foreign-born inventor (Partnership for a New American Economy, 2012). In the more high-tech–related or cutting-edge fields, the number of foreign-born patent holders is even higher.

These skilled individuals have contributed to US economic growth and competitiveness by earning degrees in science, technology, engineering, and mathematics (STEM) fields from the country's research universities. As of 2011, more than 40% of the 25,000 STEM doctorate degrees were awarded to nonresident students (Wright, 2013), and approximately 60% of natural sciences and engineering doctorates have chosen to remain in the United States after graduation (National Science Foundation, 2012).

Despite the strong link between highly skilled immigrants and the growth of the STEM field, the benefits of keeping foreign-born graduates is debatable with respect to its impact on the job market and native-born workers (Wright, 2013). Accordingly, policies on whether or not and how to secure the legal status of foreign workers (e.g., H-1B visa [a temporary, nonimmigrant visa] or permanent residency) are often part of a national debate, which has become particularly controversial under the current Trump administration. Any changes in the law will have critical impact on hiring and retaining a current highly skilled workforce (American Immigration Council, 2016; Wright, 2013).

IMMIGRANT ENTREPRENEURSHIP
AS SOCIAL ENTREPRENEURSHIP

Some immigrant entrepreneurs also are focused on making a positive impact through social entrepreneurship, which is distinguished from traditional business entrepreneurs by their primary objectives. While business entrepreneurs aim to maximize profits, social entrepreneurs aim to maximize some form of social impact by addressing an urgent need in the society (Bornstein & Davis, 2010). Social entrepreneurs are committed to social change by creating and sustaining social value in addition to private value and by solving problems on behalf of underserved, neglected, and highly disadvantaged populations (Dees, 1998; Martin & Osberg, 2007). Social entrepreneurs seek to draw up business techniques and private-sector approaches that will find solutions to social, cultural, and environmental problems, which can be seen in organizations of different sizes and with varying objectives and beliefs.

Traditionally, most research has most likely focused on immigrant businesses mainly as an economic engine for individual or local development rather than as an instrument to solve larger social problems that concern human rights, education, health, or the environment. Another potential reason for the missing link between immigrant entrepreneurship and social entrepreneurship may have to do with the characteristics of social entrepreneurship in the United States, whereby social enterprises are generally understood in the context of revenue generation by nonprofit organizations (Kerlin, 2006).

EXAMPLES OF IMMIGRANT SOCIAL ENTERPRISES IN NORTH AMERICA

To expand our current understanding and practice of immigrant entrepreneurship from business entrepreneurship to social entrepreneurship, one must be familiar with the various models of immigrant social enterprises that aim to improve the economic and social qualities of life for immigrants and, in some cases, refugees in North America. The extant literature on immigrant-founded or immigrant-targeted social enterprises is scarce. Therefore, we refer to the directory of Ashoka (the largest network of social entrepreneurs, https://www.ashoka.org/) and the report published by the Immigrant Settlement and Integration through Social Enterprise (ISISE) initiative in Canada (Chamberlain & Rosenow-Redhead, 2010) to search exemplary cases of immigrant social enterprises. Among nearly 3,000 social entrepreneur fellows whom Ashoka has selected and supported worldwide in the past 35 years, approximately 200 fellows are based in the United Sates, and, among them, eight organizations specifically target immigrant populations. In addition, the ISISE report catalogued 21 immigrant social enterprises in Canada based on a national survey. These social enterprises all share common goals to improve the living conditions of immigrants and/or refugees and gain economic, social, or legal equities for them. We discuss several examples of these social enterprises by operation structure next.

Not-for-Profit Enterprises

A majority of social enterprises that target immigrant populations operate as not-for-profit in the United States. While these organizations evidently pursue social impact, it is relatively less clear whether all of these organizations utilize a sustainable profit-making mechanism in addition to seeking funding from donations and grants, which are the two main sources of revenue for not-for-profits. In this chapter, we discuss two organizations that demonstrated mechanisms for cycling resources and money to sustain their goals.

The first example is Nuestras Raíces (NR), an organization in Holyoke, Massachusetts, a town with high unemployment and crime rates, which has hosted many new immigrants from Puerto Rico. NR transformed abandoned buildings and vacant lots into community gardens, training centers, a bakery, a greenhouse, a restaurant, and a commercial kitchen that residents can use on a time-share basis. Through this transformation, immigrants were able to grow and sell vegetables, thus expanding home-based businesses. The success of the gardens led to larger scale farming and environmental projects. The new acreage acquired has been used for small immigrant-owned farms, a youth training farm, a pig roasting business, a petting zoo, and cultural celebrations. These newly created entities support each other and create synergies: farmers sell their products to restaurants, the restaurant receives a rent discount for purchasing from NR farmers, and the farms recycle restaurant waste for livestock feed or compost. Farmers retain 70% of sales in selling their products, which adds thousands of dollars to their annual incomes. In this way, the resources and money are invested back into the cycle of revenue generation for the community and for the organization. As a result, NR has built a vibrant community that promotes healthy food and cultural pride while enabling low-income Latinos to address environmental, economic development, and food security issues.

The second example is the Mission Asset Fund (MAF). MAF is based in the Mission District of San Francisco, where the majority of low-income Latino immigrants did not have credit or banking experience. The goal of MAF was to develop financial products and services that cater specifically to low-income populations and eventually help them integrate into the financial mainstream. MAF came up with an idea to utilize lending activity that immigrant communities are already accustomed to (i.e., lending circles, *Cestas Populares* in Spanish) and to get those transactions recognized officially by the credit bureau. At the same time, MAF corrected the misinformation and misperceptions that clients had about financial institutions and banking systems. MAF encourages clients to open bank accounts and transfer loans there as opposed to handling cash. For some clients, MAF also introduces other saving services through which immigrants could save for their naturalization application. In this way, clients circulate and reinvest their money in the community while building credit history and assets to access mainstream financial services. Between 2008 and 2012, the MAF has facilitated more than $2.4 million zero-interest, zero-fee loans to more than 1,800 people of multiracial and ethnic groups. Credit scores increased on average by 168 points for the participants, and the average credit score reached 603 points at the end of the lending cycle (Reyes, López, Phillips, & Schroeder, 2013).

For-Profit Corporations

For-profit corporations seem to be a relatively rare form of immigrant social enterprise. One Ashoka social entrepreneur fellow serves this category and established a C-corporation called MicroManos in 2003. MicroManos, which stands for "Small Hands = Small Assistance," aims to tackle the same problem that MAF noticed (i.e., low access to credit and mainstream banks, and financial illiteracy among immigrants) but with a different strategy. MicroManos operates one-stop microfinance storefronts that provide various financial services that are needed by immigrants, such as remittance-transfer and savings. MicroManos offers remittance rates that are half the national average and consumer financing rates that are far lower than the effective annualized rates to which most immigrants have access. Immigrants usually first stop in to send money home, taking advantage of rates that are half those of traditional money-transfer companies, but over time begin using other financial services as well. MicroManos established a network between small, local microfinance institutions in developing countries and other international financial institutions by which families living apart across national borders utilize a more solid and sustainable financial infrastructure. Through this process, MicroManos helps clients build a formal credit history by reporting their financial activities to credit tracking companies. Beyond money transfer, this organization offers services ranging from mortgage and emergency loans and insurance products to low-cost calling cards.

For-Profit Co-operatives

Immigrant co-operative business models have been more prominently developed and researched in Canada (Canadian Community Economic Development Network [CCEDN], 2004; Canadian Co-operative Association, 2011) than in the United States. In Canada, immigrants more commonly adopted a co-operative model over other organizational structures either because they were familiar with it or because they considered it an appropriate model to address collective needs in the community (CCEDN, 2010). As of 2011, the Canadian Co-operative Association identified 52 co-operatives and 21 credit unions that are owned by and/or serve ethnocultural and immigrant communities. Ninety-two percent of the co-operatives were owned by immigrants and primarily serve their communities. Many provide services that support successful integration into Canadian society, such as language training, education, housing, healthcare brokering, financial services, Canadian culture and life skills, and business skills. Some build immigrant leadership and ethnic identity through cultural publishing and arts enterprises.

In this section, we describe the co-operative model that produces and sells a range of handcrafted goods. Examples such as SewFair and EcoEquitable in Canada represent this model. The goal of both programs is to support immigrants as they integrate into the workforce and achieve self-sufficiency. These programs train immigrant women who have experienced barriers to employment opportunities for language, cultural, or personal reasons to become competent and independent textile workers. For example, SewFair offers training and practical work experience to Muslim women who are economically dependent on social services. The training program focuses on vocational skills, life skills, and language skills that are relevant to employment and day-to-day usage. Similarly, EcoEquitable offers a 4-month training program called "Sewing for Jobs" through which multiethnic participants are active in group social activities, individual mentoring, and referrals to jobs. In addition, both of these programs introduce participants to sustainable business practices through which they can earn revenue and reinvest in the training program.

In all, the social enterprises that we discussed in this chapter, regardless of their models (i.e., not-for-profit, for-profit, corporate, co-operative), share common characteristics. These programs aim to solve economic and social problems that immigrants experience using a sustainable model of making profits and often recycling resources and reinvesting back into their communities. These programs promote the values of human dignity, self-esteem, cultural pride, and community spirit. In the long run, these programs aim to support immigrants who are developing the various skills required to transition into mainstream society.

IMPLICATIONS FOR FUTURE RESEARCH AND PRACTICE

In this chapter, we examined the current economic and social impact of immigrant entrepreneurship and the potential of linking immigrant entrepreneurship and social entrepreneurship in the context of the United States. We contend that immigrant entrepreneurship carries a critical role not only for the economic development of individuals and communities but also for social integration and cultural exchange between immigrants and mainstream society. To maximize the potential of immigrant entrepreneurship on economic and social development, we suggest that more conceptual and empirical studies be conducted to enrich our understanding of immigrant-founded or immigrant-targeted social enterprises in the United States. For example, various enterprise models and strategies can be tested to provide lessons and insights. Moreover, we propose expanding the discussion to refugee populations because research on refugee entrepreneurship is currently almost absent, yet some of the struggles that immigrants and refugees experience during the process of starting up enterprises may overlap. We argue that refugee entrepreneurship, along with immigrant entrepreneurship, will shed light on developing new models and approaches that can be beneficial for the newly arrived to succeed in enterprise management.

In practice, we advocate that immigrants and refugees receive more substantial and stable support for starting both commercial and social enterprises. Many newly arrived immigrants often experience barriers in communicating and transferring their ideas into actual enterprises due to limitations in financial and social resources. Despite their initial expectations, many immigrants and refugees have faced challenges in traditional means of employment (Orrenius & Zavodny, 2009; Frank, 2013) and have been forced to turn to entrepreneurship to create their own businesses and gain socioeconomic independence (Rajiman & Tienda, 2000; Heilman & Chen, 2003), but they often lack the support and financial resources to grow their enterprises and be successful (Lee & Black, 2017). According to a recent Canadian survey, there are a number of challenges that immigrant social enterprises experience, including lack of support from other agencies or organizations, lack of time or education, lack of awareness of social enterprise as a path to entrepreneurship or employment generation, and limited financial means and risk management strategies (CCEDN, 2010). Policy-makers and leaders in the not-for-profit or for-profit sectors must operationalize tangible ways to support immigrant enterprises. In addition, the co-operative model could be more broadly explored in the United States. For example, the federal government could provide systemic support for funding and consultation, as is the case in Canada, where anyone who is interested in developing a co-operative can contact the Co-op Development InfoService managed by Canada's national co-operative organizations. InfoService is operated with funding from the government of Canada, Co-operative Development Initiative.

The level of support for immigrants and refugees that can be offered, however, will be subject to the current political environment and immigration laws within the United States. The current Trump administration is proposing a strong-arm immigration policy that—although its long-term consequences are unknown—has already created turmoil in border security, travel procedures, refugee settlement, and legal protection of "Dreamers." The administration's stance has also impacted the approval and renewal of various types of visas, including temporary working visas for highly educated and highly skilled workforce members. The impact of these developments on immigrant entrepreneurship and innovation could be significant because the United States may experience an exodus of diverse, talented individuals, and others may be banned from entering the United and so take their skills and abilities to other countries.

CONCLUSION

For more than two centuries immigrants from all over the world have brought their talent, experience, and entrepreneurialism to the United States in hopes of bettering their lives, and the contributions these individuals have made have significantly helped to transform the landscape of the American economy both on a local as well as national basis. Immigrants have become an integral part of our society, and many immigrant entrepreneurs have had a positive impact on local and national economies. Presently, immigrant entrepreneurship has not been well established or understood in the context of social entrepreneurship despite the untapped potential that immigrant entrepreneurs can have in solving critical social problems and serving marginalized populations. In the future, with the increasing numbers of immigrants and even refugees across the globe seeking betterment in the United States, we must consider how we might best realize these individuals' talents and more readily incorporate them both economically and socially.

REFERENCES

Abrahamson, M. (1996). *Urban enclaves : Identity and place in America*. New York: St. Martin's Press.

Aldrich, H. E., & Waldinger, R. (1990). Ethnicity and entrepreneurship. *Annual Review of Sociology, 16*, 111–135. Retrieved from http://www.jstor.org/stable/2083265

American Immigration Council. (2016). *The H-1B Visa program: A primer on the program and its impact on jobs, wages, and the economy*. Retrieved from https://

americanimmigrationcouncil.org/sites/default/files/research/the_h-1b_visa_program_a_primer_on_the_program_and_its_impact_on_jobs_wages_and_the_economy.pdf

Bellows, J. (2011). The many contributions of immigrants to the American economy. *Treasury Notes.* Retrieved from https://www.treasury.gov/connect/blog/Pages/The-Many-Contributions-of-Immigrants-to-the-American-Economy.aspx

Bonacich, E. (1994). Asians in the Los Angeles garment industry. In P. Ong, E. Bonacich, & L. Cheng (Eds.), *The New Asian immigration in Los Angeles and global restructuring* (pp. 137–163). Philadelphia: Temple University Press.

Bornstein, D., & Davis, S. (2010). *Social entrepreneurship: What everyone needs to know.* New York: Oxford University Press.

Canadian Community Economic Development Network (CCEDN). (2004). *Creating opportunities—optimizing possibilities immigrant and refugee co-operatives in Canada.* Retrieved from https://ccednet-rdec.ca/files/ccednet/COOP_20Eng.pdf

Canadian Community Economic Development Network (CCEDN). (2010). *Experiences of Immigrant and Refugee Social Enterprise in Canada.* Retrieved from https://ccednet-rcdec.ca/sites/ccednet-rcdec.ca/files/ccednet/pdfs/rant_and_Refugee_Social_Enterprise_in_Canada.pdf

Canadian Co-operative Association. (2011). *Ethno-cultural and immigrant co-operatives in Canada.* Retrieved from https://d3n8a8pro7vhmx.cloudfront.net/coopontariofr/pages/46/attachments/original/1510261587/Ethnoculturalcoopsreportfinal.pdf?1510261587

Chamberlain, P., & Rosenow-Redhead, N. (2010). *Experiences of immigrant and refugee social enterprise in Canada.* Retrieved from https://ccednet-rcdec.ca/sites/ccednet-rcdec.ca/files/ccednet/pdfs/rant_and_Refugee_Social_Enterprise_in_Canada.pdf

Dana, L.-P., & Morris, M. (2007). Towards a synthesis: A model of immigrant and ethnic entrepreneurship. In L.-P. Dana (Ed.), *Handbook of research on ethnic minority entrepreneurship: A co-evolutional view on resource management* (pp. 803–812). Cheltenham, UK: Edward Elgar.

Dees, J. G. (1998). The meaning of social entrepreneurship. *Comments and Suggestions Contributed from the Social Entrepreneurship Founders Working Group.*, Durham, NC. Retrieved from http://faculty.fuqua.duke.edu/centers/case/files/dees-SE.pdf

Echanove, M. (2003). *Bed-Stuy on the move: Demographic trends & economic development in the heart of Brooklyn.* New York: Columbia University Press.

Fairlie, R. W. (2012). *Immigrant entrepreneurs and small business owners, and their access to financial capital.* U.S. Small Business Administration: Office of Advocacy. Retrieved from https://www.sba.gov/sites/default/files/rs396tot.pdf

Fennelly, K. (2005). Latinos, Africans, and Asians in the North Star State: Immigrant communities in Minnesota. In S. F. Martin & E. M. Gozdziak (Eds.), *Beyond the gateway: Immigrants in a changing America* (pp. 111–136). Lanham, MD: Lexington Books.

Fiscal Policy Institute. (2012). *Immigrant small business owners: A significant and growing part of the economy.* New York: Author. Retrieved from http://www.fiscalpolicy.org/immigrant-small-business-owners-FPI-20120614.pdf

Frank, K. (2013). Immigrant employment success in Canada: Examining the rate of obtaining a job match. *International Migration Review, 47*(1), 76–105.

Gouveia, L., & Saenz, R. (2000). Global forces and Latino population growth in the Midwest: A regional and subregional analysis. *Great Plains Research, 10,* 305–328.

Heilman, M. E., & Chen, J. J. (2003). Entrepreneurship as a solution: the allure of self-employment for women and minorities. *Human Resource Management Review,* 13(2), 347–364.

Herman, R. T., & Smith, R. L. (2010). *Immigrant, Inc.: Why immigrant entrepreneurs are driving the new economy (and how they will save the American worker).* Hoboken, NJ: John Wiley & Sons.

Hohn, M. D. (2012). *Immigrant entrepreneurs: Creating jobs and strengthening the economy.* Retrieved from http://www.immigrationpolicy.org/sites/default/files/docs/Hohn_-_Immigrant_Entrepreneurs_012512.pdf

Immigrant Learning Center (2012). *Immigrant Entrepreneurs Creating Jobs and Strengthening the Economy.* Retrieved from https://www.ilctr.org/wp-content/uploads/2017/09/Immigrant-Entrepreneur-Report-1-25-2012-FINAL1396.pdf

Kerlin, J. A. (2006). Social enterprise in the United States and Europe: Understanding and learning from the differences. *Voluntas: International Journal of Voluntary and Nonprofit Organizations,* 17(3), 246–262. doi: http://doi.org/10.1007/s11266-006-9016-2

Kershaw, S. (2005). For Schenectady, a Guyanese strategy: Mayor goes all out to encourage a wave of hardworking immigrants. *The New York Times* (July 26).

Lee, W., & Black, S. L. (2017). Small business development: Immigrants' access to loan capital. *Journal of Small Business & Entrepreneurship,* 29(3), 193–209. doi: 10.1080/08276331.2017.1297106

Light, I. H. (1972). *Ethnic enterprise in America: Business and welfare among Chinese, Japanese, and Blacks.* Berkeley: University of California Press.

Lin, J. (1998). *Reconstructing Chinatown: Ethnic enclaves, global change.* Minneapolis: University of Minnesota Press.

Lin, J. (2011). *The power of urban ethnic places: Cultural heritage and community life.* New York: Routledge.

Martin, R. L., & Osberg, S. (2007). Social entrepreneurship: The case for definition. *Stanford Social Innovation Review,* 5(2), 28–39.

National Economic Council. (2012). *Moving America's small businesses & entrepreneurs forward: Creating an economy built to last.* Retrieved from https://www.whitehouse.gov/sites/default/files/docs/small_business_report_05_16_12.pdf

National Science Foundation. (2012). *Science and engineering indicators 2012.* Arlington, VA: Author. Retrieved from https://www.nsf.gov/statistics/seind12/pdf/overview.pdf

Orrenius, P. M., & Zavodny, M. (2009). Do immigrants work in riskier jobs?. *Demography,* 46(3), 535–551.

Paral, R. (2009). Mexican immigration in the Midwest: Meaning and implications. *Heartland Papers, The Chicago Council on Global Affairs,* 1, 1–40.

Partnership for a New American Economy. (2011). *The New American Fortune 500.* Retrieved from http://www.renewoureconomy.org/wp-content/uploads/2013/07/new-american-fortune-500-june-2011.pdf

Partnership for a New American Economy. (2012). *Patent pending: How immigrants are reinventing the American economy.* Retrieved from http://www.newamericaneconomy.org/wp-content/uploads/2013/07/patent-pending.pdf

Popuch, E. D. (2009). *Empowerment zone designation and community economic development in Minneapolis, MN* (senior honors thesis). Macalester College, Minneapolis.

Portes, A. (1987). The social origins of the Cuban enclave economy of Miami. *Sociological Perspectives,* 30(4), 340–372.

Raijman, R., & Tienda, M. (2000). Immigrants' pathways to business ownership: A comparative ethnic perspective. *International Migration Review, 34*(3), 682–706.

Reedy, E. J., Teitelbaum, M. S., & Litan, R. E. (2011). The Current state of data on the science and engineering workforce, entrepreneurship, and innovation in the United States. In J. Lane, K. Fealing, J. Marburger III, & S. Shipp (Eds.), *The science of science policy: A handbook* (pp. 208–231). Stanford: Stanford University Press.

Reyes, B., López, E., Phillips, S., & Schroeder, K. (2013). *Building credit for the under-banked: Social lending as a tool for credit improvement.* Retrieved from http://cci.sfsu.edu/sites/sites7.sfsu.edu.cci/files/MAF Evaluation.pdf

Saxenian, A. (2002). Silicon Valley's new immigrant high-growth entrepreneurs. *Economic Development Quarterly*, *16*(1), 20–31. https://doi.org/10.1177/0891242402016001003

Schaid, J., & Grossman, Z. (2007). The Somali diaspora in small midwestern communities: The case of Barron, Wisconsin. In A. Kusow & S. Bjørk (Eds.), *From Mogadishu to Dixon: The Somali diaspora in a global context* (pp. 295–319).Trenton, NJ: The Red Sea Press.

US Census Bureau. (2007). *Survey of business owners.* Retrieved from http://www.census.gov/data/developers/data-sets/survey-of-business-owners.html.

US Chamber of Commerce and Immigration Policy Center. (2012). *Immigrant entrepreneurs: Creating jobs and strengthening the economy.* Retrieved from https://www.uschamber.com/sites/default/files/documents/files/Immigrant%2520Entrepreneur%2520final%25201-22-2012.pdf

Wadhwa, V., Saxenian, A., Rissing, B., & Gereffi, G. (2007). *America's new immigrant entrepreneurs.* Kauffman Foundation report. Retrieved from https://www.kauffman.org/entrepreneurship/reports/immigration-and-the-american-economy/americas-new-immigrant-entrepreneurs/

Wright, J. (2013). How foreign-born graduates impact the STEM workforce shortage debate. *Forbes* (May 28). Retrieved from https://www.forbes.com/sites/emsi/2013/05/28/how-foreign-born-graduates-impact-the-stem-worker-shortage-debate/568d3651b961

Zhou, M. (2004). Revisiting ethnic entrepreneurship: Convergencies, controversies, and conceptual advancements. *International Migration Review*, *38*(3), 1040–1074. doi: https://doi.org/10.1111/j.1747-7379.2004.tb00228.x

Zukin, S. (1995). *The cultures of cities.* Cambridge, MA: Blackwell.

CHAPTER 5

∘◇∘

Sustaining and Growing Social Innovations Using Integrated Development Models

Experiences from the United States, United Kingdom, and Japan

PAUL M. WEAVER, MICHAEL B. MARKS,
CARINA SKROPKE, LINDA MARIE HOGAN,
AND GABRIELLA SPINELLI

INTRODUCTION

In prevailing development models and development policy discourse, development is taken largely to mean economic development. Economic development has become synonymous with economic growth, which is pursued even at the expense of high social and environmental costs. While this may further benefit the rich and powerful, it does not provide for the inclusive well-being of all members of society or provide security, resilience, or sustainability, either socially or ecologically. There is a need, therefore, for new, more integrated approaches to development that begin with recognizing that human well-being is multifaceted; that economic, social, and environmental elements are important; and that these are likely to be

Paul M. Weaver, Michael B. Marks, Carina Skropke, Linda Marie Hogan, and Gabriella Spinelli, *Sustaining and Growing Social Innovations Using Integrated Development Models* In: *Social Entrepreneurship and Enterprises in Economic and Social Development*. Edited by: Katharine Briar-Lawson, Paul Miesing, and Blanca M. Ramos, Oxford University Press (2021). © Oxford University Press. DOI: 10.1093/oso/9780197518298.003.0006 secured more effectively, more equitably, and in a more balanced way when they are co-produced rather than by being pursued separately (Weaver & Marks, 2017).

This need for integrated development models that can deliver across a range of development dimensions and add to resilience and sustainability is recognized (e.g., CMEPSP, 2009) but because of political commitment to economic growth and the persistence of the prevailing growth paradigm, integrated models are likely to develop first in niche contexts. Their influence can then spread through interactions with mainstream institutions, sectors, organizations, and actors. Already, there are harbingers of integrated development models emerging bottom-up through the efforts of grassroots social innovators whose predominant concern is to deliver positive social impacts (Marks, Hogan, & Weaver, 2017; Weaver, 2017; Weaver & Marks, 2017). These form the focus of interest in this chapter.

We describe activities of social innovation organizations, drawing especially on *time banks* as an illustrative example of a social innovation that has a predominantly social mission, but one that interacts with the mainstream economy and with mainstream economic and political actors in several different ways to address societal challenges. We explore the scope for time banking to contribute to transformative change at the societal and systems levels by building complementary (secondary) economies, "preventative" infrastructures in health and social welfare, and inclusion opportunities for individuals and communities who are otherwise marginalized.

We consider development models to be integrated when they support social outcomes in ways that are economically sustainable. Achieving such integration of social and economic goals is likely to involve both novel ways of integrating unconventional with mainstream resources and new "hybrid" ways and mechanisms through which social innovation organizations secure financial resources. Integrated development models are therefore likely to be social and economic hybrids in their "means," their "modus operandi," and their "ends" and not just models that balance and trade off social and economic dimensions of development.

We therefore seek to identify integrated development models by focusing on resourcing strategies employed by time banks that seek to sustain and grow. We show how time banks interact with the mainstream economy and institutions to leverage the social impact of limited financial resources by using these to mobilize otherwise wasted or neglected resources, especially the time and talents of under-deployed people, including youth, the active elderly, and job seekers. We review how these interactions have produced integrated development models often involving the emergence of new "hybrid" entities and practices, such as social enterprises and social entrepreneurship. We use case examples of time banks drawing on time banking activities that demonstrate the integration of social and economic development and/or on time banking business models that deliver social impact and long-term economic viability.

The next section defines social innovation and considers what makes it especially interesting from the perspective of integrated development. Then, the third section reflects on the changing context within which social innovation processes play out and why, at the moment, conditions may be propitious for social innovation and perhaps also for some social innovation initiatives or aspects of them to be institutionalized. This is followed by a description of time banking. We then provide case studies of time bank resourcing activities and showcase business models that offer insight into different ways of achieving integrated socioeconomic development and delivery. This is followed by an analysis of findings from the case studies, and we develop a typology of integrated socioeconomic development models advanced through time banking. We also discuss the conflicts and tensions inherent in opting for different business and development models. This chapter concludes with a short discussion of challenges for policy development and future research.

SOCIAL INNOVATION

What Is Social Innovation?

Social innovation is a process that involves change in social relations: by extension, such processes can be considered as "socially innovative," those instigating such processes can be considered to be "social innovators," and new ways of thinking, organizing, acting and interacting emerging from such processes can be considered as "social innovations." Social innovation as a process responds to at least three different stimuli. It is a response to people's need for autonomy, social bonds, meaningful relationships, to be engaged in meaningful activities, and to contribute to what its proponents feel would be a "better" world; for example, a world that is more equal, just, and respectful of people and nature. It is a response also to perceived failings of mainstream systems and arrangements or to perceived gaps in mainstream provision (public and private). Social innovation processes and outcomes interact with their context, both responding to changes in the context and contributing to contextual change (Haxeltine et al., 2017).

Motivations for social innovation differ among initiatives, but values of communality and self-actualization are consistent and play an important role. Using approaches from the field of social psychology, Kemp et al. (2016)

explain these motivations as attempts to fulfill "innate" human psychological needs for autonomy, competence, and relatedness that are ill-served by dominant institutions. They argue that social innovation processes constitute a reaction to the dominant drivers of change in social and socioeconomic relations and the marketization and bureaucratization of society as identified and described by Polayni in his "two movements" model (Polanyi, 1944). The "humanizing" aspects of social innovations constitute a "third" movement to counter these existing long-term trends and their features, such as commodification, consumerism, and professionalization. The ultimate effectiveness of social innovation as a counter-movement is uncertain. Ultimately, much depends on whether social innovation initiatives with transformative potential can scale (up or out) and whether, in seeking to scale, they can retain their humanizing qualities (Weaver & Marks, 2017).

Social innovators often come together to form an initiative in response to a problem or unmet need that they perceive. They frame initiatives in terms of institutions that need to be transformed, and they respond to these challenges by developing new forms of organizing, acting, experimenting, and learning or by reviving and revitalizing older forms of relationships and behaviors that have lost favor. Through their initiatives, social innovators seek to demonstrate and diffuse new forms of social relations and new "proto" institutions that can challenge, alter, replace, or provide alternatives to existing institutions (Haxeltine et al., 2017). Owing to rigidities in prevailing institutions and organizations, the provision of complementary structures is seen by some analysts to offer another route (and, arguably, the most promising route) to transformative change (e.g., Longhurst et al., 2017; Loorbach et al., 2016; Pel et al., 2016; Weaver, 2014).

Most social innovation initiatives are locally situated and rooted but they are also often connected through network and membership organizations, which engage in "diffusing knowledge, exercising power and influence, building alliances with other societal actors, and securing (or creating) new resources for the network and its members" (Haxeltine, Avelino, et al., 2016). Networks can develop at various levels: local, regional, national and international. International networking among social innovation initiatives has been facilitated and the initiatives empowered by developments in Information and Communication Technology (ICT).

Various forms of social innovation offer alternatives to mainstream ways of living, working, and meeting needs, such as collective forms of living and work, local resilience initiatives and networks (such as transition towns and urban gardens), commons-based forms of production (e.g., co-maker spaces and peer-production), practices of permaculture and slow food, and autonomy-based forms of work in and outside the market economy. Some social innovation initiatives and organizations contribute to the creation of complementary economies using non-fiat community currencies and means of credit and mobilizing local resources that would otherwise remain unused. Complementary economies can offer more inclusive opportunities than the mainstream economy and a means to deliver local social security and well-being in ways that are resilient to downturns in the formal economy (Weaver, 2014; Weaver, 2016).

Why Is Social Innovation Interesting for Integrated Development?

In framing our discussion of social innovation, we consider why social innovation is potentially interesting from the perspective of integrated development. Several areas are relevant here.

First are the ways in which social innovations seek to create economic opportunities for those outside the mainstream economy. As background, social innovations focus efforts to help society to address a growing range of difficult challenges, such as urban poverty, unemployment, assimilation of economic and political migrants and refugees, aging societies, and break-down of communities. Many of these challenges are systemic. They have pathologies linked to prevailing development models and the paradigm of economic growth and are intractable to solutions developed from mainstream logics (Weaver & Rotmans, 2006). These "societal challenges" can also be viewed as development challenges requiring integrated solutions that deliver positive social outcomes in ways enabling them also to sustain themselves in economic terms.

In addressing these challenges, social innovations organize and act by working under a set of values and principles, internal "logics" and modus operandi that are not just different from those of mainstream institutions but are often diametric opposites of these. As noted by Kemp et al., this third movement involves transformation of socio-economic relationships into more humane forms, developing a "re-embedding process" where "human well-being is a more important driver of activities than maximization of profit" (Kemp et al., 2016). Approaches include reframing problems and creating novel solutions involving new social relations and proto institutions. Many social innovation initiatives are consciously designed to be open and inclusive, to foster cooperation and mutual aid, to open opportunities for those who do not "qualify" under mainstream logics, and to create and offer new choices to individuals and groups overlooked or marginalized under mainstream arrangements (Weaver, Kemp, et al.,

2016). Understanding the ways in which this philosophy and approach work alongside or outside mainstream systems to create new economic opportunities for those outside of the mainstream economy will contribute to the knowledge base of integrated development models.

Second, understanding the processes and models by which social innovation organizations sustain and grow presents interesting examples of integrated social and economic development, especially if their social impact is to be more than only minor and localized. Research shows that the resourcing needs of social innovations differ significantly from those of most mainstream organizations, especially in the early stages of their development (Weaver & Marks, 2017). This is because social innovation initiatives typically require relatively little money and make more use of otherwise wasted resources as inputs to their operations, such as volunteer labor and spare capacities. Some funds, however, are needed for day-to-day operations, and more funds are needed to finance upscaling, which entails new activities and new skills. Case examples used in this chapter will help identify viable business models used by social innovations to marry economic and social goals.

Last are the institutionalization journeys of social innovation initiatives over time. Explicitly or implicitly, social innovators organize around theories of change, and, to a lesser or greater extent, they may hold transformative ambitions; i.e., the ambition for their novel social relations and proto institutions to become mainstream (Wittmayer et al., 2015). Experiments with novel social relations also can be a precursor to wider institutional change. However, these transformative ambitions are often thwarted due to policy and institutional challenges. For example, at the start of their journeys, social innovation initiatives with transformative ambitions face frameworks of rules and regulations that do not recognize or support their proto institutions and that might even be hostile; they therefore need to find ways to change current institutional arrangements. This involves developing strategies and establishing relationships with often more powerful actors to negotiate and create new hybrid institutions (Pel et al., 2015). More knowledge is needed to better understand how these changes are made, what organizational configurations are developed, and the extent to which integrated development models can be mainstreamed and accepted within traditional systems.

THE OPPORTUNITY CONTEXT FOR SOCIAL INNOVATION

The "opportunity context" for social innovation organizations and initiatives is changing, potentially in favor of their playing a bigger role in society and in societal change, especially in postindustrial market democracies. In the first years of the 21st century, many Western countries have experienced collapse in public confidence in the formerly "bedrock" institutions that underpinned political, economic, and social arrangements during the 20th century. These include the institutions of state government, representative democracy, the tax system, finance (money and banking), and all aspects of welfare capitalism, including public services, social security, and pension provisions. The capacity of the state to act as guarantor for economic security and "order" in the forms citizens have been used to experiencing is eroding (Weaver, Kemp, et al., 2016a).

Examples of the key drivers of these changes include the breakdown of the state ability to tax capital and corporations and to intervene in domestic economies through wealth redistribution, austerity in public finances, demographic changes such as aging populations and an influx of migrants, environmental change, and technological changes that further erode the traditional need for labor. These drivers interact to exert pressures on many established systems and institutions; for example, at the same time as technological progress gives the potential to enable people to live longer, it increases the costs of medical interventions. This is driving a search for new models for delivering economic and social security and well-being fit for the 21st century (Weaver, Kemp, et al., 2016a).

The social values created by social innovation initiatives are gaining more attention in Western democracies. They offer scope for innovative new solutions to emerge (e.g., through the merging of public, private, and civil spheres and the emergence of "hybrid" solutions in delivery and finance). With diminishing confidence in state finance and "fiat" money, new forms of money and banking are emerging led by social innovation organizations, such as internet (crypto) currencies, local digital currencies, and time credits (Vora, 2015). Hybrid solutions could take advantage of these.

TIME BANKING

Against this backdrop, we now turn to the illustrative case of time banking, exploring what time banking is, the motivation for time banking, and the transformative ambitions of those involved in time banking.

What Is Time Banking?

Time banking involves service exchange among members of a network of individuals and organizations, usually within a local community. It is a values-led and asset-based approach to individual and community development. At the most fundamental (and purist) level, time banking is a mechanism for putting values of inclusion, mutual aid, equality, and reciprocity into practice through service exchange and for operationalizing its principal premise that everyone has something to contribute. In time banking all services are considered equal in value irrespective of the level of complexity or skill entailed. The unit of exchange and account is simply the time (hours) spent giving or receiving services.

In this sense, time banks establish complementary economies, usually at a very small and local scale, that use time as a complementary currency (see Cahn, 2004; Weaver, Dumitru, et al., 2016). The basic time banking mechanism is very versatile, and this gives scope for local time banks to address many different societal challenges and, in this process, for them to make contributions to broader societal projects, such as building secondary economies, building missing support systems for healthcare and well-being, and creating activities offering opportunities for social and economic inclusion for those otherwise excluded or marginalized (e.g., Drakeford & Gregory, 2010; Marks, 2012; Skropke, 2016; Skropke & Weaver, 2017; Weaver, Dumitru, et al., 2016).

Time banking values are important conceptually and practically (Weaver, Dumitru, Lema-Blanco, & Garcia-Mira, 2015; Weaver, Dumitru, et al., 2016b). Time banking proponents acknowledge that many different values and value systems exist and that different values and logics are relevant for different spheres or sectors. They distinguish especially between values relevant in the informal sphere of family, social, and civic life and those that underpin and constitute the logic of the formal economy. Of concern to them is not that there are differences between value systems and logics per se, but rather that there has been a steady and long-term incursion of values, principles, and institutions from the market economy into other spheres of social organization. The increasing importance given to the market sphere and its dominance over other activities—the marketization of society identified by Polanyi—takes focus away from the family, community, and civic spheres and the informal social support infrastructure and services it provides. An external cost of the formal economy and its influence also on state-led social welfare delivery arrangements is inadvertent damage to family, community, and civic life (Goodwin 2018).

In the perspective of time banking proponents, there is a need for a rebalancing of the market, state, and civic spheres to strengthen communities, rebuild social capital, and increase individual and community self-reliance, as well as a need to rethink the relations among these spheres to reduce negative crossover impacts and to create more positive, mutually supportive relations. Proponents argue that the importance of family, community, and civic life in delivering well-being and security is underestimated and that those who contribute to society in this sphere and their contributions are insufficiently recognized and rewarded. They also believe that strong social capital and functioning infrastructure in the family, community, and civic spheres are important in securing business and government effectiveness and efficiency (Cahn, 2004).

Time banking proponents seek less to transform existing institutions than to demonstrate that other ways of "doing" and "organizing" are necessary and possible. Time banking challenges assumptions and beliefs in the hegemony of the market economy and its institutions that are limiting and damaging to the prospects of satisfying the full range of human needs on an inclusive basis. Time bank leaders seek to rebalance the institutions of society by (re)building missing or lost social infrastructure that has an important preventative function, rebuilding social capital, and reasserting the contributions to society of cooperation, mutual aid, reciprocity, and unpaid work (Cahn, 2004).

Origins of Time Banking

The idea of time banking was developed in Japan by Teruko Mizushima in the context of the postwar breakdown of prewar institutions, including the economy, state government, fiat money, physical infrastructure, and families (Lebra, 1980; Lietaer, 2004; Miller, 2008). Mizushima set out her ideas in articles and books from 1950 onward. She created her first time bank in Osaka in 1973, and, by the end of the decade, she had developed a national network of time banks across Japan. In 1982, her organization also supported the development of a time bank among the Japanese-American community in Gardena, California, making hers also the first international time banking organization (Weaver, 2017).

Time banking meanwhile separately emerged in the United States in the mid-1970s as a self-organized initiative within poor communities in St. Louis, Missouri, under the auspices of Grace Hill Settlement House. This emergent program came later to be known under the acronym MORE (Members Organized Resource Exchange). The MORE program, and the time banking mechanism that was its core feature, attracted considerable attention from across the United States but also internationally (Wright, 1997). The underlying values, principles, and mechanism of time banking as developed by Mizushima and the women pioneers of time banking at Grace Hill Settlement were documented in books and reports. The writings of Cahn and Rowe, especially, helped spread time banking to countries around the world (Cahn & Rowe, 1992).

New time banks continue to be established. These and existing time banks are often organized into local, regional, national, or transnational networks under the umbrella of membership or support organizations that supply some services centrally, including training and access to the software programs and platforms that time banks and their members use to organize service exchanges, record transactions, and keep accounts (Weaver, Dumitru, et al., 2016b).

Why Is Time Banking Resourcing Salient in the Context of Integrated Development?

The resourcing, funding, and business models of local time banks differ between manifestations with each local time bank being (usually) an autonomous legal and financial entity. Important here is that the history of time banking, stretching now over almost 50 years, disappointingly demonstrates that few time banks survive for more than 3 years. In terms of the numbers of time banks operating in particular countries, new start-ups are broadly matched by closures of existing time banks, such that the overall number of time banks operating at any given time is constant and, in some countries, has declined from earlier peaks.

The failure of most time banks to sustain—let alone grow or spread by diffusion—has limited the contribution to transformative societal- and systems-level change that time banking has been able to make in most countries so far. At first sight, this may appear also to limit the salience of time banking to questions of integrated development and how to achieve this. But this is far from the case. What makes time banking salient is that, despite the general trend just noted, some local manifestations of time banks and some networks of time bank have not only survived long term but have thrived and grown in scale and vibrancy. As we will show, these successful initiatives employ hybrid development models that successfully integrate economic and social development activities and goals.

HISTORY, DESCRIPTION, AND RESOURCING PATHWAYS OF IDENTIFIED INITIATIVES

In this section, we use "success case" evaluation strategies (Brinkerhoff, 2003; Murphy, 2016) to understand what these long-surviving time banks do that is different and how their business strategies and development models contribute to their sustainability. Of special interest is whether their models contain lessons or have replicability potential. We describe the activities and business models of a set of time banks or mission-led organizations that use the time banking mechanism and demonstrate survivability. The set includes four activities and business models from the United States: Partners-in-Care; Portland Hours Exchange and the Portland Weatherproofing Cooperative; the Parent Resource Network of Rhode Island; and the ArchCare and predecessor time banks coordinated by Mashi Blech. It also includes two time banks from the United Kingdom: the Fair Shares time bank and its Gloucester Motorway Services venture; and Time Bank Hull and East Riding (TBHER), which is contributing to a secondary economy-building project in Hull and to a project offering immigrants social and economic assimilation opportunities. Finally, it describes some derived forms of time banking in Japan that support "incentivized volunteering" and their roles in addressing the challenges of elderly care in a rapidly aging society.

Hour Exchange Portland (HEP) in Maine, launched in 1995, is one of the longest running neighbor-to-neighbor community time exchanges in the United States and a historic leader in the time bank movement (see: www.hourexchangeportland.org). HEP has more than 500 active and diverse members that include seniors, families, and refugees, and many are low-income and/or experiencing disadvantage. Special programs include "access to the arts" in which members can use time credits to attend arts and entertainment events; mentorship workshops and participation in group marketing opportunities for artisans and crafters; and "access to education," where time credits can be used to learn new skills, take classes, or receive private tutoring. Healthcare has consistently remained the most utilized service in HEP, providing access to mental health services, therapies, nutrition counseling, childbirth support, and transportation to medical appointments paid in time credits.

HEP has been supported financially by a combination of government grants, subcontracting with partner nongovernmental organizations (NGOs), and foundation support. Of note was a subcontract and collaboration with Catholic Charities Refugee and Resettlement Programs (CCRRP) to support refugees and immigrant populations in Portland. Time exchange members assisted these populations in studying for their citizenship test or in learning English; new populations provided mutual aid to each other and exposed members to their food and culture. The subcontract was renewed annually for 15 years.

The uncertainty of funding and interest communicated by its members led HEP to explore co-developing and supporting a number of social enterprises. In the first arrangement, a weatherproofing cooperative was launched as a legally separate, tax-paying business. A successful business model was formed using the different status of two separate but collaborating organizations (HEP and the cooperative) to leverage resources for both, providing mutual support and delivering positive social and environmental impact. The cooperative, a standard fee-based business, was established to connect directly with and for HEP members. The cooperative labor force came primarily from time exchange members. This was done by the cooperative inviting time exchange members to earn hours working as "Green Teams" under the supervision of the Coop Energy Technician. Members could then spend their hours for wanted services offered within HEP. The exchange of time currency between the time exchange members needing weatherization services and cooperative staff providing services reduced the operating costs of the cooperative, resulting in competitive customer fees. The cooperative also attracted a host of in-kind and other resources through partnerships with other organizations. For example, necessary materials, tools, and equipment needed for weatherization were donated by the State of Maine, Greater Portland United Way, the local community action agency (Habitat for Humanity), and individuals.

The cooperative was not eligible to secure government or philanthropic grants or individual donations. HEP, by contrast, legally incorporated as a 501c3 (US equivalent of a charity) and was eligible for grant funding. HEP attracted grants from several foundations, banks, and individuals, which supported a staff position to coordinate work between the cooperative and the time exchange. In turn, the time exchange and its members reaped a number of benefits. The Weatherization Cooperative granted a portion of its revenue from its profits to support HEP. Interested time bank members received training in weatherizing their own homes, thus saving expenses. Also, two time exchange members gained employment in the weatherization field as a result of the training and experience they received as "green-teamers." One member was employed for a year before leaving the area; another became a manager in a private business.

The second arrangement was an off-shoot of this collaboration through which interested members of the cooperative could establish their own weatherization business. Here, the time exchange helped to incubate, grow, and sustain fledgling businesses. HEP assisted entrepreneurs by helping them start, expand, and improve their businesses, charging "time" for the support they received for mentoring, marketing, advertising, finding and securing facilities to house their business, and other essential business incubation functions. HEP members uninterested in actual weatherization but who wanted to support the businesses earned time providing transportation, lunches, or tools for the new entrepreneurs. These entrepreneurs also had access to time exchange members as potential customers for their business start-ups. In exchange, a portion of their business revenue was returned or "tithed" to the time exchange in recognition of the assistance the exchange provided.

Partners in Care (PIC) is a time exchange community that offers services to Maryland seniors and individuals with disabilities in exchange for their donated time and talents. Its diverse 3,200-person membership includes all age groups of seniors, their family members and friends, and PIC staff and community members contributing to the time exchange and to the organization. Special programs include "Ride Partners," which provides door-to-door transportation to older adults with members using their own cars; "Repairs with Care," which provides handyman support; and "Member Care," which provides individualized support such as home visits, help with paperwork, light housekeeping, pet care, and grocery shopping. Service exchanges and these specialized programs provide ways for improving the care of the current elderly and for securing care for relatives or for own care in the future, thus supplementing the nation's social security payments provided to seniors. PIC provides opportunities for everyone to contribute and benefit from elderly care regardless of income or job status. Membership in PIC is voluntary and not formally linked to national social security systems (see www.partnersincare.org).

Like HEP, PIC is supported by a combination of government and foundation grants and subcontracts with larger NGOs. In 2017, PIC had 26 different philanthropic grants to support programming as well as core operations. Despite the breadth of awards, grants are small and come with no expectations of continuity. This is because PIC maintains a deliberate policy that the organization will not become dependent on these grants or on any single funder. PIC policy deliberately assures a time gap between a grant award and submission of a new grant application. Furthermore, PIC has a policy of maintaining the share of grant funding (philanthropic and statutory) in the overall mix of organizational income at or below 40%. PIC is able to adhere to this principle in part due to the establishment of a social enterprise that it developed using the sweat equity of its time banks members.

The enterprise, the PIC Boutique, is staffed primarily by time bank members who earn hours supporting the business. The Boutique provides close to $500,000 annually (about 35% of total agency revenue) in support of PIC programming for older adults in the community. The time bank owns the profit-making boutique. PIC trains all staff who work in and who support the Boutique. Many staff members are seniors who use their banked hours for transport or handyman repair services. The network around them combats social isolation as they stay engaged by working in the Boutique, receiving mental and physical health benefits in addition to contributing to the financial health of PIC.

Moreover, PIC encourages its members to identify a service need of seniors and to address the need through its own action, not wait for the next grant opportunity. For example, members organically created "Warm Houses," which are monthly gatherings in homes to bring people together for socialization, friendship, and connectivity. Also within PIC, two members, a retired professor and a social worker who wanted to stay active in their fields, were trained in the Stanford Chronic Disease Self-Management course (in partnership with the local Area Agency on Aging). In exchange for receiving this training, the instructors facilitated classes for the benefit of other PIC members. Interestingly, PIC has leveraged these initial "in-kind" contributions to attract foundation and public funding to supplement member activities, building on initiatives self-developed by the member community. For example, the state of Maryland issued PIC a grant that funded two vans to transport nonambulatory seniors, supplementing the Rides Program for seniors provided by time bank members.

Parent Support Network (PSN) of Rhode Island, which houses the Rhode Island Time Bank, provides parent peer support services to parents with children removed from their home, involved in the justice system on probation, or placed in the Rhode Island Training School, a residential treatment provider for youth. Support is provided by PSN under a contract with Rhode Island Department of Children, Youth, and Families. Services include providing evidence-based parent education, the "Nurturing Parenting Program"; preparation and attendance at child and/or parent treatment meetings, school meetings, and special education planning meetings; and work with parents on improving their capacity to parent in order to be successfully reunified with their children. Volunteer peer support specialists, trained by PSN staff, work within PSN and other health and social service agencies in Rhode Island to provide support and services to parents and young people. PSN also has a youth group, "Youth Speaking Out" (YSO), for young people aged 13 to 17 years who have behavioral health challenges. YSO-involved youth learn leadership skills, work on community service activities, and receive training in public speaking to prepare them to testify at local government forums and hearings in support of young people and their families. Volunteers and paid peer recovery specialists support each of these projects along with other program-involved youth and families and community members, with many participating in the Rhode Island Time Bank and providing mutual aid to each other through reciprocal service exchanges (see www.psnri.org/).

PSN is almost entirely supported by government contracts and effectively operates as a commissioned service provider. It is commissioned repeatedly owing to the reliability and quality of its service offer in an area of high need. Due to its high-need target population of youth and families and their often formal involvement within the Social Services or Juvenile Justice systems, PSN has sought out and won grants from a range of federal, state, and local sources to support the organization. Funding is provided by Rhode Island's Behavioral Health Developmental Disabilities, Children Youth and Families, Human Services, and Education and Health Departments, as well as by the Federal Substance Abuse Mental Health Services Administration (SAMHSA).

Similar to the other case examples described earlier, the organization, fueled by the innovativeness and entrepreneurial nature of its time bank members and service participants, identified local needs and independently sought solutions. These home-grown initiatives then leveraged new resource opportunities for the organization. For example, PSN established a formal partnership with a substance abuse treatment provider to recruit families and young adult leaders in recovery to join the time bank and build a peer support network. Child care was identified as a need that prevented attendance at regular Narcotics Anonymous (NA) or Alcoholics Anonymous (AA) meetings. In response, three organizations, including the time bank, got together to offer on-site group respite care provided in part by Time Exchange members so that family members could attend meetings. Time Exchange hours were then used as in-kind contributions to help secure a small grant to further solidify the partnership project. Similarly, to support parents with special needs children, PSN established a Friday night group respite session where families could drop off their children for a few hours to get a break. Time Exchange members staffed the Friday program.

Another example occurred when PSN, led by its volunteer peer support specialists, became the lead partner agency to develop and implement the statewide Certified Peer Recovery Specialist (CPRS) Program. With this initiative, interested volunteer peer support specialists are now able to gain a professional certification that qualifies them for positions in the formal economy delivering peer recovery services. Due to the advocacy of its members, PSN was positioned to receive a state grant to train and place newly certified peer-support specialists in healthcare venues across the state. These efforts have contributed to the expansion and sustainability of PSN in its work of supporting direct services to youth and families, coordinating volunteer services, supporting group services for young people, advocacy, and organizing work to improve policies for youth and families.

ArchCare is the most recent of three time bank ventures operated successfully over a total period of 30 years by Mashi Blech. She has specialized in integrating time banks into large (multimillion dollar) organizations, helping these to deliver their mission by using the time bank mechanism. In each case, a time bank has been embedded into the practices of the host organization, with members recruited from the clients of the host on the basis that both members and the host organization can benefit from members being active in time banking.

Two of the host organizations that benefitted from this model are in the health sector. Elder Plan, a health insurer, benefitted by the time bank enabling elderly people to be supported longer in their own homes rather than entering residential care homes. The Visiting Nurse Service of New York was similarly supported by a time bank established to provide intergenerational support in the community, thus reducing some of the demands on visiting nurses. The embedded time banks operated for 19 and 8 years, respectively, but operations ended in each case following changes in the CEO of the host organizations. This illustrates both the strengths and weaknesses in developing embedded relationships with a larger organization: the business model can work well when the relationship holds, but its future rests on decisions of the host rather than on decisions of the time bank coordinator or its members. Reliance on a single large sponsoring organization holds a high risk. The time bank is especially vulnerable if its membership is also drawn from the clientele of the host organization, since there is no simple way for the time bank to extricate from the embedded relationship to establish an independent identity.

Mashi Blech has nevertheless successfully sustained time bank operations over long periods using this model, demonstrating that, even if precarious, this is a workable business model that can provide stability over many years. She now organizes a time bank, ArchCare, which is supported financially by the Catholic Archdiocese of New York. ArchCare in turn supports the Archdiocese in delivering its mission, especially by addressing social determinants of health, such as isolation, and organizing mutual support in the community, especially among the non–English-speaking communities of immigrants in New York who are often living without family support and have low incomes and limited access to other forms of welfare support.

Fair Shares Time Bank, established in 1998 as the first time bank in the United Kingdom, received its initial funding from local trusts and foundations, as well as from the Big Lottery Fund. The time bank now receives other Trust funding plus funding from local authorities. It sustained and grew to where it now consists of five time banks and a charity shop and is a beneficial stakeholder of a Trust funded through a social enterprise business venture that was its own initiative. The five time banks are individually operated within local communities in different parts of Gloucestershire, a rural but not particularly large county. The time banks form a local/regional network, learning from each other and exchanging experiences and lessons. To encourage broad-based membership, Fair Shares developed initiatives targeted to a number of specific marginalized populations such as single mothers, seniors, adults in prison or reentering community from prison, and people with disabilities. As the first time bank in the country, Fair Shares benefitted from a close association with the New Economics Foundation, a progressive think tank tied to policy makers that sought clarity on the legal recognition of time banks.

Fair Shares is supported in part by funds from a unique social enterprise. The establishment of the Gloucester Motorway Services occurred through the active social entrepreneurship of Mark Gale, leader of the local Fair Shares time bank, in cooperation with the Westmoreland Family and the Gloucester Gateway Trust (GGT). The Motorway Services project took 12 years to come to fruition. Its founders faced formidable bureaucratic procedures involved in securing planning permissions, building support, and fighting legal challenges from commercial companies with interest vested in conventional service station operations. Its history is one of emergence of new ways of organizing income streams for community and civil society organizations based on innovative collaboration between these and for-profit companies to create a business model centered around the idea of a strong local identity providing alternatives to the "uniformity" of standardized provision by multinational operators.

The Motorway Services project addressed a local problem by turning it into a win-win solution. It involved making use of disused land along the M5 highway, which runs through the middle of Gloucester, and turning this into an asset that serves local community interests and supports community development. The land had been part of a farm. The viability of the farm was compromised by the motorway construction when the highway cut through the farm, taking away part of the land and leaving the rest fragmented and isolated on either side of the road. The land had become disused and an eyesore. Local leaders led by Mark Gale developed a comprehensive strategic outline for their vision of a green motorway service area and searched for an investment and operating partner.

Their first move was to establish the Gloucester Gateway Trust (GGT) in 2007 as a company with charitable purpose. This brought together a group of leading local business people and social entrepreneurs. With the financial support of two trusts, the operating costs of GGT were underpinned and options were secured on the land, which was then purchased. Westmoreland Ltd., a family-owned company that had previously established a similar service station, became the business partner, provided the investment needed to develop the service station, and became its owner and operator. After 7 years spent completing the necessary planning and permitting procedures, overcoming a judicial review initiated by some major chains with national presence at motorway service stations, and a number of appeals, the project was completed in 2014. It became the first British partnership between a charity and a business united around a common interest to create benefit and value for both.

In contrast to other motorway services, Gloucester Motorway Services does not operate franchises. Instead it has local suppliers providing all services, and it operates as an outlet and showcase for local produce. Its facilities include a farm shop, gift shop, local butcher shop, and a fishmonger. The cafés and restaurants serve fresh and locally produced food. In total, the project supports more than 200 local and regional producers and provides 400 permanent jobs for local people.

Besides serving local commercial/economic interests, the service station also generates sustainable income that flows back into local communities. A share of proceeds is donated to GGT. In turn, GGT invests in six local projects. Four of these are other charities, including the Fair Shares time bank, and two are community partners. This distribution of funds secures a sustainable source of money for the projects, which provides them with sustainability and autonomy, giving the recipient projects and organizations independent control over their own operations and enabling them to maintain grassroots-driven and grassroots-controlled organizations with local identity. The synergies of the partnership are ever evolving. For example, the Growers Community Project run by the GGT provides work experience at the service station for people with learning disabilities or recovering from mental illness and who otherwise could encounter difficulties entering the regular (mainstream) labor market.

Time Bank Hull and East Riding (TBHER) is a community time bank in Kingston-upon-Hull, UK (hereafter referred to simply as Hull). Initially, TBHER received start-up funding from the local authority, Hull City Council (HCC). It has subsequently secured limited-term funding from other funders to support its transition to greater financial autonomy, and, simultaneously, it is developing activities along lines that will contribute both to its own financial sustainability and to positive social impact.

One of its initiatives involves supporting change in organizational cultures in Hull through wider take-up of the time banking principles of cooperation and mutual aid based on asset sharing. This contributes to the development of a secondary "solidarity" economy in Hull as a way to combat downturns in the mainstream economy and to the development of a circular economy, both of which support the strategic approaches of HCC to urban poverty relief based around strengthening urban resilience.

TBHER strategy toward building a secondary economy involves developing a Mutual Aid Network with thematic "hubs" of activity around core issues, including healthy and locally produced food and locally led economic development that uses local resources and assets to address local needs and challenges. These bring together organizations and their assets in projects that enable productive use to be made of spare capacities and otherwise underused resources and for collaborating partner organizations and individuals to provide mutual support, which helps all parties to reduce their costs and improve their product and service offers, including local businesses, local social enterprise start-ups, and local public service organizations.

As well as using time as a currency, TBHER envisages using a local cryptocurrency, HullCoin, to incentivize and reward participation in the Mutual Aid Network and the transactions that will enable hub activities to grow and merge over time into a coherent urban-scale secondary economy with critical mass. The programmable cryptocurrency will also enable secondary economy development to be mapped and modeled in real time.

TBHER has also established a collaborative venture with Open Doors, an initiative of the local Methodist church. The initiative seeks to improve opportunities for asylum seekers and refugees (hereafter "migrants") in the greater Hull community (Skropke & Weaver, 2017). Its purpose is to engage migrants within the wider community, support them in becoming active participants in society, and widen the set and sources of supports and services available to them while still respecting legal restrictions in the United Kingdom that prohibit asylum seekers from undertaking paid work while their asylum claims are being considered.

The context for integration and assimilation of migrants in Hull is increasingly challenging. Hull has one of the highest levels of asylum-seeker placement of any UK city. The share of ethnic minorities in Hull's population is increasing by a percentage point annually. Services are stretched as funding for public services has been reduced and is reducing. Many districts within Hull are among the most deprived in the United Kingdom, scoring in the lowest 20% of districts nationwide on the composite deprivation index. HCC reports that high shares of Hull households experience income deprivation (25.7%), employment deprivation (20.2%), and/or over-indebtedness (43.1%). The local authority has the fourth-lowest employment rate and highest benefits claimant count in the United Kingdom (Skropke, 2016). This challenging context calls for innovative ways to address isolation and assimilation that are cost-effective.

The collaboration between TBHER and the local Methodist church is an attempt to utilize the complementarity of assets and service offers of the two organizations. Open Doors provides a safe haven for asylum seekers and refugees in Hull, but those arriving also need opportunities to engage with the wider Hull community. For the mutual benefit of the host community and newcomers, it is important that there is an active assimilation process, but this needs a cost-effective assimilation mechanism. The time bank provides the important next steps: a route giving migrants access to the wider local community by joining the time bank and opportunities for honing and deploying skills and enabling migrants to contribute to the local community without taking paid employment.

The partnership fosters mechanisms for reciprocal service exchange, enabling migrants to contribute to a moneyless, mutual aid economy of service exchanges and group activities. This can help prepare migrants for inclusion in the monetary economy once their legal status is finalized. The time bank can also provide support to migrants as future entrepreneurs and microentrepreneurs by supplying labor and access to facilities and equipment as "in-kind" forms of capital on the basis of time credits, similar to methods utilized in HEP.

Japanese time banks and derivative forms of time banking also offer interesting insights. Time banking originated in Japan (Lebra, 1980). The establishment of the Volunteer Labour Bank (VLB) in 1973 and the development of its nationwide network (VLN) paved the way for the emergence of other time bank networks in Japan, each offering innovative adaptations of the original model. These adaptations emerged in co-evolutionary relation with ongoing contextual changes in Japan, especially with population aging and with public policy innovations in legal and financial arrangements (Miller, 2008).

The legal changes concerned who should assume responsibility for care of the aged and how payment for care is arranged. Important legal instruments were the Non-Profit Organization (NPO) Law and the Long-Term Care Insurance (LTCI) Law. The NPO law bestowed greater legitimacy on nonprofit organizations for taking up new roles in society, including as care providers. The LTCI law introduced a mandatory scheme of universal insurance to finance the costs of care in old age to which all those older than 40 paid premiums. This created a funding stream for organizations offering senior care.

These institutional changes enabled new time bank organizations to emerge as care providers by developing hybrid versions of time banking. These hybrids, mostly in the form of mixed currency models, created scope for members to give and receive care through the time banking arrangement, through money payments, or through a combination of time and money. This extended the appeal of time banking to actual and potential members and extended care possibilities to nonmembers, including those too frail to join as active members and already in need of care.

These arrangements helped to attract new groups into Japanese time banks and into training and certification as "carers," importantly including active retirees. Many thousands of Japanese gained official care qualifications in the first years of operating the scheme. In turn, Japanese time banks became major providers of training courses, certification, and care. Some Japanese time banking organizations have gone on to become leading institutes of research and sources of information for policy-makers and businesses about the needs and wants of the aged. Providing these services has become part of their service offer.

Time banking has traveled farther down an institutionalization pathway in Japan than in any other country. However, it is the more commercial adaptations of the model that have endured rather than the original "purist" model. Hybrid forms of time bank have become dominant in Japan, where they are considered to offer opportunities for "incentivized" or rewarded volunteering.

Interestingly, "incentivized volunteering" also has now emerged from time banking in the United Kingdom, pioneered by a social innovation organization that was originally called Spice and is now called Tempo. Tempo awards "time credits" to those who provide their time to voluntary and community sector organizations. The organizations offering volunteering opportunities form part of a time credit "earning" network. Time credits are then exchangeable for "rewards," such as entrances to leisure and sports facilities, places on courses, and rides on public transport. Tempo is supported by partner organizations and these donate their spare capacity (e.g., unsold tickets) as rewards, becoming part of a time credit "spending" network. The scheme both recognizes and rewards volunteers' contributions to community.

ANALYSIS AND DISCUSSION OF FINDINGS

In this section, we identify common features among the selected cases and develop a simple typology of pathways to financial growth and sustainability. We then discuss benefits, tensions, risks, and tradeoffs associated with each pathway.

Common Features

Turning first to common features or similarities among the case examples we note that

- While the identified initiatives differ in target group, history, and mission, a common feature is the maximum use of "non-rival" resources, especially the unused labor of community members to support and grow operations. These initiatives incorporate "citizen-organizational" co-production where community members serve as contributors and resources to further agency mission (Marks, 2009). In time bank terminology, members earn hours benefitting the host organization in some capacity and, in return, receive benefits in services provided by other time bank members or from the time bank itself.
- While having relatively low requirements for scare and rival resources, most time banks (in common with other social innovation initiatives) need some funds to cover the base-level money costs of operating and to obtain some key skills, such as to train and pay a local organizer. These funds leverage otherwise wasted community resources into productive use. Because traditional funding mechanisms are often uncertain or unsustainable, diversifying funding and/or embarking on generating an own income stream to cover basic funding needs is a common feature of those time banks that have sustained over time.
- Each of the cases involves pursuing social and economic goals simultaneously either through a single "hybrid" activity such as a social enterprise or through a combination of carefully coordinated and co-designed activities that are organized to be legally distinct but which are used together to develop and capture social and economic benefits. Different fiscal, financial, and regulatory conditions apply to different forms of legal organization. These arrangements typically require that the time bank and the social enterprise are associated functionally but are separated legally, with each having a different legal constitution (e.g., a charity plus a cooperative). This arrangement provides for the pros and cons of each

legal form to be balanced out through judicious advantage-taking of the regulatory and fiscal concessions pertaining to each (Weaver, Dumitru, et al., 2016).

• Through the process of seeking financial sustainability and growth, the more successful time banks and networks have sought institutional changes within civic, market, or state sectors. Examples of changes include developing new income streams to support and sustain the social innovation (e.g., PSN), developing new forms of cooperation across traditional sectoral lines (e.g., Fair Shares and its Motorway Project and the cooperation between community and private-sector organizations it entailed), the embedding of the social innovation in existing organizations and systems (e.g., ArchCare), and policy directions led by member advocacy and interests (e.g., PSN).

• Factors contributing to the success of initiatives include models of leadership and governance that value entrepreneurship, innovativeness, risk-taking, and contributions by all members. Also important is the early and continuous development, implementation, and adaptation of business plans that enable the time bank to reduce reliance on government income or philanthropic donations by developing own income streams and other ways to support programming using the skills and innovativeness of community members and service participants. Initiatives can take account of the context in which they operate and adapt to take advantage of contextual change (e.g., derived forms of time banking in Japan).

Pathways to Financial Growth and Sustainability

Three distinct pathways to financial growth and sustainability are evident (see also Weaver & Marks, 2017). These include (1) an external funding pathway that involves seeking investment or income from establishment actors, such as service commissioners who provide funding but set conditions on this; (2) an autonomous funding pathway through which a social innovation organization develops its own income stream to self-finance its activities and fund continuity and growth, typically through related social enterprise activity; and (3) an embedded pathway whereby the social innovation organization partners with an existing organization and receives financial support from the larger (host) organization in return for helping it deliver its mission. In addition, a strategy of using the time bank to provide foundations for schemes of rewarded volunteering or more significant forms of alternative or complementary economies is evident across the cases, based on using one or more community currencies alongside or instead of fiat currency and leveraging otherwise wasted assets into socially and economically beneficial use.

While organizations may follow more than one of these paths, one pathway is usually dominant for each organization or initiative. PSN is following a commissioned services pathway, operating as a service provider to government agencies. PIC and Fair Shares have both chosen the pathway of social enterprise to augment funding from foundations and philanthropic sources, thus diversifying their funding and developing independent income streams that allow them to maintain their autonomy and integrity to their core mission. TBHER is also developing social enterprises around its activities to promote healthy, locally produced food and nurture locally led economic development that addresses priority community concerns. ArchCare is following the embedded pathway.

It is important to note that, within the embedded pathway, there are levels of embeddedness that depend in part on the relative power of the organizations and the degree of dependency that the relation entails, but also on the compatibility of the missions of the organizations and the extent to which the embedded entity can dis-embed and still function. In the case of the time bank developed for Elder Plan, there was a high degree of mission compatibility but no scope for dis-embedding the time bank. The ArchCare time bank has integrity and is viable both within its embedded relationship with the Catholic Diocese of New York and outside that relationship.

Benefits, Risks, and Tradeoffs

The pathways are important to distinguish from each other because pathway selection is often based on the willingness and ability to take financial risk, the extent to which there is acceptance of prevailing market/mainstream systems, the nature and extent of current relationships with mainstream stakeholders, and the ability of social organization leaders to organize and engage membership to assist with organizational sustainability goals. In addition, each pathway maps onto different desired outcomes or impacts. These include prospects for transformative change, including what kinds of transformative change the social innovation can contribute toward; the extent to which the social innovation is successful in integrating its social and economic goals within its business model; the implications of financial decisions for the levels of organizational autonomy, identity, and integrity that can be maintained; and the importance that the social innovation organization attaches to scaling (see Weaver & Marks, 2017). Tables 5.1 and 5.2 illustrate these distinctions.

Table 5.1 FACTORS INFLUENCING PATHWAY SELECTION

Pathway type	Acceptance of financial risk	Acceptance of prevailing market system and logics	Relationship with mainstream institutions	Ability of leadership to organize and engage membership to contribute to organizational goals
External	Low	High	High	High
Autonomous	Medium	Medium	Low/Medium	Medium
Embedded	Medium/High	Low/Medium	Medium	Low/Medium

All three pathways involve some degree—albeit different—of acceptance of the dominant logics and modus operandi of markets and competition. Whichever pathway or pathway combination is pursued, some degree of commercialization and professionalization is unavoidable. As a result, the logics and modus operandi of the social innovation organizations are

Table 5.2 OUTCOME/IMPACT FACTORS OF IMPORTANCE

Pathway type	Achieving transformational change of existing social systems	Achieving both social and economic goals	Maintaining high levels of autonomy, identity, and integrity	Scaling/ growing the innovation
External	High	Uncertain (depends on mission compatibility)	Low	High
Autonomous	Uncertain (depends on replicability or scaling potential of the social enterprise)	High	High	Uncertain (depends on replicability)
Embedded	Uncertain (depends on degree of embedding, degree of change in the organizational culture, and replicability)	Medium	Uncertain (depends on mission compatibility and on the extent to which the embedded entity can be dis-embedded and remain functional)	Uncertain (depends on replicability)

inherently challenged and changed by the need to diversify from grant and philanthropic funding, which usually has conditions attaching to funds. Some dilution of their transformative (humanizing) ambitions is also likely (Weaver & Marks, 2017).

The external funding pathway, especially, may give scope for reforming service delivery but not necessarily along lines of the humanization ambitions and agendas initially espoused by the social innovators choosing to develop external funding relationships with service commissioners or their intermediaries. This is because accepting roles as service providers entails accepting performance standards, undertaking quality control and assurance, and meeting accountability requirements. These incur a loss of autonomy and some mission drift, especially from the transformative ambition for humanization.

Social enterprise is especially interesting as a funding pathway for social innovation organizations because it can enable an organization to maintain its identity and the integrity of its activities more readily than if finance is provided from external sources and by establishment agencies and actors that organize around mainstream market and bureaucratic logics and modus operandi. Nevertheless, social enterprise involves competing in markets with other providers, so necessarily entails embracing and engaging with the logic of the market even if social impact remains the predominant driver. Some level of bureaucracy, professionalization, and commercialization is also implied.

Last, as Table 5.2 indicates, the factors that influence the embedded pathway as well as the outcomes/impacts of selecting this as the dominant mode of sustainability are more challenging to predict. There are high risks attaching to the embedded pathway since this creates a high level of dependence of the social innovation organization on the larger (host) partner. The risk of having funding "pulled" can be high even if the host organization is financially secure since there is always scope for the management of the host organization to question the degree to which the relationship is central to its own core mission. The risk increases if the host organization itself comes into financial difficulties and must make cuts, which are often more easily imposed on partners. The risk can be reduced if the functional integrity of the social innovation operation can be maintained outside the embedded relationship. The embedded relationship may provide transformative opportunities to alter organizational practice within the larger organization and for this also to influence comparable organizations.

The likelihood is that, in the process of securing financial resources, the humanizing ambition of social innovation organizations will be moderated somewhat. Nevertheless, there is scope for new models of development to be forged in this process based on blended logics that offer economic opportunities, activities, products, and services that present a more human face. Equally, it is possible that through interaction with social innovation organizations, mainstream institutions, organizations, and actors will themselves experience change, especially toward collaborative and cooperative ways of working that cut across sectoral silos. Humanization as a movement is understood in this sense as a force that plays out within and across each of the three sectors: market, state, and civil society (Kemp et al., 2016). For example, in developing the Gloucester Motorway Services a new model of integrating marketplace and civil society actors was created and new forms of business organizations and business models emerged, with possible implications for scaling into new sites and communities.

A final point is that it is interesting to reflect on the different ways that the activities of the studied social innovation initiatives interact with the mainstream economy other than through resourcing relations. This is because there are complementary relationships between the mainstream economy and some social innovation initiatives, such that their operating together holds important implications for socioeconomic development. A growing social innovation sector is, in any event, an important counterforce to marketization. The emergence of complementary local economies using local currencies that can be used to flag and "back" demands relating to important local needs that lack "effective" demand in the mainstream (fiat money) economy makes unmet needs more transparent. These needs can then be met by nascent social enterprises and cooperatives able to address these through locally led economic development within the context of a complementary economy that makes productive use of local assets and resources that are surplus to the requirements of the mainstream economy. These assets and resources would, otherwise, go to waste.

From the case studies we see that time banks help their members to gain or maintain job readiness and employability when they are not currently in paid employment. In this sense, time banking serves the mainstream economy by maintaining the employability of citizens. But time banks also provide complementary economic and social opportunities in secondary economies. These opportunities will become increasingly important for the social and economic life of citizens as the number of jobs available in the mainstream economy reduces, as is expected, and more people find themselves surplus to market needs. The secondary economy is also part of a needed but underdeveloped "preventative infrastructure" that can deliver welfare services and, by enabling citizens to become more active, can support healthier lifestyles through offering citizens opportunities for social interactions and participation in activities they find meaningful and satisfying. This contributes to individual and community well-being while also avoiding preventable costs arising to government and its agencies. A secondary economy is increasingly important also for the social and economic inclusion of those who are administratively excluded from participation in the formal economy, which includes asylum seekers.

A secondary economy could enable society to develop new ways to organize how time is used, how shares of gross domestic product (GDP) are distributed, and how useful "work" is defined. It is likely that, in the future, new models of the life course will emerge. Instead of being committed to a working lifetime in the formal economy of 40 hours per week over 40 years, more people might move over their life course between the mainstream economy and secondary economies, spending periods in each depending on their needs for income and their needs for time to bring up children, care for frail friends and relatives, engage in personally satisfying pursuits, and contribute to civil society, community development, and environmental projects. Part-time arrangements could also increase, with more individuals undertaking several hours each week of formal and informal work.

The creation of a secondary economy would create extra "degrees of freedom" for public policy in relation to the mainstream economy by reducing societal dependence on it for jobs, output, and welfare delivery. It would also create opportunities to develop new ways for people to pay taxes "in kind" and to contribute "in kind" to their own and others' social security (Kemp, Weaver, Golland, Strasser, & Backhaus, 2017; Weaver, Kemp, et al., 2016). All of these offer scope to develop new forms and models of integrated social and economic development that can grow from secondary economy initiatives of social innovation, such as the Mutual Aid Network project in Hull.

IMPLICATIONS AND CONCLUSION

In the present context, time banks and other social innovations are actual and potential harbingers of integrated development with interest focusing especially on their business models and sustainability pathways and the relationship and interactions they develop with mainstream institutions. At one level of observation, interest lies in social innovation processes serving as incubators for social enterprises that offer approaches to socioeconomic development that are more integrated than the dominant economic models based, inter alia, on scarcity value, competition, and cost reduction. When observed at a higher level of abstraction, though, there is also a "bigger picture." Albeit on a small scale, our success cases concern initiatives that are helping to create secondary community economies that use local community currencies and operate as complements to the mainstream (fiat money) economy.

Our wider empirical work covering fail cases as well as success cases supports the notion (Moore, Westley, & Nicholls, 2012) that the financing needs of social innovations differ from usual financing needs and that usual ways of funding are less appropriate for social innovations. Social innovation organizations often require start-up funding over quite long periods to be able to test and refine ideas and develop business plans for developing them, so would benefit from scalable finance that provides secure but low levels of funding over longer start-up periods but can grow as the positive social impacts of the initiative grow. Their needs for finance also vary over different phases in the development of the social innovation. Social innovations seeking to scale require significant investment in building organizational, managerial, and technology capacities (see Marks et al., 2017).

Unfortunately, capital investment products in support of these changes are often not available (Moore et al., 2012). Social innovations are often not on the radar of traditional financial institutions who may not understand their mission and vision, may not clearly see the risk and rewards of these innovations, and may not be willing to fund innovation to support often forgotten individuals and communities (Weaver & Marks, 2017). Here, there is a funding and investment "gap" that needs to be bridged through the development of innovative and hybrid financial instruments.

Our success cases are unusual in that they have found ways to sustain and thrive in a difficult funding environment, but they have not (yet) gone to scale, either vertically or horizontally, albeit there is evidence of some limited growth within sectors (e.g., PIC, in aging) or geographies (e.g., Fair Shares, with its Gloucestershire network of time banks). Their relative success is based around a willingness to overcome silos among community sector organizations, to collaborate and cooperate in addressing needs, and to move away from only promoting a particular tool or to restricting actions to single issues, domains, or target groups. They also demonstrate relevance through willingness to respond flexibly to changing community needs and priorities. By being relevant, by becoming more effective and efficient, and by social entrepreneurship, our success cases have been able to diversify their funding sources, create recurrent income streams, and sustain their activities.

Silos constrain funding and the scaling of social innovation. The silos among voluntary and community sector (VCS) organizations, charities,

NGOs, and social innovation organizations are also not the only relevant silos here. They have their counterparts also in government departments, agencies, and statutory service providers which also tend to operate under separate and individual mandates and budgets in respect to defined issues, domains, and target groups. This has two damaging consequences. One has been a tendency for single government departments or agencies sometimes to seek to control and use a social innovation initiative instrumentally to help it deliver its mandate. This can threaten the integrity of the initiative and also be self-defeating because "capture" undermines support for the initiative at the grassroots level and thereby also its delivery capacity (Pel & Bauler, 2014). Another consequence is a lack of cross-departmental or cross-agency funding for cross-cutting social innovation initiatives whose activities contribute to delivery over multiple mandates, a situation that contributes to the funding and investment gap that needs to be bridged (Spinelli, Weaver, Marks, & Victor, 2019; Weaver, Kemp, & Hoffmeister, 2017).

Some of our cases have also accepted that sponsors and funders need verifiable evidence of activities, outcomes, and impacts. Collecting and analyzing data can be administratively burdensome for undercapacity social innovation organizations and can be counterproductive to ethos and mission, especially if the data collection is based on a deficit-based theory of change. Ways for relevant data to be collected simply, unobtrusively, and at low cost and without prejudice to asset-based approaches to community development are therefore needed. Some of our cases are using community currency software to collect data. The more advanced cases are also exploring digital community currency platforms and electronic wallets that allow for data on transactions to be collected automatically as currency passes from one electronic wallet to another. Such data can also form a valuable new community asset that can be used to develop social and economic intelligence and support smart contracting.

These insights and observations provide a basis for policy recommendations around the interlinked questions of finance, monitoring, and governance of promising social innovation initiatives and how the integrated socioeconomic development models to which they contribute might be further scaled (Svensson, Szijarto, Milley, & Cousins, 2018). Policy recommendations include the following:

- Developing new cross-departmental and cross-agency funding mechanisms—possibly using social impact methods and tools—so that government departments and agencies can pool funds and reduce risks in funding social innovation initiatives.

- Developing new forms of social impact investment and performance-based payment instruments where funds are used to help support and build the capacities of local-level intermediary organizations, whose role is to manage and coordinate contributions across multiple local social innovation and VCS organizations to meeting performance targets and achieving wanted outcomes.
- Providing social innovators and social entrepreneurs with entrées to private funders, venture capitalists, and social impact investors.
- Supporting more structured, coherent, and coordinated approaches to asset-based community development at the local level that engage individual and organizational stakeholders from all sectors, bringing their needs and assets into play and creating a critical mass and diversity of opportunities for collaboration and asset sharing in meeting local needs.
- Revising mandates of statutory service providers so these include not only meeting service demands but also taking actions to reduce service demands year-on-year, thus enabling some share of their budgets to be allocated to preventative actions in areas such as physical and mental health, including addressing socioeconomic determinants of poor health.
- Supporting development and use of digital local community currencies to stimulate, organize, and coordinate social innovation activities locally and to collect data on transactions that can be used to develop evidence of activities and impacts and to support contract specification and validation.

Research has an important role to play, especially by studying success factors and the relation of social innovation initiatives and their development to contextual factors. Matching societal needs to the social innovations and combinations of initiatives best able to help address them is also an important step in harnessing the potential of social innovation to contribute more fully to more integrated development. Important research needs are to

- Extend success case analysis to a wider set of social innovation cases with a view to better understanding the business models of successful initiatives.
- Understand better how social innovations and their business models shape each other and influence the potential of the initiatives to serve different needs of society.
- Understand how different social innovations can work together and with other organizations to serve different needs of society.

These case studies highlight the role that local complementary economies enabled by community currencies can play, making productive economic participation possible for those who are traditionally excluded from mainstream markets due to lack of regular currency or marketable skills. Complementary community economies enable critical needs that are not backed by effective demand to be signaled using community currency. They also enable these needs to be met by those whose work may not be demanded by the mainstream economy but whose skills and capacities are nevertheless relevant in a complementary economy in which participants can be recognized and rewarded through currency credits redeemable via a spending network for contributions that deliver social value or save economic costs, for example by reaching out upstream to nip problems in the bud before these manifest as demands on mainstream and statutory services. As a safeguard and safety net against the instabilities of the formal economic system, an important policy approach would be to embrace and support bottom-up initiatives that aim to create complementary local economies that operate outside the realm of the money economy (Weaver, 2014, 2017).

Worldwide, the number of complementary local community economy initiatives is growing rapidly, with a marked increase since the financial crisis of 2008 (Weaver & Spinelli, 2019). Many of the most recent initiatives are developing around the use of digital platforms, which holds out the promise of greater efficiencies in managing and attracting users following initial technology investment (Weaver & Spinelli, 2019). It is important, nevertheless, that community economies and currencies are governed locally so that they address local needs and challenges and maintain local control over local assets, including the data generated by the digital technology. National implementation strategies for community currencies risk contributing to local disempowerment and asset stripping rather than to asset-based community development (Spinelli et al., 2019). Complementary economies and currencies will be most effective if matched with local community identities as part of community-led, place-based schemes for building local resilience and creating local opportunities using (largely) local resources (Spinelli et al., 2019).

Unfortunately, policy-makers have historically taken hostile stances toward complementary economy and currency initiatives, which have often been seen by them as threats to mainstream economic and governance arrangements. The dominant policy paradigm is focused on growing only the mainstream economy (CMEPSP, 2009), the dominant systems and indicators for measuring progress are focused on GDP Stiglitz, Fitoussi

& Durand (2018), and the dominant policy approaches to economic and social inclusion seek to include and integrate people and places into the global capitalist economy (Weaver, Kemp, et al., 2016).

These imply a need for policy-makers and all societal stakeholders to reconceptualize the ways in which we think about how the well-being of citizens is secured and the roles and capacities of different sectors (state, business, civil society) and different kinds of activities and economies in securing well-being. It is important for policy-makers to recognize the potential value of local complementary economies and currencies to society as well as to the mainstream economy and mainstream services. Policy shifts and recommendations include

- Recognizing that multiple economies exist and that plurality is potentially positive, including for the mainstream economy.
- Legitimizing and sanctioning complementary currencies, economies, and key actors in their development.
- Shifting from the strong emphasis on economic growth and full employment only in the formal market economy to focusing growth efforts equally (or preferentially) on complementary economies.
- Supporting experiments with complementary economies and related infrastructural elements, including especially digital community currencies, exchange platforms, local intermediary organizations, and governance arrangement, and being open to changing dominant policy positions based on lessons learned.
- Revising regulatory frameworks and policies, especially fiscal, welfare system, and asylum seeker rules so these open opportunities for greater and freer citizen participation in complementary economies and for people to be recognized and rewarded for contributions they make without fear or risk of suffering penalties or losing benefits.
- Revising procurement rules so that organizations operating within complementary economies, including intermediary organizations and social enterprises, and their activities are eligible to be commissioned or to receive contracts issued by government, its agencies, statutory services, and service commissioners.
- Supporting new models for using time across the life course through more flexible working arrangements, which is needed to provide greater flexibility for people to move between making contributions in the formal (mainstream) and informal (complementary) economies, to balance different kinds of contributions to economic and social well-being at different phases of their lives, and to create opportunities for people

to remain active, healthy, and productive across the life course in the context of longevity societies.

It is recommended that experiments with complementary community economies and currency are conducted within a "living laboratory" framework, which serves as a methodology for experiments and data collection as well as a social foundry for the development of innovative products, services, and business models. Recommendations for research include

- Research funding organizations prioritizing research, technological development, and innovation (RTDI) investments in the establishment of living laboratory experiments involving the development of complementary economies.
- Research funding organizations focusing funds on developing enabling digital currency technology and platforms and making these freely available to local initiatives.
- Researchers studying the related aspects of digital currency platform architecture and the design of local complementary currency and economy governance arrangements.
- Research on digital currency data as a basis for developing social and economic intelligence and providing income streams to sustain new, integrated, socioeconomic development models.

REFERENCES

Brinkerhoff, R. (2003). *The success case method: Find out quickly what's working and what's not.* San Francisco: Berret-Koehler.

Cahn, E. S. (2004). *No more throw-away people: The co-production imperative.* Washington, DC: Essential Books.

Cahn, E. S., & Rowe, J. (1992). *Time dollars: The new currency that enables Americans to turn their hidden resource—time—into personal security & community renewal.* Emmaus, PA: Rodale.

CMEPSP (2009). *Report of the Commission on the Measurement of Economic Performance and Social Progress.* Retrieved from https://www.researchgate.net/publication/258260767_Report_of_the_Commission_on_the_Measurement_of_Economic_Performance_and_Social_Progress_CMEPSP

Drakeford, M., & Gregory, L (2010). Transforming time: A tool for youth justice. *Youth Justice, 10*(2), 143–156. Retrieved from https://doi.org/10.1177/1473225410369293

Goodwin, N. (2018). There is more than one economy. *Real-World Economics Review, 84*, 16–35. Retrieved from http://www.paecon.net/PAEReview/issue84/Goodwin84.pdf

Haxeltine, A., Avelino, F., Pel, B., Kemp, R., Dumitru, A., Longhurst, N., . . . Strasser, T. (2016). *A second prototype of TSI theory*. TRANSIT Project Deliverable D3.3 Retrieved from http://www.transitsocialinnovation.eu/resource-hub/transit-wp3-deliverable-d33-a-second-prototype-of-tsi-theory-deliverable-no-d33

Haxeltine A., Jørgensen, M. S., Pel, B., Dumitru, A., Avelino, F., Bauler, T., . . . Wittmayer J. M. (2016). *On the agency and dynamics of transformative social innovation*. TRANSIT working paper 7. Retrieved from http://www.transitsocialinnovation. eu/resource-hub/on-the-agency-and-dynamics-of-transformative-social-innovation-transit-working-paper-7

Haxeltine, A., Kemp, R., Cozan, S., Ruijsink, S., Backhaus, J., Avelino, F., & Dumitru, A. (2017). *How social innovation leads to transformative change: Towards a theory of transformative social innovation*. TRANSIT Project Brief 3. Retrieved from http://www.transitsocialinnovation.eu/resource-hub/transit-brief-3-how-social-innovation-leads-to-stransformative-change-towards-a-theory-of-transformative-social-innovation

Kemp, R., Strasser, T., Davidson, D., Avelino, F., Pel, B., Dumitru, A., . . . Weaver, P. M. (2016). *The humanization of the economy through social innovation*. Paper presented at SPRU 50th anniversary conference and the IST2016 conference. Brighton, UK. Retrieved from https://www.researchgate.net/publication/ 309619499['

Kemp, R., Weaver, P. M., Golland, A., Strasser, T., & Backhaus, J. (2017). Socio-economic transformations: Insights for sustainability transitions. In *Perspectives on transitions to sustainability* (Report 25, EEA) (pp. 70–94). Copenhagen, Denmark: European Environment Agency. doi: 10.2800/332443. Retrieved from https://www.eea.eu-ropa.eu/publications/perspectives-on-transitions-to-sustainability

Lebra, T. S. (1980). Autonomy through interdependence: The housewives labor bank. *The Japan Interpreter, 13*(1), 133–142.

Lietaer, B. (2004). Complementary currencies in Japan today: History, originality and relevance. *International Journal of Community Currency Research, 8*, 1–23. Retrieved from http://www.lietaer.com/images/JapanCC_2003.pdf

Longhurst, N., Avelino, F., Wittmayer, J. M., Weaver, P. M., Dumitru, A., Hielscher, S., . . . Elle, M. (2017). Experimenting with alternative economies: Four emergent counter-narratives of urban economic development. *Current Opinion in Environmental Sustainability, 22*, 1–6. Retrieved from http://dx.doi.org/ 10.1016/j.cosust.2017.04.006

Loorbach, D., Avelino, F., Haxeltine, A., Wittmayer, J. M., O'Riordan, T., Weaver, P. M., & Kemp, R. (2016). The economic crisis as a game changer? Exploring the role of social construction in sustainability transitions. *Ecology and Society, 21*(4), 1–9. doi: http://dx.doi.org/10.5751/ES-08761-210415

Marks, M. B. (2009). *A theoretical and empirical investigation of co-production interventions for involuntary youth in the child welfare and juvenile justice systems*. Doctoral Dissertation. Retrieved from Dissertation Abstracts International. (UMI No. 3345766).

Marks, M. B. (2012). Time banking service exchange systems: A review of the research and policy and practice implications in support of youth in transition. *Children and Youth Services Review, 34*(7), 1230–1236. doi: 10.1016/ j.childyouth.2012.02.017

Marks, M. B., Hogan, L. M., & Weaver, P. M. (2017). *Success case examples of sustainable social innovation resourcing strategies in the United States*. TRANSIT Working Paper 12. Retrieved from http://www.transitsocialinnovation.eu/content/original/

Book%20covers/Local%20PDFs/265%20TRANSIT_WorkingPaper%2012_Resourcing%20Straegies%20US.pdf

Marks, M. B., & Weaver, P. M. (2017). *Are social impact bonds a viable resource for social innovations?* TRANSIT Working Paper 13. Retrieved from http://www.transitsocialinnovation.eu/resource-hub/are-social-impact-bonds-a-viable-resource-for-social-innovations-a-brief-discussion-paper-transit-working-paper-13-july-2017

Miller, E. J. (2008). *Both borrowers and lenders: Time banks and the aged in Japan* (doctoral thesis). Australian State University. Retrieved from http://www.hourworld.org/pdf/Study_Time_Banks_of_Japan.pdf

Moore, M.-L., Westley, F. R., & Nicholls, A. (2012). The social finance and social innovation nexus. *Journal of Social Entrepreneurship, 3*(2), 115–132. https://doi.org/10.1080/19420676.2012.725824Innovation

Murphy, N. F. (2016). Nine guiding principles to help youth overcome homelessness: A principles-focused developmental evaluation. In M. Queen-Patton, K. McKegg, & N. Wehipeihana (Eds.), *Developmental evaluation exemplars* (pp. 63–83). New York: Guilford.

Pel, B., & Bauler, T. (2014). *The institutionalization of social innovation: Between transformation and capture*. TRANSIT Project Working Paper 2. Retrieved from http://www.transitsocialinnovation.eu/content/original/Book%20covers/Local%20PDFs/179%20TRANSIT_WorkingPaper2_Governance_Pel141015.pdf

Pel, B., Weaver, P. M., Cipolla, C., Afonso, R., Jørgensen, M. S., Elle, M., . . . Bauler, T. (2016, September). *Institutionalization dialectics in transformative social innovation: A comparative case study*. Paper presented at the 7th International Sustainability Transitions Conference, Wuppertal, Germany.

Pel, B., Weaver, P. M., Strasser, T., Kemp, R., Avelino, F., & Becerra, L. (2015). *Governance: Co-production challenges in transformative social innovation*. TRANSIT Brief 2. Retrieved from http://www.transitsocialinnovation.eu/content/original/Book%20covers/Local%20PDFs/183%20TRANSIT%20brief%20no%202%20governance.pdf

Polanyi, K. (1944). *Origins of our time: The great transformation*. New York: Farrar & Rinehart.

Skropke, C. (2016). *Timebanking to meet integration challenges of asylum seekers, refugees and migrants in the context of urban poverty in the UK: A case study* (master's thesis). Maastricht University, Netherlands.

Skropke, C., & Weaver, P. M. (2017, September). *LifeShare: An innovation partnership supporting migrant assimilation in Kingston-upon-Hull*. Paper presented at the International Sustainability Transitions Conference, Gothenburg, Sweden.

Spinelli, G., Weaver, P. M., Marks, M., & Victor, C. (2019). Making a case for creating living labs for aging-in-place: Enabling socially innovative models for experimentation and complementary economies. *Frontiers in Sociology, 4*, Article 19. Retrieved from https://www.frontiersin.org/article/10.3389/fsoc.2019.00019 DOI=10.3389/fsoc.2019.00019

Stiglitz, J., Fitoussi, J., & Durand, M. (2018). *Beyond GDP: Measuring what counts for economic and social performance*. Paris: Organization for Economic and Cooperative Development. https://doi.org/10.1787/9789264307292-en

Svensson, K., Szijarto, B., Milley, P., & Cousins, J. B. (2018). Evaluating social innovations: Implications for evaluation design. *American Journal of Evaluation, 39*(4), 459–782. Retrieved from https://doi.org/10.1177%2F1098214018763553

Vora, G. (2015). Cryptocurrencies: Are disruptive financial innovations here? *Modern Economy, 6*, 816–832. http://dx.doi.org/10.4236/me.2015.67077

Weaver, P. M. (2014, May). *The informal, alternative and 'zero marginal-cost' economies.* GLOBIS Project Policy Brief No 3. LUCSUS, University of Lund.

Weaver, P. M. (2016). Sustainable development strategies: What roles for informal economy initiatives in the Post-2015 SDGs? In R. Cörvers, J. de Kraker, R. Kemp, P. Martens, & H. van Lente (Eds.), *Sustainable Development Research at ICIS: Taking Stock and Looking Ahead* (pp. 133–144). Maastricht, Netherlands: ICIS, Maastricht University.

Weaver, P. M. (2017). *TRANSIT Project Critical Turning Points Database: FairShares, UK.* Retrieved from http://www.transitsocialinnovation.eu/sii/timebanks-1 and *Volunteer Labour Network, Japan.* Retrieved from http://www.transitsocialinnovation.eu/sii/timebanks-3

Weaver, P. M., Dumitru, A., García-Mira, R., Lema-Blanco, A., Muijsers, L., & Vasseur, V. (2016). *TRANSIT Case Study Report: Timebanking.* Retrieved from http://www.transitsocialinnovation.eu/content/original/Book%20covers/Local%20PDFs/253%20Time%20Banks%20-%20Case%20study%20report%20Time%20Banks-2017.pdf

Weaver, P. M., Dumitru, A., Lema-Blanco, I., & Garcia-Mira, R. (2015). *Transformative social innovation narrative: Timebanking.* TRANSIT Project Case Study. Retrieved from http://www.transitsocialinnovation.eu/content/original/Book%20covers/Local%20PDFs/154a1%20TSI%20Narrative_Timebanking_Upload.pdf

Weaver, P. M., Kemp, R., & Hoffmeister, L. (2017). *A review of evaluation methodologies for social innovations.* TRANSIT Project Working Paper 14. Retrieved from http://www.transitsocialinnovation.eu/resource-hub/a-review-of-evaluation-methods-relevant-for-social-innovation-with-suggestions-for-their-use-and-development-transit-working-paper-14-july-2017

Weaver, P. M., Kemp, R., Strasser, T., Backhaus, J., & Pel, B. (2016). *Transformative change for an inclusive society: Insights from social innovations and implications for policy innovation and innovation policy.* TRANSIT Project Working Paper 8. Presented at SPRU50, Brighton, UK. Retrieved from http://www.transitsocialinnovation.eu/resource-hub/transformative-change-for-an-inclusive-society-insights-from-social-innovations-and-implications-for-policy-innovation-and-innovation-policy-transit-working-paper-8

Weaver, P. M., & Marks, M. B. (2017). *Social innovation resourcing strategies and transformation pathways: A first-cut typology.* TRANSIT Working Paper 11. Retrieved from http://www.transitsocialinnovation.eu/resource-hub/social-innovation-resourcing-strategies-and-transformation-pathways-a-first-cut-typology-transit-working-paper-11-july-2017

Weaver, P. M., & Rotmans, J. (2006). Integrated sustainability assessment: What is it, why do it and how? *International Journal of Innovation and Sustainable Development, 1*(4), 284–303. doi: 10.1504/IJISD.2006.013732

Weaver, P. M., & Spinelli, G. (2019, September) *Experimenting with a structured approach to building complementary economies for community resilience and positive social impact using digital social currencies and social valuation of transactions.* Paper presented at the 5th Biennial RAMICS International Congress, Hida-Takayama, Japan.

Wittmayer, J., Backhaus, J., Avelino, F., Pel, B., Strasser, T., & Kunze, I. (2015). *Narratives of change: How social innovation initiatives engage with their transformative ambitions.* TRANSIT working paper 4. Retrieved from http://www.transitsocialinnovation.eu/resource-hub/narratives-of-change-how-social-innovation-initiatives-engage-with-their-transformative-ambitions

Wright, L. (1997). *Member organized resource exchange: A guide to replication.* Annie E. Casey Foundation, Columbia, SC.

CHAPTER 6

☙

UAlbany's Small Enterprise Economic Development (SEED) Program as an Exemplar

WONHYUNG LEE, WILLIAM BRIGHAM,
STEPHANIE H. WACHOLDER, KATHERINE BAKER,
AND BRUCE R. STANLEY

INTRODUCTION

Microlending is the provision of very small loans (microloans) to the unemployed, to poor entrepreneurs, and to others living in poverty who are not considered bankable. These individuals lack collateral, steady employment, and a verifiable credit history and therefore cannot meet even the most minimal qualifications to gain access to traditional credit. While microlending has been more widely practiced in developing countries, it is no longer new in the United States. The Aspen Institute (2014) recently reported that 418 microlenders disbursed 58,060 microloans in the United States, with the total value of $361.7 million. Global microfinance institutions such as Grameen America or Accion International are also actively serving low-income immigrant populations in major cities (Shulman, 2008).

Nonetheless, many Americans are unaware of microloans and are still unbankable. The Federal Deposit Insurance Corporation (2014) indicate that, in 2013, 7.7% of the households (nearly 9.6 million households) in the United States are *unbanked*, meaning that they do not have any kind

Wonhyung Lee, William Brigham, Stephanie H. Wacholder, Katherine Baker, and Bruce R. Stanley, *UAlbany's Small Enterprise Economic Development (SEED) Program as an Exemplar* In: *Social Entrepreneurship and Enterprises in Economic and Social Development*. Edited by: Katharine Briar-Lawson, Paul Miesing, and Blanca M. Ramos, Oxford University Press (2021). © Oxford University Press. DOI: 10.1093/oso/9780197518298.003.0007.

of deposit account at an insured depository institution. In addition, 20% (about 24.8 million) were *underbanked*, meaning that they hold a bank account but also rely on alternative financial services such as non-bank check cashing, payday loans, or pawn shops. The lack of financial assets and services is a particular problem for unemployed and low-income people because, without these resources, they have to rely on the fringe economy that charges an exorbitant rate of interest or fees (Karger, 2015). Even if they have a business idea, a lack of collateral and a verifiable credit history would not qualify them to gain access to traditional credit. The coverage shortfall is also exasperated by restrictive lending practices, such as minimum credit scores, length of time in business, gender, and small-loan principles.

While there exist a number of microlending and microenterprise development programs that aim to serve low-income populations, only a few programs practice "character-based" lending, which focuses on the character of potential clients relative to other rather traditional components (the so-called 4Cs of collateral, capital, credit, and capacity to pay back the loan). In this chapter, we discuss a program called Small Enterprise Economic Development (SEED) as an exemplar that has provided services related to both financing and technical assistance to unserved and underserved populations. Throughout this chapter, we discuss the SEED story, from the process of creating such an innovative and unique program to the current model and status, including some lessons for those who hope to replicate its model.

WHAT IS SEED?

SEED is a public–private, interdisciplinary microlending program that was established to address the specific needs of underserved entrepreneurs. The program was initiated based on the partnerships among the School of Social Welfare and the School of Business at the University at Albany (UAlbany), State University of New York; the New York State Small Business Development Center (SBDC); a regional credit union called State Employees Federated Credit Union (SEFCU); and Empire State Development. In this section we describe the motivation for the program, its development history, and its administrative characteristics.

Motivation

Small business is "big business" for the entire country. In the United States, there are between 25 million and 27 million small businesses[1] (many of these operating as microcompanies or run by solo-preneurs) that account for 60–80% of all US jobs (Sugars, 2012). In the state of New York, 65% of all business enterprises have four employees or fewer (US Census Bureau, 2015). Microenterprises[2] play an important role in local economic development as these independent businesses tend to purchase more local goods and services and hire more local people (de Renzy, 2014). The development of microenterprises is particularly critical for assisting people in poverty and further revitalizing distressed communities (Sanders, 2002).

There were a number of programs that had fostered economic growth and small business development, but what was missing was a loan fund that supported low-income people who had business ideas. A multiple-case study of US Housing and Urban Development (HUD) microenterprise development assistance programs in upstate New York found that state and local governments are generally not able to pursue a microenterprise strategy on their own, not only due to financial and staffing constraints, but also due to a potentially high failure rate and limited tax benefits in return (Bates, 2005). The same study also revealed that, for this reason, many microenterprise development programs are administered by nonprofit organizations in the United States. Even among the nonprofit programs or microlenders that provide loans to disadvantaged populations, however, the majority of them are located in New York City, according to the SBA (Small Business Administration, 2016). Only two organizations—one community development financial institution and the other a Chamber of Commerce—were providing funding to start-up and existing microsize businesses locally in the Capital Region of New York, but they are restricted from solely using character-based methodology for loans.

While developing the initial SEED proposal in July 2008, a third of the Capital Region (Albany, Schenectady, and Troy) residents survived on less than $20,650 a year, the federal poverty level for a family of four, according to census estimates. People with low income and low assets had the most difficulty in starting a self-sufficient business or expanding an existing business due to the restrictive eligibility criteria of loan funds. Low levels of income and lack of sufficient equity, combined with a prevalence of poor credit history, made any loan applications from these areas certain for denial from commercial lending institutions. In addition to not meeting the aforementioned criteria, low-income individuals are unable to meet other qualifying prerequisites, such as length of established business operations, appropriate industry profile, and referrals. This vicious cycle continues to plague poorer communities.

Development History

The initial idea of the SEED program emerged in the hope of improving local economies in the Capital Region and surrounding counties by fostering small business and microenterprise development within distressed communities. Standard funding criteria place lower income individuals at an overwhelming disadvantage. Current lending policy requires personal capital, high credit scores, and collateral unavailable to most low-income individuals. The barriers to accessing capital can be insurmountable. Successful existing microloan funds demonstrate that revolving loan funds are highly successful, especially with microenterprises, since the repayment rate is high, which in turn fosters incremental leveraging leading to successful implementation of business plans.

The necessary resources for a microenterprise in an underserved community are not limited to financial means. A structured program of technical assistance, training, mentorship, and social support is crucial to cultivating a microenterprise that is well equipped to run a business with access to capital. With appropriate assistance, community resource support, and, most significantly, a dedicated loan fund utilizing nontraditional criteria, these ventures have a much higher chance of survival and ultimate success. Along with this advancement comes the gradual economic and social improvement of the lower income communities that are participating in the program.

The SEED program was designed to recruit potential entrepreneurs from within targeted low-income populations, introduce them to business success factors through various training and mentoring programs, and inspire/reinforce the entrepreneurial spirit in the entrepreneur through ongoing assistance and supports from the program. In doing so, SEED provided a ladder to success for entrepreneurs in such distressed communities.

The key methodology for providing microloans is based on character-based lending. The strategy focuses on developing homegrown entrepreneurs and enterprises, which provides the community with a stronger economic base and more stable families and social supports, thereby lessening the flow of income out of the community as well as the flow of public monies into the community. Through microlending initiatives, low-income borrowers obtain financing that enables them to start up their businesses, gain experience, and establish a demonstrable track record. For successful microloan businesses, this translates into larger loans from conventional lenders in the future.

The loan fund for the program was established by SEFCU. To start the microlending program, SEFCU provided $2.5 million to set up a revolving loan fund that provided microloans to participating businesses. Since 2012, SEED has received financial support from Empire State Development, private donors and foundations, and UAlbany, along with in-kind services contributions from SEFCU, UAlbany's School of Social Welfare, School of Business, and SBDC for the infrastructure for the proposal, technical assistance, and capacity building for workers as they move from joblessness to entrepreneurial roles and an evaluation of the program.

Administrative Characteristics

The team. SEED is a cross-disciplinary program that involves multiple institutions and organizations. SEFCU provides funding and administers the revolving microenterprise loan fund. The UAlbany School of Business provides business mentoring for the targeted entrepreneurs. The UAlbany School of Social Welfare leads the social development and capacity-building components of this initiative. The UAlbany SBDC provides technical assistance that targets microentrepreneurs and coordinates training and mentorship components of the program. Empire State Development supported the program with infrastructure funding over a 3-year period. The collaboration draws on the talent and expertise of a major research university. The ability of university faculty, staff, and students to recruit, educate, and interact with potential entrepreneurs significantly increases the likelihood of program success and is the foundation of experiential education.

Participant selection process. The SEED program utilizes an assessment method that focuses on character rather than cash, credit, and collateral for low-income persons. The suitability of the potential participant is based on but not limited to the following criteria: personal integrity, entrepreneurial drive, the socioeconomic environment of the entrepreneur, a business model demonstrating the ability to generate revenues and profits, budgets and financial pro-formas, and a commitment to transparency and accountability on all levels.

Once the completed application package is received, each applicant is given a standardized in-person interview. All applicants for the program are asked the same exact questions in the same order. Notes are taken during the interview, and all interviews are scored based on the applicant's ability to answer the question asked, contents of the answer, and overall body language. The process is finalized with the completion of an Applicant Summary Report that provides the applicant scores on the entrepreneurial assessment and interview, interviewer's notes on character-related issues on the credit report (e.g., child support, repetitive behaviors), and an overview of information provided in the application related to the business venture and funding. A committee of SBDC Advisors meets 2 weeks prior to the start of the training session for a review of the applications and a selection of applicants for participation in the program. Following the selection committee meeting, applicants are notified of the acceptance/declination status of the program. Declined applicants are offered ongoing assistance from the SBDC for the development of their business plans and financial projections to access capital from alternative sources.

Training. To secure funding, SEED participants are required to complete an 8-week training course that includes (1) business fundamentals and business plan development and (2) social support. The business component of the training focuses on various aspects of preparing for and operating a business. The SEED Program Coordinator, SBDC business advisors, and business professionals and entrepreneurs teach the classes. The SBDC staff convenes a committee to select program applicants and provides training and business counseling services, including business plan development, financial analysis, and other management and operational issues. The training includes key components of becoming a small business owner including business planning, basic business etiquette, legal issues, marketing, budgets and financial management, accounting basics and software, taxes, management styles, and customer service.

The School of Social Welfare develops the social aspect of the training through a Peer Support Network, which is individual- and group-level social support for SEED participants. Students in the Master's in Social Welfare (MSW) program conduct participant needs assessment and lead weekly group meetings after each business training class. These meetings provide an opportunity to build stronger ties among the participants and for them to discuss their stresses, goals, fears, hopes, and issues. Prior to each class, MSW students offer both scheduled individual meetings and open office time with SEED participants to discuss individual issues in a private setting. Some of the specific assistance that social work students provide for the SEED program includes facilitating priority setting and values clarification exercises; helping SEED clients improve communication skills for the training requirements (e.g., homework, elevator speech, final presentation to SEFCU); assisting SEED clients in obtaining needed resources (e.g., child care, transportation, health insurance, housing for a client with physical disabilities, time management methods, and mindfulness and relaxation practices) and solving business-related issues by contacting community partners (e.g., business improvement districts); coordinating periodic newsletters and meetings that provide an education session based on client interests; and recruiting potential participants at various sites, including the United Way, Earned Income Tax sites, Family Support Agencies, and other community contacts such as business schools.

The Peer Support Network also involves periodic meetings for all current SEED clients and all of those SEED clients who have received a loan. These meetings include an educational component based on expressed client interests such as the mentoring program, budgeting, health insurance for small businesses, web site development, Occupational Safety and Health Administration (OSHA) compliance, and the Minority- and Women-Owned Business Enterprise Program. There is also a sharing component involving peer support through the sharing and discussion of issues important to them such as hiring good employees, stress reduction, and service networking.

In addition to formal training, SEED offers no-cost, one-to-one counseling and technical assistance in developing strategic business plans, identifying appropriate sources of funding, and providing market research and financial analysis, technical assistance, mentorship, and access to informational resources. All program participants are assigned a SBDC Business Advisor to guide them through the business planning process. The Business Advisor facilitates the development of the business plan and works with the entrepreneurs to create financial statements and assemble historical documentation.

How the loan works. While the SBDC is responsible for outreach, selection, training, application development, loan support, and all other aspects of technical assistance to be rendered to the entrepreneur, the loan fund remains the property of SEFCU and is administered in accord with program guidelines. SEFCU reviews potential borrowers' requests for loan funding, accepts or declines the loan request pursuant to underwriting criteria defined later in this chapter, originates the loan, administers loan closings pursuant to lending-recommended terms and conditions, services active loans, and reports to the program on all activities. Before a loan is issued, an existing business or prospective business completes an entrepreneurial assessment, references, and credit documentation, which is reviewed by a group of SBDC staff members in consultation with SEFCU.

The revolving loan fund serves as a financing mechanism for the development and expansion of small businesses. It is a self-replenishing pool of money, utilizing interest and principal payments on old loans to issue new ones. Loans are issued at an annual interest rate of 7%. Durations of terms usually do not vary, but may according to the use of funds. A loan used for working capital, for instance, may range from 3 to 7 years, while loans for equipment are set at the maximum 7 years. Total loan amounts range from small to mid-sized ($5,000 to $35,000). Payments are required to be made monthly.

ACHIEVEMENTS

Since the first SEED class was held in the summer of 2011, SEED has hosted 24 classes as of fall 2019. Out of 186 participants, SEFCU has provided $2,371,240 in loans to 85 participants who have created or saved 213 jobs in the Capital Region. Funded entrepreneurs represent diverse populations, including many minority- and women-owned businesses. The kinds of businesses that have been funded under the SEED program include but are not limited to beauty salons (e.g., specializing in hair care services for women of color), information technology companies, web portal advocacy services for persons with disabilities to connect and identify potential mentor arrangements, a chemical materials distribution company, a yoga studio (e.g., specializing in physical therapy for veterans), an urban youth basketball camp, environmental insulation, and composting.

Evaluation data collected by the School of Social Welfare demonstrated the effectiveness of and satisfaction with the SEED training and the Peer Support Network. All participants rated the SEED training as essential or helpful, with 91% rating it essential. The Peer Support Network met, exceeded, or greatly exceeded the expectations of 98% of the participants. The program has received positive qualitative feedback from the SEED participants as follows:

> The SEED program has been a game changer for me. I have struggled to put together a business plan in the past, but the SEED advisors helped me step by step, even with the difficult task of financial projections. With SEFCU's funding from the SEED program, I will be able to take my start-up business to the next level. Before long I will be exporting "New York-Made Larry's Southwestern Sauces" to Texas and California!

> Thanks to the SEED program, I am now in the space of my dreams and am ready to launch a Vintage & Antiques business that I have cultivated for the past 15 years. SEED classes were well worth it despite the Sunday dates as they prepared me more fully regarding how to actually run a small business and what to expect. SEFCU, SBDC, UAlbany Schools of Business and Social Welfare should be commended for being friendly, accommodating and helpful at every step. This program has given me the chance of a lifetime. Thanks again for everything!

> My experience with SEED program was a great one, the program allowed me to gain business knowledge that I was not aware of. The program inspired me to be even more on fire, overall I feel truly blessed that I was able to come in contact with the people who are involved in the SEED program. The SEED program has given me the opportunity to grow, improve, and run a business like I have always dreamed of.

SEED received the 2012 Tribeca Disruptive Innovation Award. SEED was also a finalist for the University Economic Development Association's 2012 Awards of excellence.

THE FUTURE

The SEED program is hosting its twenty-fifth business training as of winter 2019. As the program continues to move forward, the SBDC staff and affiliated faculty are planning to accomplish several goals in the following areas.

Conducting Comprehensive Program Evaluation

The SEED program has been assessing the training and support as well as the business performance and loan repayment trajectory of the program participants to consistently make the program better. The SBDC staff and affiliated faculty periodically discuss ideas to improve the program evaluation so that it can be used to assess the effectiveness of the program on multiple levels. For example, the individual-level evaluation can focus more comprehensively on how the SEED program has impacted SEED participants' entrepreneurial pursuit and trajectory, while the neighborhood-level evaluation can measure the impact of the SEED program on neighborhood- and community-level change. One of the benefits of conducting a comprehensive evaluation is to maintain long-term relationships with training participants. As the program matures, older participants may stay out of touch unless they voluntarily seek consultation with the SEED program again. A follow-up, possibly periodical, survey with SEED participants beyond the training period could benefit the relationships among the graduates, SBDC staff, and the Peer Support Network, as well as benefit from internal networks among the business owners.

Moreover, the new evaluation can examine the meaning of "character" in more depth. Although the program has implemented multiple stages that assess the character of program applicants, a systematic, replicable way of defining and assessing character has not yet taken place. Through expanded evaluation, SEED staff and affiliated faculty hope to develop tools that can measure character, which then can be incorporated into the selection process. In this way, SEED will be able to strengthen its operational model and communicate its selection standards more efficiently with potential clients and collaborators.

Expanding Collaborations

As a unique partnership program among local municipalities, non-profit organizations, and universities, collaboration is a key to the success of the SEED program. The SEED staff continues to foster collaborative partnerships with local organizations such as the United Way, local Chambers of Commerce, social service agencies, the Community Loan Fund, regional banks, and local municipalities for outreach, capacity building, and microlending. Further engagement with the local Chamber of Commerce, community and faith-based organizations, and regional and community lenders can provide referrals and infrastructure support for the program. Other organizations can help identify potential borrowers, including continuing education and vocational programs and such social service agencies and organizations as the United Way and the NYS Office for the Prevention of Domestic Violence.

Additionally, the expanded collaboration can further diversify the composition of business mentors (e.g., engineers, attorneys, lenders) who can assist in developing the skills necessary to successfully run small businesses. According to participant feedback, SEED graduates are very interested in having business mentors. Thus, further recruitment of qualified mentors and seeking other sources of knowledgeable individuals could provide program participants with expertise and support.

Bringing Experiences to the Classroom

Last, the efforts to bridge the SEED program and higher education will continue to take place. The SEED program staff and affiliated faculty members have tried their best to take full advantage of the partnership between the university and local community. For example, the UAlbany School of Business has offered opportunities to Business School students to serve the SEED program by training as business mentors. The UAlbany School of Social Welfare has not only provided the Peer Support Network, but also developed comprehensive evaluation plans. In the future, new courses could be created based on program evaluation and other empirical evidence. In addition, the SEED program offers research opportunities to the classroom and the broader academic community regarding topics such as social entrepreneurship, character-based microlending, and business development in distressed communities.

In sum, the SEED program has a great potential to be considered for scaling-up to other distressed regions. This interdisciplinary initiative provides a conceptual model that serves the disadvantaged populations and a best practice that can be applied to other regions and communities in the state.

SUMMARY POINTS

- Character-based lending creates economic opportunities to those who do not have access to credit based on traditional criteria, such as availability of collateral or a good credit score.
- The SEED program exemplifies a character-based lending model that can help clients build both business-related skills and social capacity to become successful entrepreneurs.
- Character-based lending, however, still remains in an experimental stage while there is lack of clear understanding of what "character" means. A comprehensive evaluation of various character-based approaches will be needed to integrate such an approach into regular financial practices more widely.

NOTES

1. The Small Business Administration (SBA) defines firms with fewer than 500 employees as "small." Two widely used size standards by the SBA include 500 employees for most manufacturing and mining industries and $7.5 million annual receipts for many nonmanufacturing industries. However, there are a number of exceptions. More detailed definitions are available on the SBA webpage concerning the Summary of Size Standards by Industry Sector (SBA, 2016).
2. HUD defines "microenterprise" as a commercial enterprise that has five or fewer employees.

REFERENCES

Aspen Institute. (2014). *U.S. microenterprise census highlights, FY2013.* microTracker.org. Retrieved from http://microtracker.org/assets/pdf/CensusHighlights2013.pdf

Bates, J. O. (2005). Microentrepreneurship and job creation: A multiple-case study of HUD microenterprise development assistance programs in upstate New York. *Journal of Microfinance, 7*(2), 127–147.

de Renzy, E. (2014). *Investing locally: The economic impact of microenterprise on the community.* Retrieved from https://cameonetwork.org/wp-content/uploads/2014/07/WISE-Local_Economic_Paper_FINAL.pdf

Federal Deposit Insurance Corporation. (2014). *2013 FDIC National Survey of Unbanked and Underbanked Households.* Retrieved from https://www.fdic.gov/householdsurvey/2013/2013report.pdf

Karger, H. (2015). Curbing the financial exploitation of the poor: Financial literacy and social work education. *Journal of Social Work Education, 51*(3): 425–438. doi:10.1080/10437797.2015.1043194.

Sanders, C. K. (2002). The impact of microenterprise assistance programs: A comparative study of program participants, nonparticipants, and other low-wage workers. *Social Service Review, 76*(2), 321–340. doi:10.1086/339664

Shulman, R. (2008, March 10). Small loans, significant impact. *Washington Post.* Retrieved from http://www.washingtonpost.com/wp-dyn/content/article/2008/03/09/AR2008030901617.html?hpid%3Dtopnews&sub=AR November 1, 2019

Small Business Administration. (2016). Summary of size standards by industry sector. Retrieved from https://www.sba.gov/contracting/getting-started-contractor/make-sure-you-meet-sba-size-standards/summary-size-standards-industry-sector

Sugars, B. (2012). How many jobs can your startup create this year? *Entrepreneur.* Retrieved from http://www.nbcnews.com/id/45996365/ns/business-small_business/t/how-many-jobs-can-your-startup-create-year/.V441n_krKHs

US Census Bureau. (2015). Statistics of US businesses. Retrieved from https://www.census.gov/data/tables/2015/econ/susb/2015-susb-annual.html

CHAPTER 7

֎

Failing My Way to Success

STEVE LOBEL*

NOTES ON ENTREPRENEURSHIP, SELF-KNOWLEDGE, AND REPAIRING THE WORLD

While the other chapters in this volume present the findings of scholars and researchers, this essay presents a very personal account of social entrepreneurship, a report from the trenches. In 2015, I published my memoir *Failing My Way to Success: Life Lessons of an Entrepreneur*. The book is a chronicle of my development as a businessman, tracing the arc of my career from my earliest memories of my entrepreneur father through a six-decade odyssey of misadventure and risk, defeats and triumphs. Today, as I pass 70, I am blessed with good health, a thriving family, and devoted friends. My business prospers and affords me the time and resources to contribute to philanthropic causes. I have everything to be thankful for, and that gratitude is the foundation of my book.

My life has not always been so bright. In my mid-40s, at a time when peers were hitting their mid-career stride and building their fortunes, I was the epitome of failure. I had no job, no income, no savings, and, it seemed, no future. I was tens of thousands of dollars in debt, had three liens on my house, and bankrupt. Worse, I'd brought all the misfortune on myself. I had

*This chapter is adapted from *Failing My Way to Success: Life Lessons of an Entrepreneur* by Steve Lobel (Albany, NY: F&S Publishing, 2015). The author wishes to thank his editor Timothy Cahill for his encouragement and assistance in preparing this chapter.

gambled my own and my family's security on a venture I had no business being in, then watched it go down in flames in a mere 20 months. This, in the wake of an equally devastating loss of a lucrative gourmet food market that bore my name, a store I had built from boutique market literally from scratch to regional prominence and some small celebrity for myself, only to have it wrested from my control in a contract dispute. The book depicts the winding road to my fall, and the lessons I learned that made possible my slow climb back, first to solvency and eventually to success.

From inception to publication, the memoir took more than a decade to complete as I worked with a writer and editor to shape the raw material of my life into a narrative. The book had grown out of lectures to aspiring entrepreneurs delivered at various business schools, always to enthusiastic response. I wrote it in hopes that my missteps and insights might inform and guide a wider audience. And, indeed, from millionaires to waitresses, readers have told me that my experiences resonate with their own. The reason, I have come to believe, has much to do with the book's subtitle, "Life Lessons of an Entrepreneur." I set out to write a cautionary tale for others but discovered that the book wanted first and foremost to explain myself to me.

I ended up with a more intimate story of personal weaknesses and strengths than I first conceived. More than any business savvy I might possess, it was my process of admitting my inner truths that allowed me to turn failure into success. I suppose there are successful entrepreneurs who have taken a straight road from concept to conquest without ever doubting themselves or their vision, but such a titan is hardly a model most of us can relate to. The more common experience is a trek into the unknown, sometimes on a wide and level path, but often on ways that are uphill, rutted, narrow, detoured, or blocked by barriers. I had to learn the value of good business practices to propel my journey, but I also discovered how much of entrepreneurship is an "inside job," a contest within oneself.

So, the key lesson of my book is one of the oldest and most basic truths of life: "Know thyself." The aphorism has framed Western thought from the Greek oracle of Delphi to the Hollywood hit *The Matrix*. Socrates interpreted it as meaning, "The unexamined life is not worth living." If that seems too abstract to be useful to the young entrepreneur impatient to build a company or the mid-career worker seeking to improve his or her future, think again. The old axiom is the toughest challenge you will face. And, like it or not, ready or not, it stands between you and ultimate success.

In my experience, being a successful entrepreneur, regardless of your profit or social motives, involves a gut check of personal ambitions and abilities, passions and prejudices. Why some people become entrepreneurs and others don't is almost certainly bound up in reasons beyond the reach of business school. These reasons include family background, beliefs around money and wealth, one's attitude toward others, and more. I had to lose almost everything before I began to understand the effect these forces were having on my career. Only then, after that dark reckoning, could I develop an attitude toward life and work that was sustainable and satisfying.

The route to self-knowledge tends to run through failure. The title of my book is *Failing My Way to Success*, and the spirit that permeates it is not one of defeat but resilience. As motivational speaker Zig Ziegler described it, "Failure is an event, not a person." My definition of success goes beyond the usual trappings of material goods, power, and influence. The lessons of failure and the resulting self-knowledge have made me kinder, wiser, more generous, and humbler. Our own human failings allow us to look with compassion on the humanity of others. For social entrepreneurs, care and compassion are the core values that drive the mission. I want to make these values part of the definition of success for all entrepreneurs, right alongside profitability, customer satisfaction, growth, and equity. No matter what your personal or professional net worth, if you are focused solely on self-gain and the bottom line, you haven't made it yet. In this regard, I would like all entrepreneurs to become social entrepreneurs.

The first half of my professional life was influenced by my father, Marty Lobel. No one has been a more powerful role model or pernicious obstacle. Before World War II, my father's life was one of independence and adventure in the Merchant Marine. After Pearl Harbor, he traded his maritime freedom for the cramped duty of a ball turret gunner, hunched knees-to-chin in a clear bubble on the belly of a B-17 bomber, firing twin machine guns at enemy fighters. After the war, Dad tried working a 9-to-5 job, making the commute from our new subdivision on Long Island into Manhattan. But he never took to being in harness. The daily schlep into the city chafed his autonomy. He wasn't good at following the masses down well-trodden paths. He was at heart an outsider, an army of one. Being his own boss was all that suited him, despite the stress and long hours it exacted.

One definition of an entrepreneur is someone who pursues opportunity beyond the limits of controlled resources (Eisenmann, 2013). In other words, the entrepreneur is driven by vision more than he or she is deterred by risk. This was my father. He set out on his own as a wedding and bar mitzvah photographer when I was in elementary school. He was a master with the hulking Crown Graphic press camera he used, with its 4-by-5-inch sheet film exposed one picture at a time. Unfortunately, his business skills lagged behind his creativity. He showed little interest in finance or economics, and he was naïve when it came to how money worked. I doubt these subjects were beyond his understanding. He didn't have the temperament or experience to apply himself to learning them. He bequeathed me his courage, integrity, artistry, and affability, but left me also with the lessons he failed to learn about the nuances of financial stability and profitability. I gained those the hard way, years later.

When I was 13, shortly after my bar mitzvah, my father recruited me to be his assistant. My weekends from then on were spent carrying photographic equipment, loading film holders, setting up lights, and packing and unpacking our portable studio as we moved from job to job. I watched him as he practiced his art and conducted his business. Though I did this until I graduated high school, never once did I feel I was being groomed to take over the business. Dad had other plans for me. From the time I was a young boy, he made clear his expectation that I become a doctor. Perhaps his sense of insecurity helps explain why he was so one-track about this point. He was sensitive about his own lack of education, something that showed in his subservient manner when he was around the professional men who hired his services. Whatever the reason, his message was unambiguous: as the first-born son and heir to his name, I carried the pride of the family on my shoulders. It was my fate and duty to become a physician.

The burden of this responsibility became heavier after my father had his first heart attack at age 51. It happened while we were on a job together, and I will never forget the sight of him, fallen and fragile, his skin a shocking gray-white, He survived the episode very much diminished and relied on my assistance even more afterward. I passed 16 and then 17, unable to confide in him on anything important regarding my feelings and true aspirations. How could I tell him I hated hospitals and had an aversion to studying science? At night I laid in bed sick with worry that if he found out I had neither the interest nor the aptitude to study medicine, his reaction might trigger another cardiac episode, maybe even kill him. So much for "know thyself." I was so cowed by my father's desire that, in August 1966, I entered the State University of New York at Albany enrolled as a pre-med.

Looking back at it, the deception of this outrageous act boggles my mind. I feel both chagrin and sympathy for my younger self. So bent was I on keeping the truth from my father that I kept it from myself as well. It didn't take long, however, for a storm surge of "know thyself" to roll in and knock me on my backside. I was failing all my biology and chemistry courses and cutting classes with impunity. By the end of the first semester, I was on academic probation and at risk of flunking out. Either my days of lying for my father's sake had to end, or my college career would. I went home, sat my parents down, and came clean.

Dad fell silent and more or less remained that way toward me for the rest of his life. I don't think he ever quite forgave me for betraying his dream. My mother took me aside and told me to stop worrying. "Live your life," she said. "Do what you're passionate about."

I returned to UAlbany, where I studied English, worked as a photographer for college publications, and got involved in student activism. My undergraduate years, from 1966 to 1970, were the height of the '60s student unrest. For us, nothing about the "establishment" went unchallenged. Long before strategists pressed us to "think outside the box," my generation lived that truth. We forced change by challenging everything my father's generation took for granted.

I eagerly took part in this movement. I protested the war in Vietnam, marched on Washington, shouted at demonstrations. But taking to the streets wasn't really my scene. From my father, I'd inherited an ease at working with people, and I saw that this skill could make a real difference on campus. I'm not a revolutionary, but I am a reformer. I decided I could be more effective working inside the system than I would ever be mounting the ramparts.

So, I began—with breakfast. As a sophomore, I never ate at the dining hall in the morning and resented the fact that I was paying for the meal with the one-size-fits-all meal plan that everyone had to sign up for. The plan offered no flexibility about when, where, and what you could eat, and I made it my mission to fix it. I joined the Living Area Affairs Commission, a student organization that had a say in all aspects of campus living, including the dining service. Soon I was consulting with representatives from the faculty and administration about ways to improve how we ate on campus. Our efforts were a success. By the next year, the food service offered a wider range of meal opportunities to all students.

The process taught me a lot about negotiation and networking, team building and cooperation, when to stand firm and when to compromise. I consider the meal plan reforms my first experience in entrepreneurial thinking. Our success was achieved through vision, discussion, and execution based on a plan of action. The other students and I demonstrated proof of concept and negotiated a win-win solution for both sides. The new rules allowed the food service to operate at a profit while providing a more flexible, cost-efficient service to the students. If that's not entrepreneurial, what is?

I had several other positive experiences like this while in college. You might think they would have given me valuable insight into myself and influenced my career plans post-graduation. And they might have, if not for the continuing influence of my father. The year was 1970. Vietnam was raging, and I knew I needed to continue in some sort of graduate-level education to retain my academic exemption from the draft. I could have pursued business administration, public planning, or communications, something I might have excelled in. The weight of my father's dashed hopes for a doctor son argued for a different path, though. Hoping I might win back his favor, I decided I'd become a lawyer.

I learned one thing as a result of attending Albany Law School. It had nothing to do with the law. Rather, I saw the importance of friendships and connections. I was no scholar; indeed, my grades indicated I didn't belong anywhere near law school. What helped me get accepted was the recommendation of a highly placed dean at UAlbany. He and I had worked together on student-administrative initiatives, and he wrote a glowing recommendation that I felt sure tipped the scales.

As might have been foreseen, however, my tenure in law school bore a grim resemblance to my first semester as a pre-med. I felt no connection to the thick texts or arcane rhetoric of the law, and I did everything to remain invisible in class. Rather than study contracts and torts, I spent my time teaching photography at a local community center. By the end of my first year, my grades were so bad the school informed me I could return only if I repeated the first year.

So ended my legal career. My father's disappointment was written all over his face and haunted me for the next 20 years as I strove to prove my worth. He did not live long enough to enjoy my first great triumph, but when that success went bad, I relived all too clearly the lack of belief that sat just behind his eyes. The memory stung even more when the business after that also blew up in my face.

Those events all lay in my future. I left law school ready to reinvent myself. Or, more precisely, to invent myself in my own mold. Not that I entirely knew what I wanted. All I knew for certain was what I didn't want. I had seen my father hustle and scrape as an independent businessman and desired no part of that life. I'd endured enough struggle to last a lifetime. Or so it seemed. I was newly married and wanted security, stability, and certainty.

I took a position as a retail salesman at an Albany photo-supply store. I participated significantly in the expansion to six stores, rising eventually to the level of general manager for retail operations. I was well-paid and well-liked, but despite promotion to a leadership position, it slowly became clear that I was never going to rise to the level of inner management or equity in the closely held, family-owned business. I would always be an employee. I burned inwardly at being shut out of an opportunity I felt I'd "earned" with my years of loyal service.

I am my father's son. My dissatisfaction with the photo store was in fact the restlessness of not controlling my own destiny. A new feeling stirred in my blood. The aversion I'd had to my father's way of life gave way to a more pressing instinct. I was about to unleash my inner entrepreneur.

I only knew I wanted to be my own boss. I was casting around for a business idea when an entrepreneur friend sprang a suggestion on me. Why not open a gourmet cheese shop? I looked blankly at him as he hastened to convince me the idea wasn't completely mad. It was the late 1970s. The market for upscale foods—now a multibillion dollar industry—was then just gaining a foothold. You saw it in the high-end emporiums of New York City. Albany was virgin territory. Then, cheese in New York's capital city meant American, cheddar, and maybe, for variety, Swiss.

The idea of running my own market wasn't entirely alien to me. I loved the Jewish delis I'd grown up with and had toyed with the idea of opening my own in Albany. Also, as luck would have it, my father-in-law was a good friend of the owner of a major cheese import company in New Jersey. This man traveled upstate to talk over my idea of opening a cheese shop. He liked the idea and pledged to invest $15,000 in the project, along with a line of credit for merchandise. Before I knew it, I had opened The Cheese Connection in a tiny basement-level storefront amid a row of upscale brownstone boutiques in the heart of the city.

Enthusiasm intermingled with doubt as I struggled to convince Albany it needed a specialty cheese shop. It didn't take long after opening day to recognize that there were major gaps in my business plan—like, for instance, the fact that I didn't have one. I was woefully undercapitalized and needed to turn a profit instantly in a market I had to build from scratch with no advertising budget. And then there was the small detail that I didn't know the first thing about cheese.

I fell back on my people skills and gave the best service possible. I voraciously educated myself on cheese and forged relationships with customers, caterers, and restaurateurs who sought my wares for their menus. In the first year, I grossed $125,000, a kingly sum for a niche product in that market. After expenses, however, I was only able to pay myself a salary of $9,000 for the hardest working year of my life. The healthy gross I'd made had not translated into net profits. Indeed, our financial results were in the red.

That rookie year was my introduction to the entrepreneur's complex relationship to money. As I said, my father had never been very sharp in this area, so I had no direct experience with how to manage or understand business finances. But that wasn't the half of it. Like so many people of my generation, I had come of age considering money a necessary evil and "profit" a dirty word. I understand when I meet idealistic young people who are passionate about starting a business or nonprofit but show little or no interest in grasping even the rudimentary elements of business. I tell them all the same thing. The success or failure of their vision is tied inextricably to their ability to master finances.

In my experience, it is precisely those people who become entrepreneurs solely out of commitment to a vision who are most at risk of failure. If one is selling widgets, love of the product is unlikely to cloud attention to the bottom line. It's when the vision matters above all else—when an individual or group is strictly in service to an ideal—that best business practices are neglected and succumb to wishful thinking. Earlier, I expressed the wish that everyone in business should to some degree think like a social entrepreneur. Now I will flip that formula. If you are a social entrepreneur, or starting a nonprofit of any kind, or thinking of hanging out a shingle or opening a shop, you need to make peace with a simple truth:

All business is ultimately for-profit business.

I consider this basic entrepreneurial thinking. I respect people who are driven by their mission. It gives their work special meaning. But there has to be a means to an end. You can't have a mission without the financial wherewithal to drive it. So, ultimately, even a not-for-profit venture must operate profitably. You have to consider all the elements of business. You've got to give careful, realistic attention to all the sources of revenue and add them up, and then you've got to look at all the sources of expense and add them up, and, at the end of the day, there has to be more income than outgo. That's business 101. What's left over is called *profit*.

There's nothing wrong with a not-for-profit organization being profit-driven. To my mind, the only difference between a for-profit and not-for-profit model is what you do with the profits. Obviously, they don't go into anyone's pocket. You reinvest your earnings into the mission and retain some for a rainy day—when you miss an anticipated grant, a major donor drops out, or the economy goes bad. Any number of things can happen to an organization that requires a reserve to survive.

Money may be the "root of all evil," but it is also the fertile soil of much good. It sounds so simplistic to state it like that. But I have served on non-profit boards of directors that acted as if they were not subject to basic financial best practices. Both the founders and the directors of socially conscious organizations are by definition idealists. People join boards because they are dedicated to what the organization stands for. In this capacity, they often resent fundraising and resist applying business theory to their roles in the organization. The attitude is, "this is where I leave my for-profit hat at home. I want to serve. I don't want to sell. I don't want to practice 'business as usual.'"

If you are a for-profit enterprise and end the year with a balanced budget, where income just meets expenses, you're considered to be just making it. For a nonprofit organization, however, to operate on a balanced budget is looked upon as a positive thing. It is, of course, better than operating at a deficit. And many organizations that don't have a "product" to market (beyond their mission, service, or cause), or whose product costs more to produce than market rates support, struggle to make ends meet. Their executive directors will read this and roll their eyes. My proposition that they strive to operate at a "profit" is pie in the sky. Ultimately, however, it is the mission that's served by such financial rigor. One can operate successfully on a balanced budget, but there is little room for growth under such a system, and even less for the unforeseen. Profit may not be a reality for a start-up or young organization, but it ought to be built into every organization's long-range planning. Otherwise, it will always be at risk.

After my first year as a gourmet cheese-monger, I moved The Cheese Connection to an upscale suburban shopping center and soon was thriving. Nevertheless, my business education at the School of Hard Knocks continued throughout those early years. One day, the IRS paid a call, threatening to close the shop down in 24 hours for unpaid taxes. I managed to secure an emergency loan to keep my doors open, but when my banker got a look at my books, he insisted as a condition for the money that I hire a bookkeeper and get up to speed as a businessman.

I had been flying by the seat of my pants, managing to keep my head above water from week to week and month to month. After the taxman, I began to keep precise records of my earnings and expenses. That's how I determined just how much money I was hemorrhaging in the waste of perishable foods alone—merchandise I was depositing in the dumpster because it no longer met my standards of freshness. I knew I was throwing away potential profits each night, but when I saw the figures in black and white I was stunned and instituted stringent waste and cost controls.

At the end of 8 years, my little store wasn't so little anymore. The business was comfortably profitable, and the future seemed limitless. I had indeed caught the wave of specialty and prepared foods that swept the 1980s, and, by 1987, was yearning to expand. My accountant put me in contact with another of his clients, a newly minted multimillionaire who'd made his fortune in the early years of information technology. Before anyone had heard of Whole Foods Market or Trader Joe's, and long before supermarkets routinely sold arugula, chèvre, and fresh croissants, we launched Cowan & Lobel Gourmet Marketplace, a sumptuous premium grocery in upstate New York that rivaled anything in Manhattan.

The store was an instant success and, as its public face in the media, made me something of a local celebrity. People still fondly recall Cowan & Lobel to me, although it's been closed for more than 15 years, and my association with it ended a quarter-century ago. My father had lost his first photography business to the machinations of a rapacious partner, and two and a half years after opening Cowan & Lobel, I followed in those bleak footsteps. My partner and I fell into a bitter contract dispute, and I was forced to accept a buyout and relinquish my share in the company. All at once, I was no longer part of the business I had founded and built.

I felt cast adrift, having lost not only my store and my identity, but (I felt at the time) my dignity as well. Impatient to rise again, I rushed into acquiring a business that specialized in screen-printed T-shirts and other sports apparel. As with cheese, I knew nothing about printed T-shirts. But, unlike those early days of The Cheese Connection, I wasn't responsible for just myself and a single employee. Now, I had the fortunes of a full equal partner and nearly two dozen workers at stake. I knew the business had inherent weaknesses, but against all expert advice (and there was a lot of it!), I bought it anyway. The project started going bad from Day One. We lost key employees, vendors, and retailers. Capital evaporated before my eyes. I borrowed money everywhere I could find it, including taking a second mortgage and a line of credit on my house and maxing out my credit cards. Every move I made was fruitless. It took less than 2 years for the business to come apart at the seams. One morning I showed up to find the bank had padlocked the factory doors and seized the property. It was done.

I returned home, where my wife Vivian met me at the door. Just as I had done two decades earlier with my father about becoming a doctor, I had no choice but to tell her the full truth. I had been glossing the numbers for months, hiding the worst from her. Now I revealed how deeply I had plunged us into debt. We were completely broke. The house had three liens on it, I'd incurred tens of thousands of dollars of credit card debt, and our two children's college funds might have to be liquidated. First, she cried; then a distressed silence descended.

That night, I woke up fearing I was having a heart attack. My heart was all right; the attack was the reality of my failure pulling me under like a powerful wave. Lying in the dark, I tried to make sense of what I had wrought. But nothing added up. I had worked hard and never quit. I had been faithful to my wife, supportive with my children, kind to my friends.

I did not drink, use drugs, or gamble. I had stayed loyal to my creditors, my suppliers, my employees, and my customers. I had been a successful entrepreneur and generous community volunteer. How, when I had tried to do everything right, had it all gone so wrong?

The sleepless night wore on until I accepted my reality. I had been motivated as well by a selfish need to save face and regain my pride after being forced to sell Cowan & Lobel. I had been stubborn and blinded by resentment. I'd harbored vain fantasies of staging a triumphant comeback to restore my whipped dignity. And, at a deeper level, I was still trying to impress my father and undo the past.

What I experienced in that dark night was the ultimate thrashing by the gods of "know thyself." My capacity to self-deceive had mounted its highest peak and thrown me down in utter defeat. But that moment of my worst failure also held the seeds to my redemption. The next day, I did an honest inventory of my weaknesses and strengths. I had finally to admit that I was not really chief executive material; that though I have some of the leadership and vision a CEO requires, I don't have the organizational acumen and get no pleasure from the financial and legal responsibilities.

Among my strengths I found the lifeline I needed: more than two decades of deep and loyal bonds to my community, stretching back to my college days, and developed through both business contacts and volunteer and charitable work. These friendships and professional connections helped me get back on my feet and proved to be my foundation every step of the way as I rebuilt my life and ultimately achieved prosperity.

I emphasize this point to the young entrepreneurs I mentor. I counsel them to extend their reach beyond themselves both before and after they make their fortune. I encourage those new to business to define success as doing well and doing good—building the bottom line and making a positive impact on the world. It is not a matter of choosing between one's self-interest and the community chest. The two are intertwined. I did not volunteer, serve on boards, join fundraising committees, or otherwise do philanthropic work to build business connections. I did it as a form of community service, a debt I believe we owe to each other. And yet I would be disingenuous not to admit that the connections I made as a philanthropist wove the net that saved me professionally when I was plunging into the abyss. And, ultimately, brought me resources with which I could help others.

I found my feet again working for my alma mater, eventually being named UAlbany's Assistant Vice President for Alumni Affairs. At last I'd achieved the stability and certainty I'd sought after law school. I had been forced to declare bankruptcy and diligently dug myself and my family out of debt. The house remained ours, and Vivian and I dedicated ourselves to funding our children's college educations. While at UAlbany, I became an adjunct instructor and gave the first of the lectures that eventually became *Failing My Way to Success*. As the ultimate gesture of my newly recovered self-esteem, I even cast off the hairpiece I'd hidden behind for 20 years and boldly, proudly, proclaimed my baldness.

As content as I was, however, I had begun to hear once more the distant call of the entrepreneurial life. So when my closest mentor and confidant approached me about joining his insurance firm, I listened with keen interest. Before making a move back into business, however, I insisted my friend meet first with my wife and address all her questions and concerns. She came back with her blessing. With trepidation and hope, I accepted his offer, then labored for more than 3 years to find my niche. I found it in the world of high-technology entrepreneurship. I started insuring start-up firms that no one else saw potential in. As I had been with gourmet foods, I was on the frontier of something that was about to grow exponentially.

Many of those small start-ups are now major players on the international stage. And I have established a reputation as the go-to insurance man for emerging high-tech and other entrepreneurial ventures.

What I value about selling insurance is exactly what has drawn me all my life—networking, teamwork, communication, collaboration, and, most of all, relationship building. I prize the connections I've forged through the insurance business, just as I am grateful for the financial security it has provided. My business is robust and continues to grow. Through savings and investments, I have provided for my wife and myself for as long as we live and ensured a secure legacy for our children and grandchildren. At a time when others my age are slowing down, I feel like I'm in mid-career and proudly correct anyone who assumes I am ready to retire. I report none of this to boast. Quite the opposite. When I consider my good fortune, I am filled with humility, enormous gratitude, and a measure of astonishment.

That these blessings have come through selling insurance is part of the surprise. No one thinks of the insurance industry as a vocation to capture the imagination. Yet in insurance, I found the career where my creativity, intuition, relationship skills, and business experience converged and found their full expression. In turn, the success I've found has opened the way for me to enjoy two of the most gratifying practices of my life: philanthropy and mentoring.

Philanthropically, I am guided by the Jewish ethic of *tikkun olam*, meaning "to repair the world." According to my tradition, it is the duty of every individual to make the world a better place. Philanthropic giving of time, skills, or money is not just a gesture of generosity, but an obligation we all share as members of society. Offering support to institutions that enhance community life is rewarding creatively, intellectually, and professionally.

Volunteering enables one to show his or her best skills in a "status-neutral" environment. Through my service on the boards of organizations such as Jewish Family Services, the Albany Symphony Orchestra, and the Community Foundation of the Greater Capital Region, I have contributed entrepreneurial concepts to their governance, marketing, and development. In the process, I confirmed what my truest strengths were by seeing where I had the most efficacy. Our philanthropic work dovetails with our entrepreneurial aspirations. Indeed, I would go so far as to say that philanthropy is an essential element of business activity. Be a good citizen and a good corporate citizen. The more you give the more you get, be it time, talent, and/or treasure. You don't have to be wealthy to be philanthropic.

One expression of my philanthropic activity is my work mentoring young entrepreneurs. I am a member of Eastern New York Angels, a group of successful business people who pool their resources to invest in early-stage companies. Among the several traits we use to identify the individuals and groups we take an interest in is the willingness to accept mentoring and implement constructive criticism. Confidence and humility are like twin horses pulling one carriage. A successful entrepreneur needs the boldness and self-reliance to move ahead into the unknown, but also the humility to know when to seek advice or admit an error.

Other qualities that investors require include a precise vision and the ability to effectively articulate it, passion for and commitment to an identifiable goal, a realistic view of the marketplace and how the business either fills a unique need or captures an existing market in a unique way, and a reasonable plan to monetize the product or service. We also look for evidence of intangibles, such as the ability to build and manage a team and, perhaps most important of all, the energy, perseverance, and ability to stay positive through inevitable adversity. As the term "invest" suggests, our group naturally hopes for a financial return of resources. But an equally important part of our mission is mentoring young entrepreneurs to help them succeed while benefiting our regional economy. Our greatest success comes from participating in the success and well-being of others.

Mentoring is very much an act of *tikkun olam*. Whether a business leader has already achieved success or is on the way, it's important always to remember that none of us makes it alone. When I was younger, I constantly searched for the mentor who would complete the work my father had left unfinished. In truth, I benefited immeasurably from the counsel and advice of many mentors, male and female, some of whom are no longer alive to thank. This is true for most of us. But we all have the opportunity to express gratitude and "pay it forward" by helping the next generation.

Young entrepreneurs often ask for practical advice as they set out on their careers. I have condensed mine into 10 principles gleaned from a lifetime of trial and error, failure and success.

1. *Know thyself.* Identify your deepest desires. Recognize your core skills. Understand your gifts and flaws.
2. *It takes a team.* No individual entrepreneur can provide all the skills needed to manage and grow a successful business. Surround yourself with others who share your vision and complement your strengths.
3. *Entrepreneurship is a lifestyle, not a job.* A business is a living entity that must be continuously nurtured with your time and attention.
4. *There is rarely a straight line to success.* Persistence in light of adversity is critical for survival.
5. *Learn to pivot.* While perseverance is essential, develop an instinct for when to quit against insurmountable odds or unmanageable risks. Much can be gained from a timely "pivot" or strategic change of direction.
6. *Success is fragile and uncertain.* The most important lessons I have learned came from my failures. Remember, experiencing a failure does not make you a failure.
7. *Cultivate friendships as well as contacts.* Entrepreneurship relies on salesmanship, and salesmanship is ultimately about relationships. I've learned that the people I could count on the most, in business as in life, are those I developed a close bond with. Don't just build a network of people who are "useful" to you; get to know about their lives, celebrate their successes, and stand by them during their hardships. Other than your family, your circle of friends is your strongest asset.
8. *Master the art of listening.* The best salespeople are the best listeners, and the key to listening is attention. Good listening connects you to the needs and desires of your clients and potential clients, which in turn means better, more committed business relationships. I rank the ability to be attentive and fully present with associates and clients as important to business success as core competence.
9. *The greatest compliment is referred business.* Cultivate referrals from others and make referrals whenever possible and appropriate.
10. *It's all about family.* Ultimately, my success in business pales in comparison to the love and support of my wife, children, parents, in-laws, and now my grandchildren. They are the beginning and the end of everything I do.

With these guidelines, I offer two wishes. May your failures light the way to your ultimate success. And may your success be the means by which you help repair the world.

REFERENCE

Eisenmann, T. R. (2013). Entrepreneurship: A working definition. *Harvard Business Review.* Retrieved from: https://hbr.org/2013/01/what-is-entrepreneurship.

Examples from Transitioning and Market-Based Economies

CHAPTER 8

༄

Focus on the Balkans

Social Enterprise in Albania

MICHELLE T. HACKETT AND MICHAEL J. ROY

INTRODUCTION

For those countries in the process of transitioning from a communist past to an envisioned advanced capitalist future, the social enterprise—an organization that combines social and business objectives—could appear to promise a sustainable, market-based solution to address the welfare gaps and difficult social problems that seem symptomatic of the transition process. This popular interpretation of the potential role of social enterprise in post-communist societies is, however, arguably too narrow. Rather than simply being a temporary solution for a transitioning market economy, social enterprises, by their very nature, are able to challenge ideas of what "the economy" can—and arguably *should*—look like. The "blended" social and economic value created by social enterprises can, we argue in this chapter, demonstrate a "middle way" between the excesses of both communism *and* capitalism.

Dominant conceptualizations of social enterprises and social entrepreneurship originate from Western countries, and hence the discourses surrounding these terms have been strongly influenced by neoliberal capitalist ideologies. For example, Western business schools spotlight

Michelle T. Hackett and Michael J. Roy, *Focus on the Balkans* In: *Social Entrepreneurship and Enterprises in Economic and Social Development*. Edited by: Katharine Briar-Lawson, Paul Miesing, and Blanca M. Ramos, Oxford University Press (2021). © Oxford University Press. DOI: 10.1093/oso/9780197518298.003.0009.

the charismatic "heroic" entrepreneur (Ruebottom, 2013) who employs "business models to offer creative solutions to complex and persistent social problems" (Zahra, Gedajlovic, Neubaum, & Shulman, 2009 p. 519). Correspondingly, Western governments have been promoting the value of social enterprises engaging in market-based activities as a mechanism to deliver social programs more "effectively" than the state or charity (Roy & Hackett, 2017). In Eastern Europe, however, the field is still in an early stage of development, with both internal and external factors shaping the social enterprise landscape. External powers, as we will explain, have shown interest in social enterprise's potential in Eastern Europe. Significantly, though, these actors—largely from Western countries—are arguably intent on driving Eastern European countries into "turbocharged" market economies, where social enterprises are simply a temporary solution to the "teething problems" of this transition.

An important consequence of the dominance of this "transition paradigm"[1] is that the success of social enterprise is often viewed or judged in too narrow a manner, such as the self-sustainability of the social enterprise in financial terms, and the impact, in terms of income, on the beneficiary (e.g., through employment). We argue, alternatively, that it is equally important to take sufficient account of the wider impacts and (often) structural changes to which social enterprises can contribute. We consider that social enterprises have the potential to demonstrate a "middle way" by challenging norms concerning how the economy is conceived, in that it should exist to serve society rather than the other way around—posing an alternative business framework to market fundamentalism—while also contributing to more traditional non–market-focused "social goals" such as breaking down prejudices concerning marginalized groups.

The legacies of communism and the transition agendas of various powerful (particularly transnational) actors, however, sets up myriad obstacles for the practical application of social enterprise as an effective "middle way" actor. This is apparent in the example of Albania, a country in the Balkans region of southeastern Europe which has embarked on a long process of social and economic transformation since the collapse of communism in the country in 1991.

The interplay between the potential of social enterprise as an "alternative" economic actor that may contribute to a middle way and the historical and current influences of powerful forces and paradigms will be explored through focusing on Albania. In this chapter, we analyze the discourses of key actors in an Albanian social enterprise called the Youth Albania Professional Services (YAPS) to demonstrate how social enterprises may be used as a tool to implement a smoother "free market" capitalist transition but also, and importantly, how we need to think more carefully about what we mean by "economic impacts" beyond a narrow financial perspective to highlight a different, alternative role for social enterprise in transition economies.

SOCIAL ENTERPRISE AS A "MIDDLE WAY" ACTOR IN POST-COMMUNIST COUNTRIES

On the "Transition Paradigm" and "Middle Ways"

The term "middle way" has been used since the mid-1990s to describe a variety of different economic governance forms that attempt to find an alternative to socialism and *laissez-faire* capitalism: from the "partially planned economy" of Marquis Childs and Harold Macmillan, to the embedded liberalism of Keynes (Bradley & Donway, 2010, p. 79). In the late 1990s, UK Prime Minister Tony Blair, drawing on the ideas of sociologist Anthony Giddens, used the term "third way" similarly to describe his vision for social democracy. Social enterprise in the United Kingdom was seen as emblematic of that course, as Haugh and Kitson (2007) explain. More recently, however, the concept of "middle way" has become less fashionable due in part to its association with unpopular policies and governments.

However, the term can still be valuable, we argue, if used in a more pluralistic sense; that is, by assuming that there is not one ideal "middle way" but rather a multitude of different forms of economic governance strategies that attempt to avoid what could be termed "extreme" positions, traditionally (if rather simplistically) thought of in terms of "left" and "right." Such middle ways may not necessarily be only used to describe macroscopic governance policies such as welfare policies, but also to identify "everyday"-scale ventures in alternative modes of economic operation such as social enterprise (see Gibson-Graham [2008] on the value of "diverse economies"). We consider that exploring a variety of alternatives allows for more socially inclusive forms of economic governance for post-communist societies to be imagined, found, and created.

This "middle way" position contrasts with the historically dominant "transition paradigm" of the region. The transition paradigm is treated in this study as the normative argument—championed by successive Western governments and powerful transnational actors such as the International Monetary Fund (IMF), World Trade Organization (WTO), and World Bank—that post-communist economies should ideally aim to recreate the Western capitalist market system and enthusiastically embrace so-called free market economic policies. While the transition paradigm has been criticized by many academics, particularly in the development field, it is arguably still the dominant philosophy espoused by powerful actors and international institutions operating in Eastern Europe (see Shields [2012] for a critical, transnational analysis). As noted in a United Nations Development Programme (UNDP) report, many in post-communist countries still see "the market and for-profit enterprises as the sole actors capable of rapidly filling the gap left by the withdrawal of direct state involvement in the economy" (UNDP, 2008, p. 37).

However, the "transition" to capitalism has not gone smoothly in the region, even in arguably the most Western-oriented country of Eastern Europe, the Czech Republic (Pickles & Smith, 2005, pp. 1–2). The withdrawal of state support from various sectors of these post-communist societies, for example, has exacerbated marginalization and led to high levels of unemployment (Borzaga & Spear, 2004, p. 13). There appears to be a growing understanding that neoliberal "shock therapy" policies (such as austerity) need to be tempered with more socially benign solutions (Koford, 1997, p. 31).

It is within this post-communist context that we will explore the phenomenon of social enterprise. Social enterprises, we argue, have two potential—albeit contrasting—roles to play in the wake of some of the (societal) failings of "transition." On one hand, social enterprises may help to highlight the possibility of a "middle way," a path between communism and *laissez-faire* capitalism. Contrastingly, however, they may be used by those supporting a transition agenda to smooth market reforms and reduce pressure for change. It is these two possibilities that will be further described in the following paragraphs.

Social Enterprise as an Alternative Economic Actor

While the definition of social enterprise is contested (Teasdale, 2012), with several schools of thought influencing the concept from different directions (Defourny & Nyssens, 2010), a commonality in the literature is the conceptualization of social enterprises as organizations that combine social and financial objectives, described by some as the "double bottom line" (Alter, 2007). In so doing, the social enterprise challenges the market fundamentalist ideology concerning an "exchange market economy,"[2] which is considered, somehow, to exist in a separate sphere to "society," populated only by self-interested individuals intent on pursuing profits. According to some pioneering social entrepreneurs, social enterprise— with its dual social–financial goals—offers an "improved," "sustainable," and/or "socially conscious" form of capitalism (Drayton, 2002; Emerson, 2003; Yunus, 2009). For others, social enterprise has a more radical potential, offering "a partial or a complete rejection of established 'rules' of international capitalism" (Ridley-Duff & Bull, 2011, p. 100). To varying degrees, social enterprises are thus presented as an alternative to *laissez-faire* capitalist principles in order to promote an economic system that avoids, or at least tempers, the social failings of the current reality.

For post-communist countries, similarly, we consider that social enterprises can offer an alternative to the traditional capitalist business model. With the rise in unemployment and reduction in welfare as a product of "transition," social enterprises are projected by supporters to be "one of the best solutions to the problem" (Lucas & Vardanyan, 2005, p. 2; see also Defourny, 2009). Social enterprises, with their dual missions, "are able to tackle economic and social concerns and challenges [in post-communist countries] that neither public agencies nor for-profit enterprises can address effectively" (UNDP, 2008, p. 5). Social enterprises, as small-scale actors, do not present a macroscopic alternative economic framework but instead illustrate "everyday" examples of how plotting a middle way might be possible.

Social Enterprise as a Co-Opted Transition Actor

However, in contrast to the role of social enterprise as a "middle way" actor, there is also potential for the concept to be used in the promotion of a particular form of transition. The development of social enterprise in Western and developing countries provides lessons in this respect. Alongside the potential of social enterprise to introduce a more "socially embedded" economy, it has also arguably been harnessed by actors seeking to further entrench neoliberal economic frameworks (as argued by Garrow & Hasenfeld, 2014). In the case of the United Kingdom, for example, some authors have argued that the government has promoted social enterprise as a means of plugging the gaps in provision created after spending significantly decreased on social services and/or simultaneously acting as a "smokescreen" for the privatization of state institutions such as the National Health Service (NHS) in England (see Roy, Donaldson, Baker, & Kay, 2013). In developing countries, similarly, while the concept of social enterprise has the potential to create and support alternative models of development, it has also arguably been used by international institutions, such as the World Bank with its promotion of microfinance, to marketize informal rural economies and create a new class of "bottom-of-the-pyramid" global consumers (see Weber, 2010).

In post-communist countries, there is a similar potential for social enterprise to be used as a neoliberal adjustment instrument. With the withdrawal of the state from social services post-communism, various international aid bodies have stepped in to create and fund nonprofit organizations to "fill the gaps" in welfare provision. Social enterprise could be seen as a tool for transforming these nonprofits into self-funding enterprises. Liberalization of the nonprofit sector with social enterprise creation/transformations would not only provide an "exit strategy" for international donors (Lucas & Vardanyan, 2005, p. 3), but it may also help to entrench a market-oriented approach to addressing social issues; that is, a neoliberal solution to inequalities and marginalization in transition countries. When a social enterprise (or, indeed, any other civil society actor) is pressured to conform to neoliberal priorities, this risks not only upsetting the social–financial balance that, in effect, makes an organization a social enterprise, but can also potentially have wider deleterious societal impacts (as explored by both Dart [2004] and Eikenberry & Kluver [2004]).

STUDY AIM AND METHODS
Economic Versus Social Impact Discourses

A central proposition of this chapter is that the neoliberal co-option of social enterprise in a transition strategy can be identified by the discourse employed by actors in the field—specifically, the prioritization of "economic impact" terminology. As mentioned earlier, inherent in neoliberal philosophy is the belief that the unregulated, unfettered market can support a smoothly functioning society. One consequence of this is that assessment of the "economic impact" of a project or enterprise is often given priority, either explicitly or implicitly, over and above social aims, and this can be studied through analysis of actors' discourses. For example, Haugh (2006, p. 186) identifies a variety of economic, social, and environmental outcomes—both direct and indirect—that can possibly arise from social enterprises. She argues that too much attention has been given to the direct economic outcomes of social enterprises in Western countries (Haugh, 2006, p. 180). Arguably, there are not only practical reasons (in terms of ease of measurement and so on) but also *political* motives behind this tendency to focus on the economic. This is just as true for post-communist countries as it is for Western or developing countries.

We are not arguing that economic impacts are unimportant (increased resources in low income households can obviously make a considerable difference to life quality), but rather that an exclusionary prioritization[3] of economic impacts in an actor's discourse is a possible indicator that the actor conceives of social enterprise as a market-enabling agent in a neoliberal (e.g., transition) paradigm. There is a large source of literature, for example, in the critical development field concerning the market-focused discourse of international institutions such as the World Bank as a tool for neoliberal policies and the co-option of alternatives (including less tangible concepts such as empowerment and sustainability) to a neoliberal agenda (Peet, 2003).

For social enterprises in post-communist countries, prioritization of "economic impact" could be indicated by a focus on the *financial self-sustainability* of the social enterprise itself, the ability of the social enterprise to bring *financial gain* to beneficiaries, and/or the capacity of the social enterprise to provide *employment*. To prioritize these economic outcomes over (or to the exclusion of) social goals, as evidenced by analysis of an actor's discourse, is arguably an indication of their support for social enterprise as a transition agent (or their attempt to appear so). As argued previously, increased financial sustainability of third-sector actors enables greater government withdrawal, and increased incomes and employment promote a smoother-running capitalist marketplace, both of which are neoliberal goals.

In contrast, prioritization of "social impact" may indicate that an actor conceptualizes social enterprise as a nonconventional business enterprise, one contributing to an alternative economic model. This may include a focus on the *community support* behind, or collective ownership of, the social enterprise; the building of *social capital*; the ability of the social enterprise to address the *root causes* of marginalization and disadvantage; and the *democratic governance* of the social enterprise.

Our intention in exploring these "impact" discourses is not to create a diagnostic tool for identifying neoliberal and alternative social enterprise actors: first, such a simplistic dualism is unreflective of complex reality, and, second, the economic-versus-social impact discourse is but one element in a broader discourse concerning the operations of social enterprises. Rather, we aim to bring critical attention to how the international political economy can shape—and is shaping—the social enterprise field in post-communist countries. This is important because critical exploration of social enterprise in Eastern Europe is currently sparse; indeed, the entire field of social entrepreneurship in post-communist countries is considerably underresearched (Lambru & Galera, 2015), with political analysis being particularly rare.

Case Study Analysis

The primary method of analysis of social enterprises in Albania, and in the YAPS case study in particular, was the identification of "flags," such as ideologically loaded terms and keywords, that might allow us to gain insight into the political motivations of prominent social enterprise actors in Albania. In the following sections, then, the authors' use of italics within quotes—specifically quotes from the Albania government, international actors, and prominent actors within YAPS—is intended to help the reader identify these loaded (e.g., economic or social impact oriented) terms.

Many different forms of text can be selected for discourse analysis (Jørgensen & Phillips, 2002) and so data on YAPS and social enterprise activity in Albania were gathered from organizational reports, press releases, webpages, proceedings, and other publicly available works. These data sources were supplemented with field notes taken by the authors in their role as observer-participants in two colloquia in Tirana, Albania, in April 2016,[4] where the Albanian Deputy Minister for Welfare and Youth, Partners Albania staff, several Albanian social entrepreneurs, academic experts, and representatives from numerous research institutions from around Eastern Europe communicated their positions on social enterprise in Albania (and, indeed, on other countries in the region). In addition, the Executive Manager of YAPS, Arben Shamia, was interviewed at the YAPS head office in Tirana on April 22, 2016.

The intention of this study was not to analyze the operation of YAPS per se, nor to assess the validity of any actors' statements or make judgments on their levels of "success." Rather, the aim was to explore how powerful discourses (including the neoliberal discourse)—as projected by the government and international institutions in particular—have influenced the public transcripts of key figures in YAPS and, hence, what this might mean for other social enterprises trying to negotiate the sociopolitical terrain in Albania.

THE SOCIAL ENTERPRISE FIELD IN ALBANIA

About Albania

Albania is located in the Balkans region of southeastern Europe, bordered by Montenegro and Kosovo to the north and northeast, respectively; Northern Macedonia to the east; and Greece to the south. The country was formed after the collapse of the Ottoman Empire, declaring independence in 1912. Invaded by Italy in 1939, the Kingdom of Albania became a Nazi protectorate in 1943. In 1944, a socialist People's Republic was established under the Stalinist dictator Enver Hoxha. Under communism, Albania experienced widespread social and political transformation, as well as isolation from much of the international community as one of Europe's "most ideologically repressive regimes" (Eaton & Roshi, 2014, p. 312). In 1991, the Socialist Republic was dissolved and the Republic of Albania was established.

Albania has a population of some 3 million people. Tirana, the capital and largest city, has a population of just under 500,000, although approximately 800,000 live in the broader municipality of Tirana. Economic reforms have opened the country to foreign investment, especially in the development of energy and transportation infrastructure, and it is considered an "upper-middle-income" economy by the World Bank (2019), despite high unemployment (approximately 30% youth unemployment in 2017) and a slow growth rate in recovering from the global financial crisis of 2008. Like many other countries, the consequences of economic transition involving the withdrawal or partial withdrawal of state welfare provision have had a disproportionate effect on those most vulnerable in society: marginalized groups such as young people, elderly, Roma communities, and people with disabilities. "Public spending cuts paired with slow progress on pensions, healthcare, wages and unemployment have left many citizens without vital services that contribute to overall quality of life" (TACSO, 2013, p. 65; see also Partners Albania, 2013). This has created social problems that the Albanian government continues to grapple with.

In 2009, Albania submitted its formal application for European Union (EU) membership and, in October 2012, the European Commission recommended that Albania be granted EU candidate status subject to completion of key measures of reform. In terms of "social inclusion and service delivery" measures, the European Commission focused on Albania's gender inequality in employment, marginalization of Roma in employment, education and social services, and widespread informal work and high unemployment rates as areas that the government of Albania needed to work on (TACSO, 2013, p. 21). Consequently, the Albanian government gained official candidate status in 2014 and continues, under the support and supervision of a number of transnational actors, to work on addressing key areas of social and economic development under what could be termed a new form of "transition paradigm."[5] Part of the EU's mandate is to help integrate new member states into its Single Market while also finding ways to address the social upheavals that transition has caused. For both the EU and the government of Albania, social entrepreneurship or "social business" is presented as one such solution (Rosandic & Kusinikova, 2018), as we will now explore.

Key Actors: Government of Albania

The primary vehicle by which the government of Albania articulates its position toward social enterprise is the state-owned institution *Nxitja E Biznesit Social* (NBS; "Promoting Social Business"). It was established in 2011, after the Albanian government invited Grameen Creative Lab (the European arm of the organization promoting Muhammad Yunus's concept of social business) to conduct a study in Albania to "assess the acute *social problems* and addressing them through [financially] *sustainable* and *self-financing* mechanisms" (NBS, 2014, p. 6, emphasis added). The study resulted in the creation of the NBS, with its mission to "improve *social protection policies* of the Government, *accountability* processes, and improving cooperation between the public and non-public sector" (NBS, 2014, p. 7, emphasis added). According to their public website, NBS was involved in four activities: the Social Business Incubator, where "individuals [interested in social business] were advised on how to *prepare business plans*"; a pilot investment fund "to *facilitate financing* better initiatives of social businesses"; creating partnerships with institutions; and providing advice and technical assistance to social enterprises (see www.nbs.org.al/eng/law/ ; emphasis added).

Throughout the NBS national report and website, there are references to the importance of both social and financial goals of social enterprises, though, predominantly, the "social" goals are directly related to the economic benefits for beneficiaries and employment opportunities. An early government initiative into social enterprise, for example, is presented as "a solution for the poor residents of these areas, to provide them *sustainable employment* and *growing incomes* for their families, by *economically empowering them*" (NBS, 2014, p. 6, emphasis added).

Furthermore, the primary role that the government adopts for itself is to help develop social entrepreneurs' business skills. There is, for example, a National Contest of Social Business Plans, where the NBS provides "technical assistance and consultation . . . for improving *business plans* of the semi-finalists" (see www.nbs.org.al/eng/law/; emphasis added). The focus of the government, then, as presented in its public communications, seems firmly focused on the development of business acumen within newly emerging Albanian social entrepreneurs.

International Actors

The most prominent international actors interested in and supporting so-cial enterprise in Albania to this point have been the EU and (to a far lesser extent) the Swiss government. The government's NBS national report, for example, was funded under the EU's Seventh Framework Program for Research, through an international comparative research project entitled Enabling the Flourishing and Evolution of Social Entrepreneurship for Innovative and Inclusive Societies (EFESEIIS). The Swiss Agency for Development and Co-operation, through their Regional Research Promotion Program (RRPP) for the Western Balkans, supported Partners Albania and other local nongovernmental organizations (NGOs) and think tanks involved in researching social enterprise in the region through the Challenges and Opportunities for Employment of Marginalized Groups by Social Enterprises project (Partners Albania, 2016).

Significantly, in 2014, the EU-initiated and third sector-led Belgrade Declaration was signed by stakeholders in the region; it aims to ensure that the Western Balkans and Turkey become an integral part of wider EU strategies on social entrepreneurship and social innovation develop-ment. The Albanian Ministry of Social Welfare and Youth is aware of the political implications of this—due to Albania's position as a potential fu-ture member of the EU—communicating how "the promotion of social business, in the same line with EU good practices, will be another way in achieving a fast and all-inclusive [*economic*] *growth*" (quoted in NBS, 2014, p. 12, emphasis added).

The EU Social Business Initiative is focused on improving access to credit for social enterprises, increasing their visibility, and enhancing the legal environment for social economy initiatives. The definition of a "social business" given by the Initiative includes democratic governance stipulations: social businesses are "managed in an open and responsible manner . . . [which] involves employees, consumers and stakeholders" (quoted in Defourny & Nyssens, 2012, p. 32). However, the Initiative has been criticized for being too focused on the financing of social enterprises (particularly by private investors) (EMES, 2011). In essence, this critique boils down to an uneasiness with how (neoliberal) terminology and ideas were being introduced into European discourse on social enterprise, poten-tially diluting its efficacy as a response to market fundamentalism. As one of the four head figures of the EU's Social Business Initiative states, "Social business is one of the pockets of untapped potential in our *Single Market*. Social business is a good example of an approach to business that is both responsible and contributes to *growth and jobs*" (European Commission, 2014, p. 3, emphasis added).

Shaping the Albanian Social Enterprise Field

Albania's particularly repressive communist past has played a significant role in the development (or lack thereof) of social enterprise in the country. Communist state-based cooperatives, for example, left a legacy of public distrust toward what could be termed "social enterprise principles." The majority of social enterprises in Albania are enterprising nonprofits (TACSO, 2013) that have adopted social enterprise principles less out of a belief in charting a "middle way" and more as a response to increased funding pressures by international donors. The government of Albania, however, has not focused its policies and activities on these enterprising nonprofit social enterprises, but instead focused on business-oriented "social businesses"—particularly those which aim to create jobs for marginalized people, often termed *work integration social enterprises* (WISE). Indeed, while the first attempt to draft a law for social business in Albania began in 2010, the final regulation to enact it has only just been passed, 9 years on, with many in the nonprofit sector dissatisfied with the final law (Hoxha & Haska, 2019, p. 7; UN Women, 2019).

Because the government is not a primary funder of nonprofits, it has relatively less incentive to focus on encouraging the financial self-sufficiency of nonprofits with social enterprise activities (in contrast to a country such as the United Kingdom, for example). Arguably, however, the most influential reason for the government's focus on WISE is its attempt to satisfy EU requirements, which emphasize greater employment of marginalized groups (as noted earlier; TACSO, 2013, p. 21). The government's model, interestingly, does not fit with the EU's definition of a social business as having a democratic governance model. However, significantly, the Belgrade Declaration (which is supported by the EU) has diluted this requirement, defining a social enterprise as "using democratic governance *or* participatory principles *or* focusing on social justice" (www.belgradedeclaration.net/ ; emphasis added).

In summary, the two most influential actors in the social enterprise scene in Albania appear to have a common agenda: the use of social business concepts to develop Albania's (capitalist) entrepreneurial and business expertise while dealing with the social problems that accompany transition, all in an attempt to assist Albania's accession to EU member status and participation in its Single Market. The focus on "economic" terminology and concepts, as presented in the actors' discourses, highlights the way that the social enterprise concept is, arguably, being used as a tool for smoother transition by these actors rather than as a "middle way" economic actor.

FOCUS ON YAPS

The following case study focuses on the Albanian social enterprise called YAPS to highlight how economic and social impact discourses are preferenced, or hidden, in line with the priorities (or the perceived desired priorities) of the key actors involved. This analysis will help to reveal how ideologies concerning the role of social enterprise—such as those presented earlier concerning the government and EU—may influence social enterprise actors in post-communist countries like Albania and what this means for the future of the sector.

Public "Economic Impact" Discourses

YAPS is a WISE, a form of social enterprise that focuses on the employment of groups who are marginalized from the mainstream labor markets. YAPS focuses on providing jobs for disadvantaged youths via postal delivery, repairs, maintenance, and professional cleaning services. It was initiated in 2001[6] by a nonprofit organization associated with the Roman Catholic Church, Don Bosco, and UNICEF Albania, with the aim to "engage disadvantaged youth into *productive employment* while creating *profits and project sustainability*" (YAPS, 2013, p. 2, emphasis added). It now employs more than 100 youths (17- to 21-year-olds) from disadvantaged backgrounds, such as "parentless youth, youth with special needs, migrants and Roma" (Ymeraj & Qosja, 2015, p. 6).

Executive Manager Arben Shamia highlights the financial self-sustainability of the social enterprise from a very early stage and credits this to its business connections (and contracts) with large multinational corporations (MNCs) and foreign embassies, including the US Embassy and Vodaphone. YAPS considers itself to be a successful "social business." Interestingly, according to Shamia, YAPS does not seek tax concessions, as "we live in a *free market economy*, and need to compete in a *free market economy*." In a publicly available YAPS presentation, similarly, the social enterprise highlights its role in ensuring that young people "are better able to harness some of the opportunities of an *emerging free market* for their own benefit" (YAPS, 2013, p. 2, emphasis added).

Indeed, in the public transcripts of YAPS, "economic impact" discourse appears to dominate, with the solution to complex social problems being the integration of youth into the capitalist market: "YAPS offers its help in the *softening of social problems* Albanian society is going by, through providing *employment and training* for disadvantaged youth . . . and *integrating them entirely to the society*" (YAPS, 2013, p. 6, emphasis added). YAPS also highlights the benefits for the Albanian government in its transition to a "free market" system: "As a business, YAPS has also resulted in two additional benefits: a *decrease in government welfare expenditures* and *increase in tax revenues*. Once employed by YAPS, youth are not eligible for cash benefits and assistance programs. Therefore, they are *no longer dependent on welfare*, and they have become *tax payers, active contributors to the State*" (YAPS, 2013, p. 14, emphasis added).

Other actors similarly appear to focus on the economic impact and credentials of YAPS. When introducing the different actors that helped YAPS to start up, the program flags UNICEF as the actor that "kept the focus on the 'social' aspect of social business" (YAPS, 2013, p. 4). However, for UNICEF (2001, p. 2), it appears that integration of youth into the "*free market*" is the "social" goal (emphasis added). That is, while UNICEF focuses on social impact, it is again the ability of YAPS to provide employment— integrating people into the capitalist market as productive workers—which is considered to be the means by which YAPS creates social impact.

"YAPS social businesses promote the novel concept of using the efficiency and in-built sustainability of *free markets to generate social wealth*. Through the instrumentality of commercial enterprise individuals previously considered liabilities of the State . . . have been translated into *wage earners contributing financially* to the state and producers of *social profits* that are re-directed toward social needs. In addition, and perhaps the greatest contribution to social wealth creation is the powerful effect on *deconstructing social stigmas* against the disadvantaged, minorities, disabled and homeless . . . as a result of *participating in productive work experiences*" (UNICEF, 2001, p. 2, emphasis added).

The board of YAPS is primarily composed of executives from its MNC clients, which, Shamia argues, enables their business expertise to benefit the social enterprise. It also gives YAPS access to other high-profile clients, thus providing it with a competitive advantage. The employees of YAPS have no direct involvement in this board (apart from input into how YAPS spends its charitable donations) and thus there is a clear hierarchical delineation between the employees and the executive. While some employees do have an opportunity to become involved in the "office work" of managing the daily operations of the social enterprise, they are ultimately subordinate to the decisions and direction of the board members. Rather than being conscientious about democracy in the workplace and how to challenge economic power imbalances, then, the youths are taught how to be effective capitalist workers.

Supporting a Transition Agenda?

Unlike nonprofit organizations that have adopted a social enterprise element, the daily operations of YAPS are less influenced by donors and more influenced by the business orientation of their primary clients and board members—MNCs. However, the ideologies of key powerful actors in Albania—namely the government and the EU—can arguably also be seen to influence the underlying norms of actors involved with YAPS (as appear to be presented in their public transcripts).

YAPS appears to fulfill the "ideal type" for the Albania's government: it is a WISE with "social business" origins (not previously an NGO) which is financially self-sustainable and has a "good" but not close relationship with the government, according to Shamia. The EU similarly promotes the role of WISE in the Balkans, with a focus on employment of marginalized groups in particular. For the executive board members of YAPS, their involvement with the social enterprise gives them Corporate Social Responsibility credentials with the EU and other powerful international bodies. While the nondemocratic governance model of YAPS seems at odds with the EU's promotion of democratic governance, this is still in line with the Belgrade Declaration's alternative definition.

The motivations and underlying ideological orientation of actors in YAPS are influenced by a variety of actors with their own objectives. Arguably, the transition discourse—as the medium through which the benefits of YAPS are expressed—is dominant, as explored in the "economic impact" focus of the public transcripts presented earlier. Importantly, however, this does not mean that YAPS cannot have some role to play in a "middle way."

Revealing Hidden "Social Impact" Discourses

First, as mentioned in the earlier quote by UNICEF, one of YAPS's goals is to deconstruct social stigmas against marginalized groups. According to UNICEF's (2001, p. 2, emphasis added) public transcript, this is done by enabling young people to participate in *"productive work experiences."* In the context of the text, it is implied that "working" makes youths valuable members of society, in both their own eyes and in the eyes of broader society, and it is this increased perceived "value" of the youths—as provided by their role in the capitalist marketplace—which reduces social stigma. This, arguably, is a neoliberal interpretation for how YAPS creates social impact. Alternatively, one of the less promoted initiatives of YAPS, which has the same social objective of diminishing social stigma, is via youth community building.

Every 3 months, according to Shamia, YAPS creates a social event for their employees, the point of which is to break down the barriers (and stereotypes) between the groups of youths they employ. These outings aim to bring together young men and women from a variety of disadvantaged backgrounds—Roma communities, lower income households, the disabled, etc.—and create a community or "family" environment through norm-building and practical measures (e.g., sports days, picnics, joint training, functions). In doing so, this challenges ingrained prejudices, encourages the youths to cooperate, and broadens their world view concerning marginalized "others."

Similarly, YAPS attempts to challenge gender norms within its daily operations. It does so, according to Shamia, by deliberately encouraging both male and female youths to train for delivery, repairs, and cleaning services. The practice of young women training for bike deliveries and young men training for cleaning service takes them outside their traditional gender roles and challenges their beliefs concerning their gendered position in society.

It is not the efficacy (or lack thereof) of these strategies that is of most interest here, but rather the fact that these social goals are not publicly advertised by YAPS. They were only mentioned during an in-depth interview with the executive manager and only elaborated on through further questioning by the interviewer. These social goals of YAPS potentially create social impacts that do not contribute to or conform with a neoliberal transition agenda role for social enterprise, but instead exemplify the type of roles that a "middle way" actor might provide. A "middle way" social enterprise actor, for example, could focus on how its activities might help to re-embed economic initiatives within community building and/or maintenance, such as using employee training to break down social barriers. Could YAPS, then, be inadvertently (or perhaps covertly) attempting to include objectives which do not conform to a narrow transition ideology for social enterprises? Determining the answer to such questions with only public transcripts, as we conclude next, is a hazardous undertaking.

DISCUSSION AND CONCLUSION

Public transcripts do not necessarily provide a comprehensive picture of the motivations and worldviews of actors. A social entrepreneur may concentrate on the financial sustainability of the social enterprise in an annual report or interview due to pressure to be perceived as pro-market while engaging in "hidden transcripts" concerning resistance to such priorities (Scott, 1990; see also Dey & Teasdale, 2016; Teasdale & Dey, 2019). Meanwhile, neoliberal actors may at times strategically prioritize "social capital" or "empowerment" in their public communications while still allocating funding based on "economic impact" indicators concerning, for example, the financial viability of projects. Furthermore, institutions and enterprises are not simply groups of homogeneous actors with single, static goals and ideologies, and thus the discourses arising from these groups may at times be inconsistent and/or reflect competing interpretations of the organization's cultural identity (or "institutional logics"; see Pache & Santos, 2013).

It is difficult to gauge then, even with in-depth interviews, why a particular discourse is used by an actor: Does it accurately reflect their current worldview? Or is it a pragmatic public transcript to appease supporters? A means of gaining legitimacy (e.g., a form of "tactical mimicry" viz. Dey & Teasdale [2016])? While the "true" answers to these questions are complex and arguably undiscoverable, it is enlightening to explore the differences between the public discourses surrounding social enterprises and the activities they are engaged in. It has been shown that there are several social objectives that YAPS attempts to enact, for example, which are not advertised by the social enterprise itself or its supporters, but which, arguably, further the aim of delivering a fairer, more inclusive society rather than exclusively economic growth.

Indeed, the example of YAPS encourages us to look beyond the public transcripts of other social enterprises in Eastern Europe to discover how they, too, might be enacting a broader role than is at first apparent. For social enterprise to contribute to a "middle way," though, more attention to and valuing of social (non–financially focused) goals is needed. For social enterprises themselves, this could consist of identifying and celebrating their activities that address disadvantage and, perhaps more importantly, how their own structures may challenge conventional business models. The difficulty with this, though, is the hidden and overt agendas of more powerful actors. If a transition ideology sits behind funding choices for social enterprises in Albania, then those that promote their business credentials will be more likely to survive and set the norm. Currently, these trends are insufficiently studied through critical analysis, and, without further exploration of the political influences in the Albanian social enterprise field, these tensions will remain hidden.

The research implications of this study extend beyond Albania to encompass Eastern Europe more broadly. While there is a broad range of research into social enterprises in other transition countries, there is a general dearth of political analysis that critically explores the agendas of powerful actors and the responses—both overt and hidden—of social enterprise actors.

Dey and Steyaert (2012, p. 91), when stressing the necessity for critique in social enterprise and social entrepreneurship scholarship, argue that critique is not an end in itself but rather serves as a "means to creating things (both imaginative and real), which are not possible within the matrix of the present" (see also Humphries & Grant, 2005; Kay, Roy, & Donaldson, 2016). Critical research is vital if we are to understand the influence of powerful discourses in the field and ensure that social enterprises are not set up to fail or—even worse—to advance an agenda that is the opposite of what they were created to do. We have seen that Albania is in the process of moving on from a very difficult past, and it is imperative that possibilities for social development are not foreclosed because of too firm a market focus. Indeed, this is an important lesson for social and economic development in transition economies in general.

NOTES

1. Reference to "transition" in this chapter indicates the normative neoliberal position that post-communist countries ideally ought to move toward (i.e., transition to an unregulated capitalist market economy or "free market" economy). The "free market" or neoliberal ideology involves expansion and intensification of markets while minimizing the role of government. See Harvey (2007).
2. In line with Karl Polanyi (1957) and his "substantive economy," we adopt the view that the economy is composed of modes of exchange, reciprocity, and redistribution. The term "exchange market economy" is used to indicate the component of the economy in which capitalist businesses are presumed to act (i.e., trading—exchanging goods/services for money) on the market. See Roy and Hackett (2017) for more on a Polanyian perspective of social enterprise.
3. The phrase "exclusionary prioritization" is used in this study to indicate that one concept (e.g., economic impact) is prioritized while another (e.g., social impact) is diminished or excluded.
4. The first of these was the conference The Challenges and Opportunities for Employment of Marginalized Groups by Social Enterprises organized by Partners Albania from Albania and Konekt from Macedonia, on April 20, 2016. The second

was an international scientific colloquium, Solidarity in Transition? Researching Social Enterprise in Post-Communist Societies, funded by the RRPP Western Balkans, which took place on April 21–22, 2016.

5. The EU's attempt to create a Single Market and its expansion to include post-communist states is arguably a continued (if altered) form of neoliberal transition in Eastern Europe. See Shields (2011).

6. The social enterprise was initially called the Youth Albania Parcel Services.

REFERENCES

Alter, S. K. (2007). *Social enterprise typology*. Virtue Ventures LLC. http://www.4lenses. org/setypology

Borzaga, C., & Spear, R. (2004). *Trends and challenges for co-operatives and social enterprises in developed and transition countries*. Trento: Edizioni31.

Bradley, R. L., & Donway, R. (2010). Capitalism, socialism, and the middle way: A taxonomy. *The Independent Review*, 15(1), 71–87.

Dart, R. (2004). The legitimacy of social enterprise. *Nonprofit Management and Leadership*, 14(4), 411–424. doi: https://doi.org/10.1002/nml.43

Defourny, J. (2009, June). *Concepts and realities of social enterprise: A European perspective*. Presented at the Second Research Colloquium on Social Entrepreneurship, Duke University, Durham, NC.

Defourny, J., & Nyssens, M. (2010). Conceptions of social enterprise and social entrepreneurship in Europe and the United States: Convergences and divergences, *Journal of Social Entrepreneurship*, 1(1), 32–53. doi: 10.1080/ 19420670903442053

Defourny, J., & Nyssens, M. (2012). *The EMES approach of social enterprise in a comparative perspective*. EMES Working Papers 12/03. https://emes.net/content/ uploads/publications/EMES-WP-12-03_Defourny-Nyssens.pdf

Dey, P., & Steyaert, C. (2012). Social entrepreneurship: Critique and the radical enactment of the social. *Social Enterprise Journal*, 8(2), 90–107. doi: 10.1108/ 17508611211252828

Dey, P., & Teasdale, S. (2016). The tactical mimicry of social enterprise strategies: Acting as if in the everyday life of third sector organizations. *Organization*, 23(4), 485–504. doi: 10.1177/1350508415570689

Drayton, W. (2002). The citizen sector: Becoming as entrepreneurial and competitive as business. *California Management Review*, 44(3), 120–132.

Eaton, J., & Roshi, E. (2014). Chiseling away at a concrete legacy: Engaging with communist-era heritage and memory in Albania. *Journal of Field Archaeology*, 39(3), 312–319. doi: 10.1179/0093469014Z.00000000084

Eikenberry, A. M., & Kluver, J. D. (2004). The marketization of the nonprofit sector: Civil society at risk? *Public Administration Review*, 64(2), 132–140. doi: 10.1111/j.1540-6210.2004.00355.x

Emerson, J. (2003). The blended value proposition. *California Management Review*, 45(4), 35–51.

EMES. (2011). *EMES Position Paper on the Social Business Initiative Communication*. Liege, Belgium: EMES. Retrieved from http://emes.net/publications/other-texts/emes-position-papers/emes-position-paper-on-the-social-business-initiative-communication/

European Commission. (2014). *The social business initiative of the European Commission.* Retrieved from https://ec.europa.eu/docsroom/documents/14583/attachments/3/translations/en/renditions/native

Garrow, E. E., & Hasenfeld, Y. (2014). Social enterprises as an embodiment of a neoliberal welfare logic. *American Behavioral Scientist, 58*(11), 1475–1493. doi: 10.1177/0002764214534674

Gibson-Graham, J. K. (2008). Diverse economies: Performative practices for other worlds. *Progress in Human Geography, 32*(5), 613–632. doi: 10.1177/0309132508090821

Harvey, D. (2007). *A brief history of neoliberalism.* Oxford, UK: Oxford University Press.

Haugh, H. (2006). Social enterprise: Beyond economic outcomes and individual returns. In J. Mair, J. A. Robinson, & K. Hockerts (Eds.), *Social entrepreneurship* (pp. 180–205). New York: Palgrave Macmillan.

Haugh, H., & Kitson, M. (2007). The third way and the third sector: New Labour's economic policy and the social economy. *Cambridge Journal of Economics, 31*(6), 973–994. doi: 10.1093/cje/bem027

Hoxha, J., & Haska, E. (2019). *Analysis of the legal framework on social enterprises in Albania.* Tirana: Partners Albania. Retrieved from https://partnersalbania.org/wp-content/uploads/2019/07/Analyses-of-legal-framework-on-social-enterprises-in-Albania.pdf

Humphries, M., & Grant, S. (2005). Social enterprise and re-civilization of human endeavors: Re-socializing the market metaphor or encroaching colonization of the lifeworld? *Current Issues in Comparative Education, 8*(1), 41–50.

Jørgensen, M. W., & Phillips, L. J. (2002). *Discourse analysis as theory and method.* Thousand Oaks, CA: Sage.

Kay, A., Roy, M. J., & Donaldson, C. (2016). Re-imagining social enterprise. *Social Enterprise Journal, 12*(2), 217–234. doi: 10.1108/SEJ-05-2016-0018

Koford, K. (1997). Why the ex-communist countries should take the middle way to the market economy. *Eastern Economic Journal, 23*(1), 31–50.

Lambru, M., & Galera, G. (2015, July). *An emerging policy space for social enterprises in Central and Eastern European countries?* Presented at the 5th EMES International Research Conference on Social Enterprise, Helsinki.

Lucas, J., & Vardanyan, A. (2005). *Social enterprises: An Eastern European experience.* Ann Arbor, MI: The William Davidson Institute at the University of Michigan Business School. Retrieved from http://www2.apra.am/upload/Social%20Enterprises.pdf

NBS. (2014). *Social enterprise, social innovation and social entrepreneurship in Albania: A national report.* Tirana, Albania: Government of Albania.

Pache, A.-C., & Santos, F. (2013). Inside the hybrid organization: Selective coupling as a response to competing institutional logics. *Academy of Management Journal, 56*(4), 972–1001. doi: 10.5465/amj.2011.0405

Partners Albania. (2013). *Development of social enterprises: Potential for job creation for disadvantaged groups.* Tirana: Partners Albania. Retrieved from https://partnersalbania.org/wp-content/uploads/2015/12/development_social_enterprises.pdf

Partners Albania. (2016). *Challenges and opportunities for employment of marginalized groups by social enterprises.* Partners Albania. Retrieved from https://partnersalbania.org/publication/challenges-and-opportunities-for-employment-of-marginalized-groups-by-social-enterprises/

Peet, R. (2003). *Unholy trinity: The IMF, World Bank and WTO.* London: Zed Books.

Pickles, J., & Smith, A. (2005). *Theorizing transition: The political economy of post-communist transformations*. London: Routledge.

Polanyi, K. (1957). The economy as instituted process. In K. Polanyi, C. M. Arensberg, & H. W. Pearson (Eds.), *Trade and market in the early empires: Economies in history and theory* (pp. 243–269). Glencoe, IL: Free Press.

Ridley-Duff, R., & Bull, M. (2011). *Understanding social enterprise: Theory & practice*. London: SAGE.

Rosandic, A., & Kusinikova, N. (2018). *Country report - Albania* (Social Economy in Eastern Neighbourhood and in the Western Balkans). Brussels: EU Directorate-General for Neighbourhood and Enlargement Negotiations (DG NEAR). Retrieved from https://ec.europa.eu/growth/content/social-economy-eastern-neighbourhood-and-western-balkans_en

Roy, M. J., Donaldson, C., Baker, R., & Kay, A. (2013). Social enterprise: New pathways to health and well-being? *Journal of Public Health Policy, 34*(1), 55–68. doi: 10.1057/jphp.2012.61

Roy, M. J., & Hackett, M. T. (2017). Polanyi's substantive approach to the economy in action? Conceptualising social enterprise as a public health intervention. *Review of Social Economy, 75*(2), 89–111. doi: 10.1080/00346764.2016.1171383

Ruebottom, T. (2013). The microstructures of rhetorical strategy in social entrepreneurship: Building legitimacy through heroes and villains. *Journal of Business Venturing, 28*(1), 98–116. doi: 10.1016/j.jbusvent.2011.05.001

Scott, J. C. (1990). *Domination and the arts of resistance: Hidden transcripts*. New Haven, CT: Yale University Press.

Shields, S. (2012). *The international political economy of transition: Neoliberal hegemony and eastern Central Europe's transformation*. London: Routledge.

TACSO. (2013). *Social economy in Albania - A survey on social enterprises*. Tirana: Technical Assistance for Civil Society Organizations (TACSO). Retrieved from http://www.civilsocietylibrary.org/csl/413/social-economy-in-albania-a-survey-on-social-enterprises

Teasdale, S. (2012). What's in a name? Making sense of social enterprise discourses, *Public Policy and Administration, 27*(2), 99–119. doi: 10.1177/0952076711401466

Teasdale, S., & Dey, P. (2019). Neoliberal governing through social enterprise: Exploring the neglected roles of deviance and ignorance in public value creation. *Public Administration*. doi: 10.1111/padm.12588

UNDP. (2008). *Social enterprise: A new model for poverty reduction and employment generation*. New York: United Nations Development Programme. Retrieved from https://www.undp.org/content/undp/en/home/librarypage/poverty-reduction/inclusive_development/social_enterpriseanewmodelforpovertyreductionandemploymentgenera.html

UNICEF. (2001). *Rehabilitation of vulnerable groups through social business schemes in countries in transition: The YAPS case study*. Retrieved from http://www.unicef.org/albania/YAPScasestudy.pdf

UN Women. (2019). First social enterprises in Albania to boost the employment of women and disadvantaged groups. Retrieved from https://albania.unwomen.org/en/news-and-events/stories/2019/05/first-social-enterprises-in-albania

Weber, H. (2010). Politics of global social relations: Organising everyday lived experiences of development and destitution. *Australian Journal of International Affairs, 64*(1), 105–122. doi: 10.1080/10357710903460048

World Bank. (2019). *Albania: Overview*. Washington, DC: World Bank. Retrieved from http://www.worldbank.org/en/country/albania/overview

YAPS. (2013). *YAPS - Youth Albania Professional Services*. Retrieved from https://prezi.com/dd3n2cmb6ayw/yaps-youth-albania-professional-services/

Ymeraj, A., & Qosja, E. (2015, September). *Boosting growth through social business in former communist countries: A state's or a market's function - the case of Albania*. Presented at the XXXVI Conferenza Italiana Di Scienze Regionali, University of Calabria, Italy.

Yunus, M. (2009). *Creating a world without poverty: Social business and the future of capitalism*. Philadelphia: Public Affairs.

Zahra, S. A., Gedajlovic, E., Neubaum, D. O., & Shulman, J. M. (2009). A typology of social entrepreneurs: Motives, search processes and ethical challenges. *Journal of Business Venturing, 24*(5), 519–532. doi: 10.1016/j.jbusvent.2008.04.007

CHAPTER 9

⌇⌇

Redefining Silk Roads

Social Businesses and Crafts as Approaches for Improving Women's Situations in Central Asia

JILDYZ URBAEVA

The concept of social entrepreneurship is new in Central Asian countries. However, despite its novelty, social entrepreneurship represents a promising vehicle for achieving sustainable outcomes in a region that is still developing competitive business environments. Crafts make up a small-business sector that is developing dynamically in Central Asia, and this chapter argues that they can be used for developing social businesses as well as for advancing women's agendas. This chapter outlines information about existing initiatives toward and difficulties in developing crafts and related social businesses, in addition to highlighting potential driving factors in the process.

Social entrepreneurship scholars argued that international development projects have not achieved sustainability because they have typically been driven by donors' agendas (Bornstein & Davis, 2010). However, several factors suggest that crafts is a sector that has the potential to offer sustainable social businesses in Central Asia. First, crafts do not require external expertise: craftswomen and men are the experts on local handiworks, and therefore related social businesses will not require extensive expertise

Jildyz Urbaeva, *Redefining Silk Roads* In: *Social Entrepreneurship and Enterprises in Economic and Social Development.*
Edited by: Katharine Briar-Lawson, Paul Miesing, and Blanca M. Ramos, Oxford University Press (2021).
© Oxford University Press. DOI: 10.1093/oso/9780197518298.003.0010.

from abroad. Some technologies related to the production of craft merchandise, particularly equipment, can represent challenges for developing social businesses, but overall crafts production relies on tested and relatively inexpensive techniques. Second, on a global level, there is an increased interest in natural and organic products and food: locally crafted goods in Central Asia can respond to this demand since they use natural textiles such as cotton, felt, silk, and wool. Third, social businesses based on crafts can provide employment opportunities for disadvantaged women in the region. Fourth, profits received from craft trade can be reinvested toward expanding social businesses and can also be used for social causes. Finally, the existing evidence, although limited, shows that crafts groups led by women also serve the "social consciousness" purpose suggested by Muhammad Yunus: that is, private sector enterprises driven by social purposes (Yunus & Jolis, 1999). Experts assert that many crafts businesses are created with the goal of providing employment opportunities for low-income individuals (G. Dzhunushalieva, personal communication, July 12, 2017). Crafts in Central Asia are the product of local cultures, and, as such, they are bound to local economic and social conditions. Communities where women-led crafts groups work can thereby benefit from the income generated by women and the support of such groups regarding local issues.

HISTORY OF SILK ROADS

The concept of the Silk Road usually evokes images of ancient roads, caravans with camels, riders, steppes, and deserts, and, most of all, incredible treasures from the East: textiles, ivory, jewels, and other merchandise associated with luxury and opulence. More erudite readers might imagine caravanserais, ancient oases, the conquests of Alexander the Great, and names of ancient kingdoms that no longer exist. Historically, merchandise from the East was transported to the West over land, and later over sea, by fearless merchants from territories bounded by modern Japan, Italy, Siberia, and Sri Lanka (Akiner, 1992). Merchants had to overcome countless dangers to deliver their goods to European trade centers, but they were able to sell the silk and other products for exorbitant prices.

However, the term "Silk Road" is not strictly accurate nor contemporary with the era it evokes: rather, it came to life relatively recently, despite the millennia-long trade history between the East and West, when Baron Ferdinand von Richthofen coined the term in his geographic works during the 19th century (Masuda, 1992). The Silk Road is a metaphor denoting ancient trade connections between East and West (Akiner, 1992).

It represented a network of land and maritime routes for trade between the eastern and western portions of the Eurasian landmass. And while travelers of the Silk Road had to face multiple difficulties during their travels, they also had opportunities to plan their routes (Hansen, 2017), at least in some territories.

To many people, the Silk Road represents the rich material wealth of historical cities, kingdoms, and territories overlaying trade routes. Commercial activity was, among many other exchanges, facilitated by road networks. For example, movements across trade routes facilitated transfers of technology, such as paper or silk, from East to West. Equally exciting were the constant cultural exchanges and influences occurring along these roads. Scholars indicate that, in addition to trade, technological and cultural exchanges were happening for centuries; great empires emerged and disintegrated along the way, and different actors controlled the trade networks over the course of history (Dani, 1992). The territories that made up the Silk Road have always participated in globalization as a consequence of these cultural, commercial, and technological exchanges.

Territories that now belong to modern Central Asian countries, including Kazakhstan, Kyrgyzstan, Tajikistan, Turkmenistan, and Uzbekistan, were historically part of the trade routes that made up the legendary Silk Road. Although the volume of trade operations through these roads is a contested issue among scholars because of a lack of written and material evidence (Hansen, 2017), the territories of modern Central Asian states were certainly involved in trade as well as in cultural and scientific exchanges with other parts of the globe. Sogdiana, an ancient Central Asian civilization that existed around 200 BC and through the 7th and 8th centuries AD, was centered in Uzbekistan's Samarkand and other cities of modern Uzbekistan and traded with China (Hansen, 2017). Modern Tajikistan's Khujand was first founded by Alexander the Great as a Greek settlement, and it later became a part of the northern Silk Road (Meller, 2013).

Volumes on Central Asian crafts published by reputable museums and experts (Fitz Gibbon & Hale, 1997; Meller, 2013; Watt & Wardwell, 1997) demonstrate that Central Asia has been and remains a region with a rich material culture. However, crafts saw a significant revival as trade goods after the disintegration of the Soviet Union: for example, domestic items of felt made by Kyrgyz women were made only for domestic use until recently (Bunn, 2011). In post-Soviet Central Asia, craft products have become popular among locals and visitors alike: students, businesspeople, scientists, and tourists visiting the region now leave with gifted or purchased goods that are hand-made by local craftswomen and men. Small businesses also developed because of trade proliferation, and some now successfully sell craft products such as rugs, souvenirs, clothes, and other items in Europe and North America.

CENTRAL ASIAN WOMEN IN BUSINESS

The total labor force in four Central Asian countries—Kazakhstan, Kyrgyzstan, Tajikistan, and Uzbekistan—is approximately 30 million people (World Bank, 2016). However, women have lower rates of participation in the labor market compared to men. As of 2016, the female percentage of the total labor force varied between 40.3% and 49% in these countries (World Bank, 2016). Concerning women's participation in business, the rates vary across the region (World Bank, 2012). In Kazakhstan and Tajikistan, the share of companies with women participation in ownership was 34%. In Uzbekistan, this percentage was 40%, and Kyrgyzstan reported the highest rate of firms with female ownership at 60% (World Bank, 2012). While rates of women's participation in ownership varied across the region, the percentages of women in top managerial positions within business sectors were significantly lower: 11% in Uzbekistan, 12% in Tajikistan, 23% in Kyrgyzstan, and 25% in Kazakhstan (World Bank, 2012). Furthermore, only 1.1% of all employed women in Europe and Central Asia are employers (Sattar, 2012). While Central Asian women's participation in the labor market is comparable to developed countries, their participation and influence in the private sector remains low overall.

Gender differences in productivity and earnings remain widespread across all regions of the world (World Bank, 2011). Research shows that these gender differences can be attributed to differing access to resources, such as land and credit (World Bank, 2011). Women entrepreneurs report more barriers to obtaining loans for their businesses compared to men (Sattar, 2012). Women are also less productive in labor markets and businesses because they often choose temporary jobs or positions with flexible work hours and tend to have interruptions in their employment trajectories due to childcare commitments and household responsibilities (World Bank, 2011).

The businesses that women tend to run in the region generally center around the small-scale production of goods, retail/trade, handicrafts, and the sewing and garment industries (Asian Development Bank [ADB], 2013, 2014; World Bank, 2012). Many women in the region are involved in the shuttle trade, transporting goods from one country to another: however, while this offers low entry costs for women (ADB, 2013), women also report gender-specific difficulties that arise in running cross-border businesses (ADB, 2014).

Gender differences in business sectors can be explained by the unique barriers that women face when making decisions about their careers and the limited opportunities available for developing their businesses. Women entrepreneurs tend to be concentrated in textile and garments sectors, and the companies they lead tend to be smaller scale and have more constraints in terms of capital accessibility (Sattar, 2012), leading to fewer opportunities to expand and generate higher profits. While gender-based discrimination may play a role in the lack of woman-led business advancement, women also make voluntary decisions about labor market participation that reduce their rate of participation (Sattar, 2012).

Kazakhstani women are wellrepresented in small enterprises and microbusinesses (ADB, 2013). In Uzbekistan and Tajikistan, women are less likely to be employed in the private sector (ADB, 2014; World Bank, 2013). In Kazakhstan, women entrepreneurs report that market and retail trade attract them because employment in informal sectors gives them the opportunity to combine income-generating activity with childcare and household responsibilities (ADB, 2013). Businesses also benefit from the relatively low cost of entering the informal market (ADB, 2013) since women do not need specialized training or certification to start small businesses.

However, in Uzbekistan, there are not many opportunities for women to develop their own businesses, so while some are able to save up enough money to start their own companies, many choose to migrate to Russia and Kazakhstan and pursue opportunities there (ADB, 2014). Unlike in Kazakhstan, Uzbekistani women report multiple barriers to developing small businesses, such as informal payments associated with licensing and inspections, a lack of access to financial and physical assets, loan procedures, and a lack of collateral available for commercial loans (ADB, 2014). Similarly, Tajikistani women's involvement in the private sector is limited (World Bank, 2013). Running a small business is difficult in general, and for women the constraints on developing businesses include a lack of access to credit, a lack of collateral (as women's names are not included in the list of family property owners), and a lack of education and learned skills (World Bank, 2013). However, microcrediting is becoming popular in Tajikistan, and, interestingly, women have so far tended to prefer group loans (World Bank, 2013). More experienced women also manage to re-lend money to other women who would not have access to credit otherwise (World Bank, 2013). Gulnara Dzhunushalieva has indicated that, unlike most businesses in the for-profit sector, woman-led companies in Central

Asia are very active in social entrepreneurship projects (G. Dzhunushalieva, personal communication, July 12, 2017). Since many of these projects are supported by international organizations, there is a strong motivation to ensure gender balance and women-oriented support within these ventures.

POLICY FRAMEWORKS FOR SOCIAL BUSINESSES

The terms "social entrepreneurship" and "social businesses" are not included in national legislation and, therefore, there are no policies that address social entrepreneurship directly. The legislative and policy frameworks for social businesses and crafts are underdeveloped in each country of the region. However, this does not mean that these businesses cannot be realized: social businesses can be implemented through nonprofit sector organizations, such as public foundations and community organizations, as well as through small and medium enterprises.

Nongovernmental and nonprofit organizations represent a large segment of social entrepreneurship projects (Dzhunushalieva, 2016). Dzhunushalieva, who is an expert on social entrepreneurship, has detailed the many differences in policy environments across Central Asian countries (G. Dzhunushalieva, personal communication, July 12, 2017). For instance, most nonprofit organizations in Kyrgyzstan benefit from international development funding, while in Kazakhstan nonprofit organizations are supported by local foundations, and in Tajikistan most projects are implemented by international development organizations (G. Dzhunushalieva, personal communication, July 12, 2017). Favorable policy factors include the fact that many nonprofit sector activities are tax exempt, and additional income can be reinvested by agencies involved in social entrepreneurship projects.

While the policy framework is lagging behind, there are mechanisms in place that can help artisans to market and sell their products, as well as provide the representation they need to advocate on their behalf to government stakeholders. European Union (EU) projects in Central Asia have supported the development of business intermediary organizations (BIOs) for artisans (European Commission, 2015). Organizations that can perform the role of BIOs are business associations, artisan unions, business clubs, and chambers of commerce. In Central Asia, artisans are supported by international nonprofit organizations such as the Special Agency of the Chamber of Commerce of Florence, Union of Craftsmen of Tajikistan, Bishkek Business Club, and others (Central Asian Handicraft, n.d.). These organizations help artisanal groups, often represented by women, to organize their crafts and business procedures and market their products—operations and skills that would be difficult for artisans to attain otherwise. In terms of funding, there are opportunities for concessional loans and grants from commercial banks for nonprofit organizations (G. Dzhunushalieva, personal communication, July 12, 2017).

THE CASE FOR WOMEN'S AGENDAS

It is important to consider social businesses within the economic and social context of their locality. World Bank data show that considerable numbers of people in Central Asia live in poverty: as of 2013, 34% of people in Tajikistan and 37% of people in Kyrgyzstan lived in poverty (World Bank, 2016). While the poverty rate is lower in Uzbekistan and Kazakhstan, the two largest economies in the region, overall human development indicators in countries of the region show the need for improved policies and investments in women's well-being. As health and demographic surveys show, Central Asian women have large families and have more children than most other post-Soviet nations. Many live in joint households with parents-in-law. Research demonstrates that living in joint families reduces women's autonomy in regard to making decisions related to household chores, such as purchases and visits to maternal relatives. A lack of household autonomy may be related to negative outcomes for women's health, as women are unable to make optimal decisions pertaining to their own or their children's healthcare (Furuta & Salway, 2006; Mistry, Galal, & Lu, 2009). Often women have to negotiate or request the permission of a mother-in-law and husband to seek out healthcare or use family resources for their children's needs (Allendorf, 2017; Fotso, Ezeh, & Essendi, 2009). Maternal mortality remains high in Central Asia, and it is likely that women's inferior position within the family affects their health-seeking behaviors. Protective factors that increase women's autonomy within the family are education, ownership of land and other property, and independent income.

In rural areas of Central Asia, many women are unemployed, have higher fertility rates than their peers in cities, and are more likely to live in joint households. In remote rural areas, formal employment opportunities are extremely limited for women. The lack of jobs and poor transport infrastructure leave few options for women to obtain gainful employment. In many cases they work on family land plots or engage in microtrade. This poor economic foundation does not allow women to invest in and enjoy the benefits of human development potential, such as healthcare, education for their children, and the freedom to make independent decisions for their own and their children's well-being. Muhammad Yunus (2011) inspired many people throughout the world with his model of social business for the poor. However, women-led social businesses in Central Asia would need a lot of external support to help such businesses break out of the cycle of poverty and evolve into profitable and sustainable ventures.

CASE STUDIES

In this chapter, we limit the definition of social entrepreneurship to social businesses as defined by Muhammad Yunus: "In a social business an investor aims to help others without making any financial gain himself. The SB is a business because it must be self-sustaining—that is, it generates enough income to cover its own costs. We can think about a SB as a selfless business whose purpose is to bring an end to a social problem. The company makes profit but no one takes the profit" (Yunus, 2011, p. xvii). According to an existing typology of socially engaged organizations in post-Soviet countries, few of these organizations are involved in social entrepreneurships and social businesses (Dzhunushalieva, 2016). We postulate that the cases described in this chapter have characteristics of social businesses because they aim to provide income to disadvantaged women in the labor market, they improve the social status of the women involved in the project, and some project activities serve a social purpose.

The following paragraphs describe two promising projects aimed at supporting women's crafts and entrepreneurial skills in Kyrgyzstan and Tajikistan. The first project, Improving Livelihoods of Smallholders and Rural Women Through Value-Added Processing and Exports of Cashmere, Wool, and Mohair, was funded by the International Fund for Agricultural Development (IFAD) and was implemented by the International Center for Agricultural Research in the Dry Areas (ICARDA) and regional and local organizations involved in supporting crafts development in Central Asia. The second project, Handicraft and Business Through Regional Integration and Fair-Trade Market, was funded by the European Commission (EC) and was implemented by ICARDA and other partners.

Improving Livelihoods of Rural Women

The overall goal of this project was to improve the livelihoods and income of small livestock producers and rural women through improved production of fiber in some areas of Kyrgyzstan, Tajikistan, and Iran. One of the project components focused on organizing and empowering women in project sites (Regional Program for Sustainable Agricultural Development in Central Asia and the Caucasus [RPSADCAC], n.d.). In terms of crafts and women's empowerment, the project aimed to, first, improve local wool-processing technologies so women could use the wool to make craft products; second, link women's groups producing wool crafts to local, regional, and foreign markets; and third, increase income for project participants (Central Asian Crafts Support Association's Resource Centre in Kyrgyzstan (RPSADCAC, n.d.).

The project had a positive impact on the production of high-quality mohair from goats in northern Tajikistan and supported the development of the regional market for selling cashgora fiber for small producers in southern Tajikistan. In Kyrgyzstan, the project helped local farmers improve the quality of the wool generated from sheep. All these activities increased the income of local farmers and, importantly, had a positive impact on women's income. Women learned valuable new skills and earned income from mohair yarn production, spinning yarn from goats, processing wool, and making felt goods for sale (International Center for Agricultural Research in the Dry Areas [ICARDA], 2014).

Over the course of the project, women encountered barriers that impeded their businesses. Specifically, they struggled with the maintenance of craft equipment, which requires regular repairs and updates. Additionally, it was difficult to maintain groups of women who made products. One of the external barriers was the limited volume of sales, and women's groups decided to seek marketing opportunities outside the region to confront this problem (CACSARC-kg, 2011).

Women's social status also changed as a result of their involvement in the project. First, women became wage earners, and this increased their sense of self-worth and their status within their families. Women who lost their husbands to divorce, abandonment, or labor migration to Russia were able to support themselves and their children. Moreover, family members helped women in their work: they assisted with transport and maintaining equipment for crafts. Most importantly, women's skills to sustain their businesses also evolved. For example, women in one of the project sites reinvested their profits in the project to pay designers, purchase materials for crafts and instruments, and market outside the country (CACSARC-kg, 2013). One of the pilot groups in Kyrgyzstan provided jobs to poor women and mothers of children with disabilities in their felting workshop and allocated 20% of their profits to a local kindergarten (CACSARC-kg, n.d.).

Handicraft and Regional Integration

The goals of the project were to, first, support the development of the private sector in Kyrgyzstan and Tajikistan; second, build the capacity of BIOs; and third, enhance regional cooperation between handicraft organizations (CACSARC-kg & CESVI Tajikistan, n.d.). The project also aimed to increase the capacity of BIOs with the desired outcomes of influencing state policies and advocating for handicraft-based small and medium enterprises (SME), as well as assisting handicraft SMEs in reaching regional and foreign markets (CACSARC-kg & CESVI Tajikistan, n.d.).

The project teams conducted many activities to improve the legislative environment for crafts-based businesses in both countries (CACSARC-kg, 2014). They lobbied the governments of both countries to include crafts in the list of profitable goods so that SMEs could benefit from trade agreements and improved trade regulations. Because of project activities, more than 1,500 women in Tajikistan learned traditional embroidery techniques and other craft skills (European Commission, 2015). Additionally, craftswomen received training regarding designs and the quality of their products from Italian experts, which will help them market their goods to European customers (European Commission, 2015). The project supported work on 250 craft SMEs in Kyrgyzstan and Tajikistan (European Commission, 2015). Overall, 4,000 craftswomen and men benefited from the work of BIOs in the crafts sector (European Commission, 2015).

In terms of the direct impact of project activities on women, the project partners helped 30 Kyrgyzstani and 6 Tajikistani handicraft organizations to increase their sales and reach out to new markets (European Commission, 2015). Among other planned project activities are instructing crafts organizations in fair-trade principles: while fair trade focuses on issues of environmental, social, and economic justice, the involvement of Central Asian crafts organizations with global fair trade would have positive results for developing connections within retailer markets (Ferrioli, 2014).

IMPLICATIONS AND CONCLUSION

This chapter highlighted the potential of the crafts sector for developing social businesses. The review of literatures within the fields of history, development economics, and women's studies demonstrates potential for improving women's situations using social entrepreneurship models. Crafts can be a way to connect businesses and social causes in order to improve women's situations. There are many challenges to be overcome by the business sector, communities of artisans, and advocates for women. Nonetheless, projects assisting in these areas have a chance to make lasting contributions to regional development.

One of the lessons from the long history of the Silk Road is that Central Asian territories have been involved in trade throughout Eurasian territories for centuries. Currently, crafts are experiencing a new stage of development in Central Asia. The sale of these products can support the livelihoods of artisanal communities and improve women's well-being. The overall business environment should be improved in each country of the region. One of the challenges encountered by social entrepreneurs not only in Central Asia, but in other countries as well, is the lack of financing for social businesses (Bornstein & Davis, 2010). While governments in Central Asian countries are adopting social contracting approaches, it is still difficult to receive state funding for social businesses for a number of reasons, including limited funds, complicated application procedures, and a lack of transparent criteria for selection of recipient organizations. However, even in favorable environments, governments tend to focus on accountability and short-term results, and social businesses need more time to experiment and apply flexible approaches to achieve tangible outcomes (Bornstein & Davis, 2010). These tensions between state control and the entrepreneurial spirit of social businesses, along with the limited capacity of the state to provide financing, limit achievements in the area of social entrepreneurship in Central Asia.

There is a robust dialogue regarding the development of SMEs in the region among stakeholders, but more attention needs to be paid to challenges that women encounter in the business sector. Women's agendas should be integrated into policy dialogues, and specific measures should be developed for encouraging women's participation in businesses. An additional layer of concern for developing social entrepreneurship models within the crafts sector is the integration of artisanal groups into business communities. Crafts-based businesses are at the bottom of the small-business pyramid due to the lack of financing for developing businesses, lower profits, lack of standard operating procedures, and lack of marketing skills. The role of intermediary organizations is therefore essential for developing and sustaining crafts-based businesses. Despite the strong connection between crafts work and community issues, artisans need a lot of support.

In addition to policy and external support of women-led social businesses, the socioemotional aspects of entrepreneurial advancements of women are important to consider. First is the concept of individual and collective agency. Autonomy defined as "freedom from control of others" versus having power over other people has been described in theoretical works (Schlegel, 1977), and in the Central Asian context it is an especially relevant component of women's empowerment. Being able to make decisions pertaining to their own economic well-being will support the sustainable development of businesses oriented for social causes. Another socioemotional aspect that should be acknowledged in the process of developing social businesses is collective efficacy of women. The ability to take actions and control social, economic, and political environments is necessary for ensuring sustainable and locally driven social businesses led by women. While socioemotional outcomes cannot be controlled directly with policy measures, an overall supportive environment within family, community, and state will contribute to the development of women's collective autonomy and efficacy and, ultimately, to the development of social businesses.

Existing projects supporting crafts and, specifically, women's issues, demonstrate that women-led artisanal groups are intrinsically connected to social purposes, as it is often the case that women in crafts communities are vulnerable, disadvantaged women from rural areas, without connections and expertise in the market. These groups need support from the state as well as the international and business communities. Despite small profits, some women-led craft groups manage to reinvest in their businesses and support social causes, such as helping kindergartens and people with disabilities. Because crafts are so linked to local traditions and customs of mutual support, craftswomen have the potential to connect their work to social causes within their communities. These examples also show that innovation is not a prerequisite for social businesses: as Steven Anderson asserts, successful social businesses can be developed from existing ideas (Anderson, 2014).

These case studies have shown that women's groups are willing to learn new skills and earn income to support their families, and stakeholders with expertise and experience should support them. Some examples of concrete support would include the development of a list of merchandise made by artisans approved for sale. Opportunities for tax credits could be explored as well. Policy-makers worry that artisanal groups receiving assistance from the international community will not be able to sustain their work in the long term. The complex connections between business, crafts, and women's interests require meticulous and committed cooperation between many sectors. More socially oriented businesses should be developed in Central Asian countries, and more evidence is needed to improve outcomes for women involved in these projects.

REFERENCES

Akiner, S. (1992). Significance of Silk Roads today: Proposal for a historical atlas. *Senri Ethnological Studies*, *32*, 27–32. http://doi.org/10.15021/00003096

Allendorf, K. (2017). Like her own: Ideals and experiences of the mother-in-law/daughter-in-law relationship. *Journal of Family Issues*, *38*(15), 2102–2127. https://doi.org/10.1177%2F0192513X15590685

Anderson, S. G. (2014). *New strategies for social innovation: Market-based approaches for assisting the poor*. New York: Columbia University Press.

Asian Development Bank. (2013). *Kazakhstan: Country gender assessment*. Retrieved from https://goo.gl/XdEqxL

Asian Development Bank. (2014). *Uzbekistan: Country gender assessment*. Retrieved from https://goo.gl/cj9bmN

Bornstein, D., & Davis, S. (2010). *Social entrepreneurship: What everyone needs to know?* New York: Oxford University Press.

Bunn, S. (2011). A "making point of view": Deep knowledge from local practice, with special reference to felt-makers in Kyrgyzstan. *Journal of Museum Ethnography*, (24), 23–40.

Central Asian Crafts Support Association's Resource Centre in Kyrgyzstan (CACSARC-kg). (n.d.). *Project "Improving livelihoods of small holders and rural women through value-added processing and export of cashmere, wool and mohair"* (leaflet). Retrieved from https://goo.gl/yPr2sG

Central Asian Crafts Support Association's Resource Centre in Kyrgyzstan (CACSARC-kg). (2011). *Achievements of the project "Improving livelihoods of small farmers and rural women through value-added processing and export of cashmere, wool and mohair."* IFAD Grant 1107 [PowerPoint slides]. Retrieved from https://goo.gl/b5UyQX

Central Asian Crafts Support Association's Resource Centre in Kyrgyzstan (CACSARC-kg). (2013). *Achievements of the project "Improving livelihoods of small farmers and rural women through value-added processing and export of cashmere, wool and mohair."* IFAD Grant 1107 [PowerPoint slides]. Retrieved from https://goo.gl/JdwBAH

Dani, A. H. (1992). Significance of Silk Road to human civilization: Its cultural dimension. *Journal of Asian Civilizations*, *25*(1), 72–79. http://doi.org/10.15021/00003095

Dzhunushalieva, G. (2016). The establishment of social entrepreneurship movements as a response to the transformation of governments' social policies (the case of four EAEU countries). *Journal of Business and Economic Review*, *1*(1), 17–25.

European Commission. (2015). *Central Asia Invest Boosting small business competitiveness* (brochure). Retrieved from https://goo.gl/N4tp5H

Ferrioli, A. (2014). Assessment on Kyrgyz handicrafts and their potential for the European market. Retrieved from https://goo.gl/M5eJX1

Fitz Gibbon, K., & Hale, A. (1997). *Ikat: Splendid silks of Central Asia—the Guido Goldman collection*. London: Laurence King.

Fotso, J. C., Ezeh, A. C., & Essendi, H. (2009). Maternal health in resource-poor urban settings: How does women's autonomy influence the utilization of obstetric care services? *Reproductive Health*, *6*(9). http://dx.doi.org/10.1186/1742-4755-6-9

Furuta, M., & Salway, S. (2006). Women's position within the household as a determinant of maternal health care use in Nepal. *International Family Planning Perspectives*, *32*(1), 17–27.

Hansen, V. (2017). *The Silk Road: A new history*. New York: Oxford University Press.

International Center for Agricultural Research in the Dry Areas. (2014). *IFAD Grant 1107: Final technical report*. Retrieved from https://goo.gl/Es6e7F

Masuda, S. (1992). Behind the prosperity of Silk Road. *Senri Ethnological Studies*, (32), 37–43. http://doi.org/10.15021/00003098

Meller, S. (2013). *Silk and cotton: Textiles from the Central Asia that was*. New York: Abrams.

Mistry, R., Galal, O., & Lu, M. (2009). Women's autonomy and pregnancy care in rural India: A contextual analysis. *Social Science & Medicine, 69*(6), 926–933. https://doi.org/10.1016/j.socscimed.2009.07.008

Regional Program for Sustainable Agricultural Development in Central Asia and the Caucasus (n.d.). *Programme on improving livelihoods of small farmers and rural women through value-added processing and export of cashmere, wool and mohair*. IFAD Grant 1107. Retrieved from https://goo.gl/BhoqdL

Sattar, S. (2012). *Opportunities for men and women: Emerging Europe and Central Asia*. Washington, DC: World Bank.

Schlegel, A. (1977). Toward a theory of sexual stratification. *Sexual Stratification: A Cross-Cultural View,* 1–40. New York: Columbia University Press.

Watt, J. C., & Wardwell, A. E. (1997). *When silk was gold: Central Asian and Chinese textiles*. New York: Metropolitan Museum of Art.

World Bank. (2011). *World development report 2012: Gender, equality, and development*. Washington, DC: World Bank. Retrieved from https://goo.gl/gMuuLQ

World Bank. (2012). *Gender in Central Asia: A snapshot of key issues and indicators*. Washington, DC: World Bank. Retrieved from https://goo.gl/p9BFBQ

World Bank. (2016). *World development indicators, 2016 cohort* [Data file]. Retrieved from https://goo.gl/WdBQ51

Yunus, M. (2011). *Building social business: The new kind of capitalism that serves humanity's most pressing needs*. New York: Public Affairs.

Yunus, M., & Jolis, A. (1999). *Banker to the poor: Micro-lending and the battle against world poverty*. New York: Public Affairs.

CHAPTER 10

⌀⌀

Social Entrepreneurship and Corporate Social Responsibility in the Russian Federation

RUSLAN SADYRTDINOV

The concepts of *social entrepreneurship* and *corporate social responsibility* (CSR) are among the most popular and even "fashionable" business trends in Russia today, and I believe that they can be used for future social and economic transition in this country. As Pagè (2011) noted, the economic transition that began in Russia in 1992 consisted of two very different periods: 1992–1998 was unambiguously negative, with a drop in gross domestic product (GDP) from US$516 billion in 1990 to US$96 billion in 1999; 1998–2010 experienced a return to order and reconstruction, with growth in GDP at an annual average rate of 7% until 2009. Russia experienced two main economic shocks, the first in 2008–2009 (global financial crisis) and the second in 2014 (decline in oil prices and international tensions), but began to recover from recession in 2017 (growth of GDP at an annual rate of 1.7%). This chapter outlines some of the developments in Russia related to social business and CSR and the tools used to measure them. Recommendations in support of future developments in these spheres are offered as well.

Social entrepreneurs' activity accelerates social changes by influencing long-standing institutions or organizational spheres. The ability of social

Ruslan Sadyrtdinov, *Social Entrepreneurship and Corporate Social Responsibility in the Russian Federation* In: *Social Entrepreneurship and Enterprises in Economic and Social Development*. Edited by: Katharine Briar-Lawson, Paul Miesing, and Blanca M. Ramos, Oxford University Press (2021). © Oxford University Press.
DOI: 10.1093/oso/9780197518298.003.0011.

entrepreneurs to change established norms may be even more important than solving the problems that social entrepreneurship was originally aimed to impact. A promising approach to understanding the role of social entrepreneurship in changing or generating new public practices, institutions, and structures is *institutional entrepreneurship*.

To explain the process of the emergence or change of institutions in the process of entrepreneurial activity, DiMaggio introduced the concept of institutional entrepreneurship (DiMaggio, 1988). As Fligstein notes, *institutional entrepreneurs* are defined as actors interested in changing or creating new institutional structures; they accumulate resources to create new institutions or transform existing ones (Fligstein, 1997).

Views of social entrepreneurship as a process that catalyzes social change and addresses important social needs were put forward by Mair and Martí (2006). They see social entrepreneurship as differing from other forms of entrepreneurship in the relatively higher priority given to promoting social value and development versus capturing economic value (Mair & Martí, 2006).

An interesting concept of community-based enterprise was developed by Peredo and Chrisman. They maintain that in this emerging form of entrepreneurship, typically rooted in community culture, social capital is inseparable from economic considerations, thus transforming the community into an entrepreneurial venture (Peredo &Chrisman, 2006).

The mission to change society combined with the resourcefulness of traditional entrepreneurship as inherent characteristics of social entrepreneurship are confirmed by Seelos and Mair (2005). Moreover, they argue that because it contributes directly to internationally recognized sustainable development goals, social entrepreneurship may also encourage established corporations to take on greater social responsibility (Seelos & Mair, 2005).

Considering CSR, statements about the contribution of corporations to economic growth that furthers democratic and sustainable development have increasing support in a set of papers (Fox & Heller, 2000; Nellis, 2000; Stiglitz, 1999). According to Heal (2005), the contribution of CSR to economic efficiency lies in fact that it helps the market to reconcile corporate profits and social costs.

CSR can be understood as the private provision of some public goods. Frye argues that it may increase the legitimacy of capitalism among the population in Russia and improve economic performance (Frye, 2006). Continuing this thought, Kuznetsova claims that CSR is an instrument that makes company performance meaningful in the eyes of society because it contributes to development and growth (Kuznetsova, 2009).

CSR and social enterprises have been developing dynamically in Russia since 2003–2006. At the same time, in the Russian Federation, as in most other "post-Soviet" countries, the traditions of socially oriented entrepreneurial activity have led to a confusion of these two concepts. While some recognize nonprofit organizations that have established profitable enterprises as social entrepreneurship, others consider it a kind of social responsibility of a business that implements socially significant programs through independent organizational structures (Dees, 2001).

In Russia, one of first definitions of social entrepreneurship was given by a nonprofit fund of regional social programs, Our Future (a major private initiative for social business support in this country), in 2009: "Social entrepreneurship is a pioneering work originally aimed at solving social problems in terms of self-sufficiency and sustainability" (Fund Our Future, 2009). Both for-profit and nonprofit organizations received support as social enterprises from this fund.

In 2010, the Russian government introduced the concept of "socially oriented nonprofit organizations" that can provide nongovernmental services in the social sector. In 2011, support for the development of those nonprofit organizations was entrusted to an autonomous Agency of Strategic Initiatives, which had to identify and develop promising projects of social entrepreneurship in regions of Russia. Since 2012, the state's interest in social entrepreneurship support shifted to small and medium enterprises, which are for-profit organizations. The Department of Small and Medium Enterprises in the federal Ministry for Economic Development became the main state body responsible for social entrepreneurship development. The concept of socially oriented nonprofit organizations (NPOs) still exists, and another department of the Ministry for Economic Development is in charge of it. Such a shift is explained by the difference between for-profit and nonprofit organizations in terms of their taxation, reporting requirements, and legal regulations.

Social entrepreneurship was understood by the government as business, as an entrepreneurial means for "profitable" or "for-profit" ends in Russia (Moskovskaya & Soboleva, 2016), and the only existing definition of social entrepreneurship that is given in the legislation says that it is the socially responsible activity of small and medium-sized enterprises aimed at solving social problems, including ensuring the fulfillment of the following conditions:

1. Provision of employment for disabled persons, mothers with children under the age of 3, and orphan graduates, as well as persons released from places of deprivation of liberty for 2 years preceding the date

of competitive selection, provided that the average number of these categories among their employees is at least 50% and their share in pay-roll fund is not less than 25%.

2. Provision of services/goods in the following areas:
   - Vocational guidance and employment, including self-employment
   - Social services (healthcare, physical culture and group sports, children's and youth clubs)
   - Cultural and educational activities (theaters, school-studios, musical institutions, creative workshops), including people with limited access to them
   - Involvement of socially unprotected groups of citizens (disabled, orphans, elderly people, people suffering from drug addiction and alcoholism) in social activities
   - Prevention of socially dangerous forms of citizens' behavior, or the production and (or) sale of goods that can be used solely for the prevention of disability or the rehabilitation of disabled people
   - Assistance to victims as a result of natural disasters; ecological, technogenic, or other disasters; social, national, or religious conflicts; and refugees and internally displaced persons
   - Production of periodicals as well as books related to education, science and culture

This definition was introduced by legislation to provide state support to social enterprises and is mainly used to determine the recipients of this support. Currently, this definition is given in a federal law on small and medium-sized business support. It says that only small and medium-sized businesses can be social entrepreneurs, and it must be their special, prioritized form of activity. At the same time, such organizations must meet one of the following conditions.

As a first alternative, they should provide employment for disabled people, single parents with children under the age of 7, large families, non-working pensioners, orphan graduates under the age of 21, or persons released from prison and having a criminal record provided that, based on the results of the previous calendar year, the average number of persons belonging to any of these categories (several or all of these categories) among the employees of the small and medium enterprise is at least 50% and the share of payroll funding is not less than 25%.

Federal State Statistics Service of the Russian Federation (FSSS) shows that these vulnerable groups constitute a significant part of the population and therefore the issue of their employment is important. The total population of Russia was 146.5 million people in 2016. The number of people aged 0–14 years is 17.4%; those aged 15–64 years, 68.2%; those aged 65 and older, 14.4%. The life expectancy is 71.39 years (men, 65.92 years; women, 76.71 years). The ratio of women to men in Russia is 1.157:1. There is a continued increase in the number of persons of retirement age. In fact, 30% of the population of women and men in Russia receive support from the Pension Fund of the Russian Federation. In Russia, there are about 12.5 million (8% of the population) of officially registered persons with disabilities older than 18 years of age and nearly 600,000 children with disabilities. In 2016, 13.5% of the total population lived at or below the poverty level; a large number of these include single parents with children under the age of 7 and large families (Federal State Statistics Service [FSSS], 2017).

As a second alternative, such organizations should carry out entrepreneurial activities aimed at improving the living conditions of citizens and (or) expanding their ability to independently meet their basic life needs in accordance with the list of activities specified by the government of the Russian Federation, provided that the share of income from the implementation of such activities for the previous calendar year is at least 70% of the total income volume for a small or medium-sized enterprise.

This definition helps to identify enterprises that can claim state support, but the generally accepted criteria for determining social enterprises do not correspond to the full extent of social entrepreneurship activities. In particular, there are no important criteria regarding the primacy of the social mission or of innovative activity in combining resources (which could be established through the cost of services). This lack may have the result that social enterprises not meeting the preceding two criteria might not be given state support. One alternative solution to the designation of social enterprises may be a benefit company or *B-corp certification*. This certification system appeared in Russia in 2018 and so far only one Russian company, Whatts Battery, has officially received B-corp status.

The definition of CSR is not legislated in Russia. Law regulates only some socially responsible activities such as charity, additional social programs for employees, and compensation for environmental damage. Therefore, the business sector itself tried to formulate its social mission by adopting the Social Charter of Russian Business within the Russian Union of Industrialists and Entrepreneurs (RUIE) in 2008. According to it, the social mission of business is ensuring the sustainable development of independent and responsible companies which meet the long-term economic interests of business and contribute to the achievement of social peace, security, and the well-being of citizens, preservation of the environment, and respect for human rights. At the same time, it is emphasized that CSR is diverse and multidimensional; it is continuously evolving. Attempts to normalize and put business actions into rigid standardized frameworks can lead to attenuation of this initiative (Russian Union of Industrialists and Entrepreneurs [RUIE], 2008).

Thus, we see different state approaches to the regulation of social entrepreneurship and CSR, with clear definitions for the first and the freedom for self-nomination for the latter.

CURRENT SITUATION AND SUCCESS STORIES OF SOCIAL ENTREPRENEURSHIP IN RUSSIA

Social entrepreneurship is a new phenomenon in Russia. Many people know about it, but there are still few empirical works that give a general description of the characteristics of Russian social entrepreneurship. This is due to the limited data on social enterprises in Russia. Therefore, the study of more than 1,000 social enterprises in Hungary, Romania, Spain, Portugal, Germany, Sweden, Great Britain, Russia, and China, conducted by the Social Entrepreneurship as a Force for more Inclusive and Innovative Societies (SEFORIS) consortium in the period from April to December 2015, is of undoubted interest (SEFORIS, 2016). The final report of this study presents the main findings on the state of social enterprises in Russia (based on interviews with 104 social entrepreneurs).

Another empirical study was made by Albutova, who analyzed 186 applications for financial support to social enterprises submitted to the Foundation for Regional Social Programs' Our Future in 2008–2010 (Albutova, 2013). Despite differences in method and the period of research, it is interesting to compare their results.

According to the SEFORIS report, Russian social enterprises that participated in the project are divided roughly in half according to their legal form: 51% of respondents are for-profit organizations, namely a limited liability company (LLC), and the remaining 49% are distributed among different forms of nonprofit organizations (SEFORIS, 2016). Albutova got similar results. LLCs and individual entrepreneurs make up almost 50% of the total sample, and the rest constitute various organizational and legal forms of nonprofit organizations (Albutova, 2013).

Ninety-five percent of organizations interviewed for the SEFORIS project have fewer than 50 employees (66% of organizations have fewer than 10 employees), and there are no large companies with more than 250 employees (SEFORIS, 2016). Albutova in her paper shows that the majority of social entrepreneurs are also small (97%) and medium-sized enterprises with up to 250 employees (Albutova, 2013).

According to SEFORIS, 30% of Russian social enterprises indicated education, health, employment, and training as their main activity (SEFORIS, 2016). Albutova outlines that projects related to the solution of problems of employment, education, and health made up 50% of the total sample in 2008–2010 (Albutova, 2013). This may indicate diversification of social enterprises' performance in the period of 2008–2015. Thus, it becomes difficult to determine one prevailing kind of activity for Russian social entrepreneurship.

The majority (76%) of those enterprises interviewed by SEFORIS have been in the market for 10 years or less, and the collective image of the director is of a person on average 39 years of age, with higher education (70%) and mainly (62.5%) female (SEFORIS, 2016). According to Albutova, organizations exist in the market on average for 8 years (in 2010), and the head of enterprise is on average 41 years of age, with a higher education (70%) and mainly (60%) male (Albutova, 2013). The two studies show only a small difference in average age. The difference in gender might be explained by the increased activity of women as social entrepreneurs in 2015 or differences in the methodology for selecting enterprises.

For enterprises from the SEFORIS sample, the main source of liquidity (60%) is sales revenue (mainly from customers not connected with the government), 23% of liquidity comes from grants, 12% from private donations (mainly from individuals), the rest is from investments and credit (SEFORIS, 2016). Albutova did not analyze revenue structure on average, but she analyzed several types of social enterprises depending on income source. Thus, 52% of the total sample are enterprises with their own capital, the main part of which is income from their own activities; 37% are enterprises which are dependent on government grants; and 11% are enterprises that rely mainly on borrowed capital (Albutova, 2013).

Summing up, Russian social enterprises have a clear social orientation and diversify their activities to penetrate into new sectors of the economy and social life. The majority of them are small and medium-sized enterprises existing in the market not more than 10 years. Russian social enterprises pay attention to economic indicators, preferring to rely on their own resources rather than on state support. Their leaders, social entrepreneurs, are young (on average, about 40 years old) and highly educated, which may explain why Russian social enterprises are very advanced and innovative. More than 80% of them, according to SEFORIS, implemented a significant improvement in their product or service, 70% implemented a radical innovation, and many entrepreneurs argue that they do not have any competitors on the Russian market and offer unique products/services (SEFORIS, 2016). Examples of such successful and advanced social enterprises are presented in the following case studies.

LAVKALAVKA

LavkaLavka is not a shop. It is a farm cooperative, allowing farmers to find their customers and buyers to find their farmers. It is a living social network where farmers and consumers can communicate freely. This social project is aimed at the emergence of a new agricultural and gastronomic culture in Russia and around the world. LavkaLavka has been a participant in the International Federation of Organic Agriculture (IFOAM) since 2016.

Activities of the LavkaLavka farm cooperative are aimed at supporting agriculture and popularizing environmentally friendly, natural, quality farm products. Using their website one can order a delivery of favorite products or a recipe basket that will include all necessary ingredients for a specified dish. On the website, the manufacturer's name for each product is specified, thus introducing customers to the seller. In this way, LavkaLavka has been promoting the development of a local farmers' community from Moscow, Kaliningrad, and St. Petersburg for the past 6 years.

In addition to using the Internet to market its products, LavkaLavka also opened several retail stores, holds farmers' congresses and seminars on ecology and nutrition, provides informational support to beginning farmers, and offers agricultural tourism services. It has also launched a school for young chefs and runs an online newspaper.

The project continues to develop. At the next stage, the organizers plan to enter the international market. In the framework of this cooperative history, they created the Farm Projects Development Fund, and now they are going to transfer from 3% to 20% of all sold products' profits to this fund. The fund also will receive money through grants, donations, and other social investments.

Once this fund is in place, any farmer-member of the LavkaLavka farm cooperative will be able to apply for funds to support their projects. And, as the necessary amount accumulates, the fund will give money to farmers to implement their projects in the form of a loan. The Fund will fully or partially finance projects, and farmers will be able to repay these loans with their own farm products, rather than money.

DOSPEHI

The Dospehi project was created by the LLC New Rehabilitation Technologies, Dospehi, and aimed to create and implement special orthopedic systems that help people with injuries of the spinal cord to move, stand, get up, and sit down without the help of outsiders. This system was created and patented by Aleksei Nalogin, who himself refers to those being served as wheelchair-disabled people. At the age of 14, Nalogin lost the ability to walk, and the desire to live fully prompted him to organize the production of the Dospehi (English: Armor) system. Each system is customized to order.

Moreover, Nalogin organized fundraising for those who can't themselves pay for Dospehi. This orthopedic system is designed so that people can put on and remove it on their own. In addition, Dospehi orthopedics are half the cost of Western counterparts, with comparable quality.

Dospehi is the very first project supported by the Our Future foundation. The total amount invested is about 9.5 million rubles (about US$400,000 at the average exchange rate of 2007), more than half of which (5.5 million rubles) was provided in the form of an interest-free loan (Fund Our Future, 2008). The initial number of employees in Dospehi was 11 people. The production of orthopedic systems was carried out with the cooperation and support of the medical center of the Russian State Medical University. Dospehi production expanded to the Moscow Institute of Prosthetics, the Central Institute of Traumatology and Orthopedics, and in workshops of Reutov, Volgograd, and other cities of Russia.

Nalogin continues to invent. One of his new products is an affordable carbon fiber wheelchair that weighs 5.5 kilograms (12 pounds). A regular wheelchair weighs about 20 kilograms (44 pounds), and the lightest wheelchair currently on the market weighs 11 kilograms (24 pounds). Other carbon-based wheelchairs are on the market, but they are very expensive, costing about US$12,000. Nalogin managed to make a model that costs only US$2,500.

CHARITY SHOP

Charity Shop is a social business that improves the quality of life of people and helps to decrease negative impact on the city's ecology by using resources such as unused or discarded clothes. The mission of Charity Shop is the development of the concept of sustainable consumption and social responsibility as a lifestyle. To realize its social mission, Charity Shop creates its own infrastructure to collect unwanted clothes. Ecoboxes are installed in public places, and charity stores are opened, generating sales that allow them to be sustainable. Corporate partners are involved in the collection, sorting, and transportation of clothes.

The first Charity Shop was opened in 2014 to sell clothes in excellent condition and direct its profits to charity. Very soon it became clear that not all clothes that people donate could be sold. So a program of charitable giving and processing of clothes in poor condition started. Since 2015, these programs are run by their charitable foundation Second Breath. Profit from sales at the Charity Shop is channeled to the social programs of the Second Breath Foundation. So, thanks to the buyers, tens of thousands of people in 12 regions of Russia get their clothes for free, and tons of clothing go to recycling, rather than to waste dumps.

In 2015–2016, the Second Breath Foundation redistributed more than 256 tons of unused clothes and helped more than 50,000 people get rid of unneeded clothes in the most environmentally friendly way. It distributed 143 tons of clothes to needy families living in 9 regions and sent more than 20 tons of unsuitable clothes and goods for recycling. Also it carried out actions to collect goods in the offices of 110 companies and 4 educational institutions in Moscow and opened 22 points of reception of goods in Moscow.

This project provides an opportunity for social adaptation through the employment of people who find themselves in a difficult life situation. Now Charity Shop employs 16 people from socially unprotected groups who could not get a job elsewhere. In 2017, Charity Shop started an unusual project: internships for social entrepreneurs from different cities of Russia who want to open their own charity store. Internships last several days. During this time all interns take part in all stages of the Charity Shop workflow, in the warehouse, in shops, and in partner sites.

PRIVATE AND STATE SUPPORT FOR SOCIAL ACTIVITY OF FOR-PROFIT AND NONPROFIT ORGANIZATIONS

The development and success of social entrepreneurship is primarily related to the opportunities for business development in general. If barriers to business are removed and a more favorable environment is created, then it automatically helps social businesses: they get the opportunity to develop. Also private and state support for social entrepreneurship is very important.

SEFORIS's research reveals the most important barriers to development from the point of view of social entrepreneurs themselves. Thus, for more than half of the respondents (61%), barriers are related to finance, 18% have barriers at the level of the organization, and 21% associate barriers with other problems related to the market and regulation. Fifteen enterprises from the general sample do not see any barriers at all (SEFORIS, 2016).

Financial barriers are caused by economic risks, such as the introduction of a new product and/or services and the costs of such innovation, or lack of funding and lost profits due to economic volatility. Organizational barriers are associated with lack of time, lack of qualified personnel, and/or lack of information on relevant technology and/or markets to promote a new products and services. Barriers related to regulators and institutions arise when innovation is hampered by the need to meet government regulations. Market barriers are restrictions and barriers to bringing a new product or service to market due to lack of interest and demand in the market (from potential customers).

In Russia, the first and until now main fund for supporting social entrepreneurship is the Foundation for Regional Social Programs' Our Future, a private foundation of Vagit Alekperov, founder and president of PJSC "LUKOIL". For 9 years of its existence, this fund has supported 172 socially oriented enterprises. The total amount of allocated financial resources for these purposes amounted to more than 418.3 million rubles or about US$16.7 million (2007 average exchange rate) (Fund Our Future, 2017). The Foundation established a contest, the winners of which are provided with financial and advisory support. In addition, interest-free loans are issued for a long period of time, legal and accounting services are provided at a minimum cost, and small office space is offered for rent.

Along with holding this contest, the fund has established the Impulse of Good award, which is aimed at supporting financially and morally promising projects. A total of 305 applications from 57 regions of the country were received in 2016, and 155 applicants were nominated "for personal contribution to the development of social entrepreneurship." In total, nine laureates were selected in seven nominations. The regions that sent the highest number of applications were the city of Moscow; Khanty-Mansi Autonomous District, Yugra; the Moscow region; St. Petersburg; and the Kemerovo region (Fund Our Future, 2017).

Another available support institution for social entrepreneurs is the Russian MicroFinancial Center (RMFC). It was founded in 2002 with the main aim to improve economic alternatives for low-income and socially disadvantaged people. RMFC implements microfinancing instruments that allow microcredit provision at below-market interest. Main social tasks carried out by RMFC are connected with the extension of microcredit availability in towns and villages without bank infrastructure and support for socially oriented small enterprises.

As noted earlier, another important barrier besides lack of finance is the organizational barrier. And it is not only lack of qualified personnel that form this barrier, but also lack of highly trained social entrepreneurs. To solve this problem there are some private initiatives in Russia. For example, Citibank offers grants for such training for social entrepreneurs with the support of the Graduate School of Management in St. Petersburg. The Fund Our Future acts as organizer of a training course at Moscow State University. Some Russian corporations included social entrepreneurs in the list of priority areas for implementation of socially significant programs and charitable initiatives in the regions where they do business. For example, RUSAL has support programs for the development of social entrepreneurship' projects. Another corporation, Severstal, together with local authorities, developed a project called the Urban Development Agency to support social entrepreneurs. Thus, support for social entrepreneurship by big corporations can be understood as their CSR.

The Russian state began to show a strong interest in the sphere of social entrepreneurship from 2012, when the first program for its support was adopted. Over the past 5 years more than 2 billion rubles (more than US$67 million at the average exchange rate of 2012) of subsidies have been allocated from the budget, which were provided to entrepreneurs engaged in socially oriented activities. To stimulate the entrepreneurial initiative to solve social problems, a contest, "The Best Social Project of the Year," was organized. In 2016, more than 260 applications were submitted from 54 regions of the federation, which indicates the success of the contest and the growing initiative of social entrepreneurs. A significant number of projects are related to preschool and additional education for children, social integration of disabled children and inclusive education, socialization and rehabilitation of people with disabilities, creating jobs for people in need of social support, and innovative solutions for quality social services for elder people.

At the federal level, the Ministry for Economic Development of the Russian Federation is the main office responsible for the development of social entrepreneurship. Within the framework of the Ministry's program, targeted subsidies are available to entrepreneurs. The maximum amount of subsidy is 600,000 rubles per one social enterprise (US$20,000 at the average exchange rate of 2012). Enterprises must provide co-financing in the amount of not less than 15% of the received grant.

In Russian regions, state support is given through Social Innovation Centers. Their main tasks are information dispersal; analytical and legal support for social projects; exchange of experience in supporting social initiatives; and holding seminars, workshops, and practical and lecture-based classes on social topics within the School of Social Entrepreneurship. This is a licensed educational program for social entrepreneurs and their employees based in the regional Social Innovation Centers and created in partnership with the Agency for Strategic Initiatives, regional administrations, and the business community. Training is free of charge.

In 2017, the Agency for Strategic Initiatives proposed the creation of a federal fund for social entrepreneurship support providing organizational, methodological, and financial assistance to socially significant projects. The main task of the fund is to replicate best practices and educational programs, create models of accelerated programs, and prepare tutors who will help start-ups to attract investments. The Fund will provide venture financing for start-ups in the social sphere.

ASSESSMENT OF CORPORATE SOCIAL RESPONSIBILITY IN RUSSIA

Although there were no private enterprises in the Soviet Union, elements of CSR were realized by state enterprises. Their CSR policy covered both employees and residents of the area where the enterprise operated. Some forms of its implementation were peculiar to the Soviet economy: the distribution of social benefits ranging from food to housing and a number of others, in common with many other countries; the provision of social guarantees in the form of insurance, labor, and health protection; the organization of leisure; and so on. Another form of CSR implementation was the practice of *patronage*. During Soviet times, state enterprises acquired a wide network of social sphere organizations (food enterprises, kindergartens, recreation centers for adults and schoolchildren, medical organizations, etc.). Such organizations, owned by the state enterprises, could be used by all residents of the settlements in which the enterprises were located. However, there were social benefits that were intended only for employees (e.g., some medical services, recreation centers). Svirina and Khadiullina (2017) noted that, in the USSR, employers were responsible for providing social services for their employees, while community service was a part of the state's responsibility; in the new Russia employers got rid of some social obligations they used to have under the USSR, but became responsible for providing services to the community.

Today, sponsorship and charity as ways of performing socially responsible activities are widespread within the business environment in Russia. However, only large corporations publish nonfinancial reports that create an image of socially responsible organizations for partners, customers, and investors. At the same time, many entrepreneurs do not share this information with the general public. This can be due to differences in the degree of disclosure of information about CSR activities because of the national features of the business environment. For example, in the United States firms openly state that they have invested in health, education, and employee welfare (Matten & Moon, 2008). In Europe, firms prefer not to disclose all information about their socially responsible activities because it is considered unethical to report on social services that are also provided by government agencies (Borsch, 2004).

In Russia, development of nonfinancial reporting began with the publication of the *Social Charter of Russian Business* by the RUIE in 2004. The *Social* reports by business from that time focused on personnel social benefits, charity, and regional development. In 2008, Basic Performance Indicators of RUIE were developed on the basis of the Global Reporting Initiative (GRI) that was adapted to the Russian system of accounting and statistical reporting. It allows firms to inform others about their economic, social, and environmental performance in accordance with sustainable development principles.

As an international shaper of general opinion, the UN had a certain influence on the development of social responsibility in Russia. In 2008, the launching of the UN Global Compact network, the largest initiative of the UN in the field of CSR and sustainable development, was initiated in the Russian Federation. The UN Global Compact is not a law and its purpose is not to establish requirements for CSR or to monitor the social activities of organizations—it only encourages them to join it. But joining the UN Global Compact signals, first, the intention of the organization to include the Compact's principles in its practical activities and, second, voluntary reporting. To date, 71 organizations, including the RUIE, have joined the Global Compact in Russia. All of them pledged to follow its principles.

Nonfinancial reporting in Russia continues to develop. Preuss and Barkemeyer outline the fact that companies from emerging-economy firms outperform those from industrialized nations in their coverage of GRI indicators in corporate sustainability reporting, with Russia occupying a middle position (Preuss & Barkemeyer, 2011). The dynamics of nonfinancial reports and reporting organizations, as well as the scale of public activity in this area, are evidence of it.

From 2000 to 2016, 751 nonfinancial reports were issued. Among them were 68 environmental reports, 291 social reports, 247 reports in the field of sustainable development, 120 integrated reports, and 25 industry reports. At the beginning of 2017, 164 organizations were included in the National Register of Corporate Non-Financial Reports, conducted by the RUIE (2017).

The most popular directions of social reporting development in Russia involve the gradual advancement from voluntary to systematic reports in accordance with international standards and the transfer from environmental reports to sustainable development reporting. At the same time, the low level of compliance with international business standards is connected with the underdeveloped tradition of social reporting in the business environment and a lack of legislative rules and incentives for CSR development. For example, funds directed to charity are not excluded from taxation.

The federal law, On Charitable Activities and Charitable Organizations, established tax exemption only at the amount of 3% from profits directed at charitable purposes. Furthermore, legislation has established a tax on property donations; therefore, even when donating, let's say, computers for a children's organization, a charitable company must pay taxes.

Due to incomplete data in nonfinancial reports it is rather complicated to make a cost-benefit analysis for the CSR projects of Russian companies. Thus, indicators for nonfinancial reports are selected and indices are constructed by measuring the quality and frequency of their disclosure. In most cases a content analysis research design is used.

Bashtovaya in her study undertakes a content analysis of CSR reporting in order to explain revealed differences between 10 Russian and American major players in the energy sector. American corporations compared to Russian ones report more extensively on topics of global concern in the scope of environmental performance. And Russian corporations report on areas of social performance and CSR issues related to employees and consumers more than do American companies (Bashtovaya, 2014).

Glebova, Rodnyansky, Sadyrtdinov, Khabibrakhmanova, and Yasnitskaya (2013) developed a technique to assess CSR based on a content analysis of nonfinancial reports. The following criteria were chosen, reflecting the most significant aspects of socially responsible activities, such as the mission of the company, its development strategy and social responsibility policy, activities to involve stakeholders in the process of discussing and monitoring the implementation of the development strategy, the availability of information on corporate standards and regulations on interaction with stakeholders, a description of the availability and quality of corporate governance in the field of social responsibility, comparability of data with international standards, and availability of feedback tools. Criteria are evaluated according to the grading scale (1, 0.75, 0.5, 0), depending on the quality and completeness of disclosure in nonfinancial report.

Increasing corporate transparency and developing quality management in the field of sustainable development and corporate responsibility are partly due to RUIE indices, a set of tools for independent evaluation of companies' performance. In 2017, RUIE indices in the field of sustainable development, corporate responsibility, and accountability ("Vector of Sustainable Development," "Responsibility and Openness") are included in the Global Initiative for Sustainability Ratings (GISR) international database.

The "Responsibility and Openness" index (RUIE, 2017) characterizes the actual situation regarding disclosure of corporate information on CSR in relation to the "ideal": the calculated level of disclosure correlates with the highest possible score or standard. It is calculated as

$$I_t = \frac{e}{E}$$

where *e* equals the sum of points counted for the whole sample and *E* is the maximum possible score ($E = x * m * n$, where *x* is the highest possible score for the indicator, *m* is the number of indicators, and *n* is the number of companies).

The "Vector of Sustainable Development" index (RUIE, 2017) indicates the direction of change in companies' performance in the areas of sustainable development/CSR. It is based on the ratio of positive and negative "signals," which indicate direction of changes in the array of reporting data for 3 years.

$$I_v = \frac{Q}{MN}$$

where *Q* equals the sum of signals values, *M* equals the number of signals, and *N* equals the number of companies in the sample.

In 2016, the composition of leaders in the "Vector of Sustainable Development" index almost completely coincides with results for the "Responsibility and Openness" index. This confirms once again the relationship between the social and environmental performance of companies with the development of accounting and reporting systems in the field of sustainable development and CSR, as well as the willingness of companies to engage in public dialogue about the goals and results in this area.

CONCLUSION

We discussed the implementation of "social entrepreneurship" and "corporate social responsibility" concepts in Russia. CSR and social enterprises are developing dynamically in Russia since 2003–2006, and I suggest here that they can be used to foster further social and economic transition.

Issues related to the success stories of Russian social enterprises and socially responsible corporate behavior were outlined. In Russia social enterprises have a clear social orientation and diversify their activities, penetrating into new sectors of the economy and social life. The majority of them are small and medium-sized enterprises that have been in the market for not more than 10 years. Russian social enterprises pay attention to economic indicators, preferring to rely on their own funding sources rather than on state support. Their leaders, social entrepreneurs, are young (on average, about 40 years old) and highly educated.

At the same time social entrepreneurs face significant challenges to their development, such as financial barriers, barriers at the level of the organization, and barriers related to the market and regulation. Financial barriers are caused by economic risks, such as lack of funding and lost profits due to economic volatility. Organizational barriers are associated with lack of time, lack of qualified personnel, and lack of information. Barriers related to regulators and institutions arise when innovation is hampered by the need to meet government regulations. Market barriers are restrictions and barriers in bringing new products or services to market.

An emphasis was made here on identifying government and private institutions and instruments supporting the social activity of for-profit and nonprofit organizations. There are different state approaches to the regulation of social entrepreneurship and CSR (with clear definitions of social entrepreneurship and self-nomination involving CSR). A clear definition helps to identify enterprises that can claim state support, but the generally accepted criteria for determining a social enterprise do not correspond to the full extent of social enterprise activity; thus, some social businesses might be excluded from state support.

Techniques for the assessment of CSR in Russia were described. Due to incomplete data in nonfinancial reports it is rather complicated to make a cost-benefit analysis for CSR projects. So, indicators for nonfinancial reports are selected and indices are constructed by measuring the quality and frequency of disclosure. A low level of compliance with international business standards is connected with an underdeveloped tradition of social reporting in the business environment, a lack of legislative rules, and a lack of incentives for CSR development. The most important achievements of social reporting in Russia involve a gradual advancement from voluntary to systematic reports in accordance with international standards and the movement from environmental reports to sustainable development reporting.

Policy implications for further development of the "social entrepreneurship" and "corporate social responsibility" concepts in Russia include, first, the creation of appropriate and favorable regulatory frameworks for socially active businesses, as well as the inclusion of the state in the process of financing projects at the initial stage. The existing legal framework doesn't fully reflect all the particular features that social enterprises have as opposed to traditional businesses. It is necessary to give these enterprises a specific status that will allow more active promotion of the model of social entrepreneurship. The government should also introduce mechanisms of state support. A social enterprise in most cases requires minimal investment at the initial stage. And state support in this case will have an obvious multiplicative effect: simultaneously with the solution of a certain social problem, a new source of tax revenues will be created.

The second important task for policy-makers is an active information campaign that should focus on three key audiences: the general public, representatives of regional authorities, and potential social entrepreneurs. Growing awareness of the population and authorities on the opportunities of social business will inevitably change the perception of social responsibility in the eyes of other entrepreneurs representing commercial companies from a wide range of sectors of the economy. Ideally, the outcome of this process will be a radical change in the perception of social responsibility in the business community and the formation of broad support for social entrepreneurship among the population and public authorities.

REFERENCES

Albutova, A. (2013). Social entrepreneurship in Russia: Key players and the potential of formation. *Economic Sociology, 14*(3), 109–132. Retrieved from https://ecsoc.hse.ru/data/2013/08/14/1291342150/ecsoc_t14_n3.pdf

Bashtovaya, V. (2014). CSR reporting in the United States and Russia. *Social Responsibility Journal, 10*(1), 68–84. https://doi.org/10.1108/SRJ-11-2012-0150

Borsch, A. (2004). Globalisation, shareholder value, restructuring: The (non)-transformation of Siemens. *New Political Economy, 9*(3), 365–387. https://doi.org/10.1080/1356346042000257804

Dees, J. G. (2001). *The meaning of social entrepreneurship*. Center for the Advancement of Social Entrepreneurship, Duke University's Fuqua School of Business (revised vers.). Retrieved from https://entrepreneurship.duke.edu/news-item/the-meaning-of-social-entrepreneurship/

Dimaggio, P. (1988). Interest and agency in institutional theory. In L. G. Zucker (Ed.), *Institutional Patterns and Organizations: Culture and Environment* (pp. 3–22). Cambridge, MA: Ballinger.

Fligstein, N. (1997). Social skill and institutional theory. *American Behavioral Scientist*, *40*(4), 397–405. https://doi.org/10.1177%2F0002764297040004003

Fox, M. B., & Heller, M. A. (2000). Corporate Governance Lessons from Russian Enterprise Fiascoes. *New York University Law Review*, *75*(6), 1720–1780. Available at: https://www.nyulawreview.org/wp-content/uploads/2018/08/NYULawReview-75-6-Fox-Heller.pdf

Frye, T. (2006). Original sin, good works and property rights in Russia. *World Politics*, *58*(4), 479–504. https://doi.org/10.1353/wp.2007.0007

Federal State Statistics Service (FSSS). (2017). *Russia in figures: 2017*. Retrieved from http://www.gks.ru/bgd/regl/b17_12/Main.htm

Fund Our Future. (2009). *Annual report 2009*. Retrieved from http://www.nb-fund.ru/report/db80c.pdf

Fund Our Future. (2017). *Annual report 2016*. Retrieved from http://www.nb-fund.ru/report/annual_report_2017.pdf

Glebova, I. S., Rodnyansky, D., Sadyrtdinov, R., Khabibrakhmanova, R., & Yasnitskaya Y. (2013). Evaluation of corporate social responsibility of Russian companies based on nonfinancial reporting. *Middle-East Journal of Scientific Research, 13* (Socio-Economic Sciences and Humanities), 143–148. doi: 10.5829/idosi.mejsr.2013.13.sesh.1426

Heal, G. (2005). Corporate social responsibility: An economic and financial framework. *Geneva Papers on Risk and Insurance: Issues and Practice*, *30*(3), 387–409. https://doi.org/10.1057/palgrave.gpp.2510037

Kuznetsova, O. (2009). CSR in the emerging market of Russia: Finding the nexus between business accountability, legitimacy, growth and societal reconciliation. In Satyendra Singh (Ed.), *Handbook of business practices and growth in emerging markets* (pp. 119–140). Publisher, World Scientific Publishing. https://doi.org/10.1142/6745

Mair, J., & Martí, I. (2006). Social entrepreneurship research: A source of explanation, prediction, and delight. *Journal of World Business*, *41*(1), 36–44. https://doi.org/10.1016/j.jwb.2005.09.002

Matten, D., & Moon, J. (2008). "Implicit" and "explicit" CSR: A conceptual framework for a comparative understanding of corporate social responsibility. *Academy of Management Review*, *33*(2), 404–424. https://doi.org/10.5465/amr.2008.31193458

Moskovskaya, A. A., & Soboleva, I. V. (2016). Social entrepreneurship in the system of social policy: International experience and prospects of Russia. *Studies on Russian Economics Development, 27*, 683. Retrieved from https://doi.org/10.1134/S1075700716060113

Nellis, J. R. (2000). *Time to rethink privatization in transition economies?* International Finance Corporation working paper No. 38. Retrieved from https://doi.org/10.2139/ssrn.176752

Pagè, J. (2011). Twenty years of economic transition in Russia: Results and lessons learned. *Studies on Russian Economic Development*, *22*(4), 351–353. https://doi.org/ 10.1134/s1075700711040137

Peredo, A., & Chrisman, J. (2006). Toward a theory of community-based enterprise. *Academy of Management Review*, *31*(2), 309–328. https://doi.org/10.5465/amr.2006.20208683

Preuss, L., & Barkemeyer, R. (2011). CSR priorities of emerging economy firms: Is Russia a different shape of BRIC? *Corporate Governance: The International Journal of Business in Society, 11*(4), 371–385.

Russian Union of Industrialists and Entrepreneurs (RUIE). (2008). *Social charity of Russian business 2008*. Russian Federation. Retrieved from https://rspp.ru/12/6273.pdf

Russian Union of Industrialists and Entrepreneurs (RUIE). (2017). *Responsible business practice in the mirror of accountability: Present and future*. Retrieved from http://media.rspp.ru/document/1/7/4/743222fc4c6650093518c635d0e8ecdd.pdf

Seelos, C., & Mair, J. (2005). Social entrepreneurship: Creating new business models to serve the poor. *Business Horizons, 48*(3), 241–246. https://doi.org/10.1016/j.bushor.2004.11.006

SEFORIS. (2016). *Country report Russia*. Retrieved from http://www.seforis.eu/s/SEFORIS-COUNTRY-REPORT-RU_04-APRIL.pdf

Stiglitz, J. E. (1999, April). *Wither reform? Ten years of transition* (keynote address). (1999). World Bank Annual Bank Conference on Development Economics, Washington DC. Retrieved from http://documents.worldbank.org/curated/en/448681468741326292/pdf/multi-page.pdf

Svirina, A., & Khadiullina, G. (2017). Industry CSR perception and practices: The case of Russia. In M. Aluchna & S. Idowu (Eds.), *The dynamics of corporate social responsibility: A critical approach to theory and practice (CSR, sustainability, ethics & governance)* (pp. 203–220). Cham, Switzerland: Springer. Retrieved from https://doi.org/10.1007/978-3-319-39089-5

CHAPTER 11

༄

Socioeconomic Development in India

Lessons from the Third Sector

MEERA BHAT AND SWAPNIL BARAI

CONTEXT

In 1947, India was a country of 361 million people and the first colonized nation to form a democratic government immediately following independence. Eighty-three percent of its citizens lived in rural areas, were not expected to live beyond 32.1 years, and only 18% were literate (Drèze & Sen, 2013). The preceding decade (1940s) had seen 5.1 million people die of famine as collateral damage of World War II and during the partition from Pakistan (Drèze & Sen, 2013). India's gross domestic product (GDP) growth, stymied by two centuries of colonial rule, had been stuck at 0.9% from 1901 to 1950. Consequently, a mixed economy focused on domestic institution building, self-sufficiency, and community development was thought to be the best initial recourse.

A planning commission styled after the Union of Socialist Soviet Republic's (USSR) "planned economy" laid out policy priorities and regulated the domestic private sector. The state played an active role in the economy as a major investor itself, issuing stringent industrial and import licensing norms and playing a protectionist role toward domestic public and private institutions by shielding them from global competition through their infancy (Ahluwalia, 2016). It is important to note that, at

Meera Bhat and Swapnil Barai, *Socioeconomic Development in India* In: *Social Entrepreneurship and Enterprises in Economic and Social Development.* Edited by: Katharine Briar-Lawson, Paul Miesing, and Blanca M. Ramos, Oxford University Press (2021). © Oxford University Press. DOI: 10.1093/oso/9780197518298.003.0012.

this juncture, for the first 100 years of colonial rule, India was ruled by a corporation (the British East India Company) with an armed force that fought wars and annexed and appropriated states and lands for its business interests without any process or accountability to any government (Drèze & Sen, 2013). This provides an insight into India's inward looking, protectionist economic policies and its slow transition into a liberalized global economy.

Drèze and Sen (2013) point out that the existence of an independent private and civil society sector was a marked departure from communist-type thinking. The civil society sector was a legacy of the country's non-violent, civil disobedience movement for freedom from colonial rule. It became a confluence of various ideological movements, such as (but not limited to) the feminist, labor, and *dalit* (a collective term, often a political identity used for caste groups subjected to untouchability) movements. They articulated and advocated for people's needs and existed in a creative tension with each other and the government. They played a pivotal role in making systems inclusive and accountable, and they led process and product innovations, such as microbanking, that were subsequently institutionalized by the government.

UNDERSTANDING INDIA'S ECONOMIC TRANSITION

India's inward-looking economic strategies worked, from a nation-building perspective, for about a decade and a half, as evidenced by the steady GDP growth to 4.9% by the mid-1960s (Ahluwalia, 2016). Simultaneously, significant investments were made in building strong producer cooperative networks and strengthening support infrastructure for agriculture, with food security in mind. By the mid-1960s, there was a push for economic reform, demonstrated by seven committees and reports on the issue (Ahluwalia, 2016). This thinking did not find political backing in the '60s and '70s, decades plagued by successive natural disasters, wars, and political turmoil. The policy paralysis eventually ended in the 1980s as the impact of investments made in agriculture and social infrastructure became apparent. The country registered a 30% increase in agriculture production and a 5% growth in actual agricultural wages, resulting in a visible dent in rural poverty in the country (Drèze & Sen, 2013). This stability resulted in some incremental changes in economic policy, such as liberalization of industrial and import licenses and laying down of regulatory and institutional frameworks with global financial trade in mind (Ahluwalia, 2016). The policy paralysis on economic reform ended abruptly as a "balance of payments crisis" was precipitated in 1991, followed by preconditional reforms for a structural adjustment program (SAP) loan from the World Bank and the International Monetary Fund (IMF).

The reforms received a mixed initial response from various domestic stakeholders, particularly because they were perceived as forced on the nation by the World Bank and IMF. The government refused a second SAP loan in 1993, opting for a more gradual and phased-out approach to reforms, especially in foreign direct investment and privatization of public sectors. This approach seems to have served the economy well given that India's GDP (nominal) growth has averaged 6–7% since 1991 (Drèze & Sen, 2013). While India shared some issues such as corruption and deficient infrastructure with transitioning economies of the erstwhile USSR, it differed in many ways. In contrast to post-Soviet economies, India had private-sector infrastructure, including legal and financial systems, and entrepreneurship and business skills were evolved but existed at a smaller, domestic scale.

The role of the Indian state changed, too, as it embraced—aggressively but covertly—the role of a neoliberal state, becoming a close ally of (largely domestic) private interests. Sood (2016) points out that it went further than an average noninterventionist neoliberal state by acting on behalf of private interests to dispossess people (of their means of production) and encroach on natural resources in the name of development, without public accountability or adequate repatriations. Public discourses on welfare and economic reform were decoupled even as the state remained the reference point for both and insisted that economic reform was the means to the end of proliferation of welfare. Indian state sought legitimacy by engaging in public discourse on welfare while limiting discussions on economic reform to key audiences such as industrial lobbies and chambers of commerce (Sood, 2016). Overall, public-sector funding in areas of health, education, agriculture, livelihoods has not increased, and in some cases has been reduced. The quality of physical and human resource infrastructure also has been compromised, forcing the public to gravitate toward the private sector.

The neoliberal project has received a major boost under the BJP-led NDA government elected to office in 2014, which ran on the promise of putting a CEO, rather than a prime minister in office (Sood, 2016). There has been a push in the areas of privatization of assets, under the pretext of increasing efficiency in welfare delivery by replacing government involvement with technology-led innovation, and increasing the ease of doing business. Legitimacy is no longer sought but demanded as attempts at public accountability and political discourse are drowned in a binary rhetoric that equates nationalism with economic growth.

GROWTH AND DEVELOPMENT

India is the second most populous country after China and the most populous democracy in the world, with 1.2 billion citizens. With a consistently democratic government since independence and a large youth population, it has held the attention of global business interests both as a labor and consumer resource for the past few decades. Since 1991, India's GDP (nominal) has grown from US$266.5 billion to 2.5 trillion, growing resiliently even in times of global economic crisis. It is important to acknowledge the success of India's home-grown economic reforms that have created a trillion-dollar economy in 25 years. While this a significant milestone, in a democracy the poignant question is: How have its 1.2 billion citizens been impacted by this growth? What is the societal reach of this growth? How has it improved their quality of life? Has it translated into development?

Poverty and Inequality

One common way to assess this is to look at the distribution of income, consumption, and wealth gain across the country. India's per capita income (PCI) at purchasing power parity (PPP) has gone up from US$1,140 in 1991 to US$6,490 in 2016, and the poverty head count ratio has gone down from 45.3 in 1991 to 21.9 in the 2011 census. These are both laudable gains, but it is concerning that real wages among poorer sections have not risen since the late 1980s, and the median income has worsened among the poorest sections (Himanshu, 2018). India's Gini Coefficient at 0.54 is among the worst in the world, as demonstrated by the fact that the top 1% have the fastest rising income share in the world and hold the highest income share since 1922. Seventy-three percent of the wealth generated in the past decade went to the top 1% of the population, most of whom inherited their wealthy without paying any inheritance tax and or gained it from rent-thick sectors while the wealth of the bottom 50% grew by only 1% (Himanshu, 2018). As a result, inequality in asset ownership has been exacerbated, particularly since 2000, and abides by age-old patterns of caste hierarchies. The total wealth held by billionaires increased 10-fold in the past decade and amounts to 15% of the GDP.

Consumption across the board has not gone up as much as expected but the data reveal a parity of 5.6 % in rural and 10% in urban areas between the top and bottom 10% of the population. The average monthly per capita expenditure (MPCE) as estimated by the 66th National Sample Survey was just Rs.1519 (US$33) in 2011 (National Sample Survey Office

[NSSO], 2011). The average MPCE of the poorest 10% of India's population was US$10–13 while the top 10% ranged from US$56 to US$130. Hunger and malnutrition, one of the crudest manifestations of poverty, are as widespread as in some least developed economies and pre-independence India. The urban and rural populations accessing less than adequate caloric intake has increased by about 10% since 1993–1994 and is at 65% and 68%, respectively, contradicting claims of a reduction in poverty (Patnaik, 2016). Women, children, and marginalized communities are disproportionately affected by hunger, thus amplifying the impact of other social marginalizations and disparities.

Health

India has made significant strides in health indicators, with estimated life expectancy at birth increasing from 32.1 years at independence to 60 years in 1991 and 66 years in 2011, as per census estimates. The infant mortality rate (IMR) has also declined from 180 (1951) to 74 (1991) to 44 (2011) per 1,000 live births, but 27.6% newborns are underweight, 38% children younger than 5 years were found to have stunted growth, 45.9% were underweight, and 79% were anemic (Datta, 2015). While the maternal mortality ratio (MMR) has seen a drastic decrease in numbers from 538 (1991) to 174 (2016) per 100,000 live births, 47% women were married and 16% had begun childbearing by 18 years, which is the legal age for marriage. These statistics reflect increased access to primary, reproductive, and emergency healthcare services in recent years but the disparities across geographies and communities are glaring. The lack of access to other basic needs such as potable water, sanitation, and nutrition of nearly 50% of the population, especially in rural areas and among marginalized groups, invalidates much of efforts made in other areas of healthcare provision.

Literacy and Education

India's literacy rate has come a long way from 18% people being literate in 1951 to 74% literacy in the 2011 census, but the rate of change has been slow. The gross enrollment ratio (GER) for elementary and middle schools is at 95.7% and 85.5%, respectively, owing largely to education becoming a fundamental right (for ages 6–14) in 2009. The dropout rate increases from 5.3% at age 14 to 30.2% at age 18, when education is no longer a free and compulsory entitlement, and it affects girls and minorities disproportionately. Singh and Hussain's (2016) analysis shows how cultural beliefs disincentivize education among minorities (dalit, tribal and muslim communities) through systemic biases such as wage gap, unequal employment opportunities, and diminishing returns on education for members of these communities. Enrollment figures, while important, tell us precious little about the quality of learning. The Annual Status of Education Report (ASER) sheds light on the inability of around 50% of elementary and middle school students to read in their native language, and 25% of students to do math at below grade level, as sampled across public and private schools (ASER, 2018).

Inclusive Development, Employment, and Livelihoods

Sood (2016) observes that, for growth to be sustainable, it must be inclusive. Inclusive growth cannot be reached simply by the state redistributing gains from economic growth but through the state intervening in processes that create conditions for everyone, especially disadvantaged groups, to be able to participate in that growth. This involves discussions on asset ownership, the quality as well as quantity of jobs, and the composition of growth so that there are opportunities even for the most marginalized. Poverty can be reduced and will stay reduced only if inequality is moderated. A look at India's sectoral growth points to the lack of such planning and a perpetuation of patterns of caste, class, gender, and geographical inequalities.

The agriculture sector, which is largely informal, employs an overwhelming 47% of the population and contributes about 17% to the GDP (Srinivasan & Srinivasan, 2016). This is approximately a 20% decline both in employment and economic returns since the 1980s, which, while desirable, is a consequence of a severe agrarian crisis rather than policy (Datta, 2015). A shocking total of 350,000 cultivators/farmers have committed suicide over the past two decades, citing economic distress that has resulted from increased production costs, changing climate patterns and reduced state support, and protection. The industrial sector contributes 29% of the GDP and employs 22% of the labor force, but has grown at a mere 2.3% since 1991 (Drèze & Sen, 2013). The high-skills service industry (information technology, finance), which has been a highlight of India's growth story, generated 5.8 million jobs between 2004 and 2005 and 2011 and 2012 alone and contributes almost 54% to the GDP (Datta, 2015; Drèze & Sen 2013). While the GDP continues to burgeon, the rate of employment generation in the manufacturing and service sector declined from

3.2 million per year in 1993–1994 to 1.9 million per year in 2004–2005 to 2011–2012 (Datta, 2015).

The International Labour Organization (ILO) estimated India's unemployment rate to be 3.46% in 2016, showing a slow but consistent downward trend from around 4.3% since 1993. Organized sector jobs have grown by a mere 4 million in 25 years, which is estimated to have created 44 million jobs in the informal economy, while the workforce has grown by 200 million people (Shrivastava, 2016). India's otherwise well-regarded economic transition has been dubbed "jobless growth" because of being inaccessible to large parts of its citizens. While this term is catchy, it is an oversimplification of the dire circumstances in which 93% people left in the informal economy find themselves caught. Their work is temporary, seasonal, intermittent, casual, unlegislated, and often underpaid. Many jobs in manufacturing are outsourced to "entrepreneurs" who are home-based or employed on a piece-rate, casual, or contractual basis. This allows the organized sector to invest less in infrastructure and circumvent labor and environmental laws, thus making business more profitable and life more precarious for the bottom billion.

Banerjee, Banerjee, and Duflo (2011) explain that precariousness or vulnerability manifests itself in the form of underemployment or as underpayment. They claim, based on empirical data, that in Gujarat, one of India's most industrially developed states, a casual laborer only found work between 137 and 254 days a year. This is evident in the increasing dependence on casual employment in public works, which went from 0.9 million in 2004–2005 to 6.7 million in 2011–2012 (Datta, 2015). Sixty-nine percent of rural women claim dependence on employment guarantee welfare programs, where minimum wage casual employment in public works is available for up to 100 days in a year (Datta, 2015). Banerjee, Banerjee, and Duflo (2011) claim that people living in poverty deal with this problem by "hedging jobs" to manage risk. They illustrate this by citing a survey in West Bengal, in which a median family survived by having three working members with seven different occupations (Banerjee, Banerjee, & Duflo, 2011). This tells us that there is work, but it is not full-time or remunerated enough to be called a "job," let alone a sustainable livelihood. A *livelihood* is "a means of making a living. It encompasses people's capabilities, assets, income, access and claim to resources and activities required to secure a means of living. A sustainable livelihood enables people to lead a reasonable quality of life, enhance capabilities and assets for themselves and future generations as well as cope with shocks and stresses that occur from time to time" (Srinivasan & Srinivasan, 2016). While employment statistics are important indicators to quantify growth and stability of an economy, they paint an incomplete picture of the impact of growth on society.

These trends are particularly worrisome since India's workforce of 481 million people is the second largest in the world, after China. The workforce is younger than China's, with a median age of 26.7 years; and an estimated 12 million youth between age 15 and 29 will be added to it each year for the next two decades. Much of India's growth outlook is predicated on this growing and young workforce, only 2% of which is formally skilled, which is dismally low compared to China (47%), Japan (80%), or South Korea (96%) (Swaniti Initiative, n.d.). Poverty, exacerbated by lack of opportunity and basic entitlements and glaring regional and communal disparities, seems to be pushing young middle-caste and -class Indians toward identity-based politics. As in many other parts of the world, their "economic anxiety" is being used to fuel identity-based radical right agendas that mask radically right-wing economic agendas. A popular economics magazine (*Economist*, 2018) recently lamented the unfulfilled promise of the consumerist class in India on behalf of global corporations who invested in the country. They explained that, like China, India's middle class was expected to grow in size and in their ability to spend, but instead it is shrinking. They claim that since incomes have not risen and government services have dried up or deteriorated, families are too squeezed in paying for basic necessities to be able to consume things like smartphones, cars, or even disposable consumer goods or products.

The Ministry of Skill Development and Entrepreneurship was set up in 2014 to oversee youth skill building and vocational training programs in a public–private partnership framework. Industry sets priorities with regards to the courses and curriculum being offered at training centers and contributes 5–25% of the cost. The government funds the infrastructure and provides incentives for finding job placements. Most programs also provide graduates linkages to funding, mentorship, and other infrastructure for those interested in starting their own businesses. Most of these programs are new, and success can only be measured long term but short-term data are not particularly heartening. These data point out that, in the absence of job growth, most of these trainees are not successful in keeping their job placements once the incentive period in the industry ends, and they disappear back into the informal sector (Srinivasan & Srinivasan, 2016).

In summary, while India has made great progress in terms of GDP growth when compared with other large transitioning economies such as China, Brazil, and Russia, the societal reach of this growth is strikingly limited. Many nations with significantly smaller and slower economies have overtaken India's progress in terms of malnutrition, health, education, and gender issues. Drèze and Sen (2013) explain that most of these nations invested heavily in public-sector infrastructure as soon as their economies took off, with the goal of providing basic entitlements for their citizens as a democratic duty as well as an investment for sustainable and inclusive growth. There is great disparity in human development indicators across Indian states, which directly relates to public-sector infrastructure. Those Indian states whose citizens are faring well invested well and significantly for decades in public goods and infrastructure compared to those that did not. This public infrastructure also becomes the bedrock of opportunities on which the private or civil society sector can innovate to find new or more efficient solutions to unsolved problems.

THE THIRD SECTOR

Public, private, and civil society are pillars of a democratic society whose mutual accountability forms the bedrock of democratic society. We have discussed the changing nature of the public and private sectors and its impact on Indian citizen's lives. This section discusses changes in the civil society sector, which has now come to be known as the "third sector," owing to the presence of "hybrid organizations" that often serve financial as well as civic agendas.

Indigenous Roots of Social Entrepreneurship

India's civil society sector traces its roots to the nonviolent struggle for independence, social reform, and rights-based advocacy movements. The roots of social entrepreneurship can be traced back to the pluralist public debate that prominent nationalist leaders, whom Guha (2011) calls the "makers of modern India," had about nation-building during the long struggle for independence. Among them, Gandhi and Ambedkar insisted that political freedom would mean little without economic freedom. Gandhi proposed new and powerful ideas like *Sarvodaya* (upliftment of everyone), *Trusteeship* (trustees rather than owners of wealth), and *Swaraj* (social, economic, and political self-rule) that would help build economies of permanence (Prasad, 2014). Bill Drayton, the founder of Ashoka, recognizes Gandhi's contribution in articulating and actualizing these ethics for a new world, ethics that were rooted in empathy rather than in rules (Bornstein, 2004). The ideas of *Sarvodaya, Swaraj, Tusteeship* and *Satyagraha* deeply impacted generations of change-makers, some of whom set up impactful initiatives such as the Bhoodan movement (land gift or voluntary land reform movement), the Amul cooperative dairy, the Barefoot College, the Self-Employed Women's Association (SEWA), the Bhartiya Agro Industries Foundation (BAIF), and the Honey Bee Network, among several others (Prasad & Satish, 2018). These remarkable ideas, individuals, and initiatives inspired Drayton to found Ashoka to support entrepreneurship rooted in empathy and to support these individuals through their innovation process (Prasad, 2014).

Fundamental to the idea of trusteeship was the differentiation drawn between the concepts of *wealth* and *value creation*. It insists on being guided by a strong moral framework for the generation of wealth and of wealthy people being trustees of this wealth created by the labor of other member of society. Instead of constantly accumulating material wealth, the moral approach it recommended was creating value by utilizing wealth for the greater good of society. Unlikely as it may seem, this idea was developed in consultation with business leaders of the time who stepped up to invest significant amounts of their wealth in young India's public infrastructure. What is currently and popularly referred to as the Corporate Social Responsibility (CSR) law has its roots in the concept and practice of trusteeship.

There was an understanding that technological development needed to be backed up by social innovation for it to affect social change. These ideas were accompanied by attempts to set up an ecosystem that included institutions of technological innovation, social innovation, producer collectives, and a national regulatory authority in Khadi and Village Industries Commission (KVIC) around rural livelihoods. Much like today's enterprise ecosystem, these institutions disseminated information through publications; gave out prizes to innovators; and provided technological research, funding, and networking support. Several of these institutions still exist, reaching some of the remotest parts of the country, albeit encumbered by lack of funding and political will.

From *Sarvodaya* to Social Business

Post-independence, civil society organizations were perceived as partners in conceptualizing and implementing policies as well as programs. They were adept at things that mammoth government bureaucracies struggled with, such as reaching, giving a voice to, and building sustainable relationships with marginalized communities and finding innovative solutions. They were funded through government programs, religious and philanthropic charities, and multilateral organizations.

Globalization of the economy brought with it a global consensus on poverty and development, one permeating through the civil society sector and turning it into "the third sector," filled with hybrid organizations with multiple loyalties. The *Bangladesh consensus*, as Ananya Roy (2010) terms it, shifted the onus onto people living in poverty, directing them to empower themselves and pull themselves out of poverty. The conversation, though poor-centric, became anti-welfare and, while clothed in the garb of human rights jargon, it resulted in a paradigm shift. The goals of development changed from "redistribution and equality" to "opportunity and entrepreneurialism" (Roy, 2010). It undermined the role of protective and promotive welfare entitlements that went into enabling an individual to utilize opportunity and entrepreneurialism.

Changes in the sector came in the early 2000s, with widespread acceptance of the Bangladesh consensus. It decreed that poor women were natural entrepreneurs who, with a little bit of training could run successful small-scale businesses (Roy, 2010). It was deemed the futuristic way of "making markets work for poor people" who were otherwise excluded from markets and poor as a result (Roy, 2010). Several standalone microcredit (without savings or literacy components) initiatives cropped up that marked a departure from decades of institution building around group microfinance, microentrepreneurship, and cooperatives in India. This narrative was built on by the World Bank, which assumes the role of chief arbitrator on issues of global development by controlling knowledge as well as resource generation and dissemination (Roy, 2010). By establishing standards, rankings, best practices, models, and benchmarks that valued financial viability over holistic development, it enforced the *Washington consensus* that views people living in poverty as an *asset class* with untapped market potential (Roy, 2010). Using catch phrases such as "bottom of the pyramid," "bottom billion," and "creative capitalism," widespread consensus was generated that poverty could be eradicated through profits and that funding welfare was no longer necessary. While Roy (2010) outlines the political economy of the microfinance sector, the conclusions around the creation of poverty capital hold true for the entire development sector. A report by Intellecap (2012) points out that these transitions took off around 2004–2005 when commercial microcredit was burgeoning and before the subprime microlending crisis hit in 2010.

This crisis altered expectations for both organizations and their stakeholders with respect to delivery and accountability mechanisms of development. Focus shifted from building sustainable programs with long term process-oriented engagement and impact to short-term output-oriented interventions. With leaner program funding, frontline organizations were engrossed in innovating for their self-sufficiency and survival. As a result, organizational design and legal structures that allowed for more than just nonprofit work, such as social businesses and social enterprises, were born. This also marks a change for some organizations with respect to their missions and how they engaged with the populations they served, from stakeholders to clients. Prasad (2014) details the transition of Villigro from an agency that aimed to foster innovation and experimentation among rural innovators to one that would support sustainable market-based innovations that impact rural households.

The Entrepreneurship Landscape

The entrepreneurship landscape in India consists of a variety of enterprises with a focus on innovation, business propositions, or structural change. Policies, support infrastructure and networks, funders, the entrepreneurs, and client populations are what make up the landscape.

The Policy Landscape

Policies broadly shape the contours of the entrepreneurship landscape and the behavior of players in the ecosystem. A recent study by the Natu, Singh, Shandilya, and Jaiswal (2016) enumerates 39 policies that impact the functioning of enterprises across sectors. These include policies pertaining to registration of the enterprises, financial mechanisms, taxes, and incentives, as well as sectoral policies (e.g., health or education).

The Indian government does not have a working definition for social entrepreneurship but applies policies based on the type of organization (e.g., charitable trust, cooperative, company) the entity is registered as and the sectors it is involved in. As a result, any micro, small, and medium enterprises (MSMEs) that manufacture goods or provide services may qualify themselves as social enterprises (Miles & Dutta, 2012). The National Skill Development and Entrepreneurship Policy of 2015 briefly acknowledges the existence of social enterprises in the country. Another study that asked stakeholders in the social enterprise ecosystem to define social entrepreneurship concluded that their understanding broadly centered around commercial ventures addressing social issues or engaging low-income populations (Darko, Awasthi, Gregory, & Lynch, 2015). Artisan, handicraft, or rural enterprises were conflated with income-generating livelihood programs with almost no mention of innovation or social mission–driven initiatives (Darko et al., 2015).

Nonprofits in India can register as charitable trusts, societies, or not-for-profit companies (Section 8 companies) that are publicly accountable and monitored stringently. Cooperatives and producer-owned companies are allowed to accrue profits that may be plowed back into the company or equally distributed among shareholders. For-profit businesses include private limited companies, proprietorships, public limited companies, limited liability companies, family-owned companies, and non-banking finance companies (NBFCs) that are also publicly accountable. There is a notable trend of reduction in the registration of nonprofits (73% before 2000, 7% between 2010 and 2015) compared to a drastic increase in for-profit organizations (19% in 2000, 71% between 2011 and 2015) (Natu et al., 2016).

The activities of enterprises are provisioned to be financed by debt, equity, and grants. Banks, NBFCs, and domestic development finance institutions (DFI) are the only players that are allowed to make loans to enterprises. Most MSMEs find their capital through individual or institutional investors as equity. A direct consequence of this policy is the trend of an increasing number of for-profit registrations and a decline in nonprofit enterprises as grants dry up and equity is the only available source of funding. Eighty percent of this funding, from both domestic as well as international sources, is channeled through offshore accounts to circumvent tax and repatriation laws in India (Global Impact Investing Network [GIIN], 2015). This deliberate oversight in monitoring by the government is in stark contrast to the amount of scrutiny and monitoring that charitable funders and recipients undergo to secure funding from foreign sources.

Enterprises are eligible for tax exemptions and subsidies based on specific sectoral policies and the legal structure of the enterprise. MSMEs can take advantage or reduced taxes and exemptions in the first 7–10 years of their operation and are given leniency in labor and environmental laws. This is a dangerous liberty to selectively offer to for-profit MSME enterprises in an economy where 93% workers are engaged in vulnerable informal sector jobs without legal protection which keeps them in cycles of intergenerational poverty.

CSR rules in the Companies Act of 2013 were implemented in April 2014, mandating the spending of 2% of net profits from corporations with a net worth or net profit of INR 5 billion (US$7.13 million) or revenues of INR 10 billion (US$143 million) on issues such as healthcare, education, sanitation, poverty alleviation, and livelihoods to name a few (Epstein, Sanghvi, & Yuthas, 2013). In fiscal year 2017, 92 out of the top 100 companies reported spending US$970 million on issues such as education and vocational skills (35%); hunger, poverty, and healthcare (25%); rural development; environmental sustainability; and national heritage, among other issues (Chowdhary, 2017). The Companies Act mandates philanthropy rather than promoting more progressive and sustainable standards in the spirit of trusteeship and thus creates a way to cover up shabby humanitarian or environmental impacts. It has been criticized by leaders in philanthropy as regressive because of the meek commitments it seeks from businesses and because its mandatory nature goes against the core concept of philanthropy (Bakshi, 2016).

The Enabling Ecosystem

The Indian enterprise ecosystem, though nascent, consists of a variety of stakeholders that intervene at various stages to provide access to finance, institutional support, and networks. Much like the rest of the sector, few of these enablers work exclusively with social enterprises, but they are beginning to differentiate between the nuanced needs of social enterprise, social business, and business enterprises.

Mobilizers, Incubators, and Accelerators

Mobilizers are organizations that create interest in entrepreneurship, conduct workshops for idea development, and give stipends, fellowships, or grants. They are at the forefront of the pipeline. They look for people with an interest, inclination, and ideas that might enable them to become entrepreneurs. Ashoka Foundation's Changemaker School and Youth Venture programs, Jagriti Yatra (social enterprise boot camp on a train journey across India), or the Indian government's Tinker labs for school students are some interesting examples.

Incubators are usually interested in people who have developed their ideas into plans and curate the support they provide based on the sector and stage of the enterprise (start-up, growth, mature). The support they provide includes capacity building, working space, mentorship, research, advisory services, awards, capital for idea development, conducting a pilot, seed or growth funding, and access to networks and forums. *Accelerators* work with enterprises that are stable, successful, and have the potential to grow (Miles & Dutta, 2012; Natu et al., 2016). Ashoka Innovators, the Centre for Innovation and Entrepreneurship, the Honeybee Network, Dasra Social Impact, Unltd India, and Villgro Innovation Foundation are well known in the social enterprise space.

Most incubators have been around for about a decade and are mostly concentrated in Mumbai, New Delhi, and Chennai even though most claim to have a pan-India recruitment focus (Miles & Dutta, 2012). A large number are registered as not-for-profits and depend on grants from foundations, governments, and DFIs (Miles & Dutta, 2012). Health, energy, and technology, as well as water and sanitation, dominate their sector focus (Miles & Dutta, 2012). Some of the challenges include the lack of focus at the ideas stage, a concentration in urban and well-developed geographies, a focus on technological or product-oriented solutions, and low transparency on performance data (Miles & Dutta, 2012).

Impact Investors

India is the largest impact investing market in South Asia with an estimated international investment of US$7 billion made through DFIs, investment funds, high net worth individuals, and foundations (GIIN, 2015). About 63% is directly invested by international DFIs into domestic DFIs (NABARD, SIDBI) or government programs, while an additional estimated 32% is invested indirectly by international DFIs using other channels such as investment funds (GIIN, 2015). Five and a half percent (US$438 million) comes in as private equity through investment funds, venture capitalists, angel investors, grants, or foundations. (GIIN, 2015).

On the demand side, GIIN (2015) estimates that US$1.6 billion was invested in 220 social enterprises between 2000 and 2014. Foundations that have low or no expectations of financial returns often play a catalytic role in sectors or at idea/pilot development stages, where commercial capital is unlikely to enter. Some DFIs also invest in incubators at idea or seed stages. Investment funds are largely engaged in investing at the seed-funding stage where investments range from US$20,000 to US$150,000 (Natu et al., 2016). Banks are also involved in providing debt loans at this stage and are the only source of institutionalized debt due to India's financial policies (Natu et al., 2016). Private investors invest in early growth-stage enterprises through informal networks. They also use formal networks and invest as angels or through investments funds set by venture capital or private equity firms. Investments at this stage range from US$150,000 to US$950,000. Growth-stage or scaling-up funding, which is usually more than US$950,000, is available but hard to come by, in part at least due to the nascence of the Indian social enterprise ecosystem.

Almost 70% of impact funding is invested in microfinance or financial inclusion activities, followed by renewable and nonrenewable energy, manufacturing, agro/food processing, information and communication technology, health and pharma, education, housing, and others (GIIN, 2015). It is important to note, once again, that the definitional bias in favor of social businesses applies to these data, making it impossible to separate funding for social enterprises that are mission- and innovation-driven. Studies also point to biases toward urban areas, regions with better infrastructure, in favor of entrepreneurs with a Western education, technological solutions to all problems, and large established initiatives with low overheads (Miles & Dutta, 2012; Natu et al., 2016). Sixty-three percent of investors reported third-party social and environmental impact assessments, but not many were publicly available or used a standardized framework (Miles & Dutta, 2012). Without public accountability on impact, protecting the interests of people in vulnerable situations, ensuring the development of the country, and determining the return on investment in impact for investors might be impossible.

Government policies do not incentivize or differentiate between impact investors and regular investors, thus making the competition tough for investors. This puts social entrepreneurs' nonprofits in particular at a disadvantage compared to social businesses and MSMEs. This extra cost they incur is passed along to their clients, who are already disadvantaged. This leads to people at the bottom of the pyramid (BOP) having to pay a premium price for lesser quality, also known as the "BOP penalty" (Natu et al., 2016). The client's situation is made even more precarious by the lack of policy around standards of service and standardized impact assessment (Miles & Dutta, 2012).

Networks, Forums, and Associations

The National Association of Social Enterprises is an industry association that reaches out to other ecosystem stakeholders, while the Indian Impact Investor's Association helps investors secure more opportunities. Sankalp forum and Unconvention are the two big events that bring several stakeholders to a single platform, while National Entrepreneurship Networks(NEN) support student entrepreneurship across the country. These are only a few examples of domestic networks and forums and are not meant to be an exhaustive list.

Education and Research

Social entrepreneurship is largely taught at the graduate level in business, management, and technology schools with the exception of a dedicated graduate Social Entrepreneurship program with a social science perspective at the Tata Institute of Social Sciences (TISS) (Center for Social Innovation and Entrepreneurship [CSIE], 2013). Much of the academic research available is subsumed under sectoral areas (such as health, education, livelihoods) or in business and management publications. Much of the evaluative research comes in the form of gray literature from industry conglomerates, consulting firms, or self-evaluative case studies.

POLICY IMPLICATIONS AND RECOMMENDATIONS

The absence of a policy definition of social entrepreneurship or social business leaves matters open to convenient interpretation, as reported by Darko et al. (2015). Enterprises that engage in the skill development or livelihood space make up more half of the total number, followed by education, microfinance, energy, and health services as well as a few in housing, tourism, and human rights (Natu et al., 2016). Basic data, such as on the number of organizations registered, operating, or creating wealth and value, is at best fragmented and pulled together using nonrepresentative sample studies by multilateral organizations, impact investors, and occasionally by independent or academic researchers. The lack of systematicity, leaves room for significant bias, in this case for social or commercial businesses being misrepresented as social entrepreneurship.

A definition and management information system (MIS) database much like that which exists for nonprofits and commercial businesses would allow better control over funding, nurturing, and monitoring these organizations. It would also incentivize better reach in infrastructurally lagging regions or unattractive sectors. The highest proportion of social enterprises are concentrated in metropolitan urban areas, especially in west, south, and north India. This is directly linked to the limited presence of ecosystem actors such as investors and incubators and the low quality of public infrastructure such as transport and electricity (Natu et al., 2016).

Potentially the most concerning policy area is that around standards of practice and is equally applicable to businesses, enterprises, and philanthropy. As Jochnick (2012) points out, market-based approaches are lacking in systems thinking that addresses questions of power and agency with respect to local social, economic, and political complexities. An apt example of such a failure is the subprime microlending crisis in South India, where standalone (without literacy, community organizing, and social collateral components) microlending had catastrophic results. Another looming crisis is the sweatshops hiding in the guise of small-scale manufacturing units discussed earlier in this chapter. Jochnick's (2012) version of an ecosystem includes a *watchdog entity* that looks after the interests of poor clients by scrutinizing bad services or products, excessive BOP penalty costs, or other discriminatory practices. This is crucial because, in such as system, target communities (typically composed of people with some type of disadvantage) are reduced merely to recipients or clients rather than stakeholders with a voice.

RESEARCH IMPLICATIONS AND RECOMMENDATIONS

The social entrepreneurship space is complex and quickly evolving because of the diversity of its actors as well as its interdisciplinary nature, and research has some catching up to do. Prasad and Satish (2018), through their extensive review of literature, point to a loss of focus in the sector. The focus has shifted from innovating, experimenting, and solving difficult problems in new ways to merely finding financially efficient ways of doing things or growing what is successful. Enterpreneuship in the term 'Social Entrepreneurhsip' stands for innovative, radical, out-of-the-box thinking that pushes boundaries and causes creative destruction. The idea of putting mission-driven and market-driven together is innovative in itself. The dominant discourse, is a reductive, narrow application of fiscal discipline to organizations outside the business space. As is apparent from the discussion above, it undermines the mission, all stakeholder who lives are stake as well as innovation. Researchers and thinkers, in collaboration with practitioners, must engage in this uncomfortable, abstract intellectual exercise of questioning the values and purpose of this way of doing things. They can and must cultivate the ability to advocate for innovators, funders and other stakeholders to engage with new unsolved problems, rather than merely replicating existing approaches.

The Indian context can provide interesting lessons in terms of I utilizing indigenous ethical and philosophical frameworks that co-exist with other ideologies and practices. It is particularly relevant for nations of the Global South that share colonial histories and collectivist traditions. Prasad and Satish (2018) draw attention to the fact that of all the literature on social entrepreneurship and social enterprise from 1991 to 2010, only 10% came from Asia, Africa, and Latin America collectively. While this highlights biases that most researchers know exist, it seems like a great loss to not learn from the experiences of half the world's population.

Prasad and Satish (2018) also point out that more than half of all the articles published under social entrepreneurship were covered under business and management while social science constituted less than 5% of the research. Nicholls (2006) contends that aligning social entrepreneurship with social movement and advocacy efforts in contexts like India may bring diverse perspectives and help offset the pro-market bias. This pro-market bias is visible in the fact that most research is available from industry conglomerates, in the upward trend in registration of for-profit and privately owned enterprises for social good in the past decade, and in the type and sources of funding available without government scrutiny. This fascination with the ability to use business skills in enterprises catering to excluded populations and the exclusive attention afforded to scaling them in size is taking over solving wicked cyclical problems.

Social innovation is a decentralized process of solving socially complex and wicked problems such as poverty. Social entrepreneurs and Innovators are practitioners who develop a unique perspective on the problem and engage with it until they are able to change something. Research needs to look into their black box and identify these practitioners' theories of action and the problems' theory of change. This will also contribute to the adaptive capabilities of systems and explain why some problems persist intergenerationally and across contexts (Prasad, 2014). The current reductive perspective and language referring to millions of people living in poverty and experiencing systemic oppression as an asset class must be rearticulated. Perhaps such research may help to view them as resources of knowledge on their own lives and potential sources of innovation rather than merely an asset class to sell services and goods to.

LESSONS AND CONCLUSIONS

India's enterprise sector is large, diverse, and consists of social enterprises, social businesses, and business enterprises that need to be differentiated. Organizations and processes are built on institutional values such as business discipline, innovation, or mission focus. The fact that social mission is taking a back seat is a pertinent risk, especially when funders and clients are unequal stakeholders in terms of ownership and power in an organization (Aiken, 2010). Entrepreneurship must not be allowed to become a façade for the promotion of exploitative informal sector employment or a resource drain from resource-scarce communities.

Social enterprises do fill gaps in welfare provision, but in a young and unequal democratic country like India, the broader vision and enabling environment must come from the government. It will have to set development priorities, level the playing field between powerful and vulnerable groups through democratic accountability mechanisms, and foster an environment where social enterprises can innovate to address complex, cyclical problems like poverty in a sustainable manner.

India has a long and rich history of mission-driven process and product innovations in the social sector that address causes rather than symptoms of societal problems. A large part of this innovation is driven by the idea of beneficiaries being expert stakeholders and the belief that they are crucial to sustainably solving social, economic, environmental, or political problems that surround them. A number of stakeholder-owned organizations, such as the network of dairy or artisan cooperatives, challenge the notion of trickle-down economics in favor of bottom-up economies of permanence. Policies and ecosystem actors must provide a safe environment for experimentation for social innovators willing to take on difficult societal problems.

In the livelihood sector, it is important to challenge the notion that everyone who is self-employed is a willing entrepreneur. Most people living in poverty are self-employed because their circumstances necessitate it. At the same time, self-employed people need to be supported through skill building, providing access to basic infrastructure and services, and strengthening value chains and legislation that level the playing field.

India is an important country by virtue of being one of the largest and most diverse democracies as well as economies in the world. All through her economic transition, the tightrope of growth and development has been hard to walk, with some lapses and some victories leading to a burgeoning economy with a starving population. Thus, distributing the fruits of growth will not lead to inclusive, sustainable development unless there is a redistribution of assets and entitlements. Social entrepreneurship, as a post-modern thought experiment, presents us with choice and a toolkit to build innovative solutions that allow for a just, equitable, egalitarian democratic society.

REFERENCES

Ahluwalia, M. S. (2016). The 1991 Reforms: How home-grown were they. *Economic and Political Weekly, 51*(29), 39–46.

Aiken, M. (2010). Social enterprises: Challenges from the field. *Hybrid organizations and the third sector: Challenges for practice, theory and policy*, 153–174. doi:10.1007/978-0-230-36439-4_8

ASER. (2018). *Beyond basics: Annual status of education report 2017 (Rural)*. New Delhi: ASER Centre.

Bakshi, R. (2016). *Trusteeship: Business and the economics of well-being*. Gateway House. Retrieved from https://www.gatewayhouse.in/wp-content/uploads/2016/09/Trusteeship_by_R-Bakshi_WebVersion.pdf

Banerjee, A. V., Banerjee, A., & Duflo, E. (2011). *Poor economics: A radical rethinking of the way to fight global poverty.* Public Affairs, New York.

Bornstein, D. (2004). *How to change the world: Social entrepreneurs and the power of new ideas.* Oxford, UK: Oxford University Press. doi: 361.1 B736h

Chowdhary, S. (2017). *How companies are spending on CSR projects.* Livemint. Retrieved from https://www.livemint.com/Companies/oyHdaJdn96pnmzdIFUIFNO/How-companies-are-spending-on-CSR-projects.html

Center for Social Innovation and Entrepreneurship (CSIE). (2013). *CSIE-IITM (Centre for Social Innovation and Entrepreneurship- IIT, Madras): Social enterprise ecosystem in India.* Retrieved from http://csie.iitm.ac.in/SEandSupport.html

Darko, E., Awasthi, D., Gregory, D., & Lynch, A (2015). *Social enterprise: An overview of the policy framework in India.* British Council, Social Enterprise UK, Overseas Development Institute.

Datta, S. (2015). Overview of livelihoods in India. In (Eds.). *State of India's livelihoods report 2014* (pp. 1–16). New Delhi: Oxford University Press.

Drèze, J., & Sen, A. (2013). *An uncertain glory: India and its contradictions.* Princeton, NJ: Princeton University Press. doi: 10.2307/j.ctt32bcbm

Economist. (2018). *India's missing middle: India has a hole where its middle class should be.* Retrieved from https://www.economist.com/leaders/2018/01/13/india-has-a-hole-where-its-middle-class-should-be

Epstein, M. J., Sanghvi, D., & Yuthas, K. (2013). CSR and the Companies Act, 2013: Be bold, take action. *Research Report.* Retrieved from https://www.dasra.org/sites/default/files/Be%20Bold%2C%20Take%20Action%20-%20CSR.pdf

Global Impact Investing Network (GIIN). (2015). *The landscape of impact investing in South Asia: Understanding the current status, trends, opportunities and challenges in Bangladesh, India, Myanmar, Nepal, Pakistan, and Srilanka* (pp. 223–259). Research Report. Retrieved from https://thegiin.org/assets/documents/pub/South%20Asia%20Landscape%20Study%202015/1_Full%20South%20Asia%20Report.pdf

Guha, R. (Ed.). (2011). *Makers of modern India.* Cambridge, MA: Harvard University Press.

Himanshu. (2018). *The widening gaps: India inequality report 2018.* Oxfam India. Retrieved from https://www.oxfamindia.org/sites/default/files/WideningGaps_IndiaInequalityReport2018.pdf

Intellecap. (2012). *Pathways to progress: A sectoral study of Indian social enterprises.* Mumbai. Retrieved from http://www.sankalpforum.com/wp-content/uploads/2013/04/Intellecap_Pathways-to-Progress_Revised_Web.pdf

Jochnick, C. (2012). *Systems, power, and agency in market-based approaches to poverty.* Oxfam America Research Backgrounder series. Retrieved from www.oxfamamerica.org/market-based-approaches-to-poverty

Miles, K., & Dutta, T. (2012). *Enablers for change: A market landscape of the Indian social enterprise ecosystem.* New Delhi: GIZ.

National Sample Survey Office (NSSO). Ministry of Statistics and Programme Implementation, Government of India. (2011). *Monthly per capita expenditure: NSS 66th round.* New Delhi: National Sample Survey Office. Retrieved from http://pib.nic.in/newsite/PrintRelease.aspx?relid=73098

Natu, J., Singh, D., Shandilya, D., & Jaiswal, S. (2016). *Social value economy: A survey of social enterprise landscape in India.* New Delhi: British Council. Retrieved from https://www.britishcouncil.in/sites/default/files/british_council_se_landscape_in_india_-_report.pdf

Nicholls, A. (Ed.). (2006). *Social entrepreneurship: New models of sustainable social change*. OUP Oxford.

Patnaik, P. (2016). Economic liberalization and the working poor. *Economic and Political Weekly, 51*(29), 47–51.

Prasad, C. S. (2014). Thinking through social innovation and social entrepreneurship in India. In J. Seddon (Ed.), *Social innovation in social entrepreneurship: Strengthening the ecosystem for scaling social innovation*. Villgro & IDRC, Retrieved form https://www.villgro.org/assets/img/Resource/research/social%20innovation%20paper%205.pdf

Prasad, C. S., & Satish, V. J. (2018). Embedding diversity in social entrepreneurial research: India's learning laboratories. In A. Agarwal & P. Kumar (Eds.), *Social entrepreneurship and sustainable business models: The case of India* (pp. 3–30). Cham, Switzerland: Palgrave Macmillan. doi: 10.1007 /978-3-319-7 4488-9_1

Roy, A. (2010). *Poverty capital: Microfinance and the making of development*. New York: Routledge. doi: 10.4324/9780203854716

Shrivastava, A. (2016). A-Meri-India: A note from the land of frustrated aspirants. *Economic and Political Weekly, 51*(29), 75–78.

Singh, M., & Husain, Z. (2016). Self-fulfilling equilibrium and social disparities in urban India. *Economic and Political Weekly, 51*(48), 43–51.

Sood, A. (2016). Politics of growth. *Economic and Political Weekly, 51*(29), 56–60.

Srinivasan, G., & Srinivasan, N. (2016). *State of India's livelihoods report 2015*. New Delhi, India: Oxford University Press

Swaniti Initiative. (n.d.), *Skill development in India—present status and recent developments. Policy brief.* Retrieved from http://www.swaniti.com/wp-

CHAPTER 12

❧

Where There Is No Formal Social Welfare System for an Indigenous People

Entrepreneurship, Watchmen, and the Reinvention of the Maasai Warrior

ERIC E. OTENYO, MICHELLE HARRIS, AND KELLY ASKEW

INTRODUCTION: ENTREPRENEURSHIP AND POVERTY

The underlying assumption of theoretical works on entrepreneurship is that entrepreneurs create opportunities and jobs that offer social security and a path toward the eradication of poverty. Entrepreneurship in the context of Kenya's national development referred to change agents taking risks and innovating for purposes of promoting development (Otenyo-Matanda, 2009, p. 18). From a sociological perspective, entrepreneurship is about individuals translating visions into successful, productive ventures. And although social scientists have multiple ways of specifying what constitutes entrepreneurship, attention toward understanding its linkages to the provision of opportunities for economic empowerment has been successful (Kirzner, 1997; Schumpeter, 1934; Shane & Venkataraman, 2000). Schumpeter (1934) regarded entrepreneurs as innovators who

Eric E. Otenyo, *Michelle* Harris, and Kelly Askew, *Where There Is No Formal Social Welfare System for an Indigenous People* In: *Social Entrepreneurship and Enterprises in Economic and Social Development.* Edited by: Katharine Briar-Lawson, Paul Miesing, and Blanca M. Ramos, Oxford University Press (2021). © Oxford University Press. DOI: 10.1093/oso/9780197518298.003.0013.

sustained capitalism—they take already existing resources to produce novel products. When thinking of entrepreneurial activities among indigenous peoples, Hindle and Lansdowne (2005) contend that these groups create, manage, and/or develop new ventures based on "indigenous knowledge" for the benefit of their own people. In so doing, the entrepreneurial activities are of value to their communities as well as to the entrepreneur.

Often, scholarship on entrepreneurship frames activities as driven by the need to innovate. Scholarship on indigenous entrepreneurship, however, often extends ideas about innovation to include notions of cultural heritage (and the cultural capital inherent in heritage) that is deployed in ways that create revenue and provide the necessities of life that are often not provided by nation states (Dana, 2007). The nation states of Kenya and Tanzania—where Maasai number around 1.6 million—provide very little in the way of a social safety net to aid this indigenous group but are increasingly implicated in deliberate efforts to undermine and harm Maasai life ways and their very lives.

This chapter discusses the nexus between entrepreneurship among Maasai in the context of state-induced marginalization of the community and the unfolding social transformation of what it means to be a *moran* ("warrior"). Specific examples of the reinvention of moranism in the form of watchmen (security guards) will constitute the bulk of the expose. There are five sections to this discussion. First, we describe the paucity of literature pertaining to and frameworks for understanding entrepreneurship. Second, we outline the social basis for the prevalence of the strong male warrior narrative among the Maasai. Third, we reflect on the safety net policy context in comparative terms to illustrate that social programs can change lives in all marginalized communities. Fourth, we discuss globalization and other independent variables reinforcing the status quo. The last section considers reactions to the marginalization of Maasai watchmen— entrepreneurs whose sovereignty and lifestyles are rapidly changing.

HISTORICAL CONTEXT AND SCHOLARSHIP

Historically, the colonial government discouraged African subjects from developing their own income-generating activities and instead forced them to provide cheap labor in support of the capitalist cause—profit making. Thus, at independence, most African communities had to develop policies to turn around the colonially induced anti-entrepreneurial spirit imposed through the systemic destruction of their productive capabilities. Also, colonial powers prevented "entrepreneurial groups" from taking advantage of resources deemed as reserves for "pastoralist" (traditional livestock-herding) ethnic societies (Spear & Waller, 1993). As such, exclusion made it easier for Maasai rangelands to be subjected to processes of underdevelopment. Through penetration of settlers and non-Maasai immigrants, land was expropriated for farming and wildlife conservation.

Efforts to reverse decades of prejudice against the promotion of African entrepreneurship were visible in government development blueprints, especially in sessional papers and development plans that encouraged the development of small-scale enterprises to coexist alongside foreign-owned capital investments (King, 1996; Republic of Kenya [RoK], 1986, 1997). However, most of the efforts to trigger development through small-scale enterprises did not succeed, and poverty persisted, especially in marginalized communities (Mullei & Bokea, 1998; RoK, 2005). This is clearly the case in many Maasai communities.

Scholarship on Maasai entrepreneurship is couched in resource-based perspectives which attribute entrepreneurship to the existence of specific community resources. Such resources include knowledge, organizational capacities, networks, and natural assets like water and land. Thompson and Homewood (2002) examined the use of land among Maasai around the Mara National Reserve and determined that Maasai landowners did not make decisions based on market rationale as would be expected from economic models of entrepreneurship. In their research, Maasai were involved in wildlife tourism and small-scale cultivation for household food security.

Ndemo (2007) investigated the impact of entrepreneurship among Maasai living in the Kajiado, Laikipia, Narok, and Transmara regions of Kenya. He argues that since Maasai have progressively lost land and lack capital, their entrepreneurialism has created few opportunities for income generation. And even if they tried to engage in small-scale activities, most lack the necessary education and training to be successful entrepreneurs. Because Maasai are new to entrepreneurship they face enormous challenges in separating family livelihoods from business endeavors. In Ndemo's conclusion, Maasai prefer to "retain their traditional economic system instead of integrating themselves with the rest of Kenya in a market economy" (p. 98). This is substantiated by the common practice of Maasai working in cities sending money home to purchase more cattle and to pay others to herd their livestock for them.

A rational approach to problematizing development in Africa must explore the plight of indigenous communities that are the main face of global poverty and resource misappropriation. Members of the indigenous communities are a large part of the urban poor. According to the United Nations Human Development Index, the majority of indigenous groups in

Kenya and Tanzania are classified as living below the poverty line. Critics also challenge the notion of absolute poverty among a group like the Maasai that has some wealth in cattle ownership and land.

The Maasai pastoralists are profoundly attached to their animals and, in fact, view cattle and other animals as a form of social security or functionally equivalent to money in the bank. By some estimates, cattle provide 80% of their meals and are the symbol of a man's wealth and standing in society. Because of their reliance on livestock for subsistence, Maasai have frequently suffered whenever drought (an increasingly frequent occurrence due to climate change) affects their land.

In 2009, for instance, much of Maasailand experienced severe drought leading to loss of livestock and displacement of thousands of families who had to move long distances in search of pastures. The 2009 drought was one of the key push factors that led to a proliferation of Maasai migration to urban centers in Kenya. Media accounts of losses of Maasai livestock are remarkable. In some instances, many Maasai became paupers, and *morans*, who traditionally are the defenders of the community, were unable to protect their families, with some abandoning women and children because they could not afford to provide food. Maasai women became targets of human traffickers (Njeru, 2015). Some men even committed suicide (Integrated Regional Information Networks [IRIN], 2009a). Most certainly, the prevalence of drought in Maasai community regions has the imprints of the climate change phenomenon and is a major policy issue for the marginalized areas. The reoccurrence of drought, if it is not addressed, will continue to destroy the self-image of Maasai as a strong and resilient pastoralist group.

STRONG MEN: WARRIORS' NARRATIVES

As a group, the Maasai are perhaps Africa's most globalized group. Through popular media and information and communication technologies, we picture the Maasai as an indigenous group that is attached to traditional ways of living. Gender roles are quite visible when one visits a Maasai *Enkang* or homestead, with up to 20 huts surrounded by thorny fences. Maasai culture makes good entertainment, as stories about Moranism fill advertisements, movie reels, pages of YouTube, and other Internet outlets. In those corporately manufactured images, Maasai men are seen as brave warriors, killing lions with their bare hands and crude weapons to prove that they are ready to start families and protect their women, children, and herds of livestock. The elders manage tribal affairs on a day-to-day basis. Women, for the most part, are depicted repairing their mud-plastered homes and doing other household chores. The significance of cattle is overplayed in this Maasai mythology, although protecting cattle is strongly linked to the reification of bravery among young Maasai men.

In particular, depictions of young Maasai men transitioning from boys to warriors after aesthetically rich circumcision ceremonies are now abundantly available in digital documentary film format. Conservation groups sensationalize Maasai culture as a tactic to deprive them of indigenous resources. Thus, for example, the depiction of Maasai men as mighty warriors killing lions undermines the argument that indigenous peoples have been dispossessed of resources and rendered destitute.

Sometimes Maasai themselves sensationalize the story, which frequently happens when the more educated interact with Westerners or write for Western audiences. One William Sirkobei Ole Osono who, in responding to a question raised by a student at the Village School of North Bennington, Vermont, where he was visiting, demonstrated the techniques he used to kill a lion that had threatened his animals (Carson, 2015). He even went further and stated, "We mostly hunt for fun, as warriors, to train and see how strong we are" (Carson, 2015; for related examples, see Lekuton & Viola, 2005 and Ole Saitoti, 2014). Also, through popular culture, Maasai are described as a group restricted to 19th-century customs and lacking the capabilities for modernization. Maasai men are depicted as carrying sticks, a sword, or club to symbolize their control of their environments and to separate them from women (Oduor, 2011).

Still, beneath the narratives of bravery and courage is the absence of discourse on the abject conditions of poverty in which the *morans* survive. Furthermore, government failures to provide social security and safety nets to marginalized rural communities are absent from most media accounts of policy failures. Therefore, scholarly attention to life outside moranism is sparse.

ABSENCE OF FUNCTIONAL EQUIVALENT WELFARE PROGRAMS AND NO SAFETY NETS

Perhaps greater visibility would be possible if government efforts at social transformation were successful. That is not the case, which compounds the problem and feeds into the narrative of hopelessness. National budgets in Kenya, for instance, include items purported to promote development in arid and semi-arid lands (ASAL). With development assistance from international financial institutions like the World Bank and USAID, the goal since independence has been to transform ASAL regions into "develop-ment." The record shows that the infusion of aid has not helped transform lives in rural, marginalized communities. National development plans and policy documents aimed at the elimination of poverty appear to be routine bureaucratic aspirations rather than serious implementable plans.

And even after the promulgation, in 2010, of Kenya's new "progressive" constitution, safety nets for Maasai and other pastoralist and hunter-gatherer communities are on the back burner of national priorities. One would imagine that public policy could change lives, as was seen in the 1970s in the United States. Then, poverty declined thanks to progress triggered by programs such as Aid to Families with Dependent Children (AFDC), food stamps, Medicaid, and federal welfare payments for the aged, blind, and disabled. Modest gains were also visible through the expansion of many Great Society initiatives, including the new Supplement Security Income (SSI) program. Although poverty remained intractable, social secu-rity benefits, especially for the elderly, were a major factor in lowering the numbers of those living below the poverty line in society.

From a comparative perspective, no such formal social safety nets exist in Kenya or Tanzania. The two countries, which are home to Maasai, instead pay little attention to social welfare and leave families to fend for themselves. The assumption that African society, especially in rural communities, has built-in mechanisms for taking care of the poor has carried the day. And yet the disparities between people living in urban and rural settings has grown in magnitude. The rural poor often rely on remittances from their employed relatives who live in urban areas. For the Maasai, the issue is complicated. While they are known to live in systems that encourage family support, Maasai families often risk displacement and are strangers in their own land when they return (Goldman, 2011).

In sum, African political economies have not produced welfare states by any stretch of the imagination. Programs for the marginalized typi-cally receive very minimal government funding. Social welfare has not be-come a key function of the national governments in Kenya or Tanzania. In fact, the governments cut social spending in the 1980s, at the behest of the International Monetary Fund (IMF) and World Bank, which oversaw their structural adjustment programs (SAPs). Worse, for Kenya, the po-litical elite created a dependency syndrome in which key political figures promoted the *Harambee* (pulling together fundraising) movement as a means to buy political loyalty. Funds acquired from such dealings were channeled into fund-raising activities to help construct schools, cattle dips, and other social amenities. On all those scores, politically engineered social welfare programs abysmally failed to bring about poverty reduction among the Maasai.

That the government's ASAL development effort, as an anti-poverty program, was a failure is an understatement. Poverty and homelessness, which never existed during colonial times, have become a standard feature of Maasai life. Maasai communities face severe environmental degradation occasioned by government-engineered policies. The next section discusses how progressive marginalization of Maasai communities takes place unabated.

CONTINUED MARGINALIZATION THROUGH GLOBALIZATION

The economic subjugation of Maasai peoples was consummated during the colonial period when their land was grabbed for coffee, tea, and other cash crop plantations and for tourist resorts. Later, their rights to land were further eroded as large swathes were designated as wildlife reservations and game parks. None of the benefits that accrued from the expanding and highly lucrative tourist and extractions sector were shared with the former inhabitants of the land. As a way to support the extraction agenda, railways and other forms of transportation infrastructure were developed, often at the expense of Maasai rangelands. One may speculate that the colonial regime viewed the Maasai not only in derogatory, less-than-human terms, but also as an extension of their environment (e.g., the National Geographic semi-documentary film *Man of the Serengeti* with its many scenes of Maasai amid scenes of wild animals). After all, Maasai people have been living with wildlife harmoniously for centuries. Thus, for instance, the administration's actions to desecrate the sacred hill of Endoinyo Ormoruwak (Hill of Elders) is an expression of disrespect for tribal identity, traditions, and customs. Another way in which indigenous spaces are dishonored is through the destruction of certain resources, such as trees, which have spiritual value and are used in rituals among the Maasai (Ole Kaunga, 2015).

In more recent times, the neocolonial government has continued the practice of desecrating and taking Maasai lands and ignoring their rights. For instance, resources from soda ash to rare minerals and stones have been extracted without permission, and rangelands have been co-opted for the cultivation of cash crops, sport hunting, and gaming, displacing Maasai from their traditional homes (Ndemo, 2007). The taking and exploitation of land is not just an issue of local governmental decisions, but part of the global production economy. For instance, in one case reported by Patinkin (2013), an elite United Arab Emirates-based company leased 1,500 square kilometers of long-standing Maasai land from the Tanzania government working in conjunction with tourist business interests in Kenya. The actions forcefully displaced Maasai from their lands under the guise that land was needed as a corridor for wildlife moving between Maasai Mara National Park in Kenya and the Serengeti National Park in Tanzania. Rich Arab, European, and American tourists took opportunities to hunt big game roaming around the area and rendered much of the ecosystem barren. In many instances, tourist dollars do not trickle down to Maasai residents but instead are shared among corporations and African administrators.

In absolute terms, the level of material deprivation resulting from Maasai victimization by the global production economy is staggering and worsens with the encroachment of global ecotourism industries (Johnston, 2006). If it is generally argued that African nations have some of the highest income disparities in the world, then one might assume the magnitude of poverty in indigenous African communities defies the narrative of "Africa Arising" expressed in the Western media. As many as 64% of all Maasai in Kenya and Tanzania live below the poverty line (Biocultural Conservation Institute [BCI], 2015). A majority of Maasai communities are without piped water and basic sanitation. Many of their girls have no access to education and are known to die from easily preventable diseases. Claims that globalization reduces the gap between the poor and the rich cannot be supported in this context for, if anything, it has contributed to the deterioration of Maasai culture and the environments in which Maasai live.

Three facts bear on the decline of Maasai communities and livelihoods. First, a long-term trend toward misappropriation of Maasai land through the creation of Kenya's White Highlands and multiple national parks in both Kenya and Tanzania (Masai Mara, Serengeti, Tarangire, Lake Manyara, Mkomazi, etc.) pushed the community to the margins, thereby depriving them of their traditional access to water and good pasture.

The doctrine of markets favored those who had access to finance, which disadvantaged most peasants and pastoralists. Markets could not guarantee that Maasai competed fairly since they were not well represented among the ruling elite or educated classes. Since state-directed development programs followed blueprints from the international finance institutions, the emphasis was on extraction and foreign investment rather than developing Maasai communities. Needless, to say, the SAPs were about reducing social development programs and engineering reforms that protected the interests of corporations and elites.

Second, a strong correlation exists between the growth of populations of "outsiders" and the increased poverty in regions generally accepted to be Maasai homelands. By "outsiders," we mean African communities from ethnic groups that are not indigenous to Maasai territories. Although both Kenya's and Tanzania's constitutions allow anyone to live anywhere, and although both countries are signatory states to the UN Declaration on the Rights of Indigenous Peoples (UNDRIP) that affirms the protection of indigenous land rights, the grabbing of Maasailand by powerful elites has worsened since independence in 1963. Indeed, the most prestigious estates in Nairobi, like Karen and Ngong Hills, are dominated by ruling elites who pushed Maasai inhabitants into the outskirts of the fast-growing mega city of Nairobi. The unintended consequence of the invasion of Maasai territory by non-Maasai ethnic groups has been to commercialize Maasai lands and transfer their wealth externally.

Third, the education system and other government interventions to "modernize" the Maasai were in themselves strategies for exclusion rather than development. Even when schools were built ostensibly to provide opportunities for nomadic Maasai, a great number of the beneficiaries were people from other parts of the country. And the government crushed any movement to address misappropriation of Maasailands. Thus, if policy-makers hoped to provide opportunities for Maasai to tap into "emerging global opportunities," their integration processes came from the top and were calculated to co-opt a few Maasai leaders into the mainstream ruling elite rather than cultivate a broad-based effort to eradicate poverty and create social safety nets for pastoralist groups.

JOINING THE MARKETPLACE AS WATCHMEN: THE EMERGENCE OF THE MODERN MAASAI WARRIOR?

Debates over the impact of global capitalist forces on indigenous resources and the attendant transformations of Maasai forms of livelihood continue to be discussed in social science scholarly works. An emerging trend is a shift from traditional forms of employment to modern sectors of the economy. For the Masai, the shift has been unplanned and often an unintended consequence of the dispossession of Maasai land resources, ostensibly acquired by non-Maasai for "development." Encouraged by governments of Kenya and Uganda, investors claim to be creating job opportunities on Maasai land. Yet the outcomes demonstrate a Maasai reinvention of their traditional lifestyles, often delving into occupations that do not necessarily enhance their social security and that may lead to destitution.

Undergirding the narrative of failure and destitution is the insufficient scholarly attention given to indigenous efforts to enhance development in those areas where Maasai live. A few examples will illustrate this socio-economic quandary. In Northern Tanzania, for example, Martin Kariongi Ole Sanago founded the Institute for Orkonerei Pastoralists Advancement (IOPA). IOPA has an excellent record of entrepreneurship and has nurtured successful businesses that produce milk, butter, cheese, yogurt, and ghee, among other animal products. IOPA has been successful at generating its own electricity and digging bore holes for water provisioning, which enabled other small businesses like welding to flourish. Altogether, IOPA efforts helped provide electricity to 189 households and provided water to more than a million people (Atuhaire, 2015).

Further examples of Maasai responses to changing environmental and economic conditions are captured in Mungongo and Mwamfupe's (2003) work. They describe the poverty and social conditions that force Maasai tribesmen in Tanzania to seek work outside the traditional livestock herding lifestyle. While a good number already cultivate plots of land for food consumption, including prosperous ones who now own tractors, many Maasai have taken to selling cattle and investing in shops and guesthouses. The numbers of these entrepreneur merchants are said to be on the increase in townships around Morogoro, Tanzania. In most instances, there is little or no government support for this emerging trading class. Morogoro region has seen a rise of tensions between local farmers who are trying to expand onto Maasai village lands, and there have been a number of incidences of mob looting and destruction of Maasai-owned businesses and attacks on Maasai individuals. The government response has been muted and clearly biased against Maasai in favor of the majority farmers. No investigations of those responsible for the mob attacks have occurred, and charges have only been filed against several Maasai accused of retaliatory attacks and held without charge or access to legal support (International Working Group on Indigenous Affairs [IWGIA], 2017).

Mungongo and Mwamfupe (2003) are emphatic that it is state policies, especially forced sedentarization, that drive Maasai out of their homelands. The new environments mean that Maasai have to learn new skills and adapt to alien social norms. It means, for instance, that patriarchic tendencies have had to give way to allow women greater economic control. Thus, examples of empowered and entrepreneurial women should be given as much scholarly attention as those of men.

In another well-documented example, Maasai women have been at the forefront of the adoption of solar technology. More than 200 Maasai women in Kenya's Kajiado County championed the use of renewable energy through partnerships with Green Energy Africa. The Women and Entrepreneurship in Renewable Energy Project (WEREP) provides training to women technicians to enable them to install solar panels and to promote the idea of clean energy in the community. By the end of 2014, more than 2,000 households had adopted solar technology (Obi, 2015).

The positive benefits that come with solar panels are that Maasai can now charge their cell phones rather than walk miles to the nearest charging center, save money that was previously used for purchasing kerosene, and escape the negative health impacts of kerosene fumes in the homestead. Solar energy has helped mitigate further deforestation. Still, the effort is but a drop in the ocean considering that less than 2% of the population in the country benefits from the solar panels. But it is a start of a long journey to energy independence and the creation of opportunities for the community.

There are also numerous cases of successful cultural dance groups, like the Osiligi Maasai Warriors, which have had successful tours in Europe and other parts of the world. And other Maasai have found lucrative employment in the corporate tourism sector, both as guides and drivers in the national parks such as the Serengeti (Tanzania) and Masai Mara (Kenya).

Still, a popular media depiction is of a successful Maasai man transitioning from the traditional setting to the city yet embodying the traits of the old warrior. In one example, the popular Tanzanian rapper Mr. Ebbo (now deceased) cultivated an image of being a Maasai warrior so ignorant of city rules that he didn't know how to cross a busy street, didn't know that "soda water" was an unsweetened soda (evoking ridicule when he added sugar to it), and feared the ocean and the possibility of having his body eaten by fish. In another example, a 2012 news report shared the story of Samante, an ambitious Maasai tribesman who left his village in 2005 for Nairobi to start a travel (safari) company. Here is how Samante described his experience as an entrepreneur:

> I was robbed on the first day when I came to Nairobi. I was a little bit afraid, but then I said [to myself] like a warrior surviving inside the lion, and inside the elephants, I must survive in the city for me to be capable of achieving what I wanted in my life. . . . But sometimes wearing the suit, I became so much tired. . . . There are two Moses inside me.: The Nairobi Moses and the Maasai Moses. (Al Jazeera, 2015)

Many more such stories of successful Maasai entrepreneurs exist— however, challenged by circumstance and society—especially involving women producing and selling cultural artifacts. Most traditional beads and jewelry are sold to tourists and middle- and high-income Africans. The deep-seated patriarchal attitudes in Maasai society discourage shining a spotlight on successes gained by women. The narrative of women fetching water and firewood, tending animals, and repairing houses distort the incidence of entrepreneurship among the Maasai women. This distortion masks the fact, for instance, that at Nairobi's "Maasai Market" a lot of the jewelry sold is the handiwork of Maasai women. The Maasai Market is a network of open street bazaars where African artifacts—including clothing, handbags, wall hangings, wallets, sandals, utensils, candle holders, bags, and curios—are sold (Kenyan Poet, 2014).

The transformation of Maasai men and their entry into global marketplaces took a different turn from the 1990s into 2015, when challenges to security became a major concern for both urban Kenyans and Tanzanians. A new meaning was assigned to Maasai manhood. After all, the Maasai have historically not worked outside their communities, and this change has sociological implications for their communities as well as their identity as *moran*. The complexity of climate change, globalization, and land tenure insecurity were trigger mechanisms for this emerging transformation.

After 2013, the rise of insecurity in Kenya overwhelmed the political system to the extent that, in 2010, *Foreign Policy Magazine* ruled the country as drifting toward a collapse, ranking thirteenth on the publication's "Failed States" index. Threats to security worsened after 2013, through a series of terrorist attacks that most commentators attributed to the failure of the state's security apparatus (Hidalgo, 2015; Meservey, 2015). Reactions among the business community and diplomatic corps evinced high levels of skepticism about the government's competence and ability to protect its citizens. Small businesses especially needed trustworthy security guards. Trustworthiness can be a function of ethnic stereotypes. Although debunked in empirical observations, common stereotypes hold that members of the Luhya community are disproportionately employed as watchmen and security guards because they are considered trustworthy (Githongo, 2015; Osiro, 2015). The entry of Maasai *moran* into this occupation arose because of the widespread perception that Maasai are both trustworthy and brave, which makes them more suitable for the job of security guard than other groups.

Perhaps influenced by cultural perceptions of Maasai men as fearless warriors, small businesses enterprises offered employment opportunities to thousands of the tribesmen. Maasai, clad in brightly colored *shuka* (toga-like attire), migrated to urban centers (Nairobi, Mombasa, Arusha, Dar es Salaam, Zanzibar) and townships, thereby abandoning their pastoralist traditions. The massive numbers of Maasai migrating to secure employment as night watchmen caused the Maasai Conservation of Culture and Heritage Center to use elders to vet the members of this emerging working class (Nairobi News, 2014). *USA Today* depicted the emergence of Maasai watchmen as follows:

> Today they are locked in a bitter dispute with the white farmers in the north of Kenya and the government for the return of their ancestral lands. But new research suggests the Maasai finally are reinventing themselves as an urban tribe of entrepreneurs and ferocious security guards, as they find alternative, more modern ways of proving their prowess. (Crilly, 2004)

With Maasai men joining the formal and informal security sector as watchmen (*askari*), the community signified that indigenous knowledge had meaning beyond moranism. Maasai guards and watchmen enjoyed the reputation of being committed to their employers. In Kenya and Tanzania, countries which perform poorly on Transparency International's Corruption Perception Index (Kenya and Tanzania were ranked 145 and 119, respectively, out of 175 nations in 2014), trustworthiness is an important virtue. The media is replete with information about watchmen and other security workers engaging in corrupt actions. For example, some watchmen in Mombasa are known to collect rent from sex workers who prefer to use "alleys for a few minutes at a time as a cheaper alternative to paying for hotel rooms" (IRIN, 2009b). As emerging social entrepreneurs, Maasai watchmen, however, are not generally associated with such illicit practices. Maasai men are also regarded to be ferocious and to "take pride in their manhood as a protector and provider" (Crilly, 2004).

Consistent with Ndemo's (2007) assertion that Maasai typically don't abandon entirely but rather integrate their traditional livelihoods with employment in the cash economy, most of those interviewed preferred to return to their traditional homes. After all, as Cable News Network (CNN) anchor Brooke Baldwin (2015), observed while visiting the Masai Mara, the Maasai were increasingly taking on 21st-century jobs, "but they almost always return home. Just like Joseph, our tour guide, they continue to give back, never forgetting their roots, their home." As Crilly (2004) suggests, serving as watchmen "actualizes their idea of excitement in combat and as a result of their earnings they buy cattle and therefore restore their status as herdsmen."

In fact, taking urban jobs as watchmen is often regarded as stop-gap measure, a temporary occupation to enable them to earn money for purposes of buying cattle or to resettle in their homelands. Maasai actions exemplify Michael Todaro's (1977) economic model of the "target demands" popularized by migrant workers whose sole purpose for moving from rural to urban settings is to earn money for a specific target, for example, to buy roofing materials, a bicycle, radio, or other expensive item that they could not afford if they remained working as farm laborers. Thus, to the minds of many Maasai *moran*, taking jobs as watchmen serves to fulfill a short-term social security need rather than becoming a permanent occupation. It is not a panacea for the broader economic safety of the Maasai community. And there are many socioeconomic policy consequences associated with the rise of the Maasai watchmen entrepreneurship.

A glaring consequence of this phenomenon is the resulting poor negotiations for salaries among the Maasai watchmen. Because of the informal nature of day and night watchmen, it is hard to enforce government minimum wages. According to the Kenya Wages Guide of 2013, night watchmen earn about KSh. 10,911.70 ($102 USD) in Nairobi, Mombasa, and Kisumu. They made far less in smaller towns, about KSh. 6,223.60 ($58 USD) per month. Guidelines issued after Labor Day, May 1, 2015, indicate that the minimum wage in the country was around KSh. 5, 844.20 ($54 USD) for day watchmen and KSh. 6, 970.40 ($65 USD) for night watchmen in the smaller towns. In Nairobi, the rates are more than KSh. 10,954 ($102 USD). These low figures prompted the Kenya National Private Security Workers Union to seek an audience with government officials, but no change has been reported. According to various official Ministry of Labor Gazette Notices, watchmen and other workers are entitled to housing allowances, which may add up to about 15% of the pay. Because of weak negotiating capacity, unions are unable to ensure implementation of better wages for Maasai watchmen. For example, in the Luanda, Maseno, Majengo-Vihiga area, by contrast, the average salary for Maasai watchmen was KSh. 5,000 per month (less than US$60). In other words, the temporary nature of the watchmen's positions and the large pool of Maasai available for watchman jobs resulted in pay scales that were remarkably below the minimum wages in other rural sectors. A caveat to the claim for low wages is that employers often provided housing for the Maasai watchmen. However, in most cases, the shelters are substandard and lack basic amenities.

Although Maasai men have largely internalized their jobs as temporary, the high levels of unemployment have forced them to readjust their lifestyles and have converted them into "nomadic watchmen." Thus, most Maasai watchmen move from one employer to another, often starting new jobs without formal contracts. And even when contracts were available, Maasai men consider these jobs as temporary or seasonal. Government ministries of labor have yet to recognize the informal contracts between various employers and the Maasai watchmen in urban centers and rural townships.

Informality and mobility in security sector employment have not, however, impinged on the strength of Maasai support networks. Urban Maasai watchmen have mobilized and established a resilient network, an indigenous social safety net, that—just as in the rural areas—is led by elder Maasai. It comes into play when new migrants seek to join the workforce, with established watchmen alerting new migrants to housing and job opportunities and actively recruiting Maasai from their home areas. It also comes into play when a watchman dies or is imprisoned.

In one notable case from Dar es Salaam, a watchman fell to his death in a well when he stepped on its insubstantial wooden cover in the dark. Night watchmen at the neighboring property heard a worrisome noise of wood loudly cracking and searched in vain for him, calling down the well to no reply. Emergency personnel retrieved his body from the well the following day, and it was taken to the hospital for the cause of death to be determined. Funds were raised as news of his death spread among Maasai watchmen in each and every neighborhood of Dar es Salaam, with the recognized elder of each neighborhood collecting the contributions. Over the course of 1 day, more than 4 million Tanzanian shillings (~US$1,700) had been raised, which served to transport and escort the body home, pay for the funeral, and leave a contribution to the family of the deceased, which had lost a primary income provider. The Maasai social system of strong horizontal linkages through age-sets, as opposed to only vertical linkages through familial ties, helps explain the ability of Maasai to recreate resilient social networks even when they are far from home.

Government policy in both countries does not recognize and reward the entrepreneurial spirit of the Maasai as watchmen. In comparison, Maasai *morans* are exploited for purposes of cultural tourism and have continued to experience economic marginalization through appropriation of land and other natural resources. By recognizing Maasai watchmen as social entrepreneurs, this chapter opens up the possibility for further dialogue and research in advancing knowledge on social entrepreneurship within indigenous communities. At a policy level, the local governments must provide forums that facilitate the organization of Maasai workers taking on jobs as watchmen in urban settings. There are many benefits to networking and associational decision-making. For instance, Maasai men would benefit from informational and public safety and crime prevention training development initiatives.

At employer levels, the proliferation of Maasai watchmen has to be embedded into the social and economic goals of existing partnerships between small-scale enterprises and local governments. Social entrepreneurs can function effectively when the underlying causes of poverty and marginalization are also interrogated. At independence, Maasai lifestyles were not the cause of poverty in their vast territories. Their current underdevelopment and continued participation in alien market systems has certainly not helped the community's survival and economic sustainability.

CONCLUSION

In examining the rise of the Maasai informal watchmen sector, a missing narrative is that it is directly correlated with the loss and displacement of Maasai pasture lands and the ecological destructions stemming from man-made activities. Vast areas of Maasailand were designated national park and animal reservations and placed off limits to indigenous Maasai owners who were evicted without compensation and denied access to pasture and water resources for their livestock.

From an informed economic analysis, Kenya and Tanzania both face a huge unemployment crisis. With unemployment rates exceeding 40% in both countries, entrepreneurship must be seen as a welcome gesture for the authorities. Most development experts see education and more education as one of the main ways that Maasai empowerment can be realized. Education opportunities for both men and women have to be a part of a social justice agenda that includes respect for indigenous resources and indigenous ways of life. Educator Kellie O'Brien claims that "the Maasai haven't changed because they don't have an education" (Pavin, 2015).

In 2006, O'Brien founded a primary school to empower the Maasai by offering quality education and entrepreneurial skills-building programs for women. But to attribute the strength of cultural institutions and lifestyles to inadequate education is also to deny the value that Maasai place on their way of life and the deep connectedness they feel to their herds.

From a public policy perspective, government and corporate action must match the efforts of voluntary organizations that genuinely seek to provide training and education for entrepreneurship in indigenous communities. This implies that corporations and governing elites cannot constantly talk about development while ignoring the fundamental human rights abuses meted out on indigenous peoples, including the Maasai. In the meantime, Maasai communities in Tanzania and Kenya pursue initiatives with entrepreneurial zeal, operating as agents intent on addressing the social and economic crises imposed by "development" in their nation states. Social entrepreneurs, we say, are visionary leaders who use innovative approaches, strategies, and/or technologies to solve a social problem. They continuously refine and adapt these approaches so that they can continue to make meaningful use of the resources they have in alleviating poverty and contributing to social and economic justice. We submit that Maasai watchmen are social entrepreneurs who have taken practical skills and indigenous ways of being and knowing and have renovated and deployed them in a "new" sector in order to alleviate the economic and social injustices they face.

REFERENCES

Al Jazeera. (2015, July 8). *Africa on the move*. Al Jazeera Special Series. Retrieved from https://www.aljazeera.com/programmes/specialseries/2015/07/africa-move-150708120954016.html

Baldwin, B. (2015). Finding the meaning of home in Africa. CNN Wire (July 29). Retrieved from https://www.cnn.com/travel/article/kenya-masai-mara-brooke-baldwin-feat/index.html

Biocultural Conservation Institute (BCI). (2015, October 9). *The Maasai*. Retrieved from http://www.bioguides.org/the-maasai/

Carson, D. (2015, May 8). Maasai tribe member visits Village School. Bennington *Banner*, p. A06.

Crilly, R. (2004, November 10). Maasai change lifestyle to fit modern Africa. *USA Today*. Retrieved from http://usatoday30.usatoday.com/news/world/2004-11-10-maasai-tribe_x.htm

Dana, L. P. (2007). Toward a multidisciplinary definition of indigenous entrepreneurship. In L-P. Dana (Ed.), *International handbook of research on indigenous entrepreneurship* (pp. 3–6). Cheltenham, UK: Edward Elgar.

Githongo, J. (2015, August 21). Kenya: Bitter truth about sugar, politics, and watchmen (opinion). *The Star*. Retrieved from https://allafrica.com/stories/201508210399.html

Goldman, M. J. (2011). Strangers in their own land: Maasai and wildlife conservation in Northern Tanzania. *Conservation and Society, 9*(1), 65–79.

Atuhaire, G. (2015, September 2). The Tanzania Maasai entering industrial age. Retrieved from http://www.dandc.eu/enartcle/maasai-pastoralist-tanzania

Hidalgo, P. (2015, April 12). Kenya's own worst enemy: Al Shabab isn't the real problem. *Foreign Affairs*. Retrieved from https://www.foreignaffairs.com/articles/kenya/2015-04-12/kenyas-own-worst-enemy

Hindle, K., & Lansdowne, M. (2005). Brave spirits on new paths: Towards a globally relevant paradigm of indigenous entrepreneurship research. *Journal of Entrepreneurship and Small Business, 18*(2), 131–141.

Integrated Regional Information Networks (IRIN). (2009a, June 10). Amos Lerasia, "Now the drought comes almost every year." *The New Humanitarian*. Retrieved from http://www.thenewhumanitarian.org/fr/node/246027

Integrated Regional Information Networks (The New Humanitarian, formerly IRIN News). (2009b, April 15). Kenya: Watchmen and sex workers unite. Retrieved from http://www.thenewhumanitarian.org/report/83934/kenya-watchmen-and-sex-workers-unite

International Working Group on Indigenous Affairs (IWGIA). (2017, February). *Briefing note: Violation of rights of pastoralists in Morogoro Region, Tanzania.* Retrieved from https://www.iwgia.org/en/tanzania?start=4

Johnston, A. M. (2006). *Is the sacred for sale: Tourism and indigenous people.* New York: Earthscan.

Meservey, J. (2015, January 21). False security in Kenya: When counterterrorism is counterproductive. *Foreign Affairs.* Retrieved from https://www.foreignaffairs.com/articles/east-africa/2015-01-21/false-security-kenya

Patinkin, J. (2013). Tanzania's Maasai battle game hunters for grazing land. Retrieved from http://www.bbc.com/news/world-africa-22155538

Kenyan Poet. (2014, April 4). The Maasai market open days schedule in Nairobi. *Kenyan Poet.* Retrieved from http://www.kenyanpoet.com/the-maasai-market-open-days-schedule-in-nairobi/

King, K. (1996). *Jua Kali Kenya: Change and development in an informal economy: 1970–1995.* Nairobi: East African Educational Publishers.

Kirzner, I. (1997). Entrepreneurial discovery and the competitive market process: An Austrian Approach. *Journal of Economic Literature, 35,* 60–85.

Lekuton, J. L., & Viola H. (2005). *Facing the lion: Growing up Maasai on the African savanna.* New York: National Geographic Children's Books.

Mullei, A., & Bokea, C. (Eds.). (1999). *Micro and small enterprises in Kenya: Agenda for improving the policy environment.* Nairobi: ICEG.

Mungongo, C., & Mwanfupe, D. (2003). *Poverty and changing livelihoods of migrant Maasai pastoralists in Morogoro and Kilsa districts, Tanzania.* Research Report 03.5. Dar es Salaam, Tanzania: Mkuki Na Nyota Publishers.

Nairobi News. (2014, February 22). Elders want Maasai guards vetted. *Nairobi News.* Retrieved from http://nairobinews.nation.co.ke/elders-want-maasai-guards-vetted

Ndemo, B. (2007). The Maasai: Entrepreneurship and change. In L-P. Dana (Ed.), *International handbook of research on indigenous entrepreneurship* (pp. 84–99). Cheltenham, UK: Edward Elgar.

Njeru, C. (2015, October 9). Kenya: Climate change, poverty, and tourists put Maasai daughters at risk. *Women News Network (WNN).* Retrieved from http://womennewsnetwork.net/2010/04/16/kenya-climatechange-trafficking-892/

Obi, L. (2015, June 3). Toting panels on donkeys, Maasai women lead a solar revolution. *Reuters.* Retrieved from https://www.reuters.com/article/us-kenya-solar-women/toting-panels-on-donkeys-maasai-women-lead-a-solar-revolution-idUSKBN0OJ0LX20150603

Oduor, V. (2011, January 17). The Maasai woman: A social-economic engine of Masai Life. *International Trade Centre News Bulletin.* Retrieved from http://www.intracen.org/The_Maasai_Woman_a_social_economic_Engine_of_Maasai_Life/

Ole Kaunga, J. (2015). The use of indigenous traditional knowledge for ecological and bio-diverse resource management by the Laikipia Maasai and the Samburu. In M. Roue, N. Cesard, Y. C. Adou Yao, & A. Oteng-Yeboah (Eds.), *Knowing our lands and resources: Indigenous and local knowledge of biodiversity and ecosystem services in Africa* (pp. 6–17). Paris: UNESCO.

Ole Saitoti, T. (2014). *The worlds of a Maasai warrior: An autobiography.* New York: Amazon Digital Services.

Osiro, W. (2015, July 20). And you thought all Kenyans were alike: Misconceptions Kenyan's have of one another (Blog). *The Huffington Post*. Retrieved from https://www.huffpost.com/entry/and-you-thought-all-kenya_b_7822716

Otenyo-Matanda, M. (2009). *Entrepreneurial orientation and access to new markets by small-scale earthenware manufacturers in Kenya* (doctoral thesis). School of Business, Kenyatta University, Nairobi.

Pavin, L. (2015, September 17). Moving the Maasai forward. The Doings (Clarendon Hills, IL). *Pioneer Press*, p. 35.

Republic of Kenya (RoK). (1986). *Sessional Paper No. 1. of 1986 on economic management for renewed growth*. Nairobi: Government Printer.

Republic of Kenya (RoK). (1997). *Industrial transformation to the Year 2020*. Sessional Paper No. 2. Ministry of Trade and Industry and Central Bureau of Statistics. Nairobi: Government Printer.

Republic of Kenya (RoK). (2005). *On development of micro and small-scale enterprises for wealth and employment creation for poverty reduction*. Sessional Paper No. 2 of 2005. Nairobi: Government Printer.

Schumpeter, J. A. (1934). *The theory of economic development: An inquiry into profits, capital, credit, interest, and the business cycle* (Trans. Redvers Opie). Cambridge, MA: Harvard University Press.

Shane, S., & Venkataraman, S. (2000). The promise of entrepreneurship as a field of research. *Academy of Management Review*, *25*(1), 217–226.

Spear, T., & Waller, R. (Eds.). (1993). *Being Maasai: Ethnicity and identity in East Africa*. Oxford, UK: James Currey Publishers.

Thompson, M., & Homewood, K. (2002). Entrepreneurs, elites, and exclusion in Maasailand: Trends in wildlife conservation and pastoralist development. *Human Ecology*, *30*(1), 107–138.

Todaro, M. (1977). *Economics for a developing world: An introduction to principles, problems and policies for development*. London: Longman.

CHAPTER 13

⌒〜⌒

Social Enterprise in Taiwan

Economic and Social Welfare Transition

YI-JUNG WU

INTRODUCTION

Taiwan is now considered a well-developed country in all aspects in Asia. However, there, the special colonial era in Taiwan in the past century formed the foundation of development in many perspectives. In this chapter, I introduce the nation's economic and welfare journey of the past century and discuss how the newly blossomed business model, social enterprise (SE), shapes social welfare and economic disciplines in the modern development of Taiwan.

The idea of SE has been actively applied globally in resolving social problems in the past two decades. The implication of the SE vision is an important milestone for the economic and welfare progress of Taiwan, and the country's planning process not only reveals the interdependency between economic and welfare development, but also reexamines societal progress over the past century.

The philosophy of "interdependency" also extends to public–private collaboration on resolving social problems (Executive Yuan, 2017). In civic society, it is recognized that community becomes one of the major sources of momentum in social activities (Danhardt & Danhardt, 2007). Citizen

Yi-jung Wu, *Social Enterprise in Taiwan* In: Social Entrepreneurship and Enterprises in Economic and Social Development.
Edited by: Katharine Briar-Lawson, Paul Miesing, and Blanca M. Ramos, Oxford University Press (2021).
© Oxford University Press. DOI: 10.1093/oso/9780197518298.003.0014.

participation has been an important factor driving the political system to be more responsive to the core of public interests. In contemporary society, the incentive of citizen participation is no longer driven by self-interest; it is more about mutual benefits and the sustainability of society, leading to more efficacy in social issue awareness and problem-solving (Berggren, 2016). With these major core issues in mind, the idea of SE has been active in Taiwan since 2007.

Through years of effort by the forerunners of SE, the Taiwan government decided to officially promote and support SE with some specific actions. In 2014, the government announced its phase-one 2014–2016 Social Enterprise Action Plan, recognizing the challenges and opportunities of SE and laying out relevant policies and action plans for potential funders of SE. More importantly, the government perceived the synergy for successful SE with specific support from the public sector. Therefore, the Ministry of Labor (MOL), Economic Affairs (MOEA), Interior (MOI), and Health and Welfare (MOHW) have collaborated for policy integration and action planning since then. In this phase, the government handled the steering wheel in the front seat along the path of SE development.

Although the development of SE seems to be a natural evolution in such a citizen-involved society as Taiwan, it actually took more than a century for Taiwan to begin from a humble colony of Japan to a prosperous society. Here, I briefly address the historical background of Taiwan first, and then address its progress from both economic and social welfare perspectives.

HISTORICAL ECONOMIC BACKGROUND

Taiwan has been a colony of many countries since the 17th century, during the "Age of Discovery." In addition to the governance of her ancestors from Mainland China, the Ming (1661–-1683) and Ching (1683–1895) dynasties, Taiwan was also ruled by the Netherlands (1624–1662), Spain (1626–1642, northern Taiwan only), and Japan (1895–1945) for decades. Due to the remote geographic location of Taiwan, sitting distant from Mainland China, the Ming Dynasty did not invest much to make it prosper. The Ching Dynasty began to regularly input resources and undertake efforts to activate economic activities in Taiwan, although many of these activities were forced on the Ching by other powerful countries. Several ports, including Keelung, Tamsui, and Kaohsiung, also became international ports for trade after China had been defeated by Western countries and signed the Beijing and Tianjing treaties. The open-door policy of these treaties showed, on one hand, the unfortunate "survival of the fittest" principle under the rule of international politics. On the other hand, it also opened up opportunities for economic growth for Taiwan.

Later, Taiwan was ceded to Japan as a colony from 1895 until the end of World War II. In Japan, Taiwan was considered a food provider because the weather was suitable for growing rice, the major food in Japanese daily cuisine. Therefore, during the colonial era, rice and sugar cane were the two major crops grown due to their important economic values (Wu, 2004). The historical data also showed that gross domestic product (GDP) growth in Taiwan was significant during the colonial era compared to the self-sufficient but nearly non-growth precolonial era (Wu, 2003).

In 1949, the Communist Party took over Mainland China. Chiang Kai-shek, who was the national leader at that time, moved the government to Taiwan, hoping to realize the ideal of reunification in a short time. Since then, the sovereign debate between China and Taiwan has long been a sensitive and unsolvable ideological issue on the island and internationally. However, the "ideal" of reunification never occurred, and the government decided to refocus on the economic development of Taiwan rather than strengthen its military force.

Due to the militarily strategic position of Taiwan, the United States continued to provide assistance to Taiwan after World War II, mainly in two dimensions: daily necessities (such as food and clothing; 1950–1965) and military weapons (1950–1973). These US supports were intended to later help the development of Taiwan in several aspects: first, to maintain the stability of Taiwan; second, to assist US military power in Asia; and, third, help Taiwan become self-sustaining (Jacoby, 1966). As a result, US assistance played a role in the economic revival in Taiwan for more than two decades (1950–1973). However, in 1979, due to the "One China" policy, the United States terminated its official relationship with Taiwan and established diplomatic relations with China. This became another diplomatic strike against Taiwan after it was forced out of the United Nations in 1971. The early assistance from the United States provided immediate support to help Taiwan recover from the war and that later assistance set the foundation for further economic development.

Taiwan's special historical relations with Japan and the United States helped Taiwan strengthen its international trade capacity during the 1960s and later achieve the renowned "Taiwan miracle" in the 1970s. At the same time, rapidly growing economic "miracles" were also under way in Hong Kong, Korea, and Singapore, which collectively, along with Taiwan, were referred to as the four "Asian Tigers."

In the 1980s, Taiwan's foreign reserve reached its peak and became the highest in the world. At that time, the United States was the biggest business partner to Taiwan, and almost half of Taiwanese exports (48.8%) were destined for the United States. Since then, economic growth in Taiwan has been stable. In addition, its policy-makers also designed policies that invested a great amount in researching and developing computer-related industry, leading to the establishment of the Industrial Technology Research Institute (ITRI). The Science Park and the ITRI later became an important resource and source of momentum contributing to the industrial upgrading of the 1990s.

In 1990, the Taiwanese stock market reached a historical high point (12,682 points) but also showed indicators of being a "bubble economy." The government took action to forcefully "burst" the bubble to maintain healthy and steady economic growth. Although these actions made the stock market index drop 85% (to 2,485 points) in that year and led to an annual GDP growth decrease from 8% to 5%, it was later recognized as the "necessary evil" to avoid the aftermath of the global financial crisis in 1997 (Liang & Wang, 2002).

As of September 2019, the total population of Taiwan is 23,593,783, and, with continuous progress, the GDP stands at US$25,332 per person (Department of Statistics, 2019). The postwar GDP (return to the Republic of China government) in 1945 was US$428.54, and the total population was then 4,852,000 (Wu, 2003).

Postcolonial economic planning in the past century has been dominated by the central government in Taiwan, which has a strong arm in directing economic progress. As the country reached certain economic prosperity and the concept of a civic society emerged, a more comprehensive welfare framework began to take off. Next, I introduce briefly the social welfare evolution in Taiwan over the past decade and how this history brings a once deficient society to its current status.

HISTORICAL WELFARE BACKGROUND

The Japanese colonial era lasted from 1895 until the end of World War II (1895–1945). Needless to say, as a colony, the development of social welfare was a neglected issue by the colonial administration. The powerful colonists were concerned more about their own business interests rather than the welfare of the colonized.

For the Taiwanese people, there were ambivalent emotions toward the Japanese government. On the one hand, many infrastructures were designed and implemented during the colonial era, which later accelerated the social and economic development of Taiwan after control by Japan ended.

Ending the colonial era in 1945, the welfare system in Taiwan went through three "golden decades" in the 1950s, 1970s, and 1990s. In the first two golden decades (1950s–1970s), the government completed the provision of a social insurance system and then implemented 9-year compulsory education, which set important foundations for later development. In the 1990s, the third golden decade occurred, when economic activities reached their peak and growth plateaued, resulting in a series of new regulatory formulations. It was notable that, in 1994, the first Guiding Principles for the Republic of China Social Welfare Policy was promulgated. The National Health Insurance Act, Child and Youth Sexual Exploitation Prevention Act, People with Disabilities Rights Protection Act, Sexual Assault Crime Prevention Act, and Social Worker Act were all enacted during the 1990s. As more and more welfare-relevant acts were implemented, the social welfare system in Taiwan became more comprehensive in all aspects.

Later in 2014, the compulsory education act was amended from 9 years to 12 years. The popularity of education also became a major source of momentum for economic development; this stemmed particularly from the 9-year compulsory education requirement (Ministry of Education, 2014, 2017). The 9-year compulsory education policy raised the overall educational attainment and quality of the national workforce, which was synergized with economic developmental policies. The gradual but steady accumulation of human capital and relevant policies contributed to the later advancement of the economy. The overall quality rise in human capital is deemed as a vital factor on the way to a civic society.

Moreover, in order to be connected to international trends, the International Covenant on Economic, Social, and Cultural Rights and the International Covenant on Civil and Political Rights, two UN conventions, were also passed by the Congress and then signed and ratified by the president. The two Covenants were included in the guiding principles and were expected to shape the social welfare system in Taiwan in line with an internationalized standard (Executive Yuan, 2012).

The government hoped to build on these policies to attain the next vision, a "Just Society." The vision of the "just society" was mainly about evenly distributing income to shrink income divides. The strategies that were taken were built on six perspectives. First, the government planned to raise personal average income, particularly by increasing the job opportunities and income standards for the economically disadvantaged. Second, the government reformed the national health insurance to assure the sustainability of the 22-year national policy. Third, the Congress passed a long-term care Act in 2015, which was implemented in 2017, to address Taiwan's ageing society.

In the "golden decade" vision framework, the element of "community" was always mentioned. In the 1990s, the reform pendulum in the public sector swung to the paradigm of public management, causing the private sector to part ways with the public sector on solutions to social problems. A course of "integrated community development" was proposed by the Council for Cultural Affairs in 1994 (which reorganized in 2012 and is currently housed under the Ministry of Culture). Before the direction of integrated community development was settled, welfare policies were mainly top-down and dominated by the central government. However, since the time when the top-down principle was ratified, the concept of public–private collaboration has become one of major movements in the public sector that provide another path to solutions when public resources are tightly constrained.

PUBLIC–PRIVATE COLLABORATION

With the maturity of the economy, welfare systems, and overall educational attainment, the element of community was brought in through the application of public–private collaboration. The community-based problem-solving system also allowed opportunities for citizen participation. In other words, citizens began to be proactive in solving social problems around them, and the community bridged the channels of communication and collaboration between the government and citizens in problem-solving. With the concept of "community" embedded as an element of policy, the public sector was able to line up with the community and proactive citizens to share the burden of services (Danhardt & Danhardt, 2007). The idea of a *policy community* implies that government, the private sector, not-for-profit organizations, and the public should all be included as a part of the community. Therefore, in the policy planning, formation, legalization, and evaluation stages, everyone and all sectors ought to shoulder the responsibility of forming a "safety net" in societal development.

For example, in Nanto County, Taomi Community was one of the most damaged areas following major earthquakes on September 21, 1999. After 921 earthquakes, Taomi was deserted; in order to rebuild their hometown and revive the local economy, local citizens began to plan for a series of themes and activities to make the community home again for the evacuated population. Moreover, these newly planned activities, such as local eco-system tours and tours of local farming businesses, also made Taomi a destination for many tourists. More importantly, the community also laid out many community care programs for the elderly and children, hoping to make the community a hub for mutual supportive services in Taiwan.

The Taomi community is now the "New-hometown Foundation," one of the SEs in Taiwan focused on local artistic innovation and a cultural preservation effort. Moreover, it is a good model for showcasing public–private partnerships in solving contemporary social issues and creating a common cause between the two sectors (LeRoux, 2010). A further introduction of SE development in Taiwan follows.

SOCIAL ENTERPRISE IN TAIWAN

Network, Civic Society, and Social Enterprise

The Taomi community not only shows a great transition to public–private partnership, but also represents a typical case of *network governance*. Traditionally, politicians in Taiwan hold to the rationale of "big government" to govern and deliver social services. With big government in mind, politicians and administrators are used to planning things out thoroughly for the public. However, as the contemporary government begins to face challenges of brain drain, financial shortage, and "wicked" social problems in the public sector, network governance becomes a significant solution. For the public sector, it is no longer possible for a single sector to handle all social issues due to the interdisciplinary feature of social issues.

"Wicked problems" are "not amenable to solution through traditional, linear planning, and top-down management" (Rittel & Webber, 1973)." Ultimately, solutions to wicked problems have to take place in a multiple disciplinary context. In this interdisciplinary context, players no longer operate alone (Hsia & Beyer, 2000), and it is desirable to involve players from varied professions and different sectors. In other words, the solutions should rely on the integration of financial, social, and human capitals from diverse players. Within a civic society, citizens in the community start to form their common vision and put it into action. Since citizen participation and response to neglected social needs are two important rationales of SE, the inclusion of SE seems to fit well with the idea of network governance.

To integrate all the efforts in SEs, the Ministry of Economic Affairs supported the establishment of a Social Innovative Platform (Ministry of Economic Affairs, 2020). This platform allows idea exchange and information broadcasting in the SE community. Furthermore, there is a self-registered list of SEs (innovative organizations) which continues to update the status for all stakeholders in the field, including the government, current/potential SE innovators/investors, and the interested public.

The Origin of Social Enterprise: Two Cases

In Taiwan, SE was initiated in 2007, with the first investment from a well-developed Taiwanese international business, Trend Micro Inc. The Chairman of the Board of Trend Micro, Ming-chen Chang, partnered with a popular writer, Wen-hua Wang, to establish the first venture capital SE, Flow Inc. in Taiwan. The mission of Flow is to "make money; make meaning." Flow positions itself as a consulting and service company which helps the disadvantaged to discover their own potential and develop their unique business models. Particularly, Flow intends to eliminate the physical divide of the disadvantaged through technology. It employs business information modeling (BIM) to assure the innovation of efficient and effective business models for the needy.

BIM is a model that follows three principles to help the needy be successful in the job market: first, create an appropriate business model for the disadvantaged in a cloud computing market; second, create high-value added job opportunities for the disadvantaged via technology; third, avoid reliance on government exemptions and private donations to sustain the business in the long term. Aligned with its core mission, Flow is determined to create innovative standard operating procedures (SOPs) to fit with individual competencies and resolve individual difficulties to shape the common good among customers (mainly the disadvantaged). Moreover, Flow also provides customers, who are usually needy populations, with professional training and educational mechanisms supportive of their career paths (Ministry of Culture, 2017). Flow hopes to enrich the life of the disadvantaged by finding them good job opportunities and helping them gradually climb up the career ladder for a positive "flip-over" life change.

In 2008, Aurora Social Enterprise was the first SE to use the term "social enterprise" in its name. The major mission of Aurora is to connect small-scale local farmers, particularly indigenous tribe farmers, to a stable supply chain and selling platform (Social Enterprise Insights, 2013; Taiwan Social Enterprise Organization, 2015). Like many tribal populations around the world, they face many challenges in their lives and in their careers that put them into an intergenerational cycle of poverty. The contemporary economic system forces many of tribal adults to move away from their family and children for job opportunities. This not only weakens the function of family education, but also jeopardizes the cultural reserve of the tribe.

All these issues burden the already marginalized status of the indigenous tribal population.

The founder of Aurora discovered that the major difficulty—lack of job opportunities—keeps young indigenous adults from staying in the tribe and prescribed a solution for them. The solution is to design a specific business model for the local indigenous community, from farming to selling. Aurora, as coordinator and consultant, becomes involved at the beginning of the supply chain (producing) and is active until the end (selling and customer services). Being an SE, Aurora's contracting farmers choose organic farming to produce their crops and Aurora employs the concept of fair-trade to sell the products. In addition to the supply chain of agricultural products, Aurora also lays out a series of environmental education initiatives for the public. These plans not only help promote Aurora's mission and products, but also allow the public to recognize the importance of environmental protection and fair trade (Social Enterprise Insights, 2013). Ultimately, Aurora's mission is to support indigenous people to either stay on or return to their motherland, treat the environment with respect, stabilize their family situation, and work toward a prosperous community.

The Initial Actions of Social Enterprise

Starting with the lead set by Flow's and Aurora's visions, Taiwan's SE began to grow and achieve positive attention from the public. Important trends gradually revealed some important features of Taiwan's SE: enterprises are established mostly by members of the younger generation, and the tradition of mid- and small-sized business culture in Taiwan still dominates the field of SE (Council for Economic Planning And Development, 2011). Many of the not-for-profit organizations (NPOs) also decide that moving toward the direction of self-sufficient SEs is necessary in terms of organizational sustainability (Lin, 2013). Although there may be a rugged road ahead of them, they strive to find their own niche and build from there.

After many years of efforts from the forerunners of SE, the Taiwan government decided to officially promote and support SE with some specific actions. In 2014, the government announced the Social Enterprise Action Plan, recognizing the challenges and opportunities of SE and laying out relevant policies and action plans for potential funders of SE. More importantly, the government perceived the synergy of successful SE with specific support from the public sector. Therefore, the MOL, MOEA, MOI, and MOHW all collaborate in policy integration and action planning.

In the case of SE development, MOL and MOEA are the major players. Nevertheless, MOI and MOHW also have their specific roles in supporting SE. MOL is in charge of developing job opportunities and human capital enhancement plans. It is also the leader in setting up the SE promotion platform, coordinating business alliances, providing job consultation, integrating investments, and distributing resources. Relevant policy creation and adjustments that encourage the startup of SEs are also major missions of MOEA. More importantly, it is also the major coordinator of resource integration among relevant agencies. In addition to MOEA, MOI plays a role in deregulation involving community-based coops/organizations because many SEs are small-sized and community-based. MOI is the government agency that manages organizations. Deregulation helps SEs grow with more flexibility. Moreover, many of the SEs are established with a mission of supporting a specified disadvantaged population, such as the blind and the elderly. MOHW is expected to "connect the dots" of relevant services and provide a more comprehensive support system to these SEs (Ministry of Economic Affairs, 2014).

The action plan was implemented from 2014 to 2016. The Small and Medium Enterprise Administration within MOEA was the important resource connector behind the scene of SE promotion. After the action plan expired, MOEA continued to hold SE forums to encourage current SE funders or potential funders to dialogue with one another and with relevant agencies in charge. MOEA also established a platform, the International Entrepreneur Initiative Taiwan (IEIT), to help find funders for those who have good ideas without funding sources (IEIT, 2017). IEIT not only offers funding sources to start-up SEs, but also supports a variety of services for new business start-ups. Services include a business capital monitor, evaluation of the business potential, start-up hub offices, and information exchange and consultation. IEIT coordinates and aggregates efforts to continue the services to support SE investment beginners.

In the SE Capital Monitor, a "Findit" website integrates the Global Angel and Ventures Fund to help find initial funds for an applicant and update the most current knowledge and news in the field (IEIT, 2017). To advance the business potential evaluation, IEIT draws on expertise from human resources to assure that potential SE entrepreneurs recognize their competency and can evaluate if starting up a new business is an appropriate option for them according to their business portfolios (Ministry of Economic Affairs, 2017a). Within the Start-up hub, IEIT created a start-up hub for youth, hoping to offer youth an "ecosystem" within which to start up their businesses. The hub is located in a historically well-established business district that is filled with active business ideas. The hub's "one-stop" integrated service also supports start-up entrepreneurs with customized consultation (Ministry of Economic Affairs, 2017b).

Integrated governmental services support SE with (1) personnel support in professional training and development, (2) support in sales of goods and services, (3) support for payment of rent for lands and buildings, and (4) fundraising for start-up funds (Huang, Cheng, Chen, & Wu, 2014). Although the supportive framework has been launched, the legalization of SE-relevant regulations is still not yet formalized. MOEA realizes the uncertainty in time and environment during the legalization process. If MOEA decided to set up SE related acts first and then enacted SE regulations, SE would have grown much slowly with lots of restrictions. However, MOEA decides to first support SE initiatives by flexibility, granting SE innovators with much room for discretion. This approach helps SE grow tremendously in the initial stage without too much bureaucratic restrictions.

After years of SE development in Taiwan, four typologies are recognized (Kuan, Chen, & Wang,2016; Lin, 2013). The first is *work integration or affirmative business*: this is the kind of business that builds careers for the disadvantaged. With their specific operational mission of serving low-income populations, these businesses help disadvantaged individuals find their own way to becoming self-sufficient. The second are *local community development organizations*: these attempt to resolve their community problems with their own efforts. For example, if a community had the problems of ageing citizens and a lack of job opportunities, such organizations would attempt to tackle the problem by reviving the community economy to attract the return of a younger generation. Other enterprises that fall into this category might invest their resources in promoting their local uniqueness for the purpose of cultural preservation. The third type are *social services and products*: these social enterprises sell their products to a target service group that is aligned with the SE's mission. For example, some NPOs serving the elderly are now providing long-term care services to carry out their service missions for the elderly, even as they become self-sufficient, sustainable SEs. The fourth type is a *venture capital business* created to advance other SEs. These offer a variety of professional training and development to new or potential SEs. Moreover, these enterprises also play a role as fundraising platforms to newly established SEs. The fifth type are *social coops*; these are small enterprises that operate with a noble vision. For example, they might insist on selling environmentally friendly products or mainly focus on microlending to community members.

Among the five typologies, the first is the most popular one According to Kuan, Chen, and Wang (2016), more than three-fourths (78.4%) of SEs stated that their mission was welfare services, such as providing job training and job opportunities to the disadvantaged. Most of these SEs target a service population of the physically and mentally disabled (57.4%). The survey findings reveal that SEs in Taiwan are in some ways an important transitional platform for nonprofit organizations. Under the rationale of civic society, nonprofit organizations gradually eliminate their dependence on support from donations and governmental subsidies to becoming self-supporting service/product providers. Some traditional NPOs also work to reposition themselves and open up new paths for sustainable development for the organization.

The Status of Social Enterprises

According to MOEA, there were 140 SEs registered as "social enterprise type" with the Small and Medium Business Administration by the end of 2016. The government helps sponsor more than 500 SE-related innovators share their experiences on a regular basis, adjusted 9 regulations, and held 23 SE fundraising and fund-matching meetings, with more than $4.3 million of lending capital raised. Moreover, MOEA also maintains a toll-free service line for those who are interested in starting up their own SE. Overall, MOEA plays the role of consultant and coordinator between the government and SEs (Ministry of Economic Affairs, 2017a).

As mentioned earlier, the fact of "non-legalization" serves as two-edged sword because, on the one hand, newly established SEs can be more flexible in terms of capital collection, revenue distribution, and organizational structure and thus can follow their original mission without much restriction. On the other hand, since SEs do not have explicit regulations to follow, there might also be confusion and ambiguity in the initial stage. With support from MOEA, SEs are able to overcome these initial challenges and reach the stage of developmental stability.

Kuan, Chen, and Wang (2016) surveyed 114 SEs in regard to their self-evaluation on mission achievement. The top four commonly acknowledged achievements are increasing employment opportunities for the disadvantaged (73.9%), enhancing the self-sufficiency for the SE (64.9%); increasing the income of the disadvantaged (58.6%); and helping the target population to be confident and compatible in the job market (50.5%).

In 2017, a collaborative survey was conducted in Taiwan by UDN News, Social Enterprise Insights, and DBS Bank from two perspectives: one was to understand the current status of SE in the minds of the public, and the other was to recognize the current status of SEs in Taiwan (Social Enterprise Insights, 2017). The survey findings revealed that, among the public, only

19.9% heard about SEs and most of them (43%) heard about SEs from TV. Among the "heard about SE" population, 47.2% used SE products/services and 64% were willing to pay more for the services/products. Among the "never heard about SE" population, after SE was explained, 78.6% acknowledged the mission of SE; however, only 27.7% expressed the possibility of buying SE services/products in the future. The reason for not using the services/products was mainly "too little understanding (28%)." These findings showed that promoting the idea of SE to the public was still a major effort for the development of SE in Taiwan.

The two top SEs were involved in food and agricultural initiatives (29.8%) and with SE services in remote areas and among disadvantaged populations (29%). Among the 245 surveyed organizations in Taiwan, including SEs and NPOs (with the intention to become SEs), only 21.2% of them had generated a profit, 34% could not make ends meet, and 40% were in a break-even status. The top two challenges of the surveyed SEs were the lack of human resources (26.5%) and lack of marketing venues (24.9%). A total of 31.4% of the SEs claimed that the government could help introduce the idea of SE to the public for more social recognition and actual support in the long term.

The Vision of Social Enterprise

SE has become one of the options for the younger generation to fulfill the dream of "making a difference" to society. Many of them believe that SEs are the solution to many social problems in conventional society. Passion, creativity, and action orientation are keys to becoming a change agent in the society. However, according to the Global Social Entrepreneurship Network Report (Global Social Entrepreneurship Network, 2015), only 1% of SE proposals would actually survive. This clearly show that if there is no comprehensive research done on the problems of sustainability, a clear recognition of the mission, connected resources, and a need for perseverance, most SE plans will remain a dream.

When SE was first introduced to Taiwan in the 2000s, it was a "new fad" without much solid support and understanding from the public and government. After a decade of SE development in Taiwan, SE began its "mature era," with systematic support from the government and was more widely recognized by the public.

For the next decade of SE development, SE practitioners must have certain attributes if they are to be successful and sustainable (Social Enterprise Insights, 2017). First and foremost is the ability to *listen*. SE practitioners need to listen to the problems of stakeholders if they are to understand their needs and expectations. Second, paired with listening, is *empathy*. Only by listening to customers' needs can the SE show genuine empathy for those customers who buy its products Being able to empathize is the key to good planning and service design because you can "put your feet into others' shoes." Last, a successful SE needs to *prove and improve* itself. Once it proves itself in the market, a successful SE then strives to improve with through services (Social Enterprise Insights, 2017).

After more than a decade of SE implementation, the Executive Yuan is following up with another phase: The 2018–2022 Social Innovative Action Plan. The three foci of this phase are (1) continue to modify relevant regulations on sustaining the development of SE; (2) encourage the application of a regulatory sandbox platform; and (3) promote the publicity of SE in Taiwan. SE has been recognized as an important innovation and instrument with which to initiate the concept of civic society. In this phase, the government intends to play a role as a SE resource coordinator and connector rather than a director. Moreover, starting September 16, 2019, the Social Innovative Lab has launched the database of Social Innovation Organizations where SEs can register to share and exchange more ideas and experiences. As of the end of 2019, there are 455 organizations of various sizes in the database.

Along with the missions of social innovation and sustainable development within the SE community, many SEs decide to go further in targeting their vision by becoming a B corporation ("Build a Better Business, and Be the Change"). In 2014, the first Taiwan "B corp" was recognized and certified by the international B corporation community. As of November 2019, there were 25 B corporations in Taiwan holding the vision of "a balance among profit, people, and planet" as their organizational missions. Among these 25 B corps, 8 were honored in 2019 as the best in the world in the categories of overall (3 honorees), workers (3 honorees), environment (1 honoree), and community (4 honorees).

LESSONS LEARNED IN TAIWAN

In Taiwan, the practice of SEs reveals a two-stage paradigm shift. The first stage delivers the message of public–private partnerships, which is a very different path from the traditional central government system. The second shift is not only the delegation but also the empowerment of social service problem-solving. As SEs become more stable, the role of the government gradually fades away from the problem-solving system. The power of civic society leads SEs to be self-sufficient and sustainable. This eventually serves the ultimate vision of SEs.

SE is no panacea for social problems. The SE practitioner ought to periodically self-examine the "iron triangle of SE" to assure that the original vision is still on track. The "SE iron triangle" refers to the concepts of social responsibility, organizational accountability, and business commitment. In addition to their philanthropic purposes, SEs must constantly reexamine their core "problem-solving business model." The importance of maintaining focus on the SE's original intention is the ultimate key to a successful and sustainable future for SE. Finally, public education is also crucial to the success of SEs. If the public is educated to acknowledge the vision of SEs, that vision will be sustained and the ideal solution of a mutually beneficial relationship among the public, entrepreneurs, society, and environment will be realized.

REFERENCES

Berggren, H. M. (2016). Cohousing as civic society: Cohousing involvement and political participation in the United States. *Social Science Quarterly, 98*(1), 16. doi:https://doi.org/10.1111/ssqu.12305

Council for Economic Planning and Development. (2011). Golden decade: Visionary Taiwan. *Taiwan Economic Commentary, 9*(10), 12–65.

Danhardt, J. V., & Danhardt, R. B. (2007). The new public service: Serving, not steering. Armonk, NY: M. E. Sharpe.

Department of Statistics. (2019). *R.O.C. statistics websites*. Retrieved from https://www.stat.gov.tw/point.asp?index=1

Executive Yuan. (2012). *Guiding principles for R.O.C. centenary social welfare policy towards a new society with equity, inclusion, and justice.* (1010120382). Taipei: Executive Yuan. Retrieved from https://www.sfaa.gov.tw/SFAA/Pages/Detail.aspx?nodeid=264&pid=1991

Executive Yuan. (2017). *The international trade and investment*. Retrieved from http://www.ey.gov.tw/state/News_Content3.aspx?n=1DA8EDDD65ECB8D4&s=8A1DCA5A3BFAD09C

Global Social Entrepreneurship Network. (2015). *From seed to impact - GSEN report 2015*. Retrieved from https://issuu.com/globalsen/docs/gsen_report_-_from_seed_to_impact

Hsia, H. M., & Beyer, M. (2000). *System change through state challenge activities: Approaches and products*. Retrieved from https://www.ncjrs.gov/pdffiles1/ojjdp/177625.pdf

Huang, T.-S., Cheng, S.-F., Chen, S.-J., & Wu, C.-L. (2014). Management for social enterprise. Taipei: Compass Publishing.

IEIT. (2017). Business thrives in Taiwan. Retrieved from https://sme.moeasmea.gov.tw/startup/modules/se/mod_case/

Jacoby, N. H. (1966). *U.S. aid to Taiwan*. New York: Praeger.

Kuan, Y.-Y., Chen, C.-T., & Wang, S.-T. (2016). *The governance of social enterprise: The comparative approach to Taiwan and Hong Kong* (1 ed.). Kaohsiung: Liwen Publisher.

LeRoux, K. (2010). Has public administration "repositioned" itself? Advances and inertias in transitioning to the collaborative governance paradigm. In R. O'Leary, D. M. Van Slyke, & S. Kim (Eds.), *The future of public administration around the world: The Minnowbrook perspectives* (pp. 261–266). Washington, DC: Georgetown University Press.

Liang, M.-Y., & Wang, W.-Y. (2002). *The review and re-examination of the rapid economic development of Taiwan in the past century.* Paper presented at the 6th Financial Investment and Economic Development: In memory of Professor Guo-shu Liang, National Taiwan University.

Lin, S.-H. (2013). The status and challenges of social enterprise in Taiwan: The case of the venture capital business. *Community Development Quarterly, 143,* 68–77.

Ministry of Culture. (2017). The introduction of Ministry of Culture. Retrieved from https://www.moc.gov.tw/content_246.html

Ministry of Economic Affairs. (2014). *Social enterprise action plan.* Taipei: Ministry of Economic Affairs. Retrieved from https://www.ey.gov.tw/Page/5A8A0CB5B41DA11E/ad3272ab-6b66-4c35-b02d-92c146f9fb23

Ministry of Economic Affairs. (2017a). Findit Platform. Retrieved from https://findit.org.tw/aboutV2.aspx

Ministry of Economic Affairs. (2017b). Start-up A-plus action plan. Retrieved from http://aplus.chung-chung.com/aplus/index.php

Ministry of Economic Affairs. (2020). Social innovative platform. Retrieved from https://sme.moeasmea.gov.tw/startup/modules/se/

Ministry of Education. (2014). The action plan for twelve-year compulsory education. Retrieved from http://12basic.edu.tw/

Ministry of Education. (2017). Education for primary and junior high school students. Retrived from https://ws.moe.edu.tw/001/Upload/3/relfile/6312/49637/9753b7ac-359d-42d3-aac7-d3b4daff8abb.pdf

Rittel, H., & Webber, M. (1973). Dilemmas in a general theory of planning. *Policy Sciences, 4,* 155–169.

Social Enterprise Insights. (2013). *Establish organic agriculture for the indigenous: Aurora social enterprise. YK column.* Retrieved from http://www.seinsights.asia/story/250/5/1012

Social Enterprise Insights. (2017). *Path the way: 10 lessons in social enterprise.* Taipei: Linking Publishing.

Taiwan Social Enterprise Organization. (2015). *Aroura social enterprise.* Retrieved from http://www.taiwanseo.org/business/%E5%85%89%E5%8E%9F%E7%A4%BE%E6%9C%83%E4%BC%81%E6%A5%AD/

Wu, T.-M. (2003). *The success and innovation in Taiwan economic history research: The example of economic growth.* Paper presented at the 2002 Ban-yuan foundation conference, Taipei.

Wu, T.-M. (2004). From the change of average income to see the long-term economic development in Taiwan. *Taiwan Economic Review, 32*(3), 293–320.

CHAPTER 14

⌒

Social Entrepreneurship in Argentina

The Role of Mission-Driven Organizations on the Pathway to Inclusive Growth

LEILA MUCARSEL, MEERA BHAT,
AND BLANCA M. RAMOS

INTRODUCTION

There is a growing awareness of the complexity of reducing inequalities and the need for growth that is not only smart (innovation-led) but also inclusive and green (Mazzucato & Perez, 2014). In facing this challenge, governments and other institutions around the world are acknowledging that the sustainable and inclusive development agenda can only be addressed in a comprehensive fashion and through partnerships among an array of "development actors," including the public and private sector as well as civil society organizations (United Nations 2030 Agenda for Sustainable Development). Furthermore, tackling today's unprecedented "Grand Societal Challenges," such as climate change and growing inequalities, urgently calls for profound social innovations, citizen engagement, and bottom-up participation (Mazzucato, 2015, 2018; Wu, Howlett, & Ramesh, 2018). In this context, the Argentina experience illustrates how and why social enterprises can play a strategic role in the search for inclusive growth and sustainable development.

Leila Mucarsel, Meera Bhat, and Blanca M. Ramos, *Social Entrepreneurship in Argentina* In: *Social Entrepreneurship and Enterprises in Economic and Social Development*. Edited by: Katharine Briar-Lawson, Paul Miesing, and Blanca M. Ramos, Oxford University Press (2021). © Oxford University Press. DOI: 10.1093/oso/9780197518298.003.0015.

During the last three decades of the 20th century, Argentina transitioned from an economy based on imports substitution industrialization (ISI) to an open-market model and from a welfare state to a retraction of state-sponsored social and economic welfare. The results of these transitions were very harsh for the society. The dawn of the 2000s found the country immersed in the worst political, social, and economic crisis of its history. With around 50% of the population living in poverty and increased un-employment surpassing 22% (INDEC, 2001), Argentina was no longer, the "middle-class country of Latin America," as it had been traditionally considered since the early 1940s. Notwithstanding this, from 2003 on, the country started a process of economic recovery and social development, achieving very good results in terms of tackling poverty and reducing inequalities. This chapter aims to shed light on the role that social entre-preneurship (SE) played in this context (2003–2015).

First, we begin by offering an overview of Argentina, presenting key so-cioeconomic indicators and trends. Then, we summarize the main debates around development, SE, and social enterprises in this country, within the broader context of South America. Next, as the core of our analysis, we answer the following questions: What are the key contributions that Argentina's SE organizations are bringing to the development agenda? How are these organizations contributing to the emergence of social innovations? And, what are the main stakeholders and challenges of the SE ecosystem? Last, we share some lessons learned and outline key policy implications.

ARGENTINA: A COUNTRY OVERVIEW

A former Spanish colony, Argentina gained independence from Spain in 1816, and its Constitution, preceded by more than 50 years of civil wars, was enacted in 1853. The government, within the framework of a federal system, is a democratic republic. The country is subdivided into 23 states and one autonomous city, Buenos Aires, the capital of the nation.

Argentina has been a country of immigrants for most of its history. Especially in the late19th and early 20th centuries, large numbers of immigrants came from Spain and Italy, as well as from other European and Arab countries. They were looking for a better life at a time when Europe and the Middle East were experiencing pronounced poverty or they were escaping from war and ongoing conflicts within their countries (Devoto, 1989). This was also the result of a strong policy of immigration promo-tion led by Argentina's government in its efforts to "populate the country."

In the 20th century, the main immigration waves came from the South American region, especially from Bolivia, Peru, Paraguay, and Chile, as people searched for better economic conditions and job opportunities.

Despite its extensive territory, Argentina's nearly 45 million inhabitants are mostly concentrated in urban areas, primarily in the metropolitan area of Buenos Aires (13.5 million). Currently, 89.1% of the population is urban, and the population density is 16 people per square kilometer of land area. Urbanization has been gradual since the 1950s, with a spurt occurring over the past four decades. Approximately 91% of the population has urbanized compared to about 85% in 1985, with estimates reaching 94% by 2025. One of the main drivers of this trend has been economic restructuring in the agriculture sector (Cerrutti & Bertoncello, 2003).

Argentina's fertility decline began earlier than in the rest of Latin America, occurring most rapidly between the early 20th century and the 1950s, then becoming more gradual. This can be explained by an improvement in living conditions as a result of both economic growth and a strong welfare state. Nowadays, the population continues to grow but at a very slow pace, with a steadily declining birth rate of 2.3 children per woman. The median age is 31 years and life expectancy at birth is 76 years. Life expectancy has been improving, most notably among the young and the poor as a result of the social and healthcare policies that were implemented since 2003.

While the population under age 15 is shrinking due to declining fertility rates, the youth cohort, aged 15–24, is the largest in Argentina's history and will continue to bolster the working-age population.

SOCIAL AND ECONOMIC TRENDS
IN ARGENTINA: PROGRESS AND CHALLENGES

During the 20th century, Argentina was considered an egalitarian country compared with the rest of the region (Kessler & Di Virgilio, 2010). This should be attributed not only to its economic growth and industrialization under an ISI policy, which was based on the principle of replacing foreign imports through the local production of industrialized products for the internal market, but also to the bold pro-labor and welfare policies implemented from the mid-1940s to the mid-1970s. However, this pattern changed dramatically after the mid-1970s and up to 2002, when Argentina witnessed the largest increase in inequality in the region. The Gini coefficient, used to measure inequality, increased from 0.35 in 1974 to 0.5 in 2002 (United Nations Development Programme [UNDP], 2017).

As a result of a neoliberal phase starting from the mid-1970s, through the 1980s, and particularly during the 1990s, the country went through strict structural adjustment programs comprising privatization policies, deregulation, indiscriminate trade openness, and a questionable fixed exchange rate regime (linking of the peso 1 to 1 to a strong US dollar). This phase exploded in the 2001 crisis, which was marked by a default of external debt payments.

In 2003, the country started a process of economic recovery through social inclusion. This trend continued until 2015, but slowed after 2008 due to the impact of the global financial crisis and the end of the "commodities prices boom" which had been very beneficial to Argentina as one of the world's leading food producers (World Bank, 2017).

Argentina was one of the top performers in the region in reducing poverty and inequalities during the 2003–2015 period. Incomes of the bottom 40% grew at an annual rate of 11.8% compared to average income growth of 7.6% of the total population (World Bank, 2016). The main drivers of this decline of inequality were (a) job opportunities, with around 6.5 million new jobs created during this period (Bertranou & Casanova, 2015) and improvement in wages, and (b) public policies as the country prioritized social spending through various programs, including the Universal Child Allowance, a conditional cash transfer program (educational and health conditions) that was the most important in the region in terms of reach and amount of aid. In addition, the social security system was improved and extended. In 2 years, 2 million pension recipients were added, and the elderly coverage rate rose from 68% in 2003 to nearly 90% in 2010 (Bosch & Guajardo, 2012). A large number of workers from the informal economy benefitted from this policy.[1]

Today categorized by the United Nations as a "high human development country," Argentina ranks 45th (out of 188) in the global Human Development Index (UNDP, 2016) and has a per capita gross domestic product (GDP) of US$17,848. Nevertheless, deep disparities persist between regions and social groups. In general terms, and in spite of the important advances in poverty reduction achieved during the 2003–2015 period, around a quarter of the population was still living in poverty by the end of 2015 (Salvia & Vera, 2016). It is important to note that, after 2015, under president Macri's administration, there has been a return to the neoliberal policy agenda with very negative results in terms of social indicators, almost doubling poverty and unemployment rates in 4 years (UCA, 2019). This last period has also had a profound impact on the SE sector, with numerous cooperatives and social enterprises in danger of failing or even forced by the economic crisis to stop operating.

If we look at education, although literacy and primary school enroll-ment is nearly universal, grade repetition is problematic and secondary school completion is low, with graduation rates of about 50% (UNESCO, 2014) as well as problems of fragmentation and high inequalities (Hervier et al., 2017).

The public health system is universal for everyone who does not have private coverage, but it still presents problems of fragmentation and lack of coordination. The teenage pregnancy rate was 33.7 mothers per 1,000 teenagers in 2013. This figure is above the world average and also above the levels of several countries in the region (UNDP, 2017). Maternal mortality decreased from 5.2 (among 10,000) in 1990 to 3.9 in 2015. Abortion— being penalized—is one of the main causes of maternal mortality, espe-cially for poor women (UNDP, 2017). Infant mortality rates have been systematically reduced: in 2015, they comprised 9.7 per 1,000 live births compared with 15 in 2002. Access to water and electricity is extensive, but access to sanitation infrastructure and sewage networks still present problems for some regions (UNDP, 2017).

In terms of infrastructure, the country has a significant housing deficit due to the economic constraints on families hoping to acquire to their own house. There are worrisome symptoms of residential segregation between closed neighborhoods where high-income sectors live and slums and irreg-ular settlements are present. Over a million inhabitants live in informal settlements (UCA, 2016) with no land titles and without regular access to two or more basic services such as running water, electricity, and sewers. In these settlements, 38% are children or young people up to 20 years, and 3% are older than 65 years.

Last, there are persistent inequalities in the gender equality dimension. According to Argentina's National Report on Human Development 2017 (UNDP, 2017) there are important challenges in terms of gender equality. There are significant income gaps between men and women. This gap is wider in the least educated quantile of the population, where a man earns an average 30% more than a woman. This report also highlights unequal access for women to CEO and director positions in the private sector (3 out of 10) and in public office (women represent around a 40% of repre-sentatives in the National Legislative Power, but only about 10% of local government mayors). If we look at the distribution of time use, on average, women older than 18 years are engaged in unpaid domestic tasks almost double the time of men (6.4 and 3.4 hours per day, respectively). Moreover, violence against women remains very strong and has been in the spotlight during the past years (UNDP, 2017). The feminist movement has been ex-ponentially growing during the past decade, demanding abortion rights and the end of gender-based killings of women, as well as for a broader feminist agenda. Notably, young women are currently leading this agenda through a collective that has been called in Argentina "the revolution of the daughters."

ECONOMIC STRUCTURE, LABOR MARKET, AND INFORMALITY

Argentina is the eighth-largest country in the world and is a rich country in terms of natural and human resources. Endowed with an extraordinary fertile land, it is a leading food producer in South America. The country is food self-sufficient; nevertheless, the biggest share of the food produced locally is exported. Another important economic sector is manufacturing, and, more recently, the country has started to develop high-tech industries such as software, nano, and biotechnology companies (World Bank, 2016).

Despite having an important accumulation of human capital and a modern and productive agricultural sector, labor markets are characterized by a high level of precariousness and informal (nonregistered) labor. This is due to the heterogeneous sectors of agriculture, industry, and services, where high-productivity segments coexist with small, low-productivity companies. This is very much related to the lack of enforcement of government controls over informal employment. Although labor protection laws have been in place for a long time, there are still important "black holes" in this domain.

Argentina experienced a remarkable process of employment formalization between 2003 and 2014, with a 15% reduction of what the International Labour Organization (ILO, 2014) labels as "non-registered wage employment (NWE)." This indicator, which stands for wage employment without social security contributions, moved from 49% (2003) to 34% (2012). Nevertheless, the informal employment, composed of non-registered wage employees and non-registered independent (self-employed) workers, represents an important part of the working population.

NWE constitutes more than 65% of all informal work. Nearly 35% of those workers are concentrated in productive units without a single registered worker; just over 25% perform their jobs at home, and most of them are women earning low wages.

Independent workers (self-employed) constitute 32.5% of all informal workers. While this is a heterogeneous group, one of its distinctive characteristics is low skills and poorly compensated jobs. Though the rate of informal employment may be much lower for this group of workers, they are vulnerable to problems associated with fiscal and employment slowdowns. An analysis of the sociodemographic characteristics of informal workers reveals that the groups most affected are women, young people, and those with low educational levels. NWE is present in most sectors, but with a higher composition in some sectors such as construction, manufacturing (textiles in particular), and transport. Moreover, most domestic work is informal (Bertranou & Casanova, 2015).

DEVELOPMENT, SOCIAL ENTREPRENEURSHIP, AND SOCIAL ENTERPRISES

In this section, we introduce some of the main theoretical debates around development in Argentina in the broader context of South America. We also define the key concepts and outline the defining patterns of SE.

Development

Latin America has been one of the world regions that contributed extensively to the critical debate about growth and development (Ocampo & Ros, 2011). The term "development" can be viewed by some in its most positive light as "the full realization of communities within the framework of values that sustain their identity and express their own culture (. . .) development is the path to the 'better future' that each community defines for itself" (Bernazza, 2006, p. 84, translated by authors).

There is a growing worldwide consensus, particularly in the Global South, on the fact that growth is not the same as development. Thus we see increasingly frequently the noun "growth" coupled with adjectives such as "inclusive" and "sustainable" (ECLAC, 2017; EU, 2017; OECD, 2017; World Economic Forum, 2017). This is linked with the idea that development is not something that occurs naturally or spontaneously out of economic growth. It implies induced processes that require a coordinated and strategic intervention of different stakeholders including governments, the private sector, and civil society (Coraggio, 2008; Hecker & Kulfas, 2006; Roitman, 2016).

During the neoliberal period, the pathways toward development were mostly imposed from the outside by international financial institutions (IFIs) such as the International Monetary Fund and the World Bank. They used their leverage to push debtor countries toward an externally determined policy agenda (Bulmer Thomas, 1996). In this context, the concept of "local development" appeared in the region during the 1980s and 1990s. Local territories were supposed to advance their development planning in an isolated fashion in the absence of broader regional and national development strategies. This was proved unsuccessful (Bernazza, 2007; Mucarsel, 2014).

From 2000 on, and, as a result of the deep economic and social crisis that the region faced, more critical views emerged. Visions such as the Amartya Sen development paradigm, emphasizing the importance of taking into account human capacities were widespread.

Moreover, calls for *"Buen Vivir"* (Spanish translation for the indigenous term *"Sumak Kawsay"*; literally "Good Living") emerged from South America's Andean region. This concept recovers indigenous forms of knowledge to devise alternative paths to development. The concept emphasizes the communal dimension of development, highlighting the need for a bottom-up and community-led approach. Furthermore, Nature is given a central role in these indigenous philosophies, manifested in the discussions of the *Pachamama* or Mother Earth. This revisiting of indigenous philosophies provides a framework to reflect on development with a more holistic approach (Carballo, 2015). Linked with this perspective, there have been critics highlighting inattention to the environment in the development of strategies that Latin American countries adopted since the 2000s. This is because the development model has privileged industrial growth and the export of commodities as its pillars (see Svampa, 2011, for a detailed account of these critics).

SOCIAL ENTREPRENEURSHIP IN THE CONTEXT OF CIVIL SOCIETY ORGANIZATIONS

In Argentina, the concept of *social entrepreneurship* is generally associated with the "solidarity economy" (in Spanish mostly referred as *"Economía Social y Solidaria"*). This is a people-centered socioeconomic sector where profit is not the ultimate goal but a means to achieve better living conditions for a community (Coraggio, 2008). In other words, this sector promotes an economy that creates social linkages (Roitman, 2016).

The origins of SE in Argentina trace back to two sources: (1) the European tradition of cooperatives that came with the waves of immigration from Italy and Spain and (2) the indigenous peoples' traditions and institutions (Roitman, 2016).

Notably, SE is mostly embedded in the civil society organizations (CSOs) sector: a wide sector that often includes community-based organizations

(CBOs), social movements, nongovernmental organizations (NGOs), charitable organizations, religious groups, corporate foundations, and academic institutions, among others (World Bank, 2017). Thus, in this chapter, we talk about "SE CSOs": social entrepreneurship civil society organizations.

It is also important to note that Argentina has a very strong civil society tradition. This sector is composed of a diversity of organizations, but we must underline the importance of three constituents in particular:

1. *The human rights movement*, which emerged as a response to state terrorism and is very active up to the present, comprises a wide range of CSOs. SE is generally seen as a "lighthouse" in terms of human rights promotion, popular education, and defense of democracy.
2. *Trade unions*, with a long tradition, play a key role in the fight for income distribution. Apart from traditional trade unions and workers' confederations, in recent years there has been a movement for a Popular Economy Workers Confederation (CTEP), known as the trade union of informal and "popular economy workers." This movement includes informal workers, street sellers, and "recycling co-ops." The latter are associations that have found new ways of conducting urban recycling activity collectively in partnership with the public sector.
3. *Foundations, NGOs, and other CSOs* that emerged as a response to social crisis since the 1980s and especially during the 1990s. These organizations started providing basic help and tailored services to communities. New organizations have emerged, and many have developed since 2003. They focus on issues such as child rights, citizenship promotion, environment, livelihoods, and job creation. Mostly with state support, but also with bottom-up organization and fundraising efforts, many of these are SE organizations that have developed their own schools and "capacity-building centers," delivering courses on different trades. Their missions include enhancing the employability of unemployed youth through training courses in cooperation with governments

Social Enterprises

A "social enterprise" can be defined as "an organization created to achieve specific social objectives by reinvesting its profits in its mission" (CAUSE Center, 2016). They do so by innovating and targeting areas that are otherwise outside the economic mainstream. Usually, they take a business approach and/or promote market-based solutions.

In the same line, social enterprises have been characterized as a flexible organization model whose innovative capacity promotes, through solidarity, a different way of delivering goods and services, and organizing labor, building commitment to the promotion of local capacities, transparency (being accountable to its members and to their community at large), with the preservation of the environment, and the effectiveness of its actions (Roitman, 2016, p. 15).

In the case of Argentina, development of this sector is relatively recent, with some organizations having around 10 years of experience, and there is still a long way to go. A Di Tella's University study (2013) identifies 76 social enterprises in Argentina. The study concludes that the Argentine field is in an embryonic state, identifying the following common denominators in their sample: most (89%) have annual sales of less than US$60,000, the vast majority (97%) finance their daily operations with their own resources, and most lack external investors (82%). Overall, the majority falls into the category of microenterprises and appears to share the business struggles of small enterprises. Most organizations commercialize products and services to people with vulnerabilities or some sort of social exclusion, and their impact reaches more than 1,000 people (Di Tella, 2013, in Luna, 2013).

Interestingly, since 2003, many CSOs are in a transition, moving to social enterprises. Moreover, around a third of social enterprises are part of a "multiple-organization" umbrella. A nonprofit may decide to launch a new venture for sustainability and job creation while sustaining its mission and continuing at the same time with more traditional activities

El Arca: Producers + Consumers

El Arca (Spanish for "The Ark") defines itself as a social enterprise that promotes "*Comunidades Prosumidoras*" (they coined this word in Spanish; it means communities that involve both producers and consumers). Their mission is to link small producers with networks of families, companies, social organizations, universities, and public institutions that seek to be part of fair and just trade and support their consumers. If surpluses are generated, they are invested in the community according to the mandate of their producers and consumers (Source: authors based in interview with Pablo Ordoñez, El Arca's Founder).

TRADITIONAL SOCIAL ENTREPRENEURSHIP STAKEHOLDERS

Table 14.1 presents a summary of the characteristics and challenges of the traditional stakeholders of SE.

Table 14.1 ARGENTINA'S TRADITIONAL SOCIAL ENTREPRENEURSHIP STAKEHOLDERS

	Cooperatives	"Mutuals" ("*Mutuales*" in Spanish)	Microenterprises	Small rural producers and family farms
Definition	Defined by National Law 20.337 as entities financed in self- and mutual help to provide social services. The main sectors covered by coops in Argentina are water provision, sanitation, rural areas, and food production.	A nonprofit organization formed under the principles of solidarity and mutual aid, not very common today, were very much used by immigrant communities for the provision of health and other services.	Enterprises with very low capital, usually with 5 or fewer members. Only considered as part of the solidarity economy when they are associated or integrated with microfinance groups or larger networks.	Networks and associations of small rural producers.
In numbers	21,000 coops with around 490,563 individual members.	4,000 mutuals or nonprofit agencies.	1.5 million microenterprises associated with microcredit networks. 1,500 microcredit organizations that provide funding for 150 microcredit funders.	66% (218,868) of the total rural productive units are smallholder family farms that occupy 13% of the country's agricultural area (23,196,642 hectares)
Strengths	The only legally recognized form of social enterprises in Argentina, it fosters values and principles of democratic governance.	Good results in service provision, especially in providing valuable goods and services to local consumers.	Since microcredit was incorporated in legal frameworks in 2007, there has been a steady growth of this sector providing access to credit with a positive impact on local development.	The UN Food and Agriculture Organization (FAO) highlights family farming as a food supplier. Farming plays an important role in food security and sovereignty strategies.
Main challenges	Red tape in a highly bureaucratic system in which to register and operate.	Not very popular among young generations; this sector's leaders average more than 60 years of age.	High dependence on government technical assistance and financial support.	Lack of funding, and legislative protection. Declining self-sufficiency. Land desertification.

Source: Authors' elaboration based on data from Acosta et al. (2013), Basualdo et al. (2010), and Roitman (2016).

New Stakeholders in Argentina's Social Entrepreneurship Ecosystem: The Case of "Recovered Factories"

During the past decades, SE in Argentina has grown and expanded to new sectors involving different types of social enterprises. We have also witnessed the emergence of a new stakeholder: *"Fábricas Recuperadas,"* or "recovered factories" (also called in English "workers' buy-outs").

After the economic collapse in 2001, multinational corporations pulled out of the country—literally overnight—boarding up workplaces and leaving workers without jobs. Also, a considerable number of small and medium enterprises (SMEs) went bankrupt. Workers took action and organized themselves, occupying the factories and winning the right to form cooperatives and keep the factories going. Since then, there is a "[n]ational Movement of Recovered Factories, that has shown the world how the power of regular people working together can resist globalization and create an alternative model of business where all workers earn the same amount of money, eliminating a boss who is paid a grossly disproportionate wage compared to the workers" (Pyles, 2009).

SOCIAL ENTREPRENEURSHIP ORGANIZATIONS' KEY CONTRIBUTIONS IN A NEW DEVELOPMENT SCENARIO

After the unprecedented social, political, and economic crisis that besieged Argentina in 2001, the role of the state over the next decade changed drastically. The government became a central agent in the nation's social and economic development. In this new scenario, some civil society organizations developed strong ties with the government, developing different types of partnerships and collaborations for public policy design, implementation, and assessment. This took place in a context where civil and human rights became more widespread, largely supported by the government and other civil society organizations with a long tradition in human rights defense (Blugerman et al., 2017).

Mounting evidence indicates that CSOs contribute in the search for more inclusive, transparent, and sustainable development in several ways that make their role fundamental (Talcott, 2011; World Bank, 2017). In the case of SE organizations this impact is particularly important: through their methods of operation, these organizations can influence the "direction" of economic growth (i.e., spreading inclusive and sustainable business models, practices, services, and products) and well as inform governments on the key societal challenges that need public investment, thus fostering innovative solutions, regulations, etc., and bringing "real" social and environmental challenges back to the policy debate. Moreover, at a time when very often the legitimacy of policies is at stake, this organizations foster bottom-up engagement and participation.

Drawing from the Argentina experience, we can summarize the contributions to the development of SE CSOs and social enterprises into three main categories.

1. *Improving the public sector's capacities to reach and engage the poor, vulnerable, and marginalized communities.* SE organizations have showed a great capacity to reach some of the most vulnerable sectors, which public institutions usually find hard to reach. They improve the implementation and sustainability of governmental projects by fostering better beneficiary participation, mobilizing local resources, and strengthening local institutions. As mentioned in the Argentina overview, the 2003–2015 period was characterized by the implementation of a wide range of social and pro-employment policies. Given the complex and multidimensional nature of poverty, in some cases these programs were not able to reach the most vulnerable populations. SE CSOs played a major role in both spreading the word about the existence of these programs and contributing to successful program implementation. The education sector is a good example of this contribution. When the government decided to implement a massive adult literacy program and adult schools to promote primary and secondary school competition, many CSOs hosted so-called satellite classes: they opened their offices so that the people in the neighborhood could attend a nearby school. SE CSOs have developed their own kindergarten, primary, and secondary schools (including adult education) with the legal recognition and financial support of the state (Roitman, 2016; Blugerman et al., 2017). In some states of Argentina, the schools run by this sector account for 30% of the total educational system and are mostly located in rural areas, marginal neighborhoods, and indigenous communities.

   Another example of a partnership with government institutions is the Progresar program, led by Argentina's Ministry of Labour. It is a monthly universal economic benefit for young people (18–24), subject to their attendance in training courses and school. It also includes assistance for professional training, orientation, and labor intermediation by helping the unemployed improve their profile and connecting them with employment opportunities, as well as providing childcare in some cases (ECLAC, 2017). SE CSOs participated actively in the program by providing vocational training, skill development, and capacity-building courses for young people and they also aided participants in developing their own vocational training in the organizations' offices (ILO, 2016).

2. *Piloting social innovations and streamlining methodologies for the development sector.* This is definitely one of the areas in which SE CSOs have contributed most actively and fruitfully to the development sector. Examples of this can be found in a diversity of areas. We argue that the sector is acting as a real "lab" for social innovation. Their proximity to some of the most pressing social issues and the community networks that they integrate give these organizations a better understanding of problems and potential solutions. The following cases are examples of some of the most important issues and some of the organizations where innovative solutions to social problems have been advanced and tested. These SEs include renewable energies (such as Energe), financial inclusion of the poor (numerous locally based foundations and CSOs through the Banquito de la Buena Fé Initiative), vocational training in software for underprivileged youth (such as Arbusta), coops for social housing (e.g., Tupac Amaru), access to cultural goods and services for marginalized groups for e.g. Crear Vale la Pena, adding value to local agricultural products (e.g., UST), garbage collecting and recycling through urban waste recyclers coops (usually called *Cartoneros* in Argentina), and fair trade (such as the above cited case El Arca), among many others.

3. *Participating in the definition of policy directions and government priorities through advocacy efforts and participatory governance mechanisms.* As mission-driven organizations, SE CSOs are playing a vital role in advocating for better public policies. In many cases, these institutions have been responsible for the passing of new laws and the establishment of new programs that were not within the scope of government's policy agenda before their intervention. This type of participation has been quite common since 2003, particularly in SE as well as in different fields such as livelihoods, education, and health. For example, new legislation was passed for the promotion of the Social and Solidarity Economy in the states of Buenos Aires (2014) and the Law for the Associative Productive Markets of the state of Río Negro (2009). These laws emerged as a result of long advocacy efforts by SE CSO networks. Indeed, most of the content of these laws was developed by these networks (; Roitman, 2016). SE CSOs participate actively in a diverse range of councils and policy forums locally, regionally, nationally, and internationally. Nonetheless, it has been pointed out that "CSO involvement in public policies is relatively high (e.g., in promotion of programs, laws), even when the results are variable and civil society has not a leading role in the definition of

public policies." (CIVICUS 2011, in Blugerman et al., 2017, p. 20). There is still considerable room for improvement in these regards. Particularly, there is a claim that the voices of this sector should not be part of only the social policy agenda, but also of the economic policy debate, which is usually not the case. In this way, these organizations could further influence the required "directions" for economic growth.

THE SOCIAL ENTREPRENEURSHIP ECOSYSTEM

In this section we present some of the defining characteristics and challenges of Argentina's SE ecosystem.

> *Support organizations and enabling players.* A number of support organizations and key players strengthen the foundations for the emerging SE ecosystem in Argentina. ENI Di Tella (2013) identified public "incubators" and universities as an essential support group through the various roles they play. There are also a few private incubators. Incubators are key facilitators for social entrepreneurs by providing broad support services to them, especially for nurturing their business idea. One of the drawbacks of these institutions is that they focus more on traditional business and have limited knowledge of the SE sector. There are also a few "accelerators" targeting the sector, most of which provide funding and *co-working platforms*: the use of a common office or other working environment by people from different organizations, typically to share equipment, ideas, and knowledge (Luna, 2013). The number of incubators and universities supporting the sector has also been growing in the past years. In addition, Argentina has a network of non profit organizations ("Sistema B") that certify B-corps as part as the international B Labs network (*Empresas B*, in Spanish); currently there are around 80 B-corps in Argentina (Manini, 2019).
>
> *Government institutions.* During the 2003–2015 period public institutions played a key role in providing technical support and funding to social enterprises in Argentina. The fact that this role has been played by a diversity of institutions has led in many cases to problems of coordination and overlap. The main support comes from the Ministry of Social Development, followed by the Ministries of Employment and Agriculture and, finally, with a

lower participation rate, the Ministries of Industry, Education and Science, and Technology.

Legal framework. There are still important gaps in the legal framework for this sector. There is no national law for social entrepreneurship, and only 3 of the 23 Argentina states and a few municipalities have passed laws to these ends. The main gaps occur in the lack of adequate legal frameworks for SE sector organizations and enterprises, which limits their scope of action and legal rights.

Finance. The Argentine financial system falls short: the amount of loans in the economy is very limited even when compared with its Latin American neighbors. Despite a decade of economic growth, the credit and loan resources for the private sector represented 16% of GDP in 2011, whereas it represents 40% in Brazil and 60% in Chile. Suitable credit and loan funds are difficult to obtain: few lines of credit exist and banks impose demanding requirements and guarantees.

Not surprisingly, entrepreneurs face additional difficulties. To compensate for this capital gap, the public sector created a range of financial instruments, such as subsidized credit and "patient" (long-term) capital (PNUD, 2013). This achieved discreetly encouraging results: public banks currently rank as the primary source of loans to SMEs and social enterprises (36%). Yet the state's efforts so far have not counterbalanced the shortcomings in the supply of capital. As for "microcredit," since mid-2000, Argentina has a National Microcredit Commission (CONAMI), later established by law in 2007. National microcredit funds are exempted from national taxes, and funds are allocated to developed credit portfolios with a subsidized interest rate. Pioneering entities that existed in Argentina before the enactment of the law were strengthened; namely, the micro-credit management consortiums (with the participation of CSOs and the provincial and municipal governments) and the so-called *popular banks of good faith* (local community-based organizations providing microcredit to marginalized groups, mostly women).

LESSONS LEARNED AND POLICY IMPLICATIONS

In this chapter, we presented some of the main theoretical and practical aspects of SE in Argentina today. Among the multiple factors that led to a growth of social enterprises, organizations' capacity-building and greater government support were shown to be two key elements. Indeed, once the government saw the sector as a "window of opportunity" and partnered with it in implementing an inclusion-driven development strategy, the results were very positive.

In a context of economic growth, the sector's organizations proved their ability to build bridges between social and pro-employment policies and the poor and marginalized groups. They also showed their strengths in channeling bottom-up problems and needs into the public policy agenda, bringing bold contributions in the definition of the directions needed for inclusive growth. Community-based SE organizations were in many cases the strongest "policy-advisors" in these regards. In those cases in which the sector was excluded from the policy-definition process or only invited to the table when the implementation phase was in an advanced stage, the results were not as beneficial.

Moreover, social enterprises proved to be resourceful stakeholders for catalyzing social innovations from the grassroots and linking them with other organizations, such as universities and funders, to scale-up. The 2003–2015 period also was marked by a shift from charity and philanthropy into result-oriented impact investing initiatives. While some organizations became too dependent on government support, thus forgoing their sustainability responsibilities, others were able put their focus on strengthening their capacities and designing better structures, adapting to the changing environment with great success. In this direction, developing adequate "sector-tailored" impact assessment tools is becoming a priority for some of them.

One of the main tasks ahead for both CSOs and social enterprises is to continue sharpening their business and entrepreneurial skills. It is crucial that these organizations strengthen their networks and cooperation with each other and with both the public and private sectors while defending independence and autonomy.

In the public policy arena, there have been advances in the recognition of the SE sector, specifically in new legislation that has been passed as a result of the sector's advocacy. There has also been some strengthening of government programs and institutions targeting social enterprises, but there is still a lot of room for improvement. In particular, there is a lack of "institutionalization" of this progress: some of the advances made in this field seem to be at risk in the context of state reform that is currently taking place.

To conclude, important challenges lie ahead but also enormous opportunities. The main lesson here is that if we want to tackle complex issues such as inequality and climate change and achieve the ambitious societal goals agreed upon in the UN Sustainable Development Goals, we need new avenues in the development path. The SE sector is a truly strategic partner for both setting the directions and implementing these transformations

The Argentina case showcases how the SE sector represents both a source and catalyzer of social innovation and a powerful ally in terms of envisioning, implementing, and assessing a development strategy toward smarter, more just, and more sustainable growth for all.

REFERENCES

Acosta, M. C., Levin, A., & Verbeke, G. E. (2013). El sector cooperativo en Argentina en la ú ltima década. *Cooperativismo & Desarrollo*, *21*(102), 27–39.

Basualdo, M. E., Musacchio, C. I., Masi, M., Gallo, E., Tabordo, J., & Leone, N. (2010). Participación asociativa: En un contexto de crisis la empresa se proyecta como un instrumento de la economía social. *Nueva Epoca*, *1*(8), 149–159. https://doi.org/10.14409/ne.v1i8.232

Bernazza, C. A. (2007). La planificación gubernamental en Argentina: Experiencias del período 1974–2000 como puntos de partida hacia un nuevo paradigma.

Bertranou, F., & Casanova, L. (2015). *Trayectoria hacia el trabajo decente de los jóvenes en Argentina: Contribuciones de las políticas públicas de educación, formación para el trabajo y protección social*. Organización Internacional del Trabajo (OIT). https://www.ilo.org/wcmsp5/groups/public/---americas/---ro-lima/---ilo-buenos_aires/documents/publication/wcms_454395.pdf

Blugerman, L., Darmohraj, A., & Lomé, M. (2017). *Social enterprises in Argentina*. Retrieved from http://www.lasociedadcivil.org/wp-content/uploads/2017/12/Blugerman_Darmohraj_Lome.pdf

Bosch, M., & Guajardo, J. (2012). *Labor market impacts of non-contributory pensions: The case of Argentina's moratorium* (No. IDB-WP-366). IDB Working Paper Series. https://publications.iadb.org/publications/english/document/Labor-Market-Impacts-of-Non-Contributory-Pensions-The-Case-of-Argentina-Moratorium.pdf

Bulmer-Thomas, V. (Ed.). (1996). *The new economic model in Latin America and its impact on income distribution and poverty*. Springer.

Carballo, A. E. (2015). *Re-reading Amartya Sen from the Andes: Exploring the ethical contributions of indigenous philosophies* (No. 3). DPS Working Paper Series. Retrieved from https://www.uni-kassel.de › datas › Entwicklungspolitik

CAUSE Center. (2016). Website: https://www.albany.edu/cause/

Cerrutti, M., & Bertoncello, R. (2003). Urbanization and internal migration patterns in Latin America. Conference on African Migration in Comparative Perspective, Johannesburg, South Africa, 4-7 June, 2003. *Centro de Estudios de Población. Argentin*. https://www.researchgate.net/publication/251308910_Urbanization_and_Internal_Migration_Patterns_in_Latin_America

Coraggio, J. L. (2008). La economía social y solidaria como estrategia de desarrollo en el contexto de la integración regional latinoamericana1. *Revista Foro* (66), 27–33.

Devoto, F. J. (1989). Argentine migration policy and movements of the European population (1876–1925). *Estudios migratorios latinoamericanos*, *4*(11), 135–158.

ECLAC. (2017). Non-contributory social protection programmes database. Retrieved from http://dds.cepal.org/bdilp/en/ last visited 31/01/2017

ENI Di Tella. (2013). *Primer relevamiento de actores de los negocios inclusivos en Argentina. Primera parte: Emprendimientos y pequeñas empresas (2012–2013).* Retrieved from http://www.utdt.edu/download.php?fname=_138151691174729900.pdf

Hecker, E., & Kulfas, M. (2005). *Los desafíos del desarrollo: Diagnósticos y propuestas, claves para todos.* Buenos Aires: Capital Intelectual Editorial.

Hervier, X. V., Scotta, V., Marchisio, S., & Fernández, R. M. (2017). Secondary education in Argentina: A winding road. *Economics, 5*(6), 542–552.

ILO. (2014). Employment formalization in Argentina: recent developments and the road ahead. Notes on formalization. Regional Office for Latin America and the Caribbean. International Labour Organization. https://www.ilo.org/wcmsp5/groups/public/---americas/---ro-lima/documents/publication/wcms_245883.pdf

ILO. (2015). Assessment and Perspectives on Policies for Employment Formalization in Argentina. Conclusions from the IV Seminar on the Informal Economy in Argentina. Buenos Aires, Argentina. https://www.ilo.org/wcmsp5/groups/public/---americas/---ro-lima/---ilo-buenos_aires/documents/publication/wcms_459604.pdf

INDEC. (2001). Censo Nacional de Población, Hogares y Viviendas del año 2001. Goverment Report. https://www.indec.gob.ar/micro_sitios/webcenso/index.asp

Kessler, G., & Di Virgilio, M. M. (2010). Impoverishment of the middle class in Argentina: The "new poor" in Latin America. *Laboratorium, 2.*

Luna, E. (2013). Social Entrepreneurship in Argentina. The role of networks in the quest for financial resources (Master's Thesis). Copenhagen Business School Copenhagen, Denmark.

Manini, M. (2019). Mendoza cobra importancia en el "Sistema B". Diario Los Andes.p.1. Retrieved from https://www.losandes.com.ar/article/view?slug=mendoza-cobra-importancia-en-el-sistema-b

Mazzucato, M. (2015). From market fixing to market-creating: A new framework for economic policy. Retrieved from https://doi.org/10.2139/ssrn.2744593

Mazzucato, M. (2018). Mission-oriented innovation policies: challenges and opportunities. Industrial and Corporate Change, 27(5), 803–815. https://doi.org/10.1093/icc/dty034

Mazzucato, M., & Perez, C. (2014). Innovation as growth policy: The challenge for Europe. *SSRN Electronic Journal.* doi:10.2139/ssrn.2742164 https://doi.org/10.2139/ssrn.2742164

Mucarsel, L. (2014). Hacia un nuevo modelo de planificación del desarrollo en América del Sur: Estudio comparado de los principales instrumentos de planificación del desarrollo en la Argentina y el Brasil, 2003–2013. Retrieved from https://repositorio.cepal.org/discover?query=Hacia+un+nuevo+modelo+de+planificaci%C3%B3n+del+desarrollo+en+Am%C3%A9rica+del+Sur

Ocampo, J. A., & Ros, J. (Eds.). (2011). *The Oxford handbook of Latin American economics.* New York: Oxford University Press. Retrieved from https://doi.org/10.1093/oxfordhb/9780199571048.001.0001

Pyles, L. (2009). *Progressive community organizing: The roots of social change.* New York: Routledge.

Roitman, R. D. (2016). *¿De qué hablamos cuando hablamos de economía social?* Mendoza, Argentina: Marcos Mattar Editores. Retrieved from https://bdigital.uncu.edu.ar/objetos_digitales/8617/libro-ess-completo.pdf

Salvia, A., & Vera, J. (2016). Pobreza y desigualdad por ingresos en la Argentina urbana 2010–2015 : tiempos de balance. Observatorio de la Deuda Social Argentina. Universidad Católica Argentina. http://bibliotecadigital.uca.edu.ar/repositorio/investigacion/pobreza-desigualdad-tiempos-balance.pdf

Svampa, M. (2011). Extractivismo neodesarrollista y movimientos sociales:¿ Un giro ecoterritorial hacia nuevas alternativas?. *Más allá del desarrollo*, *1*, 185–218.

Talcott, F. (2011). *Broadening Civic Space Through Voluntary Action Lessons from 2011*. CIVICUS-World Alliance for Citizen Participation. http://www.civicus.org/images/stories/resources/2011%20volunteerism%20publication.pdf

UCA. (2019). Informe del Observatorio de la Deuda Social. Retrieved 16 May 2020 from: http://uca.edu.ar/es/observatorio-de-la-deuda-social-argentina/barometro-de-la-deuda-social-argentina/informes-anuales-de-la-deuda-social-argentina

UNESCO. (2014). Revisión Nacional 2015 de la Educación para Todos: Argentina. https://unesdoc.unesco.org/ark:/48223/pf0000230307?posInSet=1&queryId=ea0d964d-3689-4d33-a9dc-39f1058e1fd5

United Nations Development Programme (UNDP). (2017). *Human development report: Argentina*. New York: United Nations. Retrieved from http://hdr.undp.org/en/countries/profiles/ARG

World Bank. (2016). Argentina Overview. Retrieved 18 April 2016, from https://www.worldbank.org/en/country/argentina

World Bank. (2017). Argentina Overview. Retrieved 15 May 2017, from https://www.worldbank.org/en/country/argentina

Wu, X., Howlett, M., & Ramesh, M. (Eds.). (2018). *Policy capacity: State and societal perspectives*. New York: Palgrave Macmillan.

CHAPTER 15

⌒∿⌒

The Odd Couple

"Incomplete Socialism" and Social Enterprises in Cuba

HENRY-LOUIS TAYLOR, JR.

This chapter interrogates the complexities of socialist construction in Cuba by examining the impact of the *2011 Lineamientos de la política económica y social del Partido y la Revolución* (the Economic and Social Policies of the Party and Revolution) of the Sixth Party Congress on Cuban society, especially Afro-Cubans and ordinary Cubanos. How should scholars and policy-makers conceptualize these economic and social reforms? Do they reflect the onset of capitalist restoration, or do they portray a new stage in the process of socialist construction? These questions are explored by examining socialist construction in multiracial Cuba during the age of neo-liberal global capitalism (Harvey, 2005).

In this chapter, I use a conceptual framework based on *incomplete socialism* and *social enterprise* to explore the character of these economic reforms and to deepen insight into their impact on Afro-Cubans and ordinary Cubanos. The incomplete socialism lens posits that market elements will always be present in socialist economies during the global dominance of capitalism, while the social enterprise lens suggests that market elements can be harnessed and used to produce socially beneficial

Henry-Louis Taylor, Jr., *The Odd Couple* In: *Social Entrepreneurship and Enterprises in Economic and Social Development*. Edited by: Katharine Briar-Lawson, Paul Miesing, and Blanca M. Ramos, Oxford University Press (2021). © Oxford University Press. DOI: 10.1093/oso/9780197518298.003.0016.

outcomes. Market dynamics in a controlled and tightly regulated socialist environment, which prioritizes social ends over economic concerns, can thus produce positive social outcomes (Alberto, 2011; Baden & Wilkinson, 2014; Campbell, 2013).

This chapter centers the complexities of socialist construction in a multiracial society with a large black population. In Cuba, socialist construction marches in tandem with the eradication of racism. The island's history of slavery and ties of intimacy with the United States interwove racism with national development, and this made anti-racism an essential component of socialist construction (Brock & Fuertes, 1998; Helg, 1995). The chapter consists of three parts. The first part explores the challenge of socialist construction, while the second part introduces the Cuban socialist revolution and examines the impact of the *2011 Lineamientos* on blacks and ordinary Cubanos in Havana. In the third part, I explore the research, policy, and practical implications of the findings.

THE CHALLENGE OF SOCIALIST CONSTRUCTION

The challenge of socialist construction cannot be understood fully without accounting for the problem of incomplete socialism. My argument is that socialist construction can never be completed in a world dominated by capitalism. It will always be incomplete during this epoch. Thus, the mere existence of market reforms in a socialist society cannot be equated with capitalist restoration. For example, the sociologist Andrew G. Walder (1996) said that market reforms vary widely in their impact on socialist society. Some market reforms can bolster economic security and egalitarianism, while others can produce disparities and inequalities. The historian Christopher Phelps (2006) argues that market elements will remain entrenched in the economy throughout the process of socialist construction.

The sociologist and economic historian Andre G. Frank (1986) suggests that political flaws that exist in socialist societies make them vulnerable to capitalist restoration. He argued that nationalism and racism create deep tensions among socialist countries as they jockey for entry into the world capitalist market system. These third-world countries, as they socialize their economies, get sidetracked, compete with each other, and inevitably resort to elitism, bureaucracy, and the repression of their own people. The "failures" of Kampuchea, Vietnam, and China caused Frank to posit that progressives should rethink the idea that socialism is a real alternative to the dehumanizing capitalist reality. Thus, regardless of how the question is posed, the discussion of socialist construction is always problematized by market dynamics (Azar, Jureidini, & McLaurin, 1978). The interpretative imperative, then, is to explain the impact of market forces on the socialist construction process. This is a *translational* question, one that grapples with understanding how market forces, including their economic, cultural, and ideological dimensions, influence the development of socialist society down on the ground, in the neighborhoods and communities where people live.

There is no blueprint on how to construct socialist societies. Vladimir Lenin, for instance, said that Karl Marx never wrote a single word about socialist construction. At the same time, Lenin believed that socialist construction was a *process* that took place over time and that the economy would contain market elements throughout the process (Phelps, 2006). Leon Trotsky also believed that an alchemy of economic structures would exist throughout the socialist construction process—pre-capitalist subsistence farming, small commodity production, private capitalism, and state capitalism (Phelps, 2006).

Lenin and Trotsky also posited that these market forces made socialism vulnerable to capitalist restoration, but they trusted the proletarian leadership to harness these market forces and use them in service of socialist goals and objectives (Phelps, 2006). Market elements thus will always be found in a socialist economy during its transition to communism. Hence, the goal for Cuba, or any other socialist economy, is to harness these market forces and use them to produce socially beneficial outcomes (Baden & Wilkinson, 2014).

The social enterprise concept is useful in explaining how socialist leaders might accomplish this goal. In this context, social enterprise refers to business firms, including self-employment and microenterprises, that use market principles to achieve socially beneficial outcomes by reducing profits. In socialist societies, the social enterprise concept can be useful in two interrelated ways. The first is to provide a framework that states can use to operationalize self-employment, microenterprise, and small business development, while the second is to encourage foreign firms to adopt a social responsibility business creed. This social enterprise concept is similar to what the Harvard economist Michael Porter called *shared value*. In this business model, companies pursue financial success in a way that also yields societal benefits (Baden & Wilkinson, 2014; Porter & Kramer, 2011). The critical issues are that socialist countries can take active measures to mitigate the adverse influence of market reforms and that all socialist countries will have market elements in them during the age of incomplete socialism.

INCOMPLETE SOCIALISM

The idea of incomplete socialism first surfaced in 1925, during a debate in the Russian Communist Party (Bolsheviks). The question was: Could socialism be built in a single country without an accompanying world proletarian revolution? Lenin and Trotsky posited that socialist construction could occur in a single country, but that it would never transition to complete socialism or communism in the absence of a world proletarian revolution. Until that happened, socialist construction would remain incomplete because the economy would contain market elements, which would also make capitalist restoration an ongoing possibility (Gaitonde, 1974; Mishra, 1976; Van Ree, 1998).

Deng Xiaoping, leader of the People's Republic of China from 1978 to 1989, provides some insight into the complexities of socialist construction. He said that every socialist state should possess five interactive characteristics: (1) public ownership of the means of production, (2) equitable distribution of wealth, (3) government of the working people, (4) a planned economy, and (5) emphasis on moral incentives to work and engage in nation-building (Hua, 1995, p. 73). These so-called characteristics are actually aspirations that cannot be realized fully in the age of global capitalism. For example, during socialist construction, the means of production will never be fully owned by the state. Some enterprises will be owned by domestic entrepreneurs, while others will be partially owned by foreign investors.

Global competition will also force countries to make concessions to keep highly trained and talented citizens from defecting. These concessions will intensify class differences, aggravate racial tensions, and complicate the equitable distribution of national wealth. Meanwhile, continued exposure to the outside world will spawn materialism, consumerism, and individualism, along with other capitalist challenges to socialist culture, especially the socialist emphasis on moral incentives. Indeed, the triumph of moral incentives over material incentives will probably never be realized during the age of incomplete socialism. The Chinese skirted the implications of these issues by simply referring to their socialist model as *market socialism* (Christensen & Bickhard, 2002; Guevara & Castro, 1989; Marable, 1984; Yang, 2000). However, back in 1959, on the eve of the triumph of the Cuban Revolution, Fidel Castro was not thinking about incomplete socialism, social enterprise, or capitalist restoration. He was only thinking about the building socialism in Cuba.

ORIGINAL INTENT: THIS TIME THE REVOLUTION IS FOR REAL

"This time the revolution is for real!" declared Fidel Castro in *Santiago de Cuba* on January 1, 1959. "This time Cuba is fortunate: the revolution will truly come to power. It will not be as in 1898 when the Americans intervened at the last minute and appropriated our country. . . . It will not be as in 1933 when the people believed the revolution was in the making and Batista . . . usurped power. . . . It will not be as in 1944 when the masses were exuberant in the belief that they had at last come in power but thieves came to power instead. No thieves. No traitors, no interventionists! This time the revolution is for real!" (Perez-Stable, 1993).

Fidel Castro (1953/2016) intended to build a society based on socio-economic justice for the *popular classes*, which included small farmers, peasants, blacks,[1] urban workers, petty bourgeoisie shopkeepers, and intellectuals (Blum, 2011; Gordy, 2015; Rosendahl, 1997). Triumphantly, he marched across the nation's 650-mile landmass, stopping along the way in hamlets, small villages, and cities, urging the masses to join him in the quest to build a new Cuba (Liberator's triumphal march, 1959). In *History Will Absolve Me*, written in 1953, as part of his defense in the Moncada Barracks attack, he outlined his program for building a people-centered society.[2]

> The problem of land tenure (agriculture), the problem of industrialization, the problem of housing, the problem of unemployment, the problem of education, and the problem of health care; we have here six concrete points to which our efforts will be directed, with resolve. (Castro, 1953)

Although not discussed in the manifesto, Fidel knew that racism and sexism must be eliminated (Barber, 2011; Benson, 2016; Castro, 1959; D'Amato 2007; de la Fuente, 2001). For example, in a March 1959 speech at a labor rally in Havana, he addressed job discrimination and its relationship to revolutionary consciousness.

> But not everybody's mentality has developed enough in a revolutionary way; a revolutionary consciousness is lagging behind the people's feelings. The people's feelings are all revolutionary, but their mentality is still not wholly so. The people's mentality is conditioned by many inherited prejudices, many vestiges of the past, and many old customs. If the people want to overcome this evil they must begin by recognizing it. If the people want to see a correct course for themselves they must accept the postulates I was talking about. (I am told?)

that battles must be won by us; the battle against unemployment; the battle to raise the standards of the lowest-paid workers; the battle to bring down the cost of living; *and one of the most just battles that must be fought, a battle that must be emphasized more and more, which I might call the fourth battle—the battle to end racial discrimination at work centers.* I repeat, the battle to end racial discrimination at work centers. Of all forms of racial discrimination, the worst is the one that limits the colored Cuban's access to jobs. It is true that there (exists?) in our country in some sectors the shameful procedure of barring Negroes from jobs. (Castro, 1959; emphasis added)

Castro conceptualized freedom and liberation in human rights terms, and he stressed the importance of improving living standards and the quality of people's lives. Achieving these goals required bolstering the quality of housing, healthcare, and education while providing access to jobs and opportunities. Castro maintained that these "human rights" problems could never be solved under capitalism. Much later, in 2005, Kofi Annan (2005), former Secretary General of the United Nations, referred to these human rights goals as the *larger freedoms*. Thus, to obtain the larger freedoms and build a just society, Castro and the *rebeldes* decided to construct a socialist society (Bobes, 2013; Draper, 1969; Dumont, 1970; Gordy, 2015; Perez, 1999).[3]

The building of socialism in Cuba centered on obtaining four interactive goals: (1) building new people-centered institutions, (2) building a vibrant socialist economy, (3) solving the core human rights problems (land tenure, industrialization, housing, unemployment, education, health, racism, and sexism), and (4) imbuing the Cuban people with a socialist culture and ideology that placed moral incentives over material ones. Since no blueprint or roadmap existed on socialist construction, each country had to find its own path. Thus, the Cuban socialist project, Castro reasoned, required ongoing experimentation in accordance with the principles of Marxism and rooted in the lived experiences of the Cuban people (Mesa-Lago, 2000).

Basking in the afterglow of victory, an exuberant but sober Fidel Castro knew that socialist construction would be a long, difficult road, filled with setbacks, disappointments, and the ever-present danger of counterrevolution, US intrigue, and capitalist restoration. He had the challenge of socialist construction in mind when he told the ecstatic masses, "This is going to be a year of work. We had a quieter life in the hills than we are going to have from now on. Now we are going to purify this country. You must all be heroes in this new time of peace. The Cuban people are intelligent enough to do what they have to do" (Liberator's triumphal march, 1959, p. 29).

Cuba became a beacon of hope to people scattered across the Global South, along with oppressed nationalities and radicals fighting for freedom in the Global North (Williams, 1962). For blacks, trampled on by centuries of slavery, colonialism, and oppression, the idea of an egalitarian multi-racial society conjured up hope and optimism (Berger, 2010; Burrough, 2016; Fanon, 1963; Hayden, 2009; Latner, 2017; Reitan, 1999; Sayres, Stephanson, Aronowitz, & Jameson, 1984). Afro-Cubans supported the Revolution because they stood to benefit from it. Positioned at the bottom of Cuban society, they had nothing to lose but their chains (Anderson, 2003).

During the early years of the Cuban Revolution, between 1959 and 1989, socialist construction took place under the most ideal circumstances. During this "Golden Age," Cuba traded mostly with the Soviet Union and the Council of Mutual Economic Assistance (CMEA) (Taylor, 2009).[4] Cuba held a "favorite son" status, which gave it favorable foreign aid and trade agreements, especially with the Soviets. During the Golden Age, Cuba's relationship with the Soviet Union and the CMEA shielded it from ongoing contact with the global capitalist marketplace because the island depended mostly on trade with other socialist countries.

Cuba prospered during this period because it had the financial resources needed to implement its socialist program.[5] Afro-Cubans, in particular, made great strides, with some enthusiastic supporters even saying the nation had eradicated racism (Cole, 1980). Cuba did not eliminate racism during the Golden Age, but it did make significant progress in removing its material basis. The *rebeldes* improved the quality of housing for all citizens and bolstered their access to jobs, medical treatment, social services, and human development. The strategy worked. A close Afro-Cuban friend, Omar Zulueta-Cardenas, once told me, "I loved my country *before* the Special Period." Life was good for Omar during the Golden Age, but the hard times spawned by the fall of the Soviet Union and the US embargo radically changed his view of Cuban society (Oppenheimer, 1992).

BUILDING SOCIALISM IN A HOSTILE WORLD: AFTERMATH OF THE SPECIAL PERIOD

Cuba's Golden Age abruptly ended in 1989 when the Soviet Union collapsed, along with the East European Socialist bloc and the CMEA (Hernandez-Reguant, 2009, pp. 1–88; Taylor, 2009). Overnight, the economy plunged into a severe depression and the nation stood on the brink of ruination. To worsen the situation, the United States intensified its economic embargo with the intention of driving Cuba over the brink. Hardship and desperation became normalized in Cuban society. The nation experienced food shortages, power outages, transportation woes, unemployment, and the absence of consumer goods and products. Fidel called this moment, *El Período Especial en Tiempo de Paz* or the Special Period in a Time of Peace, and he did two things to help the island survive the calamity. He first told the Cuban people that the economic crisis posed a grave threat to national security and called upon them to meet the challenge.

> The concept of the special period in peacetime has emerged. And we are undoubtedly already entering this special period in peacetime. . . . We will have to undergo this trial. . . . What are we trying to do and what are we doing, given this situation? We propose that if we have to face a special period in peacetime, a harsh special period, our task should not be only to survive, but even to develop. (Castro, 1990)

He then intensified the marketization of the economy and expanded self-employment or microbusiness development while fighting against the resurrection of racism (Mujal-Leon, 2011; Porter, 1990). Castro did not want to introduce market principles into the development of Cuba's socialist economy, but he had no choice. To survive, Cuba needed to find new markets for its products and acquire hard currency to operate in the global marketplace. So, Castro used international tourism to reboot the economy. *Cubanos* used to say, *"Sin azúcar no hay Cuba"*; now they say, *"sin turismo no hay Cuba"* (Without sugar, there is no Cuba; without tourism, there is no Cuba.)

Castro legalized the dollar and allowed Cubanos to receive remittances from relatives in the United States to acquire hard currency. To "capture" these dollars, the government established *mercados* (stores) where merchandise could only be bought in dollars. Last, to maintain full employment, Castro legalized the establishment of self-employment or microenterprises (Jatar-Hausman, 1999; Taylor & McGlynn, 2009). He then entered joint ventures with foreign enterprises and employed capitalist managerial principles to operate state-owned stores (Dolan, 2007; Mesa-Lago & Perez-Lopez, 2013). Concurrently, he stressed that market reforms must operate within Cuba's socialist framework, and he continued to stress egalitarianism and social development (Blum, 2011; Taylor, 2009). Although Castro did not use the term, a social enterprise framework nevertheless guided his integration of market forces into Cuba's socialist economy (O'Sullivan, 2012).

In that moment, to survive, Cuba introduced new market reforms, including the introduction of international tourism and legalization of the

US dollar. Cuba had to integrate its economy into the global market place to survive on the raging seas of capitalist domination. So, even though the Special Period ended in early 2000, Cuba still needed to shore up its economy with market reforms (Mesa-Lago, 2000).

In 2011, 52 years after the triumph of the revolution and 20 years after the onset of the Special Period, at the Sixth Party Congress in Havana, Fidel Castro's younger brother, Raúl, now president of Cuba, announced that the nation's socialist model needed updating (Castro, 2011). This introduction of these new market reforms, along with significant changes in social policy, posed two interrelated questions: (1) Was capitalism being restored in Cuba? And (2) how would the *2011 Lineamientos* impact Afro-Cubans and ordinary Cubanos?

INCOMPLETE SOCIALISM AND THE SOCIAL ENTERPRISE FRAMEWORK IN CUBA

The hardships faced by the Cuban people decreased in the 15 years between 1991 and 2006, but they did not end, and the nation continued to struggle to obtain the financial resources needed to implement its socialist program. Then, in 2006, after 47 years in power, Fidel Castro relinquished power to his younger brother, Raúl. In 2007–2008, Cuba was hit by the global financial crisis. In 2008, after he formally assumed the presidency, Raúl Castro posited that Cuba could not escape the volatility of global capitalism. For the island to survive as a socialist state, it needed to make conceptual and structural changes in the socialist model. To determine the needed reforms, he initiated a national discussion that culminated in the *2011 Guidelines for Economic and Social Policy Change* at the Sixth Congress of the Communist Party. Almost 9 million people, in more than 163,000 meetings, held by hundreds of different organizations, participated in debates on reforming the socialist model (Castro, 2011).

The *2011 Guidelines for Economic and Social Policy Change* not only altered economic policies but also changed the social policies undergirding them. For example, the guidelines replaced *egalitarianism* with "equal rights and opportunities for all citizens," and situated *material incentives* over *moral* ones. To reduce dependency on the state and develop greater self-sufficiency, the government eliminated and/or reduced fiscal support for many organizations and institutions, including the Committees for the Defense of the Revolution. Then, on the economic side, the guidelines eliminated wage caps and expanded self-employment.

One goal of the reforms was to eliminate subsidies for Cubanos who did not need them, while simultaneously they reduced social supports for those who required assistance. At the same time, Raúl Castro wanted to maintain a strong support system for Cubanos who truly needed help. He emphatically stated that no one will be left behind or needlessly suffer in Cuba.

> In Cuba, under socialism, there will never be space for "shock therapies" that go against the neediest, who have traditionally been the staunchest supporters of the Revolution. . . . The Revolution will not leave any Cuban helpless. The social welfare system is being reorganized to ensure rational and deferential support to those *who really need it*. Instead of massively subsidizing products as we do now, we shall gradually provide for those people lacking other support. . . . (Castro, 2011, emphasis added)

Raúl Castro's backing away from moral incentives and ending wage caps meant a retreat from building the new socialist citizen, but that still remained an aspiration (Guevara & Castro, 1989).[6] Cuba was continually faced with the danger of the United States luring away its most talented and highly trained citizens by offering them higher wages and an accelerated path to citizenship. The US strategy forced Raúl Castro to deemphasize moral incentives, eliminate wage caps, and provide the talented and highly trained with greater privileges. He knew that Cuba was playing with fire and that these market-based changes would intensify hardship, increase class and race inequality, and heighten the vulnerability of low-income Cubanos to social problems. Yet, at the same time, Cuba needed to make market-based changes to survive as a socialist state, and Raúl Castro trusted the national leadership to harness these market forces and use them to realize socialist goals and aspirations.

SOCIALIST CONSTRUCTION AND *2011 LINEAMIENTOS*: AFRO-CUBANS AND ORDINARY CUBANOS

The Cuban Socialist Project aimed to build a people-centered society with a robust economy capable of driving social and human development. The central question in this chapter is: How did the *2011 Lineamientos* impact Afro-Cubans and ordinary Cubanos, and the communities in which they lived? To gain insight into this issue, I examined the experiences of mostly

Afro-Cubans in 2010, and again, 5 years later, in 2015–2016, in six different areas: (1) work and income, (2) housing, (3) food, (4) health, (5) education, and (6) neighborhood life and culture.

I used focus groups, informal interviews, ethnographic field observations, and field dairies to explore the socioeconomic experiences of Afro-Cubans, along with several whites, and grouped the material into two datasets: phase-one and phase-two studies. *Phase-one studies* took place during the spring and summer of 2010, and *phase two studies* occurred in the spring and summer months of 2015 and in the summer of 2016. This approach made possible a before and after analysis of the *2011 Lineamientos* on Afro-Cubans and ordinary Cubanos. Phase one studies consisted of four focus groups and eight informal interviews. Twenty people participated in the focus groups, while informal interviews were held with an additional eight Cubanos.

The phase two studies took place in the spring and summer of 2015 and in the summer of 2016. In 2015, two focus groups and seven informal interviews took place, and 13 people participated in the focus groups and 4 in the informal interviews. One focus group was held in the summer of 2016, and six people participated in it. In total, in phase-one and phase-two studies, 36 people participated in the focus groups and 15 in the informal interviews. Five interviewees participated in both phase one and two studies. Of the 46 unique participants in this study, 43 were Afro-Cubans and 3 were white. I used a series of open-ended questions to interrogate the informants.

The phase one and phase two studies comprise a database called *Fieldwork in Havana*, which is housed at the University at Buffalo Center for Urban Studies. Snowball sampling was used to identify participants in the focus groups and interviews. The informants were friends of *habaneros* who suggested other friends who should be invited to the meeting. Snowball sampling is particularly useful—sometimes essential—when sampling hard to reach populations (Faugier & Sergeant, 1997, p. 790). The organizers of the focus groups were paid to set up the sessions. The informants, including those interviewed, held a variety of occupations, including a lawyer, school teacher, tobacco factory worker, street cleaner, unemployed worker, and student. The household structure varied, and most participants had a high school education or less. Their ages ranged from 20 to 50, with all but three being Afro-Cuban or mulatto. Two translators were used in all focus groups. The informal interviews were held in English.

All informants lived in one of three communities, Centro Habana, Habana Vieja, and La Habana del Este. These are three very different places. Centro Habana is situated adjacent to Habana Vieja and runs along

La Bahia de la Habana (Havana Bay). This densely populated community is characterized by two- and three-story buildings that are flush with the street and void of green space, and the discrete apartment buildings literally form a single wall that stretches from one end of the block to the other. Habana Vieja, the oldest community in Havana, has a built environment similar to Centro Habana, but the streets are narrower.

This is the city's prime tourist district, and the community is anchored by five different plazas which function as hubs of tourist activities. Habana Vieja's proximity to tourist venues and foreigners, combined with its animated street life, makes it a desirable living place despite its poor housing. La Habana del Este is located in the eastern part of the city and stretches along the ocean front. It is a low-density, rustic community characterized by low-rise apartments, single-family dwelling units, abundant green space, and a small-town atmosphere.

In both the 2010 and 2015–2016 studies, ethnographic fieldwork was conducted to augment the interviews. Field trips were taken to *mercados* (stores) and *cambios* or money exchanges, along with visits to the numerous shops and stores located in the neighborhood commercial districts in Centro Habana and Habana Vieja. Trips were also made to the nightclubs and restaurants frequented mostly by Cubans, as well as those that catered to tourists. I used a framework based on situational and interpretative phenomenological analysis to analyze and interpret the data from the focus groups, interviews, and fieldwork (Burgess, Ferguson, & Hollywood, 2007; Farr, 1985).

The cornerstone of the Cuban Revolution was *social inclusion* and the realization of basic human rights for its citizenry: employment, education, housing, health, and neighborhoods that promoted social, mental, and economic well-being. Cuba's success on the social and human development front legitimized the socialist project and became the nation's claim to fame (Corrales, 2012). The big question is, then: Did the *2011 Lineamientos* undermine the Cuban quest for equity, along with social and human development?

MAKING ENDS MEET: WORK AND HOUSEHOLD INCOME

The Revolution promised to end unemployment, but that pledge was complicated by the interactive relationship between work and wages. "*La vida no es fácil*" ("life is not easy") became a common refrain in Cuba after the collapse of the Soviet Union. The market-orientated reforms initiated by Fidel Castro improved living conditions, but they did not end hardship.

People had jobs, but the wages of most Cubanos were too low to make ends meet without "hustling" or holding more than one job. In 2010, about 90% of Cubanos worked in the public sector, and most obtain their income from about seven sources: public sector, moonlighting, self-employment, private sector, retirement, the informal sector, and remittances (Darlington, 2010; Taylor, 2009).

In 2010, most informants said public sector work was plentiful. In this "slack" labor market, anyone wanting a job could find one, but the wages were very low. Raúl Castro understood this, and, in a major policy speech in Camagüey on July 26, 2007, he said,

> We are also aware that, because of the extreme objective difficulties that we face, *wages today are clearly insufficient to satisfy all needs* and have thus ceased to play a role in ensuring the socialist principle that each should contribute according to their capacity and receive according to their work. This has bred forms of social indiscipline and tolerance which, having taken root, prove difficult to eradicate, even after the objective causes behind them are eradicated. (Castro, 2007, emphasis added)

Raúl Castro understood the low-wage problem but had no solution. Informants said many Cubanos dealt with the low-wage problem by moonlighting and/or working in the *economía clandestino*. "To survive in Cuba," one informant said, "you have to move like a snake." By this Cubanos meant that a person must be elusive, cunning, and deceitful to generate the financial resources needed to earn enough money to survive the city (Taylor, 2010

). In this situation, the *economía clandestino* grew in strength as increasing numbers of Cubans turned to the underground economy to buy goods and services and to find work (Ritter, 2005a, 2005b; Ritter & Henken, 2015).

The economic challenge facing Cuba was complicated. The Revolution used public-sector employment to achieve full employment, and the state ran just about everything, from factories to businesses and service industries, such as ice cream parlors, barbershops, gas stations, and shoe repair shops (Reuters, 2010; Wilkinson, 2010). The Revolution solved the unemployment problem, but, in the process, it created the low-wage problem. A professor at the Universidad de la Habana said the problem was structural (Taylor, 2010). Cuba achieved full employment by creating a profusion of useless jobs with no social value. For example, in many restaurants, public buildings, and hotels, there are people dispensing toilet paper in the restrooms (Taylor, 2010). Some people held jobs as street sweepers, who actually swept the streets with small brooms and put the debris in their push-cart. The sheer size of the public sector combined with Cuba's limited resources made it difficult for the state to pay workers a living wage. This combination of low wages and useless work proved toxic and led to problems of absenteeism, decreased labor discipline, inefficiency, poor utilization of the labor force, a severe decline in labor productivity, and unemployment. Some Cubanos preferred work in the clandestine economy to employment in the low-wage public sector (Lamrani, 2012; Smith, 1999).

The professor said the public sector needed downsizing. Her words proved prophetic. In September 2010, the government laid off 500,000 public-sector workers while simultaneously announcing the dramatic expansion of self-employment (Darlington, 2010; Wilkinson, 2010). The plan was to use self-employment to absorb laid-off workers. The government posited that self-employment would allow Cubans to use their creativity to bolster their incomes while encouraging workers in the *economía clandestino* to work in the formal economy (Mujal-Leon, 2011; NPR, 2011). Building on earlier experiences with self-employment, the government liberalized tax regulations and increased the types of businesses that workers could start.

The informants, however, said that self-employment did not work for them. In 2016, they said the cost of a business license combined with high business taxes made self-employment too expensive (Taylor, 2015/2016). The business tax was more problematic than the cost of a license. Self-employed workers were expected to pay from 25% to 50% of their gross income on taxes (BBC, 2010). The government did allow for expenses to be deducted from their taxable income, but the informants said that about 40% of their gross income consisted of business expenses. Thus, when all the taxes are paid, even with the deductions, they do not make enough money to cover all their household expenses. Therefore, for most of the informants, self-employment was beyond their economic reach (Henken, 2002; Lamrani, 2012).

One informant said the real problem was pricing. She claimed the government sets the prices for their services, and, in most instances, they set the prices too low. If you undercharge for your services, the informant said, it does not matter if you can deduct a portion of your expenses because you will still lose money. The high cost of self-employment forced some informants into the *economía clandestino,* where they could make more money. These Cubanos were typically individuals with skills in dancing, cutting hair, plumbing, repairing computers, doing hair and nails, or some other service occupation (Taylor, 2015/2016). For example, one informant tried self-employment, but could not make it work, so she started teaching dancing and doing nails and hair in the *economía clandestino* (Leonard, 2011; Ritter, 2005a).

Not everyone agrees. One self-employed informant says that owning your business can be a road to a successful and prosperous life in Cuba. But, for this to happen, the person must be willing to change—in Cuba, he says making money must become a way of life. The informant rents a table in the tourist district where he sells used books and mementos and souvenirs to tourists, as well as engages in other money-making schemes. To be successful, he says, "you must think about making money, not just working. So, if you have a job; then, in your free time, you must find ways to make more money. You must always think about how to make money. This is now the Cuban way" (Personal Communication, August 2016) (Figure 15.1).

This success story aside, the informants say that most Cubanos are not self-employed. Most people work part-time, and, to make ends meet, they have to work two or more jobs and purchase most of their goods and services in the *economía clandestino*. The informants also say that pilfering from government stores and private companies has been institutionalized and is now part of everyday life and culture. Some Cubanos would probably say that this has been the case for many years. Back in 2001, a self-employed Cuban worker said

> In Cuba, fraud and trickery have become normal parts of everyday life. Everyone is forced to cheat and lie in this system. When the government spends its time engaging in trickery against the people, the people are going to respond with more trickery. (Henken, 2002)

New employment opportunities are opening up in the private sector, but informants say that obtaining good-paying private-sector jobs is difficult, especially in the profitable tourism industry. Jobs in tourism are the

Figure 15.1 Roberto, a self-employed Afro-Cuban worker.
Source: Photo by Author (2015).

most coveted in Cuba. Not only do they pay well, but wages are typically supplemented with tips and sometimes gifts from the tourists; but tourism jobs are hard to get, especially for Afro-Cubans (Taylor & McGlynn, 2009). One white informant, laughingly said, "It is easier to go to the United States than getting a job in the tourism industry."

Not everyone agreed. An Afro-Cuban college student whose mother works in the tourism industry said tourism jobs are actually equitably distributed among whites, mulattos, and Afro-Cubans (Taylor, 2015/2016). Who is considered Afro-Cuban, however, can be a tricky question on the island. Here, physical appearance is the determinant of one's racial classification. In Cuba, some mulattos view themselves as a unique ethnic group, separate and apart from Afro-Cubans. Hence, the question of how many "blacks" are working in the tourism industry can be complicated (Assuncao & Zeuske, 1998; Snipp, 2003). This quibble notwithstanding, while the percentage of Afro-Cubans working in the formal tourism industry might be debatable, the number of Afro-Cuban tourism workers in the *economía clandestino* is not. Many Afro-Cubans are employed in this sector (Taylor, 2009).

Last, searching for satisfying work that pays a living wage is a breeding ground for frustration among a growing number of Cubans. The lack of jobs and opportunities for advancement is causing many Cubanos to consider immigrating (Krikorian, 2016; Krogstad, 2017). A white informant said, "I am 23 years old and have strong IT skills, but my opportunities are limited in Cuba. I cannot even find a full-time position. So, I want to go to the United States where opportunities are greater" (Taylor, 2015/2016). Several months after this focus group session, this young man left Cuba, and now he lives in Miami.

A growing number of Afro-Cubans view immigration as a viable option, but it does not always work out. One informant said her son now lives in Miami, but he is struggling. This Afro-Cuban informant has a large home in an exclusive part of Havana and rents out a part of the house to a private *paladar* (a small restaurant). She regularly sends her son money. The boyfriend of another Afro-Cuban informant recently went to the United States to launch a career as a hip-hop artist. She and her boyfriend sold most of their belongings to finance his trip. His visa lasts for 1 year, and then he must return to Cuba. His quest for fame is elusive. He is struggling to make ends meet in the United States.

Still another informant's ex-boyfriend married an African American woman and moved to the United States, but he never adjusted. His "hustling" skill set was not adaptable to the United States. After a year, he returned to Cuba. The informant laughingly said that he was now more socialist than Fidel (Taylor, 2015/2016). So, while immigration might work for some Cubans, it does not for others.

UNEARNED INCOME: REMITTANCE

When the Soviet Union collapsed, the legalization of remittances was one of the first market reforms initiated by Fidel Castro. This made it possible for Cubanos to receive money from friends and relatives in the United States and elsewhere (Perez-Lopez & Diaz-Briquets, 2005). Remittances, while extremely important to the Cuban economy, nevertheless have had a harmful social impact. For example, Cuba receives about USD$2.3 billion a year in remittances, with most of those dollars coming from the United States (Lobosco, 2014; Orozco, Porras, & Yansura, 2016). These dollars are an important source of "hard currency" for the government, but they are also a source of increased racial and class inequality.

Remittances are a source of *unearned income* that mostly goes to white Cubans (Archibald, 2015). For example, the majority of informants said they received no remittances, while others received them only intermittently. This unearned income widens the income gap between black and white Cubans in two critical ways (Glassman, 2011). First, remittances cause whites to be more likely than blacks to become self-employed. The unearned income brings the cost of business licenses and taxes within their economic reach. Second, it makes it possible for whites to obtain a higher living standard and quality of life than Afro-Cubans even when they reside in the same apartment buildings (Archibald, 2015; Fusion, 2015; Taylor, 2009).[7] The *2011 Lineamientos,* combined with Obama's détente policies, tended to exacerbate the problem. Obama's policies increased the allowable amount of remittances that relatives and friends can send to Cuba, which intensified the white Cuban's socioeconomic advantages over Afro-Cubans (Sullivan, 2017).

HOUSING SECURITY

Fidel Castro viewed housing as a basic human right and cultural artifact that stabilized neighborhood life and culture. The Revolution established a socialist housing market, which circumscribed the use of homeownership as a wealth-producing tool (Taylor, 2009). During the 1990s and early 2000s, homeownership was near-universal in Cuba. About 85% of the population own their homes, and rentals were capped at about 10% of a person's income (Grein, 2015). In this non-market housing system, profit-making was taken out of real estate. Consequently, people were rarely, if ever, evicted, while government regulations and the absence of a real estate class made the buying and selling of housing units difficult. This situation caused people to age in place and neighborhoods to become stable and highly organized. This situation caused the neighborhood to become a stabilizing force in Cuban society (Taylor, 2009; Zamora, 2009).

In the 2010 study, not a single informant expressed concern over housing or knew of anyone who had lost their homes for economic reasons. Also, the informants knew of no one who had been forced to move because of a change in the ownership of their rental units (Taylor, 2010). Housing security was not an issue, but housing inadequacy was a problem. Many dwellings units in Cuba are in need of major repairs, and the informants complained about housing maintenance and quality (Benitez, 2013; Diaz-Briquets, 2009; Hamburg, 1994).

Homeowners are responsible for the upkeep of their properties, but their incomes are too low to prioritize maintenance and upgrades. The government does provide technical assistance and occasionally give residents building materials, but this is not enough for them to upgrade and keep their houses in good physical conditions. On the flipside, low rents and home ownership do make housing affordable, but its low cost does not generate sufficient surplus income to cover the cost of maintenance and upgrades (Logan & Molotch, 1987). This creates a dilemma. The affordability and security of housing ensure that everyone has a home, but housing maintenance and upgrades remain a great challenge in raising the quality and making these "secure" home healthy.

THE DISPLACEMENT DANGER

Displacement is a problem in the tourist district. Tourism requires transforming the city into a commodity for consumption by visitors (Aitchison, Macleod, & Shaw, 2000). The remaking of Havana into an international tourist city required the commodification of historical sections of the city, including the waterfront. The success of the city's tourism industry revolves around the development of these locations. Habana Vieja, the old city, and the western neighborhoods adjacent to El Bahia de Habana (Havana Bay), which are mostly Afro-Cuban neighborhoods, became sites of development. To mitigate the dangers of displacement and Cuban-style gentrification, the Historian of the City conceived Habana Vieja and similar locations as "living communities," where the residences of ordinary

Figure 15.2 Food shopping at a *mercado agropecuario* in Central Havana.
Source: Photo by Author (2015).

Cubanos and the institutions serving them were integrated into the tourist venues and attractions (Figure 15.2). Eusebio Leal, the historian of the city of Havana put it this way:

> "It would be easier to make a movie set," he says. "The city must live essentially around its people. The restoration is not only a historiographical project but a project trying to recover quality of life. . . . Tourists will overwhelm the place. That's why it's important for people to work there and live there, to create spaces of silence where there aren't tourist installations but are real neighborhoods. And even in the most visited places, put schools, and little hospitals. We are trying to put up curtains in the path of the wave." (Montgomery, 2012)

Nonetheless, in the Habana Vieja plazas, many housing units were converted into restaurants, tourist shops, bars, and hotels. Some residents were allowed to remain, but many others were relocated to other parts of the city. Even so, the intermingling of ordinary Cubanos with tourist venues and attractions has nevertheless transformed Habana Vieja into a unique community. An official in the Office of the Historian once explained the challenge facing Cubans in this way: "A contradiction exists between economic and social development, and sometimes it is necessary for the economic side of the contradiction to dominate."[8] He was talking about the complexities of managing socialist construction in a world dominated by neoliberal capitalism. The social enterprise concept provides an explanatory framework for understanding this contradiction. These tourist venues function as "social enterprises," with the intent of producing the revenue required to support social development, including education, healthcare, and recreation.

A Cuban friend, within this context, explained the displacement issue with a rhetorical question. "I know it is a problem, but we need the resources. So, what can you do?" (Taylor, personal conversation, August 2016). The challenge centers on developing these "social enterprises" for revenue-generating purposes while minimizing the displacement of residents. Cuba tried to manage this problem using a "living communities" strategy, but this has met with only limited success. In Habana Vieja, many residents have been displaced from the most strategic locations within the community.

The tourist areas notwithstanding, overall, the economic and social policies enacted between 1991 and 2007 only minimally affected the housing market, but the *2011 Lineamientos* introduced some troubling market-oriented reforms. The *Lineamientos* made it easier for Cubans to buy, sell, and rent housing units (Sixth Congress of the Communist Party of Cuba, 2011). These policy changes have three important implications. First, they opened the door for the reemergence of a private landlord class and land speculation, along with evictions and other forms of involuntary displacement.

The informant who I talked with about displacement said her family was forced to move when her apartment was sold. She also said that rents are rapidly rising in Havana, particularly in the most desirable sections of the city where foreigners prefer to live (Taylor, 2015/2016). Another informant, who lives in Habana Vieja, said people in her apartment building were being asked by foreign investors to sell their units. She said her mother sold her apartment. The informants said that a growing number of foreigners were finding ways to acquire housing units in Havana. Foreigners are not allowed to buy homes directly, but informants say they use Cubans as a fictive to purchase the houses (Kahn, 2016; Peters, 2014; Taylor, 2015/2016).

Second, the new housing policies have created another income source for *habaneros*. For example, one informant owned a house when he got married. His wife also owned a house. He plans to sell his house for about USD$20,000 and move in with his wife. Another informant bought a house with a friend, and they are remodeling the unit with the intent of renting it out. Another informant has a job overseeing the remodeling of a house that was purchased by an Englishman (Taylor, 2015/2016). He hired some of his friends to do the construction work. Thus, the rehabilitation of housing units for foreign owners might become a source of income for Cubanos.

Third, these housing policies could fundamentally alter the racial and class composition of neighborhoods, especially in the most desirable parts of the city. Cuban neighborhoods are cross-class, multiracial communities, and the shift in housing policy could spawn a trend toward neighborhood homogeneity and social atomism (Taylor, 2009). These new housing policies have not eliminated housing security in Cuba, but they have endangered it. Concurrently, the long-standing problem of housing inadequacy is worsening because Cubans have even fewer resources to use for maintaining and upgrading their homes.

FOOD SECURITY

Food security is a complicated issue in Cuba. The problem exists when people do not have reliable access to a sufficient quantity of nutritious and affordable foods that meet their dietary needs and preferences (Kannan, Drev, & Sharma, 2000). In 2010, food topped the list of complaints among the informants. Food is a necessity, and the informants said that rising food prices and shortages are making it difficult for them to meet their family's dietary needs. Most informants said they spend more than 50% of their income on food, with some informants estimating that 70% of their income is consumed by food costs (Taylor, 2010).[9] Cubanos purchase food from four primary sources: the *bodega* (accepts only national money), farmers' markets (national money), the CUC *mercados* (accepts only Cuban convertible peso [CUC]),[10] and the *economía clandestino*. Cuba still has a dual monetary system that consists of the domestic peso and the CUC, which has value equal to the US dollar and is used by foreigners. On November 8, 2004, the US dollar ceased to be accepted in Cuban retail outlets and the CUC replaced it. The Cuban government still uses the Cuban peso or national money in the local economy as a shield against inflation.

In Fidel Castro's Cuba, the *libreta* played an important role in subsidizing food costs. It was part of the Cuban food distribution system, which entitled people to a basic ration of groceries (rice, bean, coffee, meats, etc.) purchased at the neighborhood *bodega* (shop) at subsidized prices. The *libreta* indicated how much each family member was allowed to buy depending on their age and gender (Claudio, 1999). The *libreta* was distributed each year by the government and reflected the composition of a family. The ration book made food affordable, but the gradual removal of food items from the *libreta* reduced its impact on the family budget Figure 15.3).

In 2010, the informants said that the *libreta* only covered about a third of their food purchases. Therefore, to make ends meet, it was necessary to

Figure 15.3 Tourist district in Habana Veija as a living community. Note the clothes hanging in the background.
Source: Photo by Author (2015).

purchase food in the *economía clandestine* (Taylor, 2010). The food shortages and price hikes may have been aftershocks from the damage caused by three hurricanes in 2008 (Gustave, on August 30; Ike, on September 8, and Paloma, on November 8–9). The Cuban government estimated that the triple hurricanes caused more than US$10 billion in damages (Davidson & Krull, 2011; Wright, 2012).

The *2011 Lineamientos* called for the elimination of the *libreta*. According to the *Lineamientos*, the *libreta* had outlived its usefulness and now threatened the socialist principle, "From each in accordance with his ability and to each in accordance with his labor." The *libreta* was issued to all Cubans regardless of their need for assistance. Raúl Castro argued that this equity principle wasted resources by giving subsidies to Cubanos who did not need them. In his report to the Sixth Congress of the Communist Party, Raúl Castro said discussions on the removal of the *libreta* dominated the national discussion on upgrading the socialist model.

> Undoubtedly, the ration book and its removal spurred most of the contributions of the participants in the debates, and it is only natural. Two generations of Cubans have spent their lives under this rationing system that, despite its *harmful egalitarian quality*, has for four decades ensured every citizen access to basic food at highly *subsidized derisory prices*. (Castro, 2011, emphasis added)

The government intended to gradually eliminate the *libreta* by slowly removing subsidized items until it was no longer useful. In 2015, informants said the food situation had worsened. Some informants said the booming tourism industry caused the food shortage. In this case, the government privileged tourists over the people in providing foodstuffs. Other informants suggested that poor food planning was the culprit (Ahmed, 2016). Regardless, the informants say that complaints about rising prices and food shortages are increasing.

Although Cubans have been complaining about the *libreta* for years, it still significantly reduced the cost of food. Thus, the elimination of the *libreta* caused an increase in food prices while wages remained stagnant or declined. Additionally, the informants said a growing number of food items could only be purchased in CUC *mercados*, where prices are higher. A combination of these two changes in the food system threatened food security while making life more difficult for the average citizen (Taylor, 2015/2016).

The informants also complained about food shortages. The inability to purchase consistently the foods they preferred was particularly aggravating. The informants said that chicken, potatoes, and some fruits were very hard to find. People are not starving, but not being able to buy the food items they desire is frustrating. The informants are angered by the seemingly endless food choices found in the tourist restaurants, which makes them believe the government cares more about foreigners than its own citizens (Taylor, 2015/2016). Food insecurity, nonetheless, is not a major problem in Cuba. People cannot always eat the foods they prefer, but no one is starving or going hungry in Cuba. I made field trips to neighborhood *mercados* and farmers' markets and found them well-stocked and filled with shoppers. Even so, the residents' frustrations are real, and those frustrations reflect a crack in the food security system. The UN Committee on World Food Security includes "food preferences" in their definition of food security.

HEALTH

Fidel Castro made healthcare a cornerstone of the Cuban Revolution and based it on a wellness model that emphasized prevention and social, mental, and physical well-being (Feinsilver, 1993). Cubans developed a three-tier healthcare system composed of (1) neighborhood-based clinics, (2) community-level *policlinics*, and (3) centralized hospitals and medical institutes. To animate the system, Cubans conceptualized doctors as frontline workers in the revolutionary struggle to build socialism and prioritized the education and training of physicians (Mason, Strug, & Beder, 2010; Taylor, 2009).

The Cuban Health system under Fidel Castro featured a decentralized approach to the delivery of healthcare services, one which the family doctor and nurse program anchored. The family doctor and nurse lived in the neighborhood, had a caseload that ranged from 120 to 150 families, and built relationships with their neighbors. Residents regularly visited their family doctor, and, when more advanced care and treatment were needed, they were referred to a policlinic or hospital (Taylor, 2009). Early in the Revolution, Castro also made medical diplomacy the cornerstone of Cuba's foreign policy (Werlau, 2013). To survive, Cuba made strategic use of its prowess in healthcare by using medical diplomacy to earn hard currency and to extend its influence throughout the Global South (Feinsilver, 2010).

The Cuban health system legitimized the Revolution, and it became a source of pride among Cubanos. However, by 2010, the informants said cracks were beginning to show in the famed Cuban health system. First, informants said the medical diplomacy program was siphoning off neighborhood doctors. Some neighborhoods no longer had family doctors, while in others the doctor's caseloads had increased, making it harder for him or her to see patients. Second, some informants said the doctor's low wages caused some physicians to use bribery to increase their income. The hustler doctor would prioritize the treatment of those patients who gave them bribes (Erisman, 2012; Taylor, 2015/2016; Trotta, 2015). According to the informants, the doctors, like everyone else in Cuba, hustled to make ends meet (Waters, 2017). The changing nature of the family doctor and nurse program caused increasing numbers of *habaneros* to bypass the family doctor and go directly to the *policlinic* for healthcare. These criticisms notwithstanding, the informants still viewed the Cuban healthcare system in positive terms, but they worried about its downward trajectory (Taylor, 2010).

The informants still spoke highly of the Cuban healthcare system in 2015, but their concerns about its downward trajectory had intensified. Most informants said good healthcare services were still available, but the system had worsened since the enactment of the *2011 Lineamientos*. Medical diplomacy was taking its toll on the domestic healthcare system. Many of the *policlinics* and hospitals were understaffed because a large number of doctors were working abroad. These doctors, informants said, made more money and had better living conditions outside the country, and they did not want to return (Taylor, 2015/2016; Waters, 2017).

The informants said medical diplomacy devastated the family doctor and nurse program. One informant said that, in 2000, there was a family doctor and nurse every two to three blocks. "The nurse even came to your house to check on you. Now, I don't even know who my family doctor is." Another informant said that, after a heart attack, her mother was taken to the *policlinic* by a neighbor, but she had to wait before being treated. "When I finally got to the clinic," the informant said, "my mother was lying on the floor dead." The informant does not know if a physician could have saved her mother's life. She only knows that her mother died on the *policlinic* floor waiting for help that never came. She blames the government. Still another informant said it is difficult finding the needed medicine. "My mother was sick; I am a nurse, and I could not find the medicine she needed" (Taylor, 2015/2016).

The Cuban healthcare dilemma speaks directly to the challenge of building socialism in a world dominated by global capitalism. Cuba is a financially strapped country that relies on medical diplomacy to generate hard currency and to create international goodwill. Since the 1959 Revolution, Cuba has exported doctors throughout the Global South—sometimes for humanitarian reasons, sometimes for cash. For example, data as of October 2009 indicate that more than 37,000 Cuban medical professionals were deployed in 98 countries and 4 overseas territories (Figure 15.4). As of February 2009, Cuban medical professionals had saved more than 1.97 million lives, treated more than 130 million patients, performed more

Figure 15.4 Number of Cuban medical aid personnel overseas.
Source: Erisman (2012). *Brain Drain Politics*: The Cuban Medical Professional Parole Programme. International Journal of Cuban studies. 4/3-4. 269-290.

than 2.97 million surgeries, and vaccinated with complete dosages more than 9.8 million people. In 2006, for example, 28%, or USD$2.3 billion of Cuba's total export earnings came from medical services (Feinsilver, 2010). To sustain these efforts, through its Latin American Medical School, Cuba has trained more than 12,000 medical personnel from developing countries, including students from the United States.

These medical services have a multiplier effect on the Cuban economy. That is, countries receiving Cuban doctors will purchase Cuban vaccines, medicines, medical supplies, and equipment. Cuba's biotech industry, for instance, holds 1,200 international patents and earned US$350 million in product sales in 2008 (Feinsilver, 2010). The point is that medical diplomacy has been a cornerstone of Cuban foreign policy since the triumph of the Revolution, and when the domestic economic crisis intensified, it became vital to Cuba's survival as a socialist state. Yet the irony is that medical diplomacy combined with the US destabilization strategy is weakening Cuba's famed healthcare system (Whitney, 2019).

EDUCATION

Primary education is another cornerstone of neighborhood life and culture in Cuba (Blum, 2011). The *rebeldes* believed that a knowledgeable citizenry with the capacity to participate fully in national life was a requisite for building a revolutionary society. So they centered universal education in socialist construction. School attendance was made compulsory for students between the ages of 6 and 16, and all primary schools were located in neighborhoods so that students could attend schools close to home. According to a 2015 World Bank report, Cuba is a world leader in education and spends nearly 13% of its gross domestic product (GDP) on education. By comparison, the United States spends only 5.4%, Canada 5.5%, and France 5.9%. A UNESCO report on education in 13 countries in Latin American ranks Cuba in first place in all subjects and stresses that a Cuban student has twice the knowledge and skills of the average Latin American student (Bruns & Luque, 2015; Lamrani, 2013). The success of its schools has become a source of pride for all Cubans.

In 2010, the informants said they were satisfied with the educational system, and those with school-aged children were happy with the quality of their child's education. Also, they were proud that children could walk to school without fear of crime and/or violence (Taylor, 2010). In 2015, not much had changed on the educational front, and people were still very satisfied with their educational system (Figure 15.5). However,

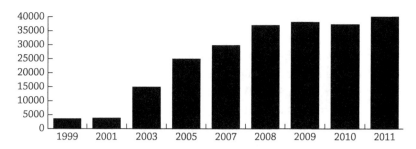

Figure 15.5 Primary school students in Habana Vieja.
Source: Photo by Author (2015).

the informants did express concern about the quality of teachers. They said an increasing number of teachers were leaving education to work in the tourism industry where they could make more money. This resulted in the hiring of inexperienced teachers, including those with questionable credentials. If this trend persisted, they said the schools could be in trouble (Taylor, 2015/2016).

The informant's observations seem to reflect events triggered by the *2011 Lineamientos*. That year, some 14,000 teachers left the classroom with medical leave certificates or requests for self-employment licenses, while during the summer of 2012 another 4,000 teachers gave up their positions without excuses (Ravsberg, 2012). Although Raúl Castro removed wage caps, teachers can still make more money in self-employment and the tourist industry. This appears to be creating an internal brain drain in the teaching profession.

NEIGHBORHOOD LIFE AND CULTURE

Fidel believed that vibrant neighborhoods were the building blocks of civil society and that such neighborhoods should be anchored by solidarity, participatory democracy, reciprocity, equitable distribution of wealth, and social justice. Castro thus centered building stable neighborhoods in the Cuban Socialist Project. Back in 2010, the bonds of trust and friendship still anchored neighborhood life (Taylor, 2009). The informants said they had lived in the same neighborhoods for many years, and, over time, they had developed bonds of trust and friendship with their neighbors. Reciprocity was a characteristic feature of neighborhood life. When someone needed help, they could always find it. One informant said, "If I am hungry or need food, I can always go to my neighbor." Another said, "If someone is sick and need help getting to the hospital, there will always be someone there to help." In Cuba, you are never alone. Someone is always there to assist, support and/or provide comfort, the informants say (Taylor, 2010; 2015/2016).

Reciprocity animated this shared experience (Scott, 1976). In a setting, where unexpected hardships were the norm, surviving the city depending on people willing to help each other. Within this context, the physical and social structure of the neighborhood supported healthy living. Most Cuban neighborhoods are replete with critical supportive institutions, along with a dense network of organizations and informal social groups. In the small Centro Habana neighborhood of Colon, for example, there were about six *mercados* (markets), a *policlinic,* and a nearby hospital, along with numerous shops and stores. This meant that residents could easily access the goods and services they regularly need.

These neighborhoods are held together by the Committee for the Defense of the Revolution (CDR), Juntos de Vicinos (neighbors group), and a core of mass organizations, including neighborhood chapters of the Federation of Women Organizations. The CDR is a formal organization that is similar to block clubs in the United States but much more powerful. It dominants every aspect of community life and is the tie that binds together the various institutions, primary schools, neighborhood health clinics, and informal organizations. Each block has a CDR, and every neighborhood resident is considered a member. The CDR leadership is democratically elected.

Some scholars view the CDR as a mechanism of social control and the extension of a totalitarian government (Colomer, 2000). This viewpoint does not reflect the reality of the Cuban CDR. This democratically based organization serves and protects the community. Its members monitor neighborhood activities and have a positive relationship with the police, but the intent is to bolster the quality of life by enhancing safety and security (Maxey, 1957). In my years of ethnographic research in low-income Cuban neighborhoods, most Cubanos I interacted with have a positive attitude toward the CDR.

The Juntos de Vicinos is a powerful informal organization in Havana's densely populated neighborhoods, where many Afro-Cubans live. Typically, the Juntos de Vicinos are found in multistory apartment buildings and bring together residents to solve mutual living problems, particularly those related to apartment building problems, resident behavior, and quality of life issues (Taylor, 2009). In some respects, there is overlap between the responsibilities of the CDR and the Juntos de Vicinos, and, in most neighborhoods, people are members of both organizations. The difference is that the Juntos de Vicinos are informal organizations that focus on living conditions in apartment buildings, while the CDR deals with broader neighborhood issues.

In 2010, the CDR was still a vibrant organization that anchored neighborhood life and culture, but the winds of change were blowing. The weight of socioeconomic change and the struggle to survive were weakening the CDR. By 2015, informants reported that the CDR had lost much of its strength. The organization still existed and almost everyone belonged to it, but participation was low and finding leadership was harder than ever. The informants said the government slashed funding for the CDR, which suggested to them that it was no longer a government priority. According to the informants, their neighbors said, "if it is not a priority for the government, it is not a priority for me."

Most important, the informants said that economic hardships caused people to become preoccupied with making money, paying bills, and trying to improve their lives. The hard reality is that Cubanos are more concerned about individual goals than community-building goals (Taylor, 2015/2016). As a self-employed informant, whom I quoted earlier, said, "In Cuba, you must think about making money. . . . You must always think about how to make money. This is now the Cuban way." This endless quest to make money and to make ends meet is eroding associational life and breaking down the bonds of reciprocity in Cuban neighborhoods. For example, a 2015 informant summed it up in this way: "In the past, if a neighbor asked for a pound of sugar, you simply gave it to them. Today, because of the high cost of food, you would have to think about it" (Taylor, 2015/2016).

These issues notwithstanding, the new housing policies represent the greatest danger to *el barrio*. Neighborhood stability and cohesiveness are the backbone of Cuban society, and, without it, the island society as we know it will not exist. The emergence of a profit-making housing market threatens that stability and cohesiveness. If higher income groups move to "better" neighborhoods, and outside investors buy up housing units in the most desirable sections, neighborhood stability, solidarity, and cohesiveness will disappear. This is a grave danger that now faces Cuba. In *Inside El Barrio*, I wrote "The development of hyper-stable and highly organized neighborhoods that are rich in social capital was the secret to the staying power of Fidel Castro. . . . The continued improvement and strengthening of the social function of neighborhoods will be critical to the survival of the revolutionary government" (Taylor, 2009).

WHAT IMPACT IS THE *2011 LINEAMIENTOS* HAVING ON AFRO-CUBANS?

The *2011 Lineamientos* represented a policy shift that the Cuban government hoped would bolster the economy, enhance social and human development, and provide the island with the financial resources needed to sustain the socialist project. The policy shift made life more difficult for Afro-Cubans, but the informants in this study accepted the new reality and found ways to adjust. Under the changed situation, they were still able to make ends meet, live a healthy life, watch their children receive a solid education, and live in stable neighborhoods. The chant, "*La vida no es facil*" did grow louder after the passage of the *2011 Lineamientos*, but that credo had been a refrain in Cuban society since the downfall of the Soviet Union. The *Lineamientos* did not create the "La vida no es facil" principle, but the government hoped that, over time, it would eliminate or mitigate the socioeconomic conditions that produced it. Life has changed for the Afro-Cubans, but the island is still the best place in the Americas for them to live.

The *2011 Lineamientos* were Cuba's response to the internal challenges produced by the socialist construction project and by the external impacts of the economic tsunami spawned by global neoliberal capitalism. The socioeconomic hardships faced by Cuba represent the challenge of building socialism in a world dominated by neoliberal capitalism. To meet this challenge, Cuban is not just infusing market elements into the economy, but, wittingly or unwittingly, the government is framing these market forces within a social enterprise context, in which the goal is to harness the market dynamics and use them in socially beneficial ways. One way to determine if this is happening is to examine Cuba's positionality in various international human development indices.

The UN 2019 Human Development Index is one such instrument. The UN Human Development Index uses a range of variables, including life expectancy, to place nations into one of four categories based on the level of human development found in their society: very high human development, high human development, medium human development, and low human development. In 2019, 8 years after passage of the *2011 Lineamientos*, Cuban ranked in the high human development category, ahead of Mexico, Brazil, China, India, and South Africa, all countries with larger and more robust economies (United Nations Development Programme, 2019).

Another important human development index is the 2016 World Economic Forum Report on Human Capital. The Human Capital Index is used to capture the complexity of education, employment, and workforce development. The index takes a life-course approach to human capital, evaluating the levels of education, skills, and employment available to people in five distinct age groups, starting from under 15 years to over 65 years. The aim is to assess a nation's investment in human capital. In this index, Cuba was the only Latin America country ranked in the top 50 countries with the highest human capital development. Cuba was ranked 36, while the United States was ranked 24 (World Economic Forum, 2016). Cuba still has the best education and healthcare system in Latin America, and it is the only country in the hemisphere without any private schools or colleges. These measures suggest that implementation of the *2011 Lineamientos* has not diminished the Cuban standard of living, nor has it lessened the nation's focus on equity and human development, all of which bodes well for the Afro-Cuban.

RESEARCH, POLICY, AND PRACTICE IMPLICATIONS

The core questions driving current debates on socialist construction, transitional economies, market socialism, and capitalist restoration centers on defining a socialist society and asks if there are any socialist countries in the world today. For example, the Cuban American writer Samuel Farber (2011) posits that Cuba is not a socialist or social-democratic society; instead, it is a modern nation. Understanding these questions is central to explaining the current status of socialist countries, projecting the future of socialist societies, and grappling with the current worldwide struggles for equity, social inclusion, and justice. I argue that an interpretative framework based on the theories of incomplete socialism and social enterprise can provide insight into these complicated questions.

This chapter, using an incomplete socialism and social enterprise framework, examined the complexities of building socialism in a multiracial society during the age of neoliberal global capitalism. In such an epoch, I argue that understanding socialist construction requires interpreting the impact of market reforms on a socialist society. The incomplete socialism lens indicates that market elements will exist in a socialist country throughout the epoch of world capitalist domination, while the social enterprise lens suggests that these market forces can be harnessed and used to achieve socially beneficial ends. There is thus a need to study socialist societies with a specific focus on their capacities to harness these market forces and use them to achieve socially beneficial ends. This method requires a translational framework in which the intent is to understand how policies and institutions impact social inclusion and social and human development down on the ground, in the neighborhoods where people live. In other words, what types of policies and socioeconomic institutions are required to harness and use market forces to achieve socially beneficial ends?

The social enterprise concept is a useful framework for understanding how market and non-market forces can complement each other and explains how capitalism can be used to save socialism. At the onset of the Special Period, an economist at the Center for the Study of the Cuban Economy reflected on the plight of his country. He said that the market alone could not provide for education, worker security, and a 100% vaccination rate for Cuban children while, at the same time, the island needed to jump-start the economy. The reason is that such a social transformation will happen only if egalitarianism, along with the goals of human and social development, are interwoven with economic development. The economist said that socialism with a market was his solution, but he ended with a vital question: How much market could Cuban socialism tolerate before it was no longer socialism at all (Gordy, 2015, p. 7)?

One way to answer the economist's question is to use a social enterprise lens to analyze the nature and character of market-based business enterprises in socialist countries. Do these businesses mirror the characteristics of social enterprises or the shared value framework outlined by Porter? Do they contribute to socialist construction, or do these business enterprises thwart the equity, social inclusion, and social and human development goals of socialism? The larger point is that scholars should move beyond the premise that market reforms equate with the decline of socialism or the restoration of capitalism to explore how the market can complement socialist development. For example, in what situations are countries able to harness market forces and use them for socially beneficial goals, and in what situations do market reforms turn ugly, spawning inequality, hardships, and capitalist restoration? Undergirding these questions is the viewpoint that the mere introduction of market reforms in a socialist society raises the threat level for capitalist restoration, but does not make it inevitable.

This premise poses an interesting sidebar: Is incomplete capitalism the flip side of incomplete socialism? If non-market reforms in a capitalist society move beyond an indeterminate threshold, will they trigger the movement of that society down the road to social democracy and socialism? To paraphrase the Cuban economist, how much non-market reforms can a capitalist state tolerate before it is no longer capitalist? Last, collectively, the theories of incomplete socialism and social enterprise create a framework for acquiring a deeper and richer understanding of the ideal of socialism, the process of socialist construction, and the future of socialism as a political economy that offers an alternative to the dehumanizing and exploitive reality of capitalism.

NOTES

1. In Cuba, the mulattos emerged as a group unto themselves. Although proud of their African decent, many still considered themselves a separate ethnic group.
2. The Moncada Barracks are military barracks in Santiago de Cuba, named after General Gullermon Moncada, a hero of the War of Independence on July 26, 1953. There is consensus that the attack on the barracks represented the start of the Cuban Revolution.
3. There exists a debate on the relevancy of civil society in Cuba. The Revolution sought to build a new type of society based on a set of assumptions about the relationship between the people and the state. Thus, the use of mass organizations associated with the state, as well as informal organizations and groups that are independent of it, are considered part of socialist civil society.
4. The Council of Mutual Economic Assistance (CMEA or Comecon) was an economic organization from 1949 to 1991 that functioned as a common market among socialist nations. The intent was to facilitate the building of socialism in a world dominated by global capitalism.
5. As expected with any country building a socialist state in the Age of Global Capitalism, Cuba encountered numerous problems developing its economic model, particularly in trying to adapt the Soviet model to the conditions in Cuban society. Yet, concurrently, it was nevertheless able to generate the revenues necessary for a robust investment in social development. The inroads made in this area won the Revolution legitimacy among the masses and made it a darling among Global South revolutionaries during the 1960s, as well as among radicals in the Global North.
6. Raúl Castro's decision has to be understood with the context of the structural crisis faced by Cuba. The issues of productivity and hardships down on the ground were causing the people to push for change. In discussing the new *gente Cubano*, Che Guevara used the term *communism*, implying complete socialism, as the place where the new *gente Cubano* would be realized. He also said of the process of creating *gente Cubano* that "the process goes forward hand in hand with the development of new economic forces" (Guevara & Castro, 1989, p. 15). Perhaps Raúl saw his retreat through this lens.
7. On the outside, an apartment building may appear rundown. On the inside, a white family might have a plasma television, expensive furniture, and other luxury items, while their next door neighbor might live a Spartans existence.
8. This comment was made by an official who works in the Office of the Historian of the City who took me on a personal tour of Plaza Vieja in Habana Vieja in June 1999. I was there teaching a summer study-abroad class on Cuban neighborhoods.
9. It should be remembered that residents spend very little on housing, and transportation costs vary depending on where in the city one lives.
10. Cuba has a dual currency, and the CUC is Cuba's international currency.

REFERENCES

Ahmed, A. (2016). Cuba's Surge in Tourism Keeps Food Off Residents' Plates. *The New York Times*. December 8. https://www.nytimes.com/2016/12/08/world/americas/cuba-fidel-castro-food-tourism.html

Aitchison, C., Macleod, N., & Shaw, S. J. (2000). *Leisure and tourism landscapes. Social and cultural geographies.* London: Routledge.

Anderson. C. (2003). *Eyes off the prize: The United Nations and the African American struggle for human rights, 1944–1955.* New York: Cambridge University Press.

Annan, K. (2005). *In larger freedom: Toward development, security and human rights for all.* United Nations. https://undocs.org/A/59/2005

Alberto, G. (2011). 'Cuba: From State Socialism to a New Form of Market Socialism?', *Comparative Economic Studies, 53*, 647–685.

Archibald, R. C. (2015, February 24). Inequality becomes more visible in Cuba as the economy shifts. *New York Times.* Online. https://www.nytimes.com/2015/02/25/world/americas/as-cuba-shifts-toward-capitalism-inequality-grows-more-visible.html

Assuncao, M. R., & Zeuske, M. (1998). Race, ethnicity and social structure in 19th century Brazil and Cuba. *Iberio-amerikanischers Archive, 24*(3/4), 375–443.

Azar, E. E., Jureidini, P. L., & McLaurin, R. (1978). Protracted social conflict: Theory and practice in the Middle East. *Journal of Palestine Studies, 8*(1), 41–60.

BBC. (2010, October 28). Cuba sets out rules and taxes for self-employed workers. https://www.bbc.com/news/world-latin-america-11625472

Baden, D., & Wilkinson, S. (2014). Socially Responsible Enterprise in Cuba: A Positive Role Model for Corporate Social Responsibility. *International Journal of Cuban Studies, 6/1*(Spring), 55–86.

Barber, S. (2011). *Cuba since the revolution of 1959: A critical assessment* (chapter 5). Chicago: Haymarket Books.

Benitez, C. (2013, July 9). Cuba's housing situation: The coming crisis. *Havana Times.Org.* https://havanatimes.org/features/cubas-housing-situation-the-coming-collapse/.

Benson, D. S. (2016). *Antiracism in Cuba: The unfinished revolution.* Chapel Hill: University of North Carolina.

Berger, D. (Ed.). (2010). *The hidden 1970s: Histories of radicalism.* New Brunswick, NJ: Rutgers University Press.

Blum, D. F. (2011). *Cuban youth and revolutionary values: Educating the new socialist citizen.* Austin, TX: University of Austin Press.

Bobes, V. C. (2013). Cuban civil society during and beyond the special period. *International Journal of Cuban Studies, 5* (2), 168–183.

Brock, D., & Fuertes, C. (1998). *Between race and empire: African-Americans and Cubans before the Cuban Revolution.* Philadelphia: Temple University Press.

Bruns, B., & Luque, J. (2015). *Great teachers: How to raise student learning in Latin America and the Caribbean.* Washington, D.C.: World Bank Group.

Burgess, M., Ferguson, N., & Hollywood, I. (2007). Rebels' perspectives of the legacy of past violence and of the current peace in post-agreement Northern Ireland: An interpretative phenomenological analysis. *Political Psychology, 28*(1), 69–88.

Burrough, B. (2016). *Days of rage: America's radical underground, the FBI, and the forgotten age of revolutionary violence.* New York: Penguin.

Campbell, A. (2013). Finding a New Road (Again) to a Socialist Economy and Socialist Well-Being in Cuba. In A. Campbell (Ed.), *Cuban Economists on the Cuban Economy* (pp. 1–22). Gainesville, FL: University Press of Florida.

Castro, F. (1953/2016). *History will absolve me: Castro's court argument.* New York: RosettaBooks (Original work published in 1953).

Castro, F. (1959, March 23). No hope for the counterrevolution. Speech at Havana Labor Rally, Havana. *Castro Speech Data Base.* Retrieved from http://lanic.utexas.edu/project/castro/db/1959/19590323.html

Castro, F. (1990, September 28). Speech given at 30th CDR Anniversary. *Castro Speech Database*. Retrieved from http://lanic.utexas.edu/project/castro/db/1990/19900929.html

Castro, R. (2007, July 26th). Speech at the celebration of the 54th anniversary of the attack on Moncado. *Rock Around the Blockage*. https://www.ratb.org.uk/raul-castro/147-speech-by-raul-castro-ruz-at-the-main-celebration-of-the-54th-anniversary-of-the-attack-on-moncada-and-carlos-manuel-de-cespedes-garrisons-at-the-major-general-ignacio-agramonte-loynaz-revolution-square-in-the-city-of-camagueey-july-26th-2007.

Castro, R. (2011, April 16). Central report to the 6th Congress of the Communist Party of Cuba. *Cuba Debate*. Retrieved from http://en.cubadebate.cu/opinions/2011/04/16/central-report-6th-congress-communist-party-cuba/

Christensen, W. D., & Bickhard, M. H. (2002). The process dynamics of normative function. *The Philosophy of Biology, 85*(1), January, 3–28.

Claudio, L. (1999). The challenge for Cuba. *Environmental and Health Perspective, 107* (5), A246–A251.

Cole, J. B. (1980). Race toward equality: The impact of the Cuban revolution on racism. *The Black Scholar, 11* (8), 2–24.

Colomer, J. M. (2000). Watching neighbors: The Cuban model of social control. *Cuban Studies, 31*, 118–138.

Corrales, J. (2012). Cuba's "Equity Without Growth" dilemma and the 2011 Lineamientos. *Latin American Politics and Society, 54*(4), 157–184.

D'Amato, P. (2007). Race and sex in Cuba. *International Socialist Review, 51*. https://isreview.org/issues/51/cuba_race-sex.shtml

Darlington, S. (2010, September 14). Cuba to lay off 500,000 in 6 months, allow private jobs. CNN. http://edition.cnn.com/2010/WORLD/americas/09/13/cuba.economy/

Davidson, M. J., & Krull, C. (2011). Adapting to Cuba's shifting food landscape: Women's strategies of resistance. *Cuban Studies, 42*, 59–77.

de la Fuente, A. (2001). *A nation for all: Race, inequality, and politics in twentieth-century Cuba*. Chapel Hill: The University of North Carolina Press.

Diaz-Briquets, S. (2009). The enduring Cuban housing crisis: The impact of hurricanes. *Cuba in Transition, 19*, 429–441.

Dolan, B.C. (2007). *Cubaonomics: Mixed economy in Cuba during the special period*. Department of History, Emory University. http://history.emory.edu/home/documents/endeavors/volume1/Brendans.pdf

Draper, T. (1969). *Castroism: Theory and practice*. New York: Frederick A. Praeger.

Dumont, R. (1970). *Cuba: Socialism and development*. New York: Grove.

Erisman, H. M. (2012). Brain drain politics: The Cuban medical professional parole programme. *International Journal of Cuban Studies, 4*(3/4), 269–290.

Fanon, F. (1963). *The wretched of the Earth*. New York: Grove.

Farber, S. (2011). *Cuba since the revolution of 1959: A critical reassessment*. Chicago: Haymarket Books.

Farr, J. (1985). Situational analysis: Explanation in political science. *The Journal of Politics, 47*(4), 1085–1107.

Faugier J., & Sargeant, M. (1997). Sampling hard to reach populations. *Journal of Advanced Nursing, 26*, 790–797.

Feinsilver, J. M. (1993). *Healing the masses: Cuban health politics at home and abroad*. Berkeley: University of California Press. 1–7.

Feinsilver, J. M. (2010). Fifty years of Cuba's medical diplomacy. *Cuba Studies, 41*, 96–98.

Frank, A. G. (1986). Kampuchea, Vietnam, China: Observations and reflections. *Contemporary Marxism, 12*(13), 107–119.

Fukuyama, F. (1989). The end of history? *The National Interest, 16*(Summer), 3–18.

Fusion. (2015, April 15). Historic poll: 94% of Cubans who receive money from friends and family abroad use it to cover everyday expenses. *Splinter*. https://splinternews. com/historic-poll-94-of-cubans-who-receive-money-from-fri-1793846952

Gaitonde, V. A. (1974). An answer to the theory of convergence. *Social Scientist, 3*(5), 38–51.

Glassman, N. (2011, June 22). Revolutionary racism: Afro-Cubans in an era of economic change. *Southern Social Movement Newswire*. CETRI. https://www.cetri. be/Revolutionary-Racism-Afro%E2%80%91Cubans?lang=fr

Gordy, K. (2015). *Living ideology in Cuba: Socialism in principle and practice*. Ann Arbor: University of Michigan Press.

Grein, J. (2015). *Recent reforms in Cuban housing policy*. Law School International Immersion Program Papers, No. 7. Chicago: University of Chicago.

Guevara, C., & Castro, F. (1989). *Socialism and man in Cuba*. New York: Pathfinder Press.

Harvey, D. (2005). *A brief history of neoliberalism*. Oxford: Oxford University Press.

Hayden, T. (2009). *Long sixties: From 1960 to Barack Obama*. New York: Routledge.

Helg, A. (1995). *Our rightful share: The Afro-Cuban struggle for equality 1886–1912*. Chapel Hill: University of North Carolina Press.

Henken, T. (2002). Condemned to informality: Cuba's experiments with self-employment during the special period: The case of bed and breakfast. *Cuban Studies, 33*, 1–29.

Hernandez-Reguant A. (2009). *Cuba in the special period: Culture and ideology in the 1990s*. New York: Palgrave.

Hua, S. (1995). *Scientism and humanism: (1979–1989)*. Albany, NY: SUNY Press.

Jatar-Hausmann, A. J. (1999). *The Cuban way: Capitalism, communism, and confrontation*. Sterling, VA: Kumarian Press.

Kahn, C. (2016, October 19). Amid a struggling, economy, Cuban real estate is booming. *NPR*. https://www.npr.org/sections/parallels/2016/10/19/498399652/amid-a-struggling-economy-cuban-real-estate-is-booming

Kannan, K. P., Drev, S. M., & Sharma, A. N. Concerns on Food Security (2000). *Economic and Political Weekly, 35* (45), 3929.

Hamburg, J., (1994). *The Dynamics of Cuban Housing policy*. Dissertation. Columbia University.

Krikorian, M. (2016, January 18). The Cubans are coming! *National Review*. https://cis. org/Cubans-Are-Coming

Krogstad, J. M. (2017). Surge in Cuban immigration to US continued through 2016. Pew Research Center. https://www.pewresearch.org/fact-tank/2017/01/13/cuban-immigration-to-u-s-surges-as-relations-warm/

Lamrani, S. (2012). Reforming the Cuban economic model: Causes and prospects. *International Journal of Cuban Studies, 4*(1), 1717–1735.

Lamrani, S. (2013). *Cuba: Les médias face au défi de l'impartialité. Paris Star*, p. 38.

Latner, T. (2017). *Irresistible revolution: Cuba and American radicalism, 1968–1992*. Durham: University of North Carolina Press.

Leonard, A. (2011, September 29). Inside the shadow economy: A growing bazaar. *The Louisiana Weekly*. http://www.louisianaweekly.com/inside-the-shadow-economy%E2%80%94a-growing-underworld-bazaar/

Liberator's triumphal march through an ecstatic island. (1959, January 19). *Life Magazine*, 28–32.

Lobosco, K. (2014, December 17). Americans send $3 billion a year to Cuba. *CNN*. https://money.cnn.com/2014/12/17/news/economy/cuba-remittances/index.html

Logan, J. R., & Molotch, H. L. (1987). *Urban fortune: The political economy of place* (pp. 99–146). Berkeley: University of California Press.

Mason, S. E., Strug, D. L., &, Beder, J. (2010). *Community health care in Cuba*. Chicago: Lyceum Books.

Marable, M. (1984). Race and democracy in Cuba. *The Black Scholar, 15* (3), 22–37.

Maxey, A. B. (1957). The block club movement in Chicago. *The Phylon Quarterly, 18* (2), 124–131.

Mesa-Lago. (2000). *Market, Socialist, and Mixed Economies: Comparative Policy and Performance: Chile, Cuba, and Costa Rica*. Baltimore: John Hopkins University Press.

Mesa-Lago, C., & Perez-Lopez, J. (2013). *Cuba under Raul Castro: Assessing the reforms*. Boulder: Lynne-Rienner.

Mishra, R. (1976). Convergence theory and social change: The development of welfare in Britain and the Soviet Union. *Comparative Studies in Society and History, 18*(1), 26–56.

Montgomery, D. (2012, May 20). Eusebio Leal: The man who would save Old Havana. *The Washington Post*. https://www.washingtonpost.com/lifestyle/style/eusebio-leal-the-man-who-would-save-old-havana/2012/05/20/gIQAAW31dU_story.html

Mujal-Leon, E. (2011). Survival, adaptation and uncertainty: The case of Cuba. *Journal of International Affairs, 65*(1), 149–168.

NPR. (2011, January 11). Cuba issues thousands of self-employment licenses. https://www.npr.org/2011/01/18/133020988/cuba-issues-thousands-of-self-employment-licenses

Oppenheimer, A. (1992). *Castro's Final Hour: The Secret Story Behind the Coming Downfall of Communist Cuba*. New York: Simon & Shuster.

Orozco, M., Porras, L., & Yansura, J. (2016). *The continued growth of family remittances to Latin America and the Caribbean in 2015*. Inter-American Dialogue. http://www.thedialogue.org/wp-content/uploads/2016/02/2015-Remittances-to-LAC-2122016.pdf

O'Sullivan, M. (2012). The economic reforms in Cuba: Strengthening the country's essential socialist character or a transition to capitalism? The impact on educated youth. *International Journal of Cuban Studies, 4*(3/4), 321–346.

Perez, L. A., Jr. (1999). *On becoming Cuban: Identity, nationality, and culture*. Chapel Hill: The University of North Carolina Press.

Perez-Stable, M. (1993). *The Cuban revolution*. Oxford: Oxford University Press.

Perry, M. D. (2016). *Negro Soy Yo: Hip and citizenship in neoliberal Cuba*. Durham: Duke University Press.

Peters, P. (2014, February). *Cuba's new real estate market: Latin America initiative working paper*. Washington, D.C.: Brookings Institution.

Peters, P. (2012). A chronology of Cuba's updating of the socialist model. *International Journal of Cuban Studies, 4* (3/4), 385–390.

Phelps, C. (2006). C.L.R. James and the Theory of State Capitalism, in American Capitalism: Social Thought and Political Economy in the Twentieth Century. University of Pennsylvania Press, 157–174.

Porter, G. (1990). The Transformation of Vietnam's world-view: From two camps to Interdependence. *Contemporary Southeast Asia, 12* (1), June, 1–19.

Porter, M. E., & Kramer, M. R. (2011). Creating shared value: How to reinvent capitalism and unleash a wave of innovation and growth. *Harvard Business Review,* 89/1-2 (January/February), 62–77.

Ravsberg, F. (2012, October 25). In Cuba, the teachers are leaving. *Havana Times.* https://havanatimes.org/opinion/in-cuba-the-teachers-are-leaving/

Reitan, R. (1999). *The rise and decline of an alliance: Cuba and African American leaders in the 1960s.* East Lansing: Michigan State University Press.

Reuters. (2010, April 12). Cuba: Employees take ownership of hair salons. *New York Times.* https://www.nytimes.com/2010/04/13/world/americas/13briefs-Cuba.html

Ritter, A. R. M. (2005a). *Cuba's underground economy* (unpublished manuscript). Carlton University, Canada. https://carleton.ca/economics/wp-content/uploads/cep04-12.pdf

Ritter, A. R. M. (2005b). Survival strategies and economic illegalities in Cuba. *Cuba in Transition.* https://www.ascecuba.org/c/wp-content/uploads/2014/09/v15-ritter.pdf

Ritter, A. R. M., & Henken, T. A. (2015). *Entrepreneurial Cuba: The changing policy landscape.* Boulder: First Forum Press.

Rosendahl, M. (1997). *Inside the revolution: Everyday life in socialist Cuba.* Ithaca, NY: Cornell University Press.

Sayres, S., Stephanson, A., Aronowitz, S., & Jameson, F. (1984). *The sixties without apology.* Minneapolis: University of Minnesota Press.

Scott, J. C. (1976). *The moral economy of the peasant: Rebellion and subsistence in Southeast Asia.* New Haven, CT: Yale University Press.

Sixth Congress of the Communist Party of Cuba. (2011, April 18). *Resolution on the guidelines of the economic and social policy of the party and the revolution.* http://www.cuba.cu/gobierno/documentos/2011/ing/l160711i.html

Smith, B. (1999). The self-employed in Cuba: A street level view. *Cuba in Transition, 9,* 49–59.

Snipp, M. (2003). Racial measurement in the American census: Past practices and implications for the future. *Annual Review of Sociology, 29,* 563–588.

Sullivan, M. P. (2015). Cuba: US restrictions on travel and remittances. *Congressional Research Service,* 7-5700, 10 April 2015. https://www.google.com/search?q=sullivan+Cuba+www.crs.gov&rlz=1C1GCEU_enUS894US894&oq=sullivan+Cuba+www.crs.gov&aqs=chrome..69i57.39134j0j9&sourceid=chrome&ie=UTF-8

Taylor, H. L., Jr. (2009). *Inside El Barrio: A bottom-up view of Castro's Cuba.* Sterling, VA: Kumarian Press.

Taylor, H. L., Jr. (2010). *Fieldwork in Havana, Phase one studies.* U.B. Center for Urban Studies, University at Buffalo.

Taylor, H. L., Jr. (2015/2016). *Fieldwork in Cuba, Phase two studies.* Buffalo, NY: University at Buffalo, Center for Urban Studies.

Taylor, H. L., Jr., & McGlynn, L. (2009). International tourism in Cuba: Can capitalism be used to save socialism? *Futures, 41*(6), 405–413.

Trotta, D. (2015, December 1). Cuba reinstates limits on doctors leaving the country. *Reuters.* https://www.reuters.com/article/us-cuba-usa-migrants-healthcare/cuba-reinstates-limits-on-doctors-leaving-the-country-idUSKBN0TK58B20151201

United Nations Development Programme. (2019). *Human Development Report: Beyond Income, beyond averages, beyond today: Inequities in human development in the 21st century.* New York: United Nations.

Van Ree, E. (1998). Socialism in one country: A reassessment. *Studies in East European Thought, 50*(2), June, 77–117.

Walder, A. G. (1996). Markets and Inequality in Transitional Economies: Toward Testable Theories. *American Journal of Sociology, 101*(4), 1060–1073.

Whitney, Jr., W. T. (2019, May 19). Brain drain. Senators urge revival of U.S. program to entice Cuban doctor defectors. *People's World.* https://www.peoplesworld. org/article/brain-drain-senators-urge-revival-of-u-s-program-to-entice-cuban-doctor-defections/

Waters, R. (2017, February 8). The Cuban hustle: Doctors drive cabs and work abroad to make up for meager pay. *STAT.* https://www.statnews.com/2017/02/08/ cuba-doctors-meager-pay/

Werlau, M. C. (2013). Cuba's health-care diplomacy: The business of humanitarianism. *World Affairs, 175*(6), 57–67.

Wilkinson, S. (2010). Cuba's exceptional road to reform. *International Journal of Cuban Studies, 2*(3/4), 197–2000.

Williams, R. F. (1962). *Negroes with guns.* New York: Marzani & Munsell.

World Economic Forum. (2016). *The human capital report.* New York: World Economic Forum.

Wright, J. (2012). The little-studied success story of post-crisis food security in Cuba: Does lack of international interest signify lack of political will? *International Journal of Cuban Studies, 4*(2), 130–153.

Yang, M. M. (2000). Putting global capitalism in its place: Economic hybridity, Bataille, and ritual expenditure. *Current Anthropology, 41*(4), 477–509.

Zamora, A. R. (2009). Real estate development in Cuba: Present and future. *ISLA Journal of International and Comparative Law, 15*(3), 605–627.

Toward More Integrative Economic and Social Development

Selective Barriers and Facilitators

CHAPTER 16

༄

Integrating Economic and Social Development

Rationale, Models, and Limitations

KATHARINE BRIAR-LAWSON AND MIZANUR R. MIAH

This chapter addresses the need for more comprehensive approaches to development, a process by which nations and communities evolve and build both human and economic capacities in support of their citizens. The array of nations facing transitions in both their social and economic structures warrants an examination of new mechanisms for 21st-century economic and social development supports. We feature the interconnections between economic and social development with concerns about the need for integration and sustainability. Offering overviews on the integration problem, we make recommendations for more intentional approaches that foster both economic and social improvements. We argue for progressive development to offset the harms of distorted development and to promote human and community well-being (Midgley, 1995, 2014). We believe that integrative approaches will advance more tailored attention to the human side of development and to the social protections needed as nations and communities undergo economic transitions.

Too often the burden of survival and livelihood development falls on workers and their families. Market economies are driven by competition,

Katharine Briar-Lawson and Mizanur R. Miah, *Integrating Economic and Social Development* In: *Social Entrepreneurship and Enterprises in Economic and Social Development*. Edited by: Katharine Briar-Lawson, Paul Miesing, and Blanca M. Ramos, Oxford University Press (2021). © Oxford University Press. DOI: 10.1093/oso/9780197518298.003.0017.

jobs, and capital. Jobs and capital can move with ease to other regions and nations, leaving in their stead wasted human talent, rising economic insecurity, human suffering, and decimated communities. These realities, along with the absence of inclusive norms regarding economic and social development, place workers and their families at risk. If one cannot get a job or develop a livelihood through one's own entrepreneurial means, they one may have to turn to the state for benefits for survival. If such social welfare benefits, in the form of social protections, are not available or are not in sync with changing economies, labor markets, and jobs, then increasing numbers of individuals, families, and communities may face irreparable harms or demise and, in some cases, may perish. Social protections comprise social welfare interventions to buffer the destabilizing effects of ineffective or changing labor markets involving limited entrepreneurial or related livelihood and job opportunities. They may derive from governmental entitlements and supports or from select employers in the form of occupational social welfare.

Segregated spheres of social and economic development may impede necessary tailored thinking as well as the policy and program development needed to reduce the hardships that fall on individuals, families, and communities victimized by unstable and transitioning economies. In the face of such realities, the International Labour Organization (ILO, 2018) predicts that, globally, unemployment will remain high and that jobs continue to be low-paying. Thus, efforts to advance social entrepreneurship and related enterprise supports through combined economic and social development may help create jobs and work opportunities while cushioning the hardships of poverty, failed enterprises, and debilitating consequences.

We begin our look at integrative approaches by examining the authors who have historically been at the forefront of such arguments. Authors such as Midgley (1995, 2014), Sen (1999), Stiglitz (2016), Miah (2003), Pawar and Cox (2010), and others have been writing about various aspects of more integrated thinking and practices for several decades. Even so, the challenge of balancing, coordinating, and harmonizing these domains of development creates unusual hurdles for policy leaders and practitioners. Moreover, such integrative practices may not even be recognized as necessary by some leaders. In fact, some of the institutional and political structures that might foster such interconnected planning, investments, and progress charting are divided as well by separate practices and spheres of economic versus social development. Augmenting this is the fact that the academic disciplines that might inform such integrative thinking are impeded by their circumscribed and separate knowledge bases. These may seem not only disparate but even antithetical—such as a focus on profits and profit maximization versus a focus on meeting basic needs through social protections.

We argue that the tensions between the two strategies of social versus economic development, when addressed with more comprehensive thinking and practices, may yield improved results with fewer human and community disparities and preventable human costs if not causalities. In more inclusive practices, some of the consequences of distorted development, such as income inequality, joblessness, poverty, dislocation, and related disparities in underutilized human capacity, along with sustainability shortfalls, may be reduced as human and community well-being becomes a more focused agenda for action and progress charting (Stiglitz, 2016).

DEFINITIONS: UNTANGLING APPROACHES

We begin with some definitional challenges. On the one hand, the two concepts of development—social versus economic—may span vastly different domains. On the other hand, writers and theorists may subsume one under the other, thus making the terms murky and unclear.

For our purposes, the definition of *economic development* comprises activities which spur incomes and jobs, including job retention, and lead to increases in some key indices of economic well-being such as an improved tax base, gross domestic product (GDP), and life quality. On the other hand, *social development* is defined as prioritizing human needs and capacities in societal growth. This includes social protections and social welfare benefits including health, education, income, and employment supports along with the promotion of norms that govern social interaction and the advancement of diverse institutions to create a civil society. While economic development is often about goods, services, and jobs, the social development side of the ledger focuses on human capacity; the individual, family, and community aspects of economic investments; and overall human and community well-being.

Even with some definitional clarity, there are ambiguities and overlap. For some theorists and policy analysts, social development subsumes and thus comprises economic development (Khinduka, 1987; Midgley, 1995, 2014). For others, economic development comprises and thus includes social development (Todaro & Smith, 2015). Despite such potential to subordinate one strategy under the other, both are explicitly needed. We contend that more intentionally integrative practices may foster the development of inclusive societies in which all are valued and supported through various income streams for the roles and the contributions they are able to make.

APPROACHES TO SOCIAL AND
ECONOMIC DEVELOPMENT

Social workers such as Khinduka (1987) and Midgley (1995) may see social development as the overriding and most comprehensive concept inclusive of jobs and social protections along with new institutional models to deliver key policies, programs, and services (Lowe, 1995). Midgley (1993, 1995, 1997) has conceptualized four types of social development strategies. These include enterprise, communitarian, statist, and institutional approaches (Lowe, 1995; Midgley 1993,1995, 1997). *Enterprise-based arrangements* foster individual entrepreneurship with minimal government involvement in development activities. The enterprise approach primarily depends on informal sectors including small business development to promote healthy income generation and rising standards of living. *Statist approaches* involve governmental control of social development activities comprising planning, financing, and implementation. Vast bureaucracies are needed to plan, deliver, and administer these programs. *Communitarian approaches* (Midgley, 1997) arose in response to statist regimes, with their corruption, resource waste, bureaucratic barriers, and a singular exclusion of people from local communities in planning, designing, and implementing social development programs. The *institutional approach* comprises a synthesis of all three, thus ensuring a more coherent and integrated whole. In what Midgley (1997) calls *managed pluralism*, this institutional approach maximizes participation of individuals, the community, and the market. Government roles include coordination and management.

Unlike Midgley, some others see economic development as the solution to social development. This includes authors such as Todaro and Smith (2015). For example, they believe that poverty eradication depends on progress in economic development, more businesses, more trade, and more private-sector investments.

Sen (1999), a development economist, has made the case that human "capability" should be the overriding concern in development and that jobs, economic supports, social welfare resources, and social protections are subsumed under this human capacity frame of reference. He, too, calls for more integrative thinking, norms, and practices. To address the fact that economic development may not be a panacea for human and community well-being, Sen argued for an integrated index to measure growth and development. In this tradition Nussbaum (2000) has argued from a feminist perspective that "capabilities" rather than a "capability" approach should govern thinking about human development. At the core is every individual's right to develop in people-centered development. Nussbaum

(2011) lists some of these capabilities; they include rights to life longevity, health, mobility, safety and freedom from abuse, education, material goods and property rights, and political participation. Hers is a focus on constitutional rights. Both have informed the Human Development Index (HDI) adopted by the United Nations to measure progress across the globe (Comim, 2016; Stanton, 2007).

Such an index was adopted by the UN in 1990 and has been used since then to capture the human aspects of a nation's functioning. As a result, the UN has played a key role in advancing more integrative thinking, as seen in their annual *Human Development Reports*.

Integrative Scholars: The Limits of Economic Development and Social Development

Integrative thinking is not limited to economics or social work. It can be found in other disciplines such as sociology, anthropology, political science, philosophy, and business.

Several specialties of economics also demonstrate some aspects of these more holistic conceptions. One is *social economics*. This addresses market-based decision-making and behavior within a social ecological frame, namely the social forces that impinge on individuals and families (Costa-Font & Macis, 2017).

Development economics is another branch of economics that also approximates some of this synthesis in thinking and research. Development economics has sought to aid primarily developing nations. In development economics, for example, some social welfare supports are seen as relevant to economic development, such as health, education, workers' rights, and safe working conditions (Kuznets,1980; Sachs, 2005; Sen, 1999; Stiglitz, 2016). In the same vein, we see in the social work community several key supports for economic and asset development proffered by scholars and leaders such as Midgley (2014), Sherraden (1991), and Soifer, McNeely, Costa, and Pickering-Bernheim (2014). Most recently, Nandan, Bent-Goodley and Mandayam (2019) have made a very strong case for social innovation and social entrepreneurship as key social justice resources and tools for social work.

UNITED NATIONS INTEGRATIVE INDICES

The HDI is used to gauge the condition of peoples and nations around the world. The HDI measures inequality, life expectancy, per capita incomes, education, human capacity including untapped human assets reflected in unemployment, and the level of inclusionary practices. Such an index allows for continued progress charting and quality monitoring of country, regional, and global progress on integrated outcomes. Moreover, the human development focus is one means used to synthesize economic and social development in favor of people-centered or human-centered development. In the Human Development Report for 2016 (United Nations Development Program [UNDP], 2016) the concept of *universalism*, fostering inclusion, is a core principle. In addition to the HDI, UN indices also include gender inequality and gender development measures. More recently these indices have undergone a review to determine how best to integrate the Sustainable Developmental Goals with them (United Nations [UN], 2018).

WHY CARE?

Why do we care about integrative approaches? To address the importance of integrative approaches we draw on economic development investments in the United States and elsewhere in which the federal and state governments provide, for example, tax credits; subsidies; financial "bail outs" to large, troubled companies and industries; workforce development for a skilled workforce; and aid with trade and related governmental supports. Such governmental investments may generate more goods, services, and profits. However, job creation and related benefits such as social welfare supports for local communities and cultures may be given short shrift given the beliefs, held by some (including many policy-makers) that once businesses are supported they will elevate and increase local tax bases, generate local jobs, and foster more community well-being and workforce improvement. Such assumptions may not be borne out, as argued by Reich (2007) and Stiglitz (2016). Investments and tax breaks for companies may prove to have an elusive effect on the local community and its labor force. Moreover, given capital flight to other regions or nations where labor is less costly amid fewer taxes and environmental controls, companies have demonstrated that they can pick up and move at will (Reich, 2007). In their wake may grow ghost towns comprised of dejected workers and their families, trapped by falling house prices, falling tax bases, fewer services, small business foreclosures, and growing poverty (Goldstein, 2017). Such workers have lost not just their jobs but their livelihoods, some of which may have been intergenerational. In fact, workers' offspring have often been raised to expect to work in the industry which dominated their town and their family livelihood. As noted earlier, these companies may have benefited earlier from tax credits and financial incentives to locate to a region, only to later move where profit maximization may be more lucrative, thus keeping stockholders sanguine and workers' lives decimated.

In the same vein, we see similar shortfalls with social development. For example, investing in the poor and the jobless through welfare, employability supports, and short-term training programs may not yield sufficiently prepared workers for the kind of jobs and labor markets in place in various parts of a nation or community. In some cases, such programs may protect labor market attachments through training and job search supports, but fall short of moving people into jobs (Ahn, 2017). In effect, workers may not drop out of the labor market as "discouraged workers" but keep working in a training program or at job seeking. In this capacity they are seen as marginally attached, often through no fault of their own.

Social development also includes education and health, as well as social protection or welfare programs. Since such benefits are often not entitlements and may be constrained by time limits on use, be means-tested for poverty level eligibility, or not be available to all, such programs may make little impact in high-need areas. For example, in the United States, labor market programs are designed to help low-income persons access jobs. Yet the training and human capacity building programs may have little discernible benefits and reach only a fraction of those in need (Ahn, 2017). While there may be cost-effective outcomes for some, at least in the United States, there may be insufficient programs to reach all those in need (Orr et al., 1996).

Public and nonprofit social service sectors often do not connect service users to jobs or see their social service roles as advancing employment or entrepreneurial activities. Few social service providers may help service users develop social enterprises or businesses that create jobs. Absent these focused and integrated investments in social supports, jobs, and benefits, the creation of a skilled, healthy workforce as well as strong families and communities may be further impeded.

To advance basic human rights, nations are under pressure to build if not guarantee supports so that their members have opportunities to build a livelihood for self- and family sustenance and sustainability. Few nations provide income guarantees for life. Thus, as trickle-down job creation is less likely to provide a job and thus income resource for most, the alternative is self-employment and entrepreneurship. Given the high rate of failure of many small businesses, with their attendant human costs such as divorce, bankruptcy, stigma, and sometimes prolonged joblessness, it is all the more imperative that supports that heighten entrepreneurial success be advanced in conjunction with social welfare or social protection benefits.

Over the years, some forms of development have come under heavy criticism. This includes government-controlled strategies that disproportionately have benefited the privileged class while increasing inequity and the expansion of poverty (Birdsall, 1993; Haque, 1999; UN, 2004). In fact, unbridled capitalism has often fostered wealth maximization and poverty aggravation (Adelman & Morris, 1973). This is especially the case in developing nations (Amin, 1990; Preston, 1985). However, inequality in nations like the United States is the greatest that the nation has seen since the 1920s, before the Great Depression. In fact, in the 1970s, the top 1% of the US population earned 10% of the income and now they earn 20%, whereas the bottom 50% earned 20% in the 1970s and now only 12% (Desilver, 2014; Saez, Piketty, & Zucman, n.d.; Stone, Trisi, Sherman, & Taylor, 2018). Children in the United States used to be able to exceed the earning power of their parents; that may no longer be possible.

Such gross distortions and disparities leading to income inequality are a direct byproduct of unbalanced social and economic development. Unfettered market forces, instead of reaching the many, have fostered labor market dropouts. Such disparities in access to employment warrant more attention to the distorted development problem. Moreover, in the United States in the mid-1990s, when the labor market was robust, welfare as an entitlement was ended and replaced by time-limited life benefits. Such benefits may be no more than for 2 years and a maximum of 5 years. This then has left the nation with no substantial safety net. This situation continues to this day, despite the Great Recession of 2008 and its aftermath. Thus, absent more attention to benefits that are integrated with and tailored to local labor conditions, many workers and their families are consigned to struggle to survive.

INTEGRATIVE UN WORLD AGENDAS

We see the beginnings of more integrated thinking about social and economic development in the Copenhagen Declaration of 1995, in which the UN called for more statist developments. This included expectations of poverty eradication; more inclusion and social integration in support of full employment; finding ways to protect human rights and foster gender equality and equity; addressing social development in structural adjustment programs; increasing political, cultural, economic, and legal environmental supports to foster social development; advancing universal and equitable access to primary healthcare and education; and strengthening cooperation for social development through the UN (1999).

A World Summit held in 2005 launched an even more comprehensive policy framework based on equity and equality (UN, 2005). Goals were adopted for poverty eradication, employment, and social integration as well as socially, culturally, and environmentally sustainable social development. Other goals included addressing hunger, infant and child mortality, health, and literacy. Known as the UN Millennium Declaration fostering Millennium Development Goals (MDGs), nations were expected to fulfill these by 2015. The UN called for "engaged governance," compelling non-governmental organizations (NGOs) and civil society to be part of the advancement of effective social development strategies (UN, 2004, p. 27).

As expected, tensions between states and individual, family, and community goals have been prevalent in the implementation of programs to advance such millennial goals. In fact, the MDG agenda was fraught with centralized bureaucratic problems, along with corruption and an irreconcilable gap between the rich and the poor. Given the prior criticisms of this statist approach, a preferred, emergent strategy promoted small-scale, autonomous free-market approaches to microfinance and microcredit initiatives.

The model promoted was that of the *Grameen Bank*. Designed and implemented by 2006 Nobel Peace Laureate, Professor Muhammad Yunus (1995, 2003), this model demonstrated that microfinance and microlending could extend to the poorest of the poor, including teams of poor women in Bangladesh. Serving as an integrative mechanism for both social and economic development, the Grameen Bank, through its microenterprise development among the poor, added new significance to microfinance activities as a social and economic enterprise model. In fact, the Grameen Bank microcredit/ microenterprise model inspired a global movement (Miah, 2003; Miah & Tracy, 2001; Mizan, 1994; Yunus, 1995, 2003). Such a model demonstrated that economic and social development could be fostered simultaneously from the ground up instead of from the "trickle down" approach of large corporate and governmental investments.

The Grameen Bank and its microfinance, microlending, and microenterprises exemplified Midgley's proposed institutional and integrative approach to social development (2014). It involves lifting people out of poverty, using the mechanisms of the market and government legal structures, and empowering collectives, namely women, who band together to acquire loans and supports for their social enterprises.

Not only did the millennial goals comprise both social and economic improvements, but they saw health, nutrition, and education problems as impediments to economic growth. As further evidence of the integrative thinking, the Department of Economic and Social Development (DESA) has operated within the UN since 1997. Within DESA the integrative council, the Commission on Social and Economic Development (ECOSOC), is charged with promoting a "balanced integration of the economic, social and environmental dimensions of sustainable development" (https://www.un.org/development/desa/en/about/desa-divisions/ecosoc-support.html).

Along with DESA, ECOSOC, and the Commission on Economic and Social Development, UN projects such as the Millennium Goals and their sequel, the Sustainable Development Goals (SDGs) (https://www.un.org/ecosoc/en/ecosoc-integration-segment), all seek to foster social, economic, and environmental improvements in member nations throughout the world.

The SDGs adopted by the UN in 2015 involve 17 initiatives that address ending poverty, protecting the environment, and ensuring prosperity. Some of these broad goals compel universal healthcare, quality education, and women's empowerment, along with work, water, climate, and related inclusionary initiatives (UN, 2015). These SDGs are far-reaching in the scope and outcomes sought. For example, they include no extreme poverty; zero hunger; the promotion of food security and sustainable agriculture; good health and well-being; gender equality, especially in wages and work, including women's unpaid labor in the family; reduced inequalities; decent work and economic growth, including inclusive and sustainable economic growth; full, productive employment; climate action; clean water and sanitation; and clean energy. Such inspiring and yet necessary goals are agenda setters for more equitable social and economic development. The focus on gender rights is especially pertinent since it has been argued that microenterprises are often the best if not only route for women in some nations to gain employment. This is due in part to the fact that traditional employment involving the private and public sectors may have privileged men (Issac, 2017; McCarter, 2006; Organisation for Economic Cooperation and Development [OECD], 2017).

WHO ARE THE "PLAYERS" IN ECONOMIC AND SOCIAL DEVELOPMENT?

Unlike the UN, which oversees global progress charting with its integrative council, at national and local levels, many of the leaders and practitioners who advance economic development are not the same as those who oversee social development. In many nations, accountability for social and economic outcomes may rest with a prime minister or a president, but the systems, agencies, and policies that address social development versus economic functioning are seen as very different and even antithetical. In economic development, the policy analysts and implementers are often economists, business leaders, and entrepreneurs along with regional or state economic development councils and policy leaders. In social development, players may be educators, social workers and related human services practitioners, health providers, and pension and related benefit staff.

Integrative Structures

Unlike the integrative structure and thinking at the UN, as reflected in their Commission on Social and Economic Development, some nations segregate these two domains of economic and social supports, often seeing them as antithetical. For example, in industrialized nations, there may be in the executive branch a Council of Economic Advisors but not a Council of Social Advisors. There may be a Department of Health and Human Services disconnected from Departments of Labor or Commerce. In the legislative branch, there may be legislative committees on social concerns such as family needs, poverty, education, and healthcare and a separate committee on economic development focusing on incentives and supports for private-sector developments. There is no model that approximates an ideal integrative set of structures. One can envision an ideal-typical type, however. This would include a vertical integration of policy and programs that support the social as well as economic needs of individuals, families, communities, regions, and nations. In the future, such integrative structures might help to harmonize social and economic development with more well-articulated social and economic supports at the worker and community levels.

Building from the model developed at the UN through DESA, there would be councils of economic and social advisors to national leaders, and the executive and legislative branches all might have departments and committees, respectively, with dual-purpose orientations to foster social welfare and economic development. At the state or regional level and in local jurisdictions, similar coordination if not syntheses of social and economic development initiatives would be in place. And to aid the entrepreneur, the supports would be financial, relevant to economic success, as well as social, including assistance with an array of personal efficacy and family and social support strategies.

OTHER INTEGRATION MECHANISMS

In more recent years, Mohammed Yunus (2016) has developed the concept of social businesses as an extension of his Grameen Bank innovations. He claims that social businesses have triple aims: financial, social, and environmental. Building stakeholders instead of shareholders, social businesses are concerned with ending poverty. They harness the same innovations as traditional business ventures but have the goal of meeting human needs, with their profits enabling the expansion of the social business, thus furthering the triple aims. According to Yunus, social businesses are a missing link between nonprofit organizations and businesses. Nonprofits and NGOs seek foundation and public funds to operate. Social businesses operate as social enterprises but with business-based revenue-generating goals. According to Yunus, partners become essential in the social business model as companies may seek to divest some of their stockholder franchises in favor of a stakeholder, which involves social (anti-poverty) rather than financial returns. *The Social Business Journal* from Australia depicts models from around the world and delineates how the hybrid of social and business values are realized. Some models of social businesses are government-funded while others have funding from the private or philanthropic sector.

The *Ericsson Social Business Report* offers an array of businesses that have intentionally been designed as social businesses. Such social enterprises harness business tactics to advance both a social good and a business or commercial good. In some cases, these can be solely for social good and not seek a profit-making goal. They can be undertaken through for-profit or nonprofit organizations.

While many corporations have corporate responsibility goals, and some even start a charitable foundation, these are different from the end goals being advanced by social enterprises. This is because in social enterprises, or what Yunus calls "social businesses," the social good and impact is the overriding concern rather than profits. In the United States, examples are Toms Shoes, Start Something That Matters, Patagonia, and the Body Shop. Their profits are invested in social welfare or environmental protection ventures. Venture funds, such as Legacy Venture, require that all their investments go to entities with philanthropic goals. Multiple US states have passed legislation to allow corporations to register as benefit companies (B-corps), which puts the interest of the community, workers, and environment ahead of financial profits.

Integrative and Inclusive Missions

In the past decade, the World Health Organization (WHO), World Bank (WB) (2009), the International Monetary Fund (IMF), and the World Economic Forum (2017), among others, have begun to address inclusion. In doing so they call for varying forms of integrative approaches to economic and social development. For example, the WHO (World Health Organization, 2016) argues that supports for health and education are prerequisites for inclusive growth. Inclusive growth at the WB (World Bank, 2009) entails equity, equality of opportunity, and protection in the market and in employment transitions. The IMF (International Monetary Fund, 2017) has addressed inclusion through its work on income inequality. Growing income inequality around the world is seen as a threat to economic development. These bodies are, in one way or another, calling for more integrative thinking as they seek better outcomes through access to education, health, and related social protection and social welfare programs. Increasingly the concern is one of more equitable opportunity.

GROWTH AND INCLUSIVE ECONOMIES

The Rockefeller Foundation, the Ford Foundation, and the Brookings Institution have fostered new thinking about inclusive economies. Inclusive indices include growth, prosperity, and inactivity. For example, using an index developed by Brookings (2018), few communities in the US meet the threshold of inclusivity.

Philanthropic bodies such as Rockefeller Foundation have also funded some of these more inclusive developments. Like others, they criticize trickle-down and pro-poor economic growth as being too limited if not ineffectual. They promote an extensive framework for inclusive economies (Rockefeller Foundation, 2018). This comprises five broad domains: they are equitable (e.g., equal access to ecosystem goods and services), participatory (e.g., all can participate in economy as consumers, business owners, and workers), growing (e.g., good jobs with material well-being, intergenerational income mobility), stable (e.g., resilience to shocks and stressors), and sustainable (social and economic well-being). They use 54 indicators to discern the extent to which some of these efforts are under way, including access to early childhood education, sanitation, higher education, and gender equity in wealth sharing. Here again we see that the comprehensive definition of inclusive economies comprises many social welfare and related supports along with the right to jobs and small business ownership.

Inclusive growth, as measured by the UN, requires reaching the poor and the most vulnerable. In all cases this comprises not just jobs and job creation but also social protections through social welfare programs. Such inclusive goals help to compel societies to create economies which comprise both job opportunities as well as social safety nets. Given the rise of what is described as the "gig economy" (short-term jobs, no benefits, contracts that neither employ nor support self-employment) in nations such as the United States, it is increasingly urgent for governments to build their social safety nets through more social welfare supports rather than relying on "occupational social welfare." Occupational social welfare involves employment-contingent benefits such as healthcare, pensions, and family and medical leave protections. Increasingly, some of these occupational benefits are on the decline as companies seek to pass on to the government some of these benefit responsibilities.

Linking Social and Economic Supports to Entrepreneurs

Since growth and especially inclusive growth depend on the initiative and risk-taking of entrepreneurs, it may be time for a paradigm change in which the financial and related supports used to spur growth prioritize, from the ground up, the entrepreneurs themselves.

The risk-taking involved in the United States and in most communities around the globe may result in failure. Some entrepreneurial and small business failures run as high as 95% in the first year. Such failure rates vary by location, but, in the United States, the average is about 80% after the first year (Wagner, 2013). The Aspen Institute has supported the Aspen Network of Development Entrepreneurs (ANDE). Most recently the Ford Foundation has also joined it to helped foster entrepreneurship work as part of the inclusive economies agenda (ANDE, 2018). This network advances entrepreneurship and small business startups across 150 nations. ANDE sees small business development as key to anti-poverty efforts globally. They have classified economies in terms of entrepreneurship readiness. However, most of the variables they reference include business and not social protection–related supports. This is problematic given the fact that entrepreneurs often use their own funds for startups and then face predictably high rates of failure. If they fail, then what individual or family resources do they use for survival?

The Babson Global Entrepreneurial Monitor shows that entrepreneurship and job creation globally are on the rise, and many new initiatives arise from opportunity and not just necessity (GEM, 2018). While infrastructure supports noted by ANDE are important if not critical to survival, so may be the social protections to which these innovators can turn for themselves and their families if they fail. In fact, some might argue that the demand for social protection programs has never been greater given the need for more low-income entrepreneurs to join in the social enterprise and entrepreneurial development opportunities.

Major tax breaks and subsidies position big business to thrive while the core of job creation in emerging and transitioning economies may be borne by many low-income entrepreneurial workers and their families. Because of the high failure rate and the human costs of risk-taking for job creation, it would follow that similar rates of subsidies and social protections would be available to low- and moderate-income entrepreneurs. Yet that is not the case. In the United States, it is estimated that corporate subsidies are greater than $100 billion a year (Reich, 2015). Yet this "corporate welfare" estimate is an undercount (Laird & Reich, 1998). A new US law now requires full disclosure of the subsidies and a subsidy tracker has been established (Good Jobs First, 2017). Such a tracker may reveal the disparities in large corporate investments and tax breaks versus what small business and social entrepreneurs are able to garner in supports. In New York state, as the Small Enterprise Economic Development (SEED) microlending program was being developed for low-income microentrepreneurs, it was estimated that the cost per job in New York state investments in new companies coming to the region was more than $100,000 per job versus $1,000 per job for a microentrepreneur using SEED.

While concerns among some analysts are that subsides may be disincentives for poor and low-income entrepreneurs, the fact remains that the allocation of incentives and supports skew toward the cumulative advantage of large companies. Since serial entrepreneurship is seen as one way to offset the predictably high challenges of failure with the first enterprise, it might be argued that more systematic serial supports to help resilient and persistent entrepreneurs are warranted.

While there are few studies of the human costs of entrepreneurial failure, we know that, among some, especially those who study enterprises, failure is normalized. Moreover, the human costs of financial stress and related job loss (from any source) can create scarring and irreversible mental and physical health problems, divorce, loss of homes and vehicles, and domestic violence (Briar, 1988). There are some who claim that bankruptcy is a tool to help entrepreneurs who cannot pay back their loans and bills and cope with related financial burdens, but such tools are limited. They may not help the entrepreneur stay resilient. Just as national and international bodies seek environmental and related sustainability, so, too, do sustainability concerns affect the well-being of entrepreneurs, especially those who will be repeat or serial entrepreneurs. While some of these entrepreneurs can learn from their failure, others may remain overly optimistic. This is, in fact, seen as a trait in serial entrepreneurs and one that potential investors in new ventures seek to spot for any risks (or success) as they continue to take on new ventures. In fact, because they may be unyielding in their optimism, some of these serial entrepreneurs may pose a threat to their investors (Ucbasaran, Westhead, & Wright, 2011). Some of the same optimism has been seen in the jobless who, after a year or more of joblessness and with resources and relationships depleted, still believe that a job may be just around the corner (Briar, 1978).

The gendered nature of small business failure is also of concern. Business performance research suggests that women entrepreneurs are less successful than men (Fairlie & Robb, 2009). While the human costs of their failure in the form of effects on children and their family functioning are unknown, the risks they may endure and failure consequences warrant more policy attention.

Systems of capitalism do not offer many alternative options to most workers, especially entrepreneurs. If they believed that failure will lead to financial and family-related disasters, they might not attempt such ventures. Welfare and leaving the job market may not be an option. Currently in the United States, for example, there has been a drop in new startups and thus in entrepreneurial activity. Thus, to preserve and invest in more successful entrepreneurial undertakings, more research is warranted on what the variables may be for success, especially in testing integrative economic and social welfare supports for low-income entrepreneurs.

In summary, if trickle-down economics were the solution to community and human welfare through company-provided jobs and benefits, the need for entrepreneurship would not be so pronounced. However, economies in transition, especially those that have undersupported social entrepreneurship and small business development, have a missing domain for investment and support. Given the potential for higher rates of risk taking and even enterprise survival, the social enterprise sector of the economy requires tailored and sustainable investments.

LIMITATIONS AND CAUTIONS

While bodies like the UN and others have called for more inclusive practices and policies, including more integrative approaches combining social and economic ends, there are pitfalls and key concerns to be addressed. First of all, the rise of social entrepreneurship has paralleled the decline in some nations (United States, European nations) of social protections. It is possible that the expectations that nonprofits raise their own funds through entrepreneurial ventures may supplant governmental and donor support.

Moreover, the decline in government-provided social protections, seen in a number if nations, also parallels the cuts in social insurances linked to the workplace (health, disability, retirement). Thus, the focus on inclusion in social entrepreneurship requires more systematic investments. The next section lists some activities that might help cushion risk-taking while advancing more entrepreneurial activities that also advance the social good.

SUMMARY

This chapter explored the need for more interconnections if not integration between economic and social development. In doing so, we examined some of the frameworks and approaches of different scholars, disciplines, and branches of government. We showcased some of the work of the UN as an integrative exemplar.

We contend that to advance improved integration at the level of the entrepreneur who is combining his or her entrepreneurship with a social benefit, that more social protections and supports might advance their success. In an age of risk and uncertainty in transitioning economies, such integrative supports may cushion some of the hardships that fall on the entrepreneurial worker and family and even accelerate their success. Too often the benefits and protections are directed at large companies offering the trickle-down benefits of new jobs coming to an area. By contrast, investments in inventive and often community-minded local social entrepreneurs may help to balance the scales and ensure more sustainable and successful social entrepreneurship.

The following list suggests some of the programs that may aid in more integrative programming and policy.

- Social protection programs (housing, food, income supports) offered as part of universal benefits rather than being employment-based only and involving select employers and occupations
- Healthcare and education provided as universal benefits
- Low- and moderate-income social entrepreneurs receive start-up subsidies, mentoring
- Entrepreneurial education and training provided along with peer supports, mentors
- Financial supports through loans offered with more inclusive criteria than credit scores alone
- Family-centered supports provided to social entrepreneurs, such as child care, elder care

- Social entrepreneurs receive small cash supports in cases of failure (criteria-based, similar to farm subsidies) and for serial social entrepreneurial undertakings

REFERENCES

Adelman, I., & Morris, C. T. (1973). *Economic growth and social equity in developing economies.* Cambridge, UK: Cambridge University Press.

Ahn, S. (2017). *The effects of employment and training programs on low-income workers' labor market outcomes: Evidence from the Survey of Income and Program Participation* (unpublished dissertation). University at Albany, New York.

Amin, S. (1990). *Maldevelopment: Anatomy of a global failure.* Tokyo: United Nations University Press.

ANDE. (2018). SBD Sector Issue Briefs. Retrieved from http://www.andeglobal. org/page/Ford_USAID_Partner/New-Alliance-Formed-to-Expand-Inclusive-Economies-.htm

Birdsall, N. (1993). *Social development is economic development.* Washington, DC: World Bank.

Briar, K. H. (1978). *The effect of long-term unemployment on workers and their families.* San Francisco, CA: R & E Research Associates.

Briar, K. H. (1988). *Social work and the unemployed.* Silver Spring, MD: NASW Press.

Brookings Institute. (2108). *Metropolitan monitor.* Washington, DC. Retrieved from https://www.brookings.edu/research/metro-monitor-2018/

Comim, F. (2016). *Beyond the HDI? Assessing alternative measures of human development from a capability perspective* (background paper). UNDP Human Development Report. Retrieved from http://hdr.undp.org/en/content/beyond-hdi-assessing-alternative-measures-human-development-capability-perspective

Costa-Font J., & Macis, M. (2017). *Social economics: Current and emerging avenues.* Cambridge, MA: MIT Press.

Desilver, D. (2014). *5 Facts about economic inequality.* Pew Research Center. Retrieved from https://www.pewresearch.org/fact-tank/2014/01/07/5-facts-about-economic-inequality/

Fairlie, R. W., & Robb, A. M. (2009). Gender differences in business performance: Evidence from the Characteristics of Business Owners Survey. *Small Business Economics, 33,* 375–395.

GEM. (2018). *Most entrepreneurs start businesses out of opportunity not necessity.* Babson Park, MA: Babson College. Retrieved from http://www.babson.edu/news-events/babson- news/Pages/2018-babson-global-entrepreneurship-monitor-report.aspx

Goldstein, A. (2017). *Janesville: An American story.* New York: Simon and Schuster.

Good Jobs First. (2017). Tracking subsidies, promoting accountability in economic development. https://www.goodjobsfirst.org/subsidy-tracker

Haque, M. S. (1999). *Restructuring development theories and policies.* Albany, NY: State University of New York Press.

International Labor Organization (ILO). (2018). *World employment and social outlook—trends 2018.* Retrieved from http://www.ilo.org/global/research/global-reports/weso/2018/lang--en/index.htm

International Monetary Fund (IMF). (2017). *Fostering inclusive growth*. Hamburg, Germany: IMF. Retrieved from https://www.imf.org/external/np/g20/pdf/2017/062617.pdf

Issac, J. (2014). *Expanding women's access to financial services*. World Bank. Retrieved from https://www.worldbank.org/en/results/2013/04/01/banking-on-women-extending-womens-access-to-financial-services

Khinduka, S. K. (1987). Development and peace: The complex nexus. *Social Development Issues, 10*(3), 19–30.

Kuznets, S. (1980). *Growth, populations and income distribution*. New York: W.W. Norton & Company.

Laird, F. (2001) Controversy: The rhetoric of corporate welfare. *American Prospect*. Dec. 19. https://prospect.org/economy/controversy-rhetoric-corporate-welfare/

Lowe, G. R. (1995). Social development. In *Encyclopedia of social work* (19th ed., pp. 2168–2173). Washington, DC: NASW Press.

McCarter, E. (2006). Women and microfinance: Why we should do more. *University of Maryland Law Journal on Race, Religion, Gender & Class, 6*(2), article 7. Retrieved from https://digitalcommons.law.umaryland.edu/rrgc/vol6/iss2/7

Miah, M. R. (2003). Empowerment zone, microenterprise, and asset building. In *Encyclopedia of social work* (19th ed.). Washington, DC: National Association of Social Workers.

Miah, M. R., & Tracy, M. B. (2001). The institutional approach to social development. *Social Development Issues, 23*(1), 58–64.

Midgley, J. (1993). Ideological roots of social development strategies. *Social Development Issues, 15*(1), 1–14.

Midgley, J. (1995). *Social development: The developmental perspective in social welfare*. Thousand Oaks, CA: Sage.

Midgley, J. (1997). *Social welfare in global context*. Thousand Oaks, CA: Sage.

Midgley, J. (2014). *Social development: Theory and practice*. London, UK: Sage.

Mizan, A. (1994). *In quest of empowerment: The Grameen Bank impact on women's power and status*. Dhaka, Bangladesh: The University Press.

Nandan, M., Bent-Goodley, T. B., & Mandayam, G. (Eds.). (2019). *Social entrepreneurship, Intrapreneurship, and social value creation relevance for contemporary social work practice*. Washington, DC: NASW Press.

Nussbaum, M. C. (2000). *Women and human development: The capabilities approach*. Cambridge, UK: Cambridge University Press.

Nussbaum, M. C. (2011). *Creating capabilities: The human development approach* (pp. 33–34). Cambridge, MA: Harvard University Press.

Organisation Economic Cooperation and Development (OECD). (2017). *Do women have equal access to finance for their business*. Retrieved from https://www.oecd.org/gender/data/do-women-have-equal-access-to-finance-for-their-business.htm

Orr, L. L., Bloom, H. S., Bell, S. H., Doolittle, F., Lin, W., & Cave, G. (1996). *Does training for the disadvantaged work? Evidence from the National JTPA study*. Washington, DC: The Urban Institute Press.

Pawar, M. S., & Cox, D. R. (2010). *Social development: Critical themes and perspectives*. New York: Routledge.

Pawar, M. S., & Cox, D. R. (Eds.). (2010). Conceptual understanding of social development. In D. R. Cox & M. S. Pawar (Eds.), *Social development* (pp. 13–36). London, UK: Routledge.

Preston, P. W. (1985). *New trends in development theory*. London, UK: Routledge & Kegan Paul.

Reich, R. B. (2007). *Supercapitalism*. New York: Vintage Books.

Reich, R. B. (2015). End corporate welfare. Retrieved from http://robertreich.org/post/119938747675

Rockefeller Foundation. (2018). *The five characteristics of an inclusive economy: Getting beyond the equity-growth dichotomy*. New York: Rockefeller Foundation. Retrieved from https://www.rockefellerfoundation.org/blog/five-characteristics-inclusive-economy-getting-beyond-equity-growth-dichotomy/

Sachs, J. D. (2005). *The end of poverty*. New York: Penguin.

Saez, E., Piketty, T., & Zucman, G. (n.d.). *Economic growth in US: A tale of two countries*. Washington Center for Equitable Growth. Retrieved from https://equitablegrowth.org/economic-growth-in-the-united-states-a-tale-of-two- countries/

Sen, A. (1999). *Development as freedom*. Oxford, UK: Oxford University Press.

Sherraden, M. (1991). *Assets and the poor: A new American welfare policy*. Armonk, NY: M. E. Sharpe.

Soifer, S., McNeely, J. B., Costa, C., & Pickering-Bernheim, N. (2014). *Community economic development in social work*. New York: Columbia University Press.

Stanton, E. A. (2007). *The human development index: A history*. Working Papers Series, 127. Amherst, MA: University of Massachusetts Political Economy Research Institute. Retrieved from https://scholarworks.umass.edu/cgi/viewcontent.cgi?article=1101&context=peri_work ingpapers

Stiglitz, J. E. (2016). Inequality and economic growth. *The Political Quarterly, 86*(S1). Retrieved from https://www8.gsb.columbia.edu/faculty/jstiglitz/sites/jstiglitz/files/Inequality%20za nd%20Economic%20Growth.pdf

Stone, C., Trisi D., Sherman, A., & Taylor, R. (2018, May 15). *A guide to statistics on historical trends in income inequality*. Center on Budget and Policy Priorities. https://www.cbpp.org/research/poverty-and-inequality/a-guide-to-statistics-on-historical-trends-in-income-inequality

Todaro, M. P., & Smith, S. C. (2015). *Economic development* (12th ed.). New York: Pearson.

Ucbasaran, D., Westhead, P., & Wright, M. (2011). Why serial entrepreneurs don't learn from failure. *Harvard Business Review*. Retrieved from https://hbr.org/2011/04/why-serial-entrepreneurs- dont-learn-from-failure

United Nations. (1999). *The Copenhagen Declaration*. United Nations/Division for Social Policy and Development. Retrieved from https://www.un.org/en/development/desa/population/migration/generalassembly/docs/globalcompact/A_CONF.166_9_Declaration.pdf

United Nations. (2004). *Report on the follow–up of the World Summit for Social Development: State and globalization, challenges for human development, Bangkok, 17–19 December, 2003*. New York: United Nations.

United Nations (2005). *The social summit: Ten years later*. New York: United Nations Department of Economic and Social Affairs.

United Nations. (2015). *Transforming our world: The 2030 agenda for sustainable development*. New York: United Nations. Retrieved from https://sustainabledevelopment.un.org/post2015/transformingourworld

United Nations. (2018). *World employment social outlook*. Geneva, Switzerland: ILO. Retrieved from: http://www.un.org/sustainabledevelopment/blog/2018/01/unemployment-remain-high-quality-jobs-harder-find-2018-un-labour-agency/

United Nations Development Program (UNDP). (2016). *Human development report 2016: Human development for everyone*. New York: United Nations.

Wagner, E. T. (2013). *Five reasons eight out of ten businesses fail*. Forbes. Retrieved from https://www.forbes.com/sites/ericwagner/2013/09/12/five-reasons-8-out-of-10- businesses-fail/679262a36978

World Bank. (2009). What is inclusive growth? Retrieved from http://siteresources.worldbank.org/INTDEBTDEPT/Resources/468980- 1218567884549/WhatIsInclusiveGrowth20081230.pdf

World Economic Forum. (2017). *The inclusive growth and development report, 2017*. Retrieved from http://www3.weforum.org/docs/WEF_Forum_IncGrwth_2017.pdf

World Health Organization. (2016). Communiqué: Meeting of the High-Level Commission on Health Employment and Economic Growth. Retrieved from http://www.who.int/hrh/com-heeg/communique/en/

Yunus, M. (1995). Grameen Bank: Experiences and Reflections. *Impact*, *30*(3/4), 13–25.

Yunus, M. (2003). *Banker to the poor: Micro-lending and the battle against world poverty*. New York: Public Affairs.

Yunus, M. (2016). *Yunus social business 2016 impact report*. Retrieved from http://www.yunussb.com/wp-content/uploads/2017/07/YSB-2017_digital_small.pdf

CHAPTER 17

࿋

Selected Observations and Lessons Learned for 21st-Century Supports for Social Entrepreneurship and Social Enterprises

KATHARINE BRIAR-LAWSON, PAUL MIESING, AND
BLANCA M. RAMOS

As social enterprises grow in popularity, there are risks and warning signs that also emerge from this sphere of innovation. Some of these warning signs include the potential displacement and rolling back of welfare state programs in favor of more market-oriented solutions. Such retrenchment often targets the poor and disadvantaged, promoting entrepreneurship as a substitute for jobs in the private sector or welfare state support in the form of income or in-kind subsidies. We underscore this by asserting that social enterprises are not a panacea for state-supported social protections and public services (Driver, 2012).

We have seen state-run economies like Cuba introduce market supports for enterprise development. Moreover, we have examples of varying kinds of policy and in some cases multiple-level supports in market-driven economies such as in Taiwan. Some of our illustrations from varying country snapshots illustrate that when entrepreneurship is on the rise there may be few if any supports for workers and their enterprises (Chapter 9 by Jildyz Urbaeva). This is in sharp contrast to the variety of tax

Katharine Briar-Lawson, Paul Miesing, and Blanca M. Ramos, *Selected Observations and Lessons Learned for 21st-Century Supports for Social Entrepreneurship and Social Enterprises* In: *Social Entrepreneurship and Enterprises in Economic and Social Development*. Edited by: Katharine Briar-Lawson, Paul Miesing, and Blanca M. Ramos, Oxford University Press (2021). © Oxford University Press. DOI: 10.1093/oso/9780197518298.003.0018.

and related subsidies provided for corporations (totaling more than $800 billion in the United States) (Chapter 16 by Briar-Lawson, Miah). Large corporations enjoy benefits that small businesses and social enterprises rarely access. For example in the US the recent $2.2 trillion Coronavirus Aid, Relief, and Economic Security (CARES) Act was intended to help small US businesses and employees negatively impacted by the coronavirus pandemic. While they received around $349 billion from the Paycheck Protection Program, most of these funds went to the largest corporations and wealthy individuals (Gibson, 2020). Thus, in the spirit of more equitable supports, this final chapter argues that if workers and their families are to be drivers of social enterprises and expanded social businesses that generate jobs and address unmet needs, they require more systematic investments that aid in their success.

Glimpses into the status of social entrepreneurship and innovation in various nations have revealed the need for more social protections and social welfare benefits in support of workers and their families as they undertake their entrepreneurial work. In many cases, entrepreneurial activity is required for survival; in other cases, it may be a path to pursue an idea, a dream, and a sense of felt need in a community. Such pioneering missions may exact major costs if failure rates are high, along with supplanting if not exhausting financial resources on which family members rely. On the other hand, successful enterprises serve as role models for aspiring entrepreneurs.

Augmenting the gaps and challenges faced in social entrepreneurship is the paucity of systematic research. Thus, it is our hope that some of the findings and observations offered in this book may foster an agenda for future policy and practice developments, and more evaluative research. To build the agenda and to foster more research and experimentation through demonstration projects and related innovations, we offer some recommendations and summary statements culled from the chapters in this book. These can be thought of as preliminary recommendations and, in some cases, propositions for the decades ahead. To set the stage, we first lay out some key premises emerging from the book. Then we offer propositions for policy, practice, and research. Finally, we suggest the need for developing a "system of supports" for social entrepreneurship at local, state, national, and international levels. From the key lessons learned involving gaps and needs, we extract some suggestions for building systems that support social enterprises and social entrepreneurs (see Table 17.1). In fact, efforts that support social enterprises around the world, as reflected in these country and regional snapshots, all share the same dilemma: There is no "system" in place to enable the building of social enterprises. This

Table 17.1 FRAMING CONTEXTUAL AND RELATED SUPPORTS FOR SOCIAL ENTREPRENEURSHIP (SE)

Premises	Contextual issues	Balancing social and economic development for human well-being	Moving from grand vision to social entrepreneurship and social enterprise development	Social enterprises, social entrepreneurship and social inclusion	Lessons learned for enterprises and social entrepreneurs	Research and evaluation
Integrative mechanisms for social and economic development	SE no substitute for welfare and social protections	Organized structural supports are needed	International, national, local regulatory and facilitating structures	SE can foster inclusion, cooperation, mutual aid	Use of teams for mentors, peer supports, investors	Assess entrepreneurial orientation in social missions
Source of social innovation but proactivity requires more supports	SE no panacea for societal response to social problems	Secondary economy addressing local needs and using complementary (nonconvertible) currency may aid in the process	Seed funds, start-up hubs	SE can address non-market social goals	Sound fiscal plans	Integrated development requires more research on social innovations (complementary community currencies, secondary economies)
Addresses jobs, inclusion, income inequities	SE can be problematically used as a neoliberal adjustment instrument	Microlending using character loans is promising	Incubators	SE can catalyze grassroots	Integrate mission into all aspects of SE	Social impact variables need better studies
		Address immigrants, the poor, indigenous populations, and asylum seekers	Mentors, peer supports	SE can improve women's situations	Build on social and cultural capital	Character-based lending requires more specified definitions and research
		Confront racism in market forces	Organizational partners	SE can rebalance market, state, civil spheres		
			Income supports			
			In-kind benefits (food, housing)			
			Secondary economy and resource exchanges			

includes the absence of a coherent framework of policy and related fiscal and organizational resources to help advance promising, socially relevant ideas into successful and sustainable undertakings with cushions and social protections for risk-taking entrepreneurs and their families.

KEY LESSONS FROM CHAPTERS

Premises

- Social enterprises constitute integrative mechanisms for social and economic development (Chapter 1 by Miesing).
- Social enterprises have filled the gap where other sectors (government, charities, and for-profit businesses) have failed (Chapter 1).
- Social enterprises may reduce income disparities in emerging and transitioning economies (Chapter 1).
- Transitioning nations may find social enterprises promising, with integrated social and economic outcomes (Chapter 8 by Hackett & Roy).
- Risks of failure remain the same with both social and commercial enterprises (Chapter 1).
- Multiple partners must be mobilized to address social problems such as economic disparities and joblessness (Chapter 1).
- Social entrepreneurship may advance more just, sustainable, and inclusive growth (Chapter 14 by Mucarsel, Bhat, & Ramos).
- Risk-taking innovation and proactivity require more supports (Chapter 3 by Wales & Gupta).
- Trusteeship involves a moral framework so that wealth created by the labor of others must create value for the greater good of society (Chapter 11 by Bhat & Barai).
- Social enterprises and entrepreneurship can help advance the United Nations Sustainable Development Goals[1] (Chapter 16 by Briar-Lawson & Miah, and Chapter 14; see also https://sustainabledevelopment.un.org/).

Contextual Issues

- Social enterprises are not an alternative for social protection (Chapter 8).
- Social enterprises are no panacea for social problems (Chapter 13 by Wu).
- We need to guard against reductions in international aid as social enterprises emerge (Chapter 8).

- Neoliberal market dynamics may polarize economic versus social development (Chapter 15 by Taylor).
- Rather than developing local communities, these communities instead may experience resource extraction facilitated by the state and international investors (Chapter 12 by Otenyo, Harris, & Askew).
- Public-sector infrastructure can serve as a bedrock of sustainable development (Chapter 11 by Bhat & Barai).
- Even in socialist countries market forces may emerge and must be managed (Chapter 15).
- Structural adjustment programs may reduce social development programs while enhancing the interests of corporations and elites (Chapter 12).
- Social enterprises cannot replace societal responsibility for social problems (Chapter 13).
- Materialism, consumerism, and individualism will be alluring even in socialist states (Chapter 15).
- International institutions may turn informal rural economies into markets with "bottom-of-the-pyramid" global consumers (see Weber, 2010, as cited by Hackett & Roy in Chapter 8).
- Social enterprises (in post-communist countries) run the risk of being used as neoliberal adjustment instruments, implicating the nonprofit sector (Chapter 8).
- The social enterprise concept is a useful framework for understanding how market and non-market forces can complement each other and explains how capitalism can be used to save socialism (Chapter 15).
- Social entrepreneurship, as a postmodern thought experiment, presents us with choice and a toolkit to build innovative solutions that allow for a just, equitable, egalitarian democratic society (Chapter 11).
- Indigenous groups can be co-opted by modernization plans, including the misappropriation of their lands (Chapter 2 by Gross and Chapter 12).
- Regulatory policy frameworks need to be revised and recognize that there are multiple and complementary economies (Chapter 5 by Weaver, Marks, Skropke, Hogan, & Spinelli).

Balancing Social and Economic Development for Human Well-Being

- There is untapped potential in developing immigrant entrepreneurship, and we must acknowledge its new role in solving social problems (Chapter 4 by Lee & Black).

- Women's crafts advance feminine conditions as their businesses are integrated with social causes, mutual supports, and local traditions (Chapter 9 by Urbaeva).
- Intermediary organizations are critical to financing, developing business operations, and marketing skills (Chapter 9).
- Indigenous communities compel more economic and social investments to address poverty (Chapter 12 by Otenyo, Harris, & Askew).
- Secondary economies with nonmonetized exchanges can foster social and economic development (Chapter 5 by Weaver et al.).
- Microfinance using character-based loans and peer supports shows promise in serving distressed communities (Chapter 6 by Lee, Brigham, Wacholder, Baker, & Stanley).

Moving from Vision to Social Entrepreneurship and Social Enterprise Development

- Far fewer social enterprises are envisioned without actual creation than implemented (Chapter 13 by Wu).
- The iron triangle (social responsibility, organizational accountability, business commitment) along with the "philanthropic" mission must be addressed simultaneously (Chapter 13).
- Active information campaigns are needed to focus on three key audiences that advance an awareness of the opportunities of social businesses: the general public, representatives of regional authorities, and potential social entrepreneurs (Chapter 10 by Sadyrtdinov).
- At their core social enterprises need to continually assess their "problem-solving business model" (Chapter 13).
- A regulatory framework is needed for corporate social responsibility in socially active businesses along with start-up funding (Chapter 10).
- More clarity and legal standing will aid with model development for social entrepreneurship (Chapter 10).
- Collaboration and partnerships among local financial, educational, and government programs may be key to developing microfinance and character-based loans (Chapter 6 by Lee et al.).
- Social enterprises require a mutually beneficial relationship among the public, entrepreneurs, society, and sustainability, industry, government, etc. (Chapter 13).
- Well-being has economic, social, and sustainability, industry, government, etc. elements which are likely to be secured in a more balanced way when they are co-produced rather than pursued separately (Chapter 5 by Weaver et al.).

- Fostering social innovations can transform relations so that human well-being is more important than profit maximization (Kemp et al., 2016, as cited in Chapter 5).
- Postindustrial market economies may especially benefit from social innovation organizations (Chapter 5).
- Secondary economies may foster more social inclusion of marginalized populations (Chapter 5).
- Social innovations offer ways to build social capital, cooperation, mutual aid, reciprocity, and unpaid work (Cahn, 2004, as cited in Chapter 5).

Social Enterprises, Social Entrepreneurship, and Social Inclusion

- Social innovations can foster more inclusion, cooperation, and mutual aid (Weaver et al., 2016a, as cited in Chapter 5 by Weaver et al.).
- Social enterprises offer an alternative business framework to address non-market "social goals" such as breaking-down prejudices concerning marginalized groups (Chapter 8 by Hackett & Roy).
- Market forces may have embedded racism (Chapter 15 by Taylor).
- A secondary economy may aid groups such as asylum-seekers (Chapter 5).
- Social enterprises can be resourceful stakeholders for catalyzing social innovations from the grassroots and linking them with other organizations such as universities and funders to scale-up (Chapter 14 by Mucarsel, Bhat, & Ramos).
- There is potential for improving women's situations using social entrepreneurship models (Chapter 9 by Urbaeva).
- Women-led artisanal groups are intrinsically connected to social purposes, as women in crafts communities often are from vulnerable and disadvantaged rural areas (Chapter 9).
- Time banking may help rebalance market, state, and civic spheres (Chapter 5).
- A secondary economy can redefine work, reorganize how time is used, and how gross domestic product (GDP) is distributed (Chapter 5).
- Character-based lending creates economic opportunities for those with no access to funding and who lack collateral or a good credit score (Chapter 6 by Lee et al.).

Lessons Learned for Entrepreneurs and Social Entrepreneurs

- The problems, needs, and expectations of stakeholders and potential customers need to be understood (Chapter 13 by Wu).

- Addressing formal and informal networks, local traditions, and stakeholder ownership is key for developers and social entrepreneurs (Chapter 2 by Gross).
- Government and corporate action must match the efforts of voluntary organizations that genuinely seek to provide entrepreneurial training and education in indigenous communities (Chapter 12 by Otenyo, Harris, & Askew).
- Developers and social entrepreneurs need to address capital, transportation, and physical supports for their projects (Chapter 2).
- Developers and social entrepreneurs need to address problem loans and high financial risks by advocating for improved policy with reasonable loan rates and outcomes (Chapter 2).
- Entrepreneurship requires a team with complementary skills and visions (Chapter 7 by Lobel).
- Entrepreneurship is more than a job: it is a lifestyle that requires ongoing development and attention (Chapter 7).
- Persistence in the face of adversity is essential (Chapter 7).
- Most entrepreneurial business opportunities are developed through social networking and thoughtful relationships (Chapter 7).
- Prerequisites for social entrepreneur success are sound financial plans and adequate financing for the first several years (Chapter 1 by Miesing).
- Social mission-driven operations inspire employees (Chapter 1).
- Entrepreneurship must not be allowed to become a façade for promoting exploitative informal sector employment or a resource drain from resource-scarce communities (Chapter 11 by Bhat & Barai).
- Target markets need to be well understood and offered a unique value proposition (e.g., quality, reliability, cost of delivery, level of convenience and service, engineering innovation and design, image, overall satisfaction) (Chapter 1).
- The social enterprise practitioner ought to periodically self-examine that the "iron triangle" of social responsibility, organizational accountability, and business commitment are on track (Chapter 13 by Wu).

Research and Evaluation

- We need to conceptualize and research more on the role of entrepreneurial activity and entrepreneurial orientation in social enterprises (Chapter 3 by Wales & Gupta).
- The antecedents and outcomes of entrepreneurial orientation need to be specified in social enterprises (Chapter 3).
- Organizational entrepreneurship needs to be better studied within the context of social enterprises (Chapter 3).

- Organizations with impactful change-making missions need to be better studied and not seen as merely being led by solo entrepreneurial heroes (Chapter 3).
- We must identify more of those social enterprise activities that address disadvantage and how their own structures may challenge conventional business models (Chapter 8 by Hackett & Roy).
- Refugee entrepreneurship needs to be better understood through conceptual and empirical studies (Chapter 4 by Lee & Black).
- Successful social innovations and their business models need further study as they shape each other and can simultaneously serve multiple needs of society (Chapter 5 by Weaver et al.).
- A more comprehensive understanding of character-based lending models can inform financial practices more widely (Chapter 6 by Lee et al.).

CONCLUSION

What is necessary to advance social entrepreneurship and social enterprises, based on the chapters in this volume and the propositions just suggested, is a globally-shared system comprised of policies, social protections, financing, intermediary support organizations, training, coaching, and peer supports, along with research and evaluation of the process. We have seen in several chapters glimpses of loan funds that address character rather than credit (Small Enterprise Economic Development [SEED]); governmental offices in support of social enterprises, as in Taiwan and Argentina; and new approaches to developing a secondary economy using complementary currencies, such as time banks and local digital currencies.

In many cases, however, venturing social entrepreneurs are often on their own. This means risking their own family savings (often resources for their family's survival) to advance a new enterprise (with both economic and social impact) that runs a high risk of failure despite offering classes and mentoring on how to build a small business. Thus, if such desired contributions to the economic and social goals of a family, community, and nation are to succeed, it is evident that more benefits and supports are warranted in the form of a system of policies (including legal frameworks), financing, organizational and related infrastructure, and services. Some of the features may include a formal office in government, such as we have seen in Taiwan. Financing can be ensured using some of the principles of the Grameen Bank model (Yunus, 2007) or from SEED. Services can include training, such as peer and related coaching and its supports, as is done by SEED. None of these necessarily guarantees success, but they may be key variables to be tested and evaluated as a research base builds locally, nationally, regionally, and globally.

In addition, some of our chapters introduced ideas about some facets of a system of supports, which unfortunately seem nonexistent in many of the snapshots from the nations illustrated. These need to dovetail with a safety net. In fact, if there is no set of social protections, then the entrepreneur runs the risk of not only losing personal resources, but also many future resources in support of their own survival and that of their family members. While the research remains scant, beginning studies suggest that family-focused planning with the social entrepreneur may aid in success (Aldrich & Cliff, 2003).

It is notable that debates have emerged in Sweden about the loss of jobs through robots and the threat that this might augur for innovators. Yet the response is reported to be positive because of safety nets and related protections against the harms of joblessness in that country (Goodman, 2017). In fact, one leader argues that safety nets are good for entrepreneurship because they serve as cushions and buffers (Goodman, 2017). Nations may increasingly discover that countries like Sweden lead the way in teaching us about the need for safety net cushions and buffers if social innovations and entrepreneurial risk-taking are to flourish.

Given the earlier concerns raised by Miesing about disparities and the role of social entrepreneurship in helping close the gap, one can wonder whether the countries that have the best social safety net will also be those that are able to embrace and support social entrepreneurship and innovation. In fact, some have suggested that social policies along with investment funds and intermediary support organizations to aid social enterprises are key to success. Absent the infrastructures, any scale-up of such integrated social and economic development may fall short of expectations.

Because social enterprises promise a double bottom line of economic as well social benefits, policy and investments might prioritize social entrepreneurship over traditional business as well. In fact, consulting firm McKinsey recently reported why companies pursuing environmental sustainability, social responsibility, and corporate governance can outperform their competition (Henisz, Koller, & Nuttall, 2019).

Thus, incentives and more rigorous supports to advantage social enterprises could inform if not guide future policy deliberations. Ultimately, the social impact factor—figuring so prominently in social enterprises—provides a model for traditional businesses. And while we see in Russia and elsewhere businesses focusing on corporate social responsibility and the growth of social businesses, this suggests that the critical variable is the social impact orientation regardless of where a business may fall on the continuum laid out by Miesing. Given the multiplier effects of a double bottom line, as well as the potentially inclusive and socially beneficial impacts, it would seem that the social impact agenda for all businesses—not merely emergent social enterprises—could represent a global policy and practice campaign. In fact, social impact expectations and accountability might become a more prominent goal for 21st-century development worldwide. Such an agenda would further the attainment of the UN Sustainable Development Goals and the UN Global Compact that encourages all businesses everywhere to adopt and report on their sustainable and socially responsible practices.

NOTE

1. See https://sustainabledevelopment.un.org/.

REFERENCES

Aldrich, H. H., & Cliff, S. E. (2003). The pervasive effects of family on entrepreneurship: Toward a family embeddedness perspective. *Journal of Business Venturing, 18*, 573–596.

Driver, M. (2012). An interview with Michael Porter: Social entrepreneurship and the transformation of capitalism. *Academy of Management Learning & Education, 11*(3), 421–431. http://dx.doi.org/10.5465/amle.2011.0002 Retrieved from https://www.sharedvalue.org/sites/default/files/resource-files/Interview%20 with%20Porter_AMLE%20Social%20Entrepreneurship%20and%20the%20 Transformation%20of%20Capitalism.pdf

Gibson, C. (2020). Workers Are Getting the Short End of the Stick from the Cares Act. *Barron's* (April 15). Retrieved from https://www.barrons.com/articles/ cares-act-workers-companies-unfair-coronavirus-aid-51586983332

Goodman, P. S. (2017, December 27). The robots are coming and Sweden is fine. *New York Times*. Retrieved from https://www.nytimes.com/2017/12/27/busi-ness/the-robots-are-coming- and-sweden-is-fine.html

Henisz, W., Koller, T., & Nuttall, R. (2019). Five ways that ESG creates value. *McKinsey Quarterly*, November 14. https://www.mckinsey.com/business-functions/ strategy-and-corporate-finance/our-insights/five-ways-that-esg-creates-value?cid=other-eml-alt-mcq-mck&hlkid=54e6f8d1486340c6a2afeb3d9f0211a 8&hctky=1957082&hdpid=e0e63416-b7dd-41c8-bba8-3bfef96816f5

Yunus, M. (2007). *Creating a world without poverty: Social business and the future of capitalism*. New York: Public Affairs.

INDEX

Tables, figures and boxes are indicated by *t*, *f* and *b* following the page number

For the benefit of digital users, indexed terms that span two pages (e.g., 52–53) may, on occasion, appear on only one of those pages.